How the World
Remade Hollywood

How the World Remade Hollywood

Global Interpretations of 65 Iconic Films

Ed Glaser

McFarland & Company, Inc., Publishers
Jefferson, North Carolina

ISBN (print) 978-1-4766-8403-1
ISBN (ebook) 978-1-4766-4467-7

LIBRARY OF CONGRESS AND BRITISH LIBRARY
CATALOGUING DATA ARE AVAILABLE

Library of Congress Control Number 2022007934

© 2022 Ed Glaser. All rights reserved

No part of this book may be reproduced or transmitted in any form or by any means, electronic or mechanical, including photocopying or recording, or by any information storage and retrieval system, without permission in writing from the publisher.

Front cover: Levent Çakır (standing with gun) and Emel Özden in the 1973 Turkish film *Yarasa Adam* (Nuran Film Company)

Printed in the United States of America

*McFarland & Company, Inc., Publishers
Box 611, Jefferson, North Carolina 28640
www.mcfarlandpub.com*

Table of Contents

Acknowledgments — viii

Introduction — 1

Why Didn't They Get Sued? — 5

1. Capes, Conquerors, and Comic Books — 9
    3 Dev Adam (Three Giant Men) 9
    Ator l'invincibile (Ator the Fighting Eagle) 13
    Darna 16
    Kızıl Maske ("The Phantom") 20
    La Mujer Murciélago (Bat Woman) 23
    Supaidāman (Spider-Man) 26
    Superman 30
    Süpermen Dönüyor ("Superman Returns") 34
    Supersonic Man 38
    Tarzan İstanbul'da ("Tarzan in Istanbul") 41
    Wurideul-ui Chingu Pawo 5 ("Our Friend Power 5") 44
    Yarasa Adam: Bedmen ("Batman") 48
    Zashchitniki (Guardians) 52

2. Muscles, Magnums, and Machismo — 56
    7 Belalılar ("7 Troublemakers") 56
    1990: I guerrieri del Bronx (1990: The Bronx Warriors) 59
    Altın Çocuk ("Golden Boy") 62
    Black Cobra 66
    Cellat ("The Executioner") 69
    Den' D ("D-Day") 73
    Dhoom ("Boom") 76
    The Intruder 79
    Khoon Khoon ("Blood Blood") 82
    Korkusuz (Rampage) 85
    OK Connery 89
    Qayamat: City Under Threat 92

3. Family, Fantasy, and Fairy Tales — 96
    Aabra Ka Daabra: The School of Magic 96
    Badi ("Shorty") 99

    Os Carrinhos em: A Grande Corrida (*The Little Cars in the Great Race*) 102
    Ge wu qing chun (*Disney High School Musical: China*) 105
    Kuzhandaiyum Deivamum ("Children and God") 108
    Lassie—Eine abenteuerliche Reise (*Lassie Come Home*) 111
    Maugli (*The Adventures of Mowgli*) 115
    Pamuk Prenses ve 7 Cüceler ("Snow White and the 7 Dwarfs") 119
    Os Trapalhões e o Mágico de Oróz ("The Tramps and the Wizard of Oróz") 122
    Vinni-Pukh ("Winnie the Pooh") 125

4. Monsters, Maniacs, and the Macabre   130
    Aatank ("Terror") 130
    Anyab ("Fangs") 133
    Bach ke Zara ("Tread Carefully") 135
    Drakula İstanbul'da ("Dracula in Istanbul") 138
    Kader Diyelim ("Let's Say It's Fate") 142
    Kingu Kongu no Gyakushū (*King Kong Escapes*) 144
    L'ultimo squalo (*The Last Shark*) 148
    Mahakaal ("Time of Death") 151
    La Momia Azteca (*The Aztec Mummy*) 155
    Paranōmaru Akutibiti Dai 2 Shō: Tōkyō Naito (*Paranormal Activity 2: Tokyo Night*) 158
    Şeytan ("Satan") 161
    Xingxing wang (*The Mighty Peking Man*) 166
    Zapatlela ("Possessed") 169

5. Androids, Aliens, and the Apocalypse   174
    Baytekin Fezada Çarpışanlar ("Flash Gordon's Battle in Space") 174
    The Bionic Boy 176
    Computer Haekjeonham Pokpa Daejakjeon (*Savior of the Earth*) 180
    Dünyayı Kurtaran Adam (*The Man Who Saves the World*) 183
    Pembalasan Ratu Pantai Selatan (*Lady Terminator*) 187
    Robo Vampire 190
    Robowar 194
    Shocking Dark 197
    Starcrash 201
    Time of the Apes 204
    Turist Ömer Uzay Yolunda ("Ömer the Tourist in Star Trek") 208
    Uchū kara no Messēji (*Message from Space*) 212
    Warrior of the Lost World 216

6. Outlaws, Outsiders, and Oscar Winners   220
    12 220
    Akounak Tedalat Taha Tazoughai ("Rain the Color of Blue with a Little Red in It") 224
    Cemo ile Cemile ("Cemo and Cemile") 227
    Fight Club: Members Only 231
    Kara Şimşek ("Black Lightning") 234
    Kartal Yuvası ("Eagle's Nest") 238
    Kılıç Bey ("Mr. Kılıç") 242
    Lim jing dai yat gik (*First Shot*) 245

Masoyiyata / Titanic ("My Beloved / Titanic") 248
Pi li da niu (*Girl with a Gun*) 251
Pyaar Tune Kya Kiya... ("Love... What Have You Done") 254
Sangharsh ("Conflict") 257
Sarkar ("Overlord") 261
Yurusarezaru mono (*Unforgiven*) 264

Bibliography and Filmography 269

Index 281

Acknowledgments

First and foremost, I wish to thank Mehmet Alemdar, İrfan Atasoy, Adite Banerjie, Levent Çakır, Tanuja Chandra, Richard Chen Yao-chi, John P. Dulaney, Çetin İnanç, Engin İnanç, Murat İnanç, Serdar Kebapçılar, Ravi Kishan, Raul Filippo Mattei, Ramdas Padhye, Shyam Ramsay, Salim Raza, Haven Tyler, Kunt Tulgar, David Worth, and Sönmez Yıkılmaz for sharing their personal memories of many of the films contained within these pages.

Thanks to cult cinema aficionado Todd Stadtman who gave me the inspiration and the organizational tools to start writing a book in the first place. His wisdom and encouragement provided the initial momentum that got this ball rolling.

I owe an enormous debt of gratitude to my friend and colleague Iain Robert Smith for his unflagging belief in this project and superhuman tolerance for being bothered. Over the course of writing, I must have pestered him with a hundred questions about everything from finding specific research materials to the proper capitalization of Italian movie titles to the minutiae of his own work. He also generously reviewed and offered his advice on much of this book from its earliest stages.

I'm eternally grateful to my honorary elder brother Ali Murat Güven who graciously gave so much of his time, expertise, and resources to an aspiring film historian. He was my hospitable host during a research trip to Istanbul in 2016 and introduced me to many of the filmmakers and actors whose movies are featured in this book. His encyclopedic knowledge of Turkish cinema has been priceless, and the access to his archive of historical material equally so. But both pale in comparison to his patience and generosity.

My sincere thanks to Kaya Özkaracalar for sharing his incredible knowledge of film, comics, and Disney in Turkey, and for responding so kindly to a barrage of questions about the debuts of superheroes in his home country.

I'm indebted to Alem Dauletkulov, who made a substantial quantity of Russian-language material accessible by dint of his generous research and translation. He was also kind enough to cast his expert eye over several of my entries. *Spasibo!*

An additional thank you to Aditi Sen and Beth Watkins for contributing their immense Indian cinema knowledge, providing valuable research, and offering notes on many of the items in this book.

This volume would not have been possible without the expertise of so many world cinema scholars, critics, and journalists. I would like to extend my warmest thanks to Savaş Arslan, Umut Tümay Arslan, Heike Behrend, Carol Borden, R.L. Cagle, Aseem Chandaver, Fatih Danacı, Shamya Dasgupta, Rayna Denison, Nicholas Diak, Austin Fisher, Gökay Gelgeç, Cem Kaya, Ayman Kole, Fred Kudjo Kuwornu, Andrew Leavold, Mike Leeder, Jesús Manuel Pérez Molina, Pınar Öğünç, Phelan Porteous, Utku Uluer, and Can Yalçınkaya for allowing me to pick their brains in person and over email.

For their help with various translations involved in this book, my thanks to Fatima Eldes, Julia Ghoulia, and Yasuka Kawakami.

I also wish to acknowledge Mike Barnum and Tim Paxton for kindly contributing images from their archives.

I'm grateful to my agent Christopher Hermelin for his guidance, advice, and enthusiasm for pop culture obscurities. Additional thanks to the team at McFarland, particularly my editor Susan Kilby, for their patience and assistance in molding this book into its final form.

Finally, extra special thanks to my amazing wife, Meagan. From offering ideas and encouragement to reading early drafts to keeping me sane as I navigated the stresses of a first-time author, she was as instrumental in the creation of this book as I was. Madam, you are the best.

Introduction

For a century Hollywood has dispersed films throughout the globe like dandelion seeds on the wind. When they landed in other countries and took root in new soil, something remarkable happened. Thanks to enterprising local filmmakers, hybrids began to emerge: an *Exorcist* (1973) remake set in a Muslim nation, an anime-style *Tron* (1982) produced in Korea, Captain America wrestling an evil Spider-Man in Istanbul, and an Indonesian *Terminator* (1984) without a single robot.

I first discovered this phenomenon in college when it was brought to my attention by a noted psychiatrist and cannibal. I had just read Thomas Harris's original *Hannibal* trilogy, and as a follow-up I decided to marathon the various film adaptations. I knew that *Red Dragon* had been made twice, including in 1986 as *Manhunter*, and I was curious if there was some obscure version of one of the others of which I was unaware.

I was in luck. According to the Internet Movie Database, *The Silence of the Lambs* (1991) had been remade as something called *Sangharsh* (1999)—in India. That is to say, "Bollywood." This was a place where, I had been reliably informed, all movies were musicals. Bewildered, I tracked it down on eBay and hammered "Buy It Now." The moment the disc arrived, I rang up my friends: "You guys!" I blurted gleefully. "*Silence of the Lambs: The Musical!* Who's in?"

Two hours and twice as many pizzas later, it was over. It had changed my life.

You haven't lived until you've seen Hannibal Lecter sing and dance in a Zorro costume. Because in *Sangharsh*, that happens. And that's hardly all. In many ways you might not even recognize the story. It replaces serial killer and lotion enthusiast Buffalo Bill with a psychotic bald kidnapper in a sari. It features a love triangle between Hannibal, Clarice, and Clarice's astronomer friend. And moreover, Hannibal himself—depicted here as handsome, sweaty, and smoldering—is not even explicitly a cannibal. Rather, the film is conspicuously coy about the nature of his crimes. By the standards of any right-thinking fan of the series, then, *Sangharsh* gets it hopelessly wrong.

Presently, however, I realized: this film wasn't made for me, an American fan of a Hollywood franchise. More likely it was aimed at an audience that had never seen *The Silence of the Lambs* and would have had nothing to compare it to. And on its own merits, *Sangharsh* is a genuinely enjoyable movie. It's well shot and well acted, the songs are mostly colorful and entertaining, and the action sequences are terrific. So I began to wonder: in that case, what were the causes or criteria for the film's many changes? Was it a case of cultural factors? Industry norms? Censorship? Budget? Whim?

So I dug. At the time I knew very little about Bollywood. I had no idea who director Tanuja Chandra or star Akshay Kumar were, or that producer Mahesh Bhatt had worked on Bollywood remakes of everything from *On the Waterfront* (1954) to *An American Werewolf in London* (1981). But I read and I watched. And each revelation inspired further questions. Yet one loomed largest of all: how many other international remakes of Hollywood movies were out there?

Only hundreds.

Welcome to the world of "remakesploitation"—weird, wild, and often highly unauthorized international remakes, rip-offs, and remixes of popular Hollywood films. Since the 2000s they've begun to resurface via cherry-picked, out-of-context YouTube clips that pull in hundreds of thousands of views apiece. Titles like "Turkish *Star Wars*" top lists of "the worst movies ever made." But for all their newfound Internet fame, their origins are rarely investigated. Why and how were these movies made? Who made them? What was the context in which they were produced? And how did the filmmakers avoid lawsuits?

Answering these questions is the *raison d'être* of *How the World Remade Hollywood: Global Interpretations of 65 Iconic Films*.

Initially those questions spurred me in a slightly different direction. After years of DVD collecting and research, in 2010 I launched the award-winning video series *Deja View* as a way to draw attention to some of these gems. Each episode spotlighted a different international remake and explored its origins and production. This book, then, is an extension of that journey.

There is, of course, no single motivation behind the hundreds of homegrown adaptations and reworkings. Some simply capitalized on the local success of Hollywood films. Some allowed filmmakers to circumvent movie import restrictions by making their own versions. Some jettisoned unrelatable Americentric plots or taboo subject matter for something that hit closer to home. And some allowed a beloved Hollywood franchise to reiterate. This book plucks these films from the contextless, ironic sphere of the Internet and presents them in a new light alongside their fascinating behind-the-scenes stories.

These remakes tend to get a bum rap as mere "imitations" or "copycats." Reviews dwell on the extent to which their production values or plots (fail to) measure up to the originals. But that's a losing proposition. If you treat an "original" film as a Platonic ideal and the remake as its shadow, you deny the latter any voice or perspective of its own. You also fail to acknowledge the many inspirations—literary, cinematic, or otherwise—that almost certainly influenced the earlier film.

International remakes are part of a much more interesting and complex cultural exchange of ideas. In his terrific book *The Hollywood Meme: Transnational Adaptations in World Cinema*, Iain Robert Smith explores this exchange in detail. His title refers to a term coined by Richard Dawkins; a "meme" is a unit of culture in the same way that a gene is a unit of heredity. Though commonly used today to refer to an amusingly-captioned image shared widely online, a meme is simply an idea transmitted from one brain to another, like the genetic material inside those dandelion seeds floating to a new patch of soil. It's Rambo's iconic costume and rocket launcher. A visually spectacular scene from *The Matrix* (1999). A planet ruled by apes. And if the conditions are right, the meme replicates in its new environment. Thus, aspects of *The Godfather* (1972), *The Evil Dead* (1981), or *Thunderball* (1965) resonate with filmgoers and filmmakers around the world and spawn new, local variations. And just as the dandelions that grow from those seeds are not exact clones of the parent weed, neither are the remakes identical copies. Consider the case of Dashiell Hammett's American gangster novel *Red Harvest*, which traveled to Japan and was adapted as the iconic samurai film *Yojimbo* (1961), which in turn emigrated to Italy and was remade as quintessential Spaghetti Western *Per un pugno di dollari* (*A Fistful of Dollars*, 1964).

Remakes are also, to put it simply, fun. We humans are fond of variations on a theme. Mozart composed Twelve Variations on "Ah, vous dirai-je, Maman" (aka "Twinkle, Twinkle, Little Star") because he enjoyed hearing the tune in new and interesting ways. Shakespeare dusted off the well-known Scandinavian folktale of Amleth and retold it to appreciative crowds in iambic pentameter as *Hamlet*. And how many times has Batman's origin story been retooled and republished in comic books alone? There's something appealing about reliving something familiar, but with a novel twist.

To be sure, the sampling of remakesploitation examined in this book is cherry-picked. The titles highlighted in these pages—including versions of *Captain America* (1944), *King Kong* (1933), *A Nightmare on Elm Street* (1984), *12 Angry Men* (1957) and *The Wizard of Oz* (1939)—were chosen because they're based on popular franchises, blockbusters, and cinematic touchstones that have become woven into the fabric of American popular culture. In other words, these are familiar household names unexpectedly put to new, unfamiliar faces, and these often-imaginative renovations force us to question how much we really know about our favorite characters after all.

Admittedly, a few of the films in this book are not *technically* remakes in the usual sense. *Drakula İstanbul'da* ("Dracula in Istanbul," 1953), for example, was not based on Universal's *Dracula* (1931), nor was *Vinni-Pukh* ("Winnie the Pooh," 1969) a remake of Disney's *Winnie the Pooh and the Honey Tree* (1966). Rather, they were separate adaptations of the same literary source material. They still offer fascinating alternate takes on familiar Hollywood fare, but in such instances I've referred to the films in these pages as "counterparts" of American films rather than "inspired by" them.

Incidentally, allow me to clarify one thing this book isn't. It is not a collection of reviews. I'm not rating these movies on a four-star or two-thumb scale. I decline to judge them as good or bad. Nor, for that matter, am I fond of the label "so bad it's good"—a phrase I find snobbish, condescending, and frequently just plain inaccurate. Whether you enjoy these films or not is a matter of taste, but each one has a story that makes it worthy of examination.

Nor do I make value judgments on the industries that made the films. Each of the countries discussed in this book has a rich cinematic heritage of its own. In fact, it's worth noting that Yılmaz Güney, the star of Turkey's take on *The Magnificent Seven*

(1960), was one of his country's most celebrated actor-directors, lensing numerous social issues films and winning the Palme d'Or at Cannes for his controversial *Yol* ("The Road," 1982). Fukasaku Kinji, director of an unabashed *Star Wars* (1977) cash-in, brought to Japanese cinema a number of highly original yakuza pictures and samurai films as well as the chilling dystopian classic *Batoru Rowaiaru* (*Battle Royale*, 2000).

So if anything, my hope is that the movies discussed in this book might serve as "gateway films," giving the curious Hollywood-centric reader something familiar to anchor to, while simultaneously broadening their horizons toward new and rewarding cinematic experiences.

A brief note about naming conventions. For consistency, all of the movie titles in this book are written in (or transliterated from) their original language. Non-English titles are followed by the English equivalents in parentheses. Official English titles are presented in Italics, and when those do not exist, a literal translation is provided in quotes. Additionally, the Japanese, Chinese, and Korean names of people are presented in the traditional format, surname first. I've made exceptions for Chinese actors and filmmakers who are also well-known by Western given names. In those cases, I've followed the standard practice of displaying the Western given name first, followed by the surname, and then the Chinese given name (e.g., Maggie Cheung Man-yuk).

So pop some popcorn, fry up some samosas, grab a bag of dry sardines, or tear open a package of salty licorice. It's time for our feature presentation!

Why Didn't They Get Sued?

In any discussion of remakesploitation films, the question inevitably arises, "How did they get away with it?" That is, how was a producer in another country able to make and release a film that infringes on someone else's copyright without facing legal action? Because this is always a point of great interest, it seems worthwhile to address it up front. The most common answers to the litigation conundrum have to do with a studio's awareness of the film in question, the profitability of legal action, variations among international copyright laws, and popular misunderstandings about copyright infringement.

First of all, before a Hollywood studio can even consider pursuing legal action against a film, it has to know that the film exists. Many of the movies covered in this book were only released in and around their home countries. For example, Brazilian comedy troupe Os Trapalhões, which produced versions of *The Wizard of Oz* (1939), *Planet of the Apes* (1968), and *Star Wars* (1977) in the 1970s and '80s, was a strictly local phenomenon. *Anyab* ("Fangs," 1981), Mohamed Shebl's indie take on *The Rocky Horror Picture Show* (1975), was unlikely to have been seen outside of its native Egypt. And the USSR's counterpart of *Winnie the Pooh and the Honey Tree* (1966) was quite literally screened behind the Iron Curtain. It wasn't until the mid-2000s, with the advent of video-sharing websites like YouTube, that many of these films began to receive worldwide attention—often, ironically enough, thanks to piracy. And by that time, the production companies that made them might well have become defunct.

Moreover, it has to be worth a studio's while to seek damages, and that's not always the case. Certainly Lucasfilm and 20th Century-Fox probably eventually learned about the notorious "Turkish *Star Wars*," *Dünyayı Kurtaran Adam* (*The Man Who Saves the World*, 1982), which incorporated unlicensed footage from *A New Hope*. But as the film had only 1/37th the budget of *Star Wars* and box office receipts likely to match, it would hardly have been worth the time or expense to go after its producers for a pittance. Similarly, *Mahakaal* ("Time of Death," 1993), the Ramsay Brothers' unauthorized Indian remake of *A Nightmare on Elm Street* (1984), grossed just $600,000 worldwide—chicken feed compared to *Elm Street*'s $25.5 million take. And box office flop *Aabra Ka Daabra* (2004), India's 3D riff on *Harry Potter and the Sorcerer's Stone* (2001), pulled in less than $250,000—an 86 percent loss—compared to *Harry Potter*'s $317 million. In other words, these were not deep pockets.

Furthermore, not all countries' intellectual property laws were created equal. For decades Turkey had firm IP legislation governing works of art produced domestically, but unclear laws regulating copyrights on foreign works. This fostered an environment ripe for plagiarism with local films lifting plots, music, and even footage from Hollywood films. It wasn't until 1995 when, as part of its candidacy for accession into the European Union, Turkey's IP laws were amended to be comparable to the rest of Europe's.

Even when copyright laws are effectively identical, complications can still arise when American-filed lawsuits are tried in foreign countries. India, for example, has intellectual property laws much like those in America, but a lackluster track record of enforcing them in court and a judicial system criticized for sluggishness. Factors like these can deter Hollywood studios from pursuing their cases with vigor—or at all.

Then there's the question of whether a particular film is legally actionable in the first place. Most international copyright laws protect the expression of an idea, but not the underlying idea itself. That means that a rip-off would have to materially copy the source film, not just its concept, to warrant a lawsuit. Thus *Zashchitniki* (*Guardians*, 2017), Sarik Andreasyan's Russian take on *The Avengers* (2012), was unlikely to get slapped with a suit since it has little in common with its U.S. counterpart beyond a national team of superheroes—even though the film owes much of its fame to comparisons with the Marvel franchise. And while the Italian sci-fi epic *Starcrash* (1978) was explicitly commissioned as a copy of *Star Wars*, the actual similarities are mostly superficial—laser-swords, a Galactic Empire, hyperspace, mind-probes, and androids. Its story is completely different. This important distinction explains why several remakesploitation movies have been widely and legally distributed without incident even in the United States.

Every once in a while, however, studios *do* pursue legal action. When Film Ventures International attempted to release Italian *Jaws* (1975) knock-off *L'ultimo squalo* (*The Last Shark*, 1981) in American theaters, Universal Pictures smelled blood and successfully filed for an injunction. And in 2009, 20th Century–Fox sued Indian production company BR Films, alleging that its film *Banda Yeh Bindaas Hai* ("This Guy is Cool") was an infringement of *My Cousin Vinny* (1992)—a case that was eventually settled out of court.

But nowadays more and more studios are side-stepping the problem by getting into the international remake business themselves. In 2010, as part of a bid to reach the lucrative Chinese market, Walt Disney Pictures teamed up with Shanghai Media Group and Huayi Brothers Media Corporation to co-produce *Ge wu qing chun—Disney High School Musical: China*—an official remake of its hit TV movie. And in 2014 Fox Star Studios, a joint venture between 20th Century–Fox and STAR India, produced *Bang Bang!*, a Bollywood version of Fox's Tom Cruise/Cameron Diaz actioner *Knight and Day* (2010). Following that film's success, its director Siddharth Anand then went on to make a deal with U.S.-based Millennium Films for the rights to the Rambo franchise—along with four other titles—for an authorized modern update.

In recent years, the internet and the global economy have done a great deal to close the loopholes that enable unauthorized remakes. But there still remains an extraordinary back catalog of remakesploitation films from around the world that exist in various states of limbo. Some of these are legally available in specific countries only; for example, you can still buy an official DVD of "Turkish *Star Wars*" in

Turkey or *L'ultimo squalo* in Sweden. Others were once for sale on videotape but are now long out of print, having become rare and valuable collectors' items. And a few never received any kind of consumer release and are only obtainable via the gray market, through torrent sites and sellers of home-burned DVDs. But whatever their legal status, the audience for these films remains voracious, and where there's a will, there's usually a way.

1

Capes, Conquerors, and Comic Books

3 Dev Adam (*Three Giant Men*)

INSPIRED BY: *Captain America* (1944)
COUNTRY: Turkey
YEAR: 1973
PRODUCTION: Tual Film
DIRECTOR: Tevfik Fikret Uçak
WRITER: Doğan Tamer
STARS: Aytekin Akkaya, Deniz Erkanat, Yavuz Selekman, Tevfik Şen, Doğan Tamer, Mine Sun, Altan Günbay

Istanbul is in the grip of a crime wave. An international villain has descended upon Turkey, plundering precious artifacts and butchering anyone in his way. Fortunately, the heroic Captain America (Aytekin Akkaya) is hot on his heels. Joining forces with his Mexican colleague, the masked luchador and crime-fighter El Santo (Yavuz Selekman), Cap travels to Istanbul to hunt down his arch-nemesis, that diabolical red fiend….

Spider-Man.

This unfriendly neighborhood Spidey (Tevfik Şen) controls a global counterfeiting operation in which the stolen artefacts play a crucial role. Running down a pair of leads, Captain America's girlfriend Julia (Deniz Erkanat) investigates a fashion show that's been playing host to some suspicious foreigners, while El Santo tracks the owner of a mysterious post office box to a shady karate dojo.

Julia is captured at the fashion show while photographing some documents, but a homing device brings Cap to her rescue, bursting through the wall like the Kool-Aid man. Meanwhile, sneaking into the dojo office, Santo discovers fragments of a letter and a wad of counterfeit money, escaping with them only after battling a handful of karateka.

While waiting for the police lab to reconstruct the letter, which turns out to contain addresses of robbery targets, Cap stakes out the post office once again and trails a courier to a creepy mannequin factory. He and Santo burst in to find the evildoers' counterfeiting equipment and a pack of gobsmacked gangsters.

The final threads lead to a technicolor strip club operating as a front for the baddies, where Julia naturally has to go undercover, and the next robbery target, where Cap and Santo ambush Spider-Man, though he nevertheless eludes them. The chase culminates in a warehouse showdown with Spider-Man, who turns out to be much more than he seems....

~~~

3 Dev Adam was made during the heyday of Yeşilçam. Turkish for "Green Pine," Yeşilçam is simply the name of the Istanbul street where most Turkish production companies had their offices. However, it really refers to a particular, wild, fruitful era in Turkey's film industry between the 1950s and '80s. Struggling to meet an increasing demand for local films with hardly any infrastructure to back them up, filmmakers churned out movies at a whirlwind pace. They wrote, shot, edited, and released titles all in less than two months. Budgets were minuscule. Film stock was rationed and, due to restrictions on spending foreign currency, difficult for producers to import on their own. Casts and crews worked under every possible hardship. And yet, at its peak, Yeşilçam was the third most productive film industry in the world, cranking out 300 movies in 1972 alone.

Turkish one-sheet for *3 Dev Adam* (1973). Spider-Man is drawn much more like his comic book counterpart than he actually appears on screen.

One of the most popular genres in the 1960s and '70s was masked hero films. These featured do-gooders like Batman, The Phantom, and Spy Smasher as well as anti-heroes like Killing, the sadistic, skeleton-clad criminal of popular Italian photo-novels. Benefiting from lax copyright protections for foreign media, these unauthorized adventures were churned out in great numbers to delighted audiences, particularly in rural areas.

Filmmaker Tevfik Fikret Uçak was eager to capitalize on these successes. He was no stranger to comic book movies, having already adapted the Turkish fantasy-adventure comic *Tarkan*, about a Hunnic warrior of yore, in *Tarkan: Camoka'ya Karşı* ("Tarkan: Against Camoka," 1969). With his new project, however, he wanted to do something to one-up his competition. He proposed a movie with *multiple* masked heroes, a novel concept for 1973. The end result would be the world's first comic book crossover film, pitting Captain America against Spider-Man 43 years before Hollywood's *Captain America: Civil War* (2016). Uçak also added Mexican wrestler El Santo into the mix for good measure. The silver-masked luchador had made the transition from the ring to the screen in 1958, and by 1973 he had appeared in dozens of adventure films as a cinematic costumed crime-fighter in his own right. El Santo's movies were distributed overseas and found an appreciative audience in Turkey, making him a logical candidate for Uçak's superhero romp.

However, the way Uçak presented his heroes was not exactly how fans might remember them. With Captain America, the filmmaker appears to have made some curious adjustments. Superficially, he stripped the hero of his trademark shield and helmet wings. More fundamentally, though, he downgraded the crime-fighter from a World War II-era super soldier to an ordinary police officer in a costume. Yet Uçak and his team were not precisely responsible for these transgressions against canon. The real culprit was Hollywood.

Captain America was one of the first comic book superheroes to be adapted for the silver screen, headlining a 15-chapter Republic movie serial in 1944. Originally, Republic had planned to adapt Fawcett Comics' Mister Scarlet, but a split with Fawcett necessitated a hasty rewrite with a new hero. Cap was substituted, but because of the scramble he differed greatly from his comic book origins. He became, like Mister Scarlet, a middle-aged district attorney who moonlighted as a vigilante. His costume was also revised, omitting—can you guess?—the shield and wings. This is the version of the character that Turks would have been familiar with in 1973. *Captain America* comics wouldn't be introduced to Turkey until 1975, but the Republic serial had already been distributed nationally by Kemal Film as *Yıldırım Yüzbaşı*—"Captain Lightning." When Uçak and company set out to adapt him, then, this was the version they would likely have drawn from.

However, the real aberration is the sinister Spider-Man. With Captain America and El Santo on the case, Uçak and his team wanted an especially powerful foe to oppose them. Their solution was to transform another major superhero into a super-*villain*. Like Cap, Spider-Man's comics wouldn't arrive in Turkey until the mid-'70s, and then only briefly, before reappearing more regularly in the '80s. He also wouldn't receive a big-screen adaptation until 1977, when the American TV pilot was released as a theatrical feature for the foreign market. Therefore, since Turkish audiences were only minimally familiar with the character, Uçak and screenwriter Doğan Tamer were able to take as many liberties as they wished. Hence, *3 Dev Adam*'s Spider-Man became a sadistic, murderous crime lord cast in the same mold as Italy's Killing. He was also given the superhuman but distinctly un-spider-like ability to spontaneously duplicate himself! Uçak and screenwriter Doğan Tamer re-envisioned Spidey as a kind of malicious, self-replicating virus. This conceit allowed him to battle both heroes simultaneously and even be killed several times during the film's final act—yet always reappear, laughing merrily.

Such high-concept-but-low-cost ideas (all you need to clone Spider-Man is another guy in a duplicate costume) made the most of the film's limited resources,

Spider-Man (Tevfik Şen), El Santo (Yavuz Selekman), and Captain America (Aytekin Akkaya) duke it out. Santo lifts one of the evil Spidey's clones, portrayed here by a dummy.

which was always an issue for Yeşilçam cinema. Effects and techniques that Hollywood took for granted had to either be imitated for pennies on the dollar or abandoned entirely. Even demonstrating Cap's bulletproof suit was a challenge. In order to achieve the effect of rebounding bullets, the team had a crew member blow seeds at Akkaya's chest through a straw.

Another cost-saving measure was the use of lifted Hollywood soundtracks. Given the short amount of time in which films had to be turned around, the prohibitive cost of composing and recording an original orchestral score and, again, Turkey's lenient copyright laws, filmmakers found it more expedient to pull albums of existing film music from their personal libraries to score their movies. Uçak used this approach for *3 Dev Adam*, and the attentive listener will notice, among other cues, the main theme from the James Bond flick *Diamonds Are Forever* (1971).

Despite containing what Tamer called the four essential elements of a profitable Turkish action film—violence, sex, sadism, and heroism—the film nevertheless went months without financial success. Finally, Uçak rented a booth at a film festival where he found an international distributor who, among other feats, turned *3 Dev Adam* into the first Turkish movie sold in Tanzania.

Unfortunately, due to unsafe storage methods, the original negatives of *3 Dev Adam* were destroyed in a fire. Nearly all of the prints have been lost as well. Today the film primarily exists in the form of low-fidelity videotape transfers. In fact the first 16 seconds were thought to be lost entirely until distributor Vassilis Barounis of

Onar Films discovered them on a 20-year-old Greek VHS tape and restored them for the film's only official DVD release in 2006.

Ator l'invincibile (*Ator the Fighting Eagle*)

INSPIRED BY: *Conan the Barbarian* (1982)
COUNTRY: Italy
YEAR: 1982
PRODUCTION: Filmirage
DIRECTOR: David Hills (Aristide Massaccesi)
WRITERS: José María Sánchez, Aristide Massaccesi
STARS: Miles O'Keeffe, Sabrina Siani, Ritza Brown, Dakar, Edmund Purdom, Laura Gemser

In an ancient time, frightened peasants live in the shadow of the all-powerful High Priest of the Spider (Dakar). Their only salvation lies in a prophecy that foretells the birth of a savior—a warrior who will one day overthrow the tyrant and kill his spider god. On the day the child is born, recognizable by a sacred birthmark, the rebel Griba (Edmund Purdom) flees with it to a distant village to prevent it from being slaughtered by the High Priest's soldiers. There Griba turns the child over to a peasant couple to raise.

Eventually the boy, Ator (Miles O'Keeffe), comes of age and is about to marry his beloved, Sanda (Ritza Brown). However, on the day of the wedding, the High Priest's scouts spy Griba keeping watch nearby. Presently a horde of soldiers thunders into the village. They kill Ator's parents, decimate his homeland, and abduct his new bride. Shattered, Ator vows revenge.

Griba therefore takes him under his wing and teaches him to fight. Once Ator is suitably proficient at combat, he sets out on his own for the Temple of the Spider God in search of Sanda—only to be immediately captured by a tribe of Amazon warriors. The women duel for the privilege of killing Ator—after first conceiving his child. But fortunately, his champion, Runn (Sabrina Siani), agrees to spare his life (and virginity) in exchange for allowing her to accompany him on his mission. Runn is a thief by profession, and the Temple of the Spider God is said to contain countless treasures.

However, their journey is rife with the obligatory fantasy trials and dangers. Ator is captured and hypnotized by a witch (Laura Gemser) who tricks him into believing that Sanda has willingly joined the spider worshippers. Escaping from her, he and Runn must then navigate the Land of the Walking Dead—an army of zombified soldiers. From there they venture into a volcanic cave to retrieve a magic shield guarded by blind warriors and a shadow clone of Ator—literally a shadow cast on the wall.

Finally they arrive at the Temple of the Spider God. They sneak in, and once they dispatch the guards, Runn must decide whether treasure or loyalty mean more to her as Ator prepares for his perilous final showdown with the High Priest.

～～～

In 1982, director John Milius and Universal Pictures released *Conan the Barbarian*, inspired by the fantasy stories of Robert E. Howard and the popular comic book series published by Marvel. Recounting the tale of the moody Cimmerian warrior and his quest for revenge against the snake cult leader who murdered his parents, the film was made for $16 million and earned nearly ten times that much worldwide. Needless to say, those numbers inspired the envy of producers everywhere and, subsequently, a flood of similar sword-and-sorcery flicks in the 1980s. Aimed at the insatiable home video rental market, a great many of these cash-ins were produced in Italy. This was only natural, however, since Italians had essentially been making Conan movies since before Conan was born.

The year of 1914 had marked the release of Italian silent epic *Cabiria*, a sprawling adventure set in ancient Rome which introduced the world to Herculean hero Maciste. It

Italian four-sheet for *Ator l'invincibile* (1982).

was the birth of the *peplum*, better known as the sword-and-sandals film, which featured beefy, superhuman strongmen of the old world doing battle with tyrants, gods, and mythological beasts. *Cabiria* was renowned for its quality and splendor, but the peplum didn't truly become a phenomenon until Pietro Francisci's more modest *Le fatiche di Ercole* ("The Labors of Hercules") in 1958, starring former Mr. Universe Steve Reeves as Hercules himself. American producer Joseph E. Levine picked up the low-budget spectacle for $120,000 and then spent $1 million marketing it. His gamble paid off fivefold and sparked a peplum frenzy in Italy, resulting in dozens of films that trumpeted the adventures of Hercules and rival supermen Samson, Ursus, and *Cabiria*'s Maciste in numerous encore performances.

By the end of the '60s the fad had mostly petered out. But when *Conan* arrived little more than a decade later, Italian producers must have experienced a profound sense of déjà vu. An ancient setting, a routed village, a mighty hero swearing vengeance, a torturous mill wheel, a despotic ruler with a cruel religion—these were all hallmarks of the peplum! To capitalize on *Conan*'s popularity, then, Italian producers had only to restart the sword-and-sandals machinery and swap their heroes' togas for furs. Helming these new productions, predictably, were some of the genre's old hands, including Umberto Lenzi, Francesco Prosperi, and Tonino Ricci.

Ator l'invincibile, on the other hand, was the work of Aristide Massaccesi, an unlikely choice for a sword-and-sorcery epic. His only peplum credit was as an assistant camera operator on Mario Bava's *Ercole al centro della Terra* (*Hercules in the Haunted World*, 1961). He was better known for making low budget horror and erotic films. But Massaccesi was also an opportunist, and many of his movies rode the coattails of more famous work. His *Emanuelle* series, for instance, was a cash-in on the success of Just Jaeckin's original *Emmanuelle* (1974) and Bitto Albertini's *Emanuelle nera* (1975). His later films piggybacked on such disparate sources as *Mad Max* (1979), *Caligula* (1979), and *Flashdance* (1983). As long as he had a template—like, say, *Conan*—Massaccesi could be at home in any genre. Thus, over the course of *Ator l'invincibile*, the eponymous hero teams up with a fiery blonde thief, just like Conan; is seduced by an evil witch, just like Conan; and must rescue a young woman from an evil cult leader, just like Conan.

Subtext, however, was another matter. Central to *Conan the Barbarian* were themes of religion and cultism. Snake cult leader Thulsa Doom strongly echoes the infamous Rev. Jim Jones, who instigated the mass suicide of 900 followers in Jonestown, Guyana just four years prior to *Conan*'s release. Massaccesi, by contrast, was content to dispense with allegory in the service of a more straightforward adventure tale.

However, in a clear nod to James Earl Jones's Thulsa Doom, Massaccesi cast

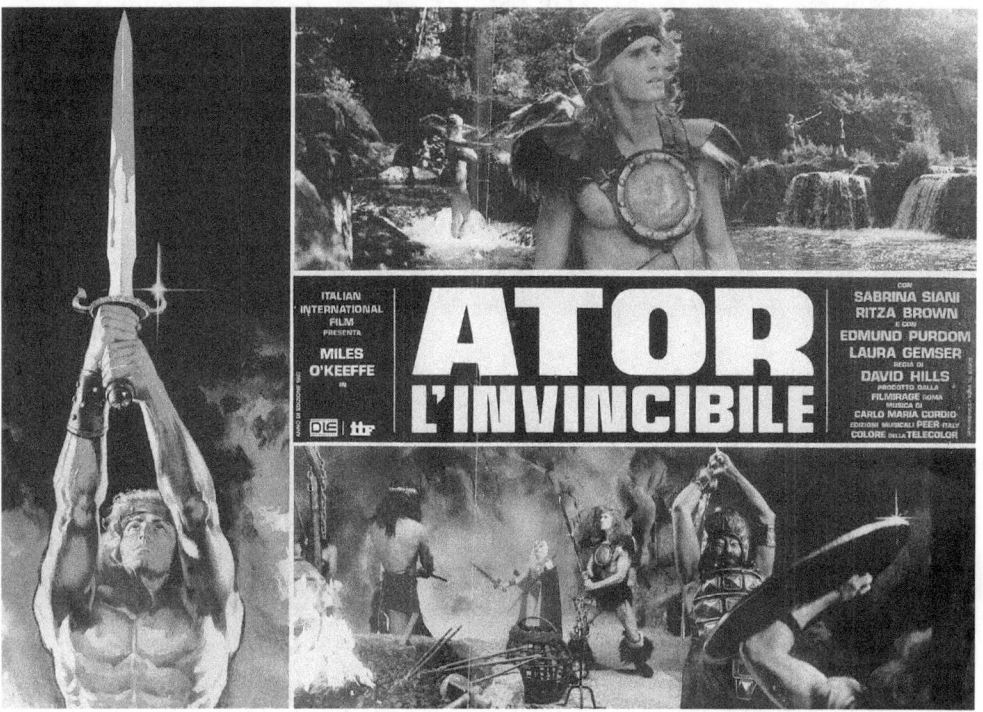

Italian lobby card depicting several sequences from *Ator l'invincibile* (1982).

brawny, dark-skinned, Peruvian-born Dakar, an actor and wrestler, as his equivalent High Priest of the Spider. Moreover, Dakar's voice in the English-language dub is a respectable imitation of Jones's basso profundo.

Massaccesi may have been pleased with his casting of Dakar, with whom he had worked before, but he was less so with his ersatz Conan. Miles O'Keeffe, a former American football player, had earned a degree of fame starring in John Derek's *Tarzan, the Ape Man* (1981), thanks in part to his steamy love scenes with co-star Bo Derek. Massaccesi hired him on the recommendation of his American business partner, but he quickly regretted the decision. Author Michele Giordano quoted the filmmaker lamenting that his star "was very shy and walked like a paralytic," and that he "would not attempt to change his expression even slightly." And despite O'Keeffe's impressive physique, the director felt that it was only through the colossal efforts of the master of arms, Franco Ukmar, that he was able to perform his fight scenes successfully.

But Massaccesi might have taken solace in his movie's array of attractive, convenient, and inexpensive filming locations. Whereas *Conan* had to travel to Spain for its Hyborian kingdoms, *Ator*'s prehistoric world consisted of picturesque landmarks in Rome's own backyard. These included the town of Manziana, the Monte Gelato waterfalls, and the excavated amphitheater at Tusculum for the Temple of the Spider God—although why the temple appears to be an ancient ruin even in ancient times is left unexplained.

Ator l'invincibile was successful enough that it spawned three sequels of its own: *Ator 2: L'invincibile Orion* (*The Blade Master*, 1982), *Ator il guerriero di ferro* (*Iron Warrior*, 1987), and *The Lord of Akili* (*Quest for the Mighty Sword*, 1990). Entering production before *Conan*'s sequel, *Ator 2* was instead inspired by *The Quest for Fire* (1981), featuring clans of murderous cavemen. The third entry, which is substantially more psychedelic, features an opening scene that replicates in remarkable detail the Kryptonian trial sequence from Richard Donner's *Superman* (1978)! And the final installment, heavily inspired by Richard Wagner's *Der Ring des Nibelungen*, reuses the goblin masks from the notorious horror film *Troll 2* (1990), causing it to be released in some territories as *Troll 3*—and therefore leading to far more confusion than seems strictly necessary for a series of otherwise modest *Conan* rip-offs.

Darna

INSPIRED BY: *The New Original Wonder Woman* (1975)
COUNTRY: Philippines
YEAR: 1991
PRODUCTION: Viva Films
DIRECTOR: Joel Lamangan
WRITER: Frank G. Rivera
STARS: Nanette Medved, Edu Manzano, Pilar Pilapil, Tonton Gutierrez, Nida Blanca, Bing Loyzaga

In 1900 South America, archaeologist Dominico Lipolico (Edu Manzano) uncovers a mystical amulet that grants him immortality and powerful dark magic. Seventy-five years later, a young girl named Narda, living with her grandmother

(Nida Blanca) and two younger brothers, is visited by an angel who bestows upon her a small white stone. When Narda swallows the stone and says the name "Darna," she transforms into a mighty superheroine.

Fast-forward to the present day as an adult Narda (Nanette Medved) holds down a day job in the city as a journalist. She works alongside her love interest, George (Tonton Gutierrez), who takes no particular notice of Narda but is smitten with her alter ego. The two reporters start off their day with an assignment to cover a couple of celebrities. One is Valentina (Pilar Pilapil), the "first Filipina fashion designer and international model." The other is Dominico Lipolico, who has become a famous "philanthropist, businessman, artist, and playboy" and is contributing a fortune to local development projects.

Lipolico holds a debauched party at his lavish estate to celebrate the donation. He has specifically invited Valentina to the bash, and as soon as she arrives he whisks her away to his chamber. There, using the power of the amulet, he transforms the fashionista into an obedient gorgon. Lipolico also puts the moves on a schoolteacher (Bing Loyzaga), transmogrifying her into the harpy-like Impakta and sending the creature to wreak havoc on the city.

Lipolico next turns his attention to his greatest obstacle to world domination: Darna. With Valentina's help he captures the superheroine and begins a ritual that will turn her evil. Unfortunately for the dark magician, Narda's brothers come to the rescue just in time, forcing Lipolico to resort to other tactics.

When Impakta fails to defeat Darna, Valentina kidnaps Narda's grandmother

Darna (Nanette Medved) sports bullet-repelling bracelets and a Wonder Woman–like tiara designed especially for this film.

and holds her hostage. If Darna wants to get her grandma back and save the world, she'll have to battle the sinister snake woman and contend with Lipolico's diabolical powers.

~~~

One glance at Nanette Medved in her red and gold Darna outfit is enough to put even the most casual fan of American comics in mind of a certain Amazing Amazon. It's not surprising, then, that the character is frequently saddled with the label "the Filipina Wonder Woman." But while Darna's connection to the DC universe is undeniable, it's also fairly complicated.

During World War II, the *Superman* comics brought to the Philippines by American soldiers inspired writer and cartoonist Mars Ravelo to develop a female counterpart for his own country. He conceived the character, initially called Suprema, in 1939—two years before the debut of Wonder Woman. Ravelo based her in part upon the woman he considered a real-life superhero: his mother. He continued to tinker with the character over time, eventually renaming her Varga after the "Varga Girl" pin-ups popular with GIs. Along with the name change came something borrowed from another American hero, Captain Marvel. Rather than being a permanently superpowered woman, Varga became the alter ego of a young, mortal *barrio* girl. With the help of an amulet, she could transform at will into the adult superheroine.

It was a long road from conception to publication. Ravelo offered the character to several magazines but none were interested. A female superhero wouldn't sell, he was told, even as the remarkably similar *Wonder Woman* hit American newsstands in 1941. He had to fight until 1947 before Varga finally debuted in *Bulaklak* ("Blossom") magazine. Illustrated by Ravelo, *Bulaklak*'s Varga battled the forces of evil in a winged helmet and one-piece costume emblazoned with the sun and stars of the Philippine flag. Before long, though, she'd trade in that outfit for a star-decorated bikini with a loincloth—a look that would outlast her. The comic ran for less than two years, at which point Ravelo left *Bulaklak* over creative differences. The magazine kept the rights to the Varga name—but not to the image.

So when Ravelo went to work for *Pilipino Komiks* shortly thereafter, he simply recreated the character with a new moniker. Varga became Darna—in the same bikini, loincloth, and helmet—and young Narda could transform into her by swallowing a magical stone and saying the name. Her first story, illustrated by Nestor Redondo and debuting on May 13, 1950, introduced the world not only to the revamped hero, but also to her arch-nemesis and most enduring foe, the snake-haired Valentina. An apparent freak of nature born to ordinary human parents, Valentina sought to destroy humanity and replace it with a civilization of serpents in a throwback to the days of the dinosaurs.

Before the first story had even run its course, Darna became a movie star. Royal Films quickly snapped up screen rights to the comic and produced a film directed by the esteemed Fernando Poe, Sr., with a screenplay by Mars Ravelo himself. An adaptation of the then-running serial, *Darna* (1951) put the title character up against Valentina once more, this time on the big screen. Starring the Philippines' "Original Movie Queen" Rosa Del Rosario, the film was a tremendous success and helped establish Darna as the Philippines' premiere superhero. It also launched a string of further cinematic adventures that would be the envy of her American rivals for decades.

In 1975, however, Darna's most obvious rival scored a major coup. After a failed attempt to bring DC Comics' Wonder Woman to television in 1974 with an off-model pilot starring Cathy Lee Crosby, the ABC network tried again with the telefilm *The New Original Wonder Woman* (1975). Starring Lynda Carter in a comics-accurate red, blue, and gold costume—including her tiara and bullet-deflecting bracelets—it was a ratings hit. It kicked off a television series that lasted three seasons and significantly boosted the American heroine's fame abroad.

Before long, Wonder Woman's Filipina counterpart began exhibiting some curious changes. The screen version, at any rate. The 1980 *Darna at Ding* ("Darna and Ding") featured Vilma Santos, in her fourth outing as the title character, wearing new spangled blue briefs with her classic red-and-gold top. The overall effect was conspicuously like Lynda Carter's Wonder Woman. And in 1986, Sharon Cuneta's cameo as Darna in *Captain Barbell* (based on another Mars Ravelo comic) featured the heroine in a red, gold, and blue one-piece that pushed her look even further in that direction.

For 1991's *Darna* reboot, director Joel Lamangan returned Darna to a more traditional red-and-gold bikini, but that's not to say he didn't also have *Wonder Woman* on his mind. For the first time, Darna's helmet was swapped for a gold tiara, and her bracelets became a tool to deflect bullets—a curious choice when the character was already impervious to that particular brand of lead poisoning.

In fact, these tweaks were just part of an overall script by Frank Rivera that offered a hodgepodge of

Original poster for *Darna* (1991). Note Valentina's snake familiar Vibora in the bottom-center; she's stolen the heroine's magic stone and gets her own little Darna costume!

non-canon revisions. Narda's day job as a mild-mannered reporter with a coworker crush is pure Superman, not at all like the *Darna* comic. And instead of living in a poor rural village, Narda and her family (with an extra sibling) have been relocated to a comfortable house in the city. Meanwhile, her nemeses Valentina and Impakta received alternate origins as sidekicks to a newly-created villain—with Valentina's snake familiar Vibora reimagined as a sassy talking puppet. In other words, the version of Darna presented by Rivera and Lamangan was something of an oddity all-around.

It's also important to note that the connections and similarities between Wonder Woman and Darna—in Lamangan's film as well as other incarnations—are not only mostly superficial, but they cut both ways. For example, Darna was invulnerable and could fly decades before Wonder Woman gained the same powers. A Darna fan might also have looked askance at Lynda Carter's Wonder Woman when she donned a red helmet with gold wings for a 1978 episode about skateboarding. And the feature films starring Gal Gadot and comic incarnations like the "Rebirth" design by Tony Daniel have recently incorporated a loincloth element into the Amazon's costume. So to paraphrase Iain Robert Smith's *The Hollywood Meme*: if we're going to call Darna the "Filipina Wonder Woman," we might consider why we're not calling Wonder Woman the "American Darna."

Kızıl Maske ("The Phantom")

COUNTERPART OF: *The Phantom* (1943)
COUNTRY: Turkey
YEAR: 1968
PRODUCTION: Atadeniz Film
DIRECTOR: Çetin İnanç
WRITER: Çetin İnanç
STARS: İrfan Atasoy, Sezer Güvenirgil, Yıldırım Gencer, Faruk Panter

A shadowy international syndicate meets in a darkened conference room, each member hidden beneath a numbered white hood. The organization determines to focus its sinister efforts on Turkey, where Professor Asım Bilginer (Haydar Karaer) has just invented a miraculous and valuable formula for an enlarging ray.

After surviving an assassination attempt, the professor sends his daughter Sezer (Sezer Güvenirgil) to appeal for help from The Phantom. However, the masked hero is getting too old for such adventures, so he passes the torch—and the mission—to his son (İrfan Atasoy). Thus, together with his muscular sidekick Panther (Faruk Panter), the new Phantom sets out with Sezer to meet Prof. Bilginer.

Meanwhile, the syndicate has sent assassins to plant a timebomb in the professor's home. The Phantom and Panther arrive with Sezer in time to dispatch the hoodlums, but they don't notice the bomb until moments before it explodes. Everyone escapes, but the professor's house and laboratory are completely demolished. The Phantom therefore invites the professor and his daughter to stay with him at his home in Istanbul.

Elsewhere, mafia boss "Al Capone" Arif (Yıldırım Gencer) arrives in Istanbul to represent the interests of the syndicate. His first order of business is to send two

Faruk Panter and İrfan Atasoy leap after the bad guys. Fans will hardly recognize The Phantom in his revamped black leather outfit, but for the illustration his jacket and cowl were colored a comics-accurate red.

henchmen to The Phantom's home in the guise of police officers to take care of the professor. But The Phantom smells a rat and tricks them into giving themselves away. Incapacitating and interrogating the goons, he learns that Arif is operating out of a local nightclub. He and Panther break into the club and tangle with a throng of mafia henchmen, but Arif manages to escape.

Eager for revenge, Arif once more sends henchmen to The Phantom's home. Another melee ensues, kickstarting a perilous chase across the rooftops of Istanbul. The heroes win out, only to discover that this was part of a trap; The Phantom, Panther, Prof. Bilginer, and Sezer are all captured.

Arif strings up Phantom and Panther, then leaves for the train station with Prof. Bilginer, intending to sell the scientist to none other than the insidious Fu Manchu! (In this universe, however, the notorious Chinese villain is Arabian.) With great effort and superhuman contortions, Phantom and Panther escape their bonds and pursue Arif, praying that they make it in time.

∼∼∼

For those who came in late, The Phantom is an American comic strip hero created in 1936. He dwells in the jungles of Africa devoting his life to the destruction of piracy, greed, and cruelty. Every generation his mantle is passed from father to son so that The Phantom always appears to be the same man—the mythic "Man Who Cannot Die." His swashbuckling exploits have inspired a movie serial, a Hollywood film, two TV pilots, and a couple of animated series. And those are just the legitimate entries.

He was also wildly popular in Turkey, where he was dubbed "Kızıl Maske"—"Red

Mask." For although he may be known in the States for his purple bodysuit and cowl, that wasn't precisely by design. In the original black-and-white daily strip, The Phantom's costume was explicitly gray; in fact, he was very nearly called "The Gray Ghost." But when a full-color Sunday edition began in 1939, the colorist arbitrarily tinted the suit purple, much to creator Lee Falk's confusion. To complicate matters further, international publishers had the freedom to color the strips however they chose, so in Scandinavia he was blue, in Australia green, and in Turkey and much of Europe he was red.

This scarlet Phantom first appeared in Turkey in 1939. His strips were published in children's magazines and comics periodicals like *1001 Roman* ("1001 Novels") and *Haftalık Albüm* ("Weekly Album") rather than newspapers. And they weren't always ported over in their original form. Sometimes they were abridged or censored (redrawing women's dresses to be more conservative, for instance), and occasionally bootleg publishers would even pawn off cheap tracings. But regardless of the form or format, *The Phantom* was popular enough to warrant three separate unauthorized film adaptations. What's more, two of them—this one among them—came out in the same year from competing companies.

Well-known heroes occasionally appeared in "dueling" adaptations thanks to ready-made fan bases and few copyright concerns. And in truth, they weren't really competing. These films made their money in rural areas, playing second-tier theaters or open-air cinemas—the equivalent of American drive-ins. Their audiences had a ravenous appetite for films, which were their primary form of escapism. So two exciting Phantom adventures was a bonus, not a dilemma.

Of course, being unofficial productions, they also boasted varying degrees of fidelity to the source material. Director Çetin İnanç, at the very beginning of his extensive career, wasn't much of a comic book fan, and as a result his depiction of the title character tended to miss the mark. In his biography *Jet Rejisör*, İnanç described his thought process for reimagining The Phantom for Turkish audiences:

> Let's say a family in Istanbul has been wronged, and the man is going to avenge it. Let's also say that the man is a lawyer. For him to take revenge as a lawyer isn't very stylish; it would look bad. So what's going to happen? The man will disguise himself; he'll become The Phantom to take care of his business. The Phantom is essentially like Zorro.

İnanç didn't give himself quite enough credit; the origin of his Phantom isn't quite so off-base as he suggests. But his statement does indicate the kind of irreverent attitude that went into determining how to domesticate the character. İnanç felt that the hero needed a love interest, so he invented one in the person of the scientist's daughter. But The Phantom of the comics already had a love interest—Diana Palmer, who had been a recurring character since the very first strip. Furthermore, the elder Phantom of İnanç's film lives not in a remote African jungle, but in a nearby Turkish cave, presumably somewhere in Anatolia. And we get only a glimpse of his signature costume, since his son, in taking over the family business, opts instead for a black hood and matching leather jacket—when he bothers to wear a disguise at all.

Suspiciously, these new duds are almost identical to those of the hero in *Casus Kıran* ("Spy Smasher," 1968), a film İnanç worked on the same year, and *Demir Pençe:*

Korsan Adam ("Iron Claw: The Pirate," 1969), which he would direct the following year. And most tellingly, all of these mimicked the Italian film *Mister X* (1967) from the previous year. İnanç and company apparently found Mister X's costume ideal for the modern Turkish superhero and copied it indiscriminately.

The "and company" was primarily producer Yılmaz Atadeniz, İnanç's boss and mentor. A longtime fan of comics and adventure serials, he was the pioneer of superhero films in Turkey, kicking off the craze in 1967 with *Kilink İstanbul'da* ("Killing in Istanbul"), based on the popular Italian photo-novel *Killing*—but with the addition of a Captain Marvel-inspired superhero. İnanç assisted Atadeniz on several such films before the master handed the student the reins of *Kızıl Maske*. In fact, the scene of the hooded cabal at the beginning of the film is actually footage from Atadeniz's *Kilink: Soy ve Öldür*

The Phantom (İrfan Atasoy) takes aim while Panther (Faruk Panter) hangs in there.

("Killing: Strip and Kill," 1967) redubbed to match the new plot. It was a trick İnanç learned from the boss, and one he'd use many times in the years to come.

Ultimately, Turkey's lax attitude toward intellectual property had a twofold effect on superhero cinema. On one hand, any movie producer could respond to the demands of fans to see their favorite comic book characters on screen. But it also meant that the filmmakers had carte blanche to adapt and alter those characters, for better or worse, in any way they saw fit. So it was just a matter of chance, when the cinema patron paid for his ticket, whether he was really going to see The Phantom—or, as İnanç suggested, just a Phantom-flavored Zorro.

La Mujer Murciélago (Bat Woman)

INSPIRED BY: *Batman* (1966)
COUNTRY: Mexico
YEAR: 1968

PRODUCTION: Cinematográfica Calderón S.A.
DIRECTOR: René Cardona
WRITER: Alfredo Salazar
STARS: Maura Monti, Roberto Cañedo, Héctor Godoy

Acapulco's wrestlers are being systematically murdered. Their corpses are turning up in the sea with their pineal glands depleted. Baffled, police captain Mario Robles (Héctor Godoy) calls in special agent and costumed crime-fighter Bat Woman (Maura Monti) to infiltrate the wrestling circuit and discover who's behind it all.

The prime suspect is neurosurgeon Dr. Eric Williams (Roberto Cañedo). The authorities don't know it yet, but aboard his yacht *Reptilicus*, Williams is using the athletes' precious pineal fluid to create a superhuman gill man. To obtain his victims, Dr. Williams has one of his henchmen impersonate a blind lottery ticket seller who secures the wrestlers excellent deals on fishing boats. Then, while the unsuspecting musclemen are angling peacefully, four more henchmen in scuba suits sneak on board and abduct them. It's a complicated arrangement but it works.

Bat Woman sneaks aboard the *Reptilicus* to investigate Williams. In his below-deck office she discovers a scientific paper on the pineal gland, but she's unprepared for what she witnesses when she looks through the keyhole of his laboratory: a miniature aquatic man in a fish tank! Before she can learn more, Williams's henchmen seize her and present her to their boss. Williams snatches a scalpel to dispense with the intruder quickly, but Bat Woman splashes acid in his face and escapes.

To avoid his secret getting out, the scarred Williams sends a squad of goons after Bat Woman, but she handily fights them off. Then, taking Robles along, the hero sets out again for the *Reptilicus* to gather more evidence. This time, though, the doctor sees her coming and unleashes the now-fully-grown and deadly gill man, forcing the duo to retreat.

That night at Bat Woman's wrestling match, the "blind" henchman plants a radio transmitter on her to attract the monster. She spots the device but allows the game to play out. Predictably, the gill man abducts her and carries her to the shore, but Robles rescues her in the nick of time. Changing tactics, Williams kidnaps Robles, using him as bait to lure Bat Woman back to the yacht so that he can turn her into his newest creation: the first gill woman....

∽∽∽

In 1966, ABC TV series *Batman* BIFFed, POWed, and ZAPPed its way into American living rooms. Influenced by the camp appeal of the *Batman* movie serials of the 1940s, which had been re-released in '65 to enthusiastic and irreverent crowds, this new series played the Dark Knight exclusively for laughs. Featuring cartoonish villains, far-out production design, off-the-wall gadgets like the anti-mesmerizing bat-reflector, and the idiosyncratic stylings of star Adam West, the show was an instant pop culture—and pop art—phenomenon. Its creators, seizing their moment, quickly parlayed its success into *Batman: The Movie* (1966), a $1.4 million theatrical outing with a broad international release. Immediately, "Batmania" went global.

Just south of the border, prolific director René Cardona saw an opportunity. This groovy, gaudy take on Batman would be an ideal mixer for the colorful world of lucha libre, Mexican professional wrestling, which had fast become a cinematic sensation of its own.

Lucha libre is best known for the vibrant masks worn by many of its combatants—a tradition that began in 1934. Never appearing in public unmasked, these luchadores, with larger-than-life names like El Santo ("The Saint") and Blue Demon, quickly gained a mystique and influence beyond the boundaries of the ring. By the 1960s they had become full-fledged superheroes, starring as themselves in films and serials battling mad scientists, vampires, mummies, Martians, and more. These were quickie, low budget productions with lots of action—in the same tradition as the cliffhangers that inspired *Batman '66*. And that resemblance made "lucha Batman" a shrewd proposition.

It didn't matter that Batman wasn't a real-life wrestler. Although lucha libre movies began as a way to capitalize on the popularity of real-world athletes, new characters were sometimes invented just for the screen in order to satisfy the public's appetite. Such muscular personages as Huracán Ramírez and Neutron the Atomic Superman, for example, began in fiction, though both would eventually break out of the screen and into the ring.

Moreover, René Cardona and screenwriter Alfredo Salazar had a unique, signature variation on the lucha film: the luchadora. A sexy twist on the formula, the duo's femme-focused *Las Luchadoras contra el Médico Asesino* ("The Wrestling Women vs. the Murderous Doctor") debuted in 1962 and begat five sequels, including *Las Mujeres Panteras* ("The Panther Women," 1967) and *Las Luchadoras contra el Robot Asesino* ("Wrestling Women vs. the Killer Robot," 1969). In the wake of those successes, it was entirely plausible that Bat*man* might be even more profitable as Bat *Woman*.

Gender notwithstanding, Salazar and Cardona conceived a heroine very much in the mold of her male counterpart. Like Bruce Wayne, Gloria (Bat Woman's

"Vigilante! Brave! Seductive! Reckless! Invincible! Audacious!" Original Mexican one-sheet for *La Mujer Murciélago* (1968).

alter ego) is a wealthy socialite and accomplished athlete. Her shiny blue cape and cowl unmistakably emulate Adam West's, even though the rest of her costume consists of little more than a matching bikini and opera gloves. And her alternate full-body wrestling uniform—designed to conceal the figure of her stuntwoman—mimics the '60s Caped Crusader even more closely. As for accessories, she's equipped with an obligatory goofy gadget—a gun disguised as a makeup compact—and her stylish black convertible bears a distinct resemblance to the official Batmobile.

By this time, so-called "Mexploitation" films were well known for mining ideas from Hollywood. Universal horror classics like *Dracula* (1931), *Frankenstein* (1931), and *The Mummy* (1932), for example, were frequent sources of inspiration, particularly for screenwriter Salazar. Case in point, *Bat Woman*'s gill man is an obvious riff on *The Creature from the Black Lagoon* (1954)—though its appearance uncannily resembles the Sleestak from not-yet-created TV series *Land of the Lost* (1974)! Perhaps the only real novelty in this "monster vs. wrestler" offering, then—a well-tread genre by 1968—is Bat Woman herself.

Remarkably, Cardona's film wasn't even the first unauthorized cinematic Batwoman. The year of 1966 saw American filmmaker Jerry Warren's *The Wild World of Batwoman*. That movie, however, strayed much further from its inspiration, conceiving Batwoman as a kind of flamboyant sorority-housemother-cum-Pinkerton's-chief. It was unquestionably zany, but it had little else in common with the *Batman* series.

On the other hand, Cardona's *La Mujer Murciélago* is much closer to the spirit of the show. In fact, considering the series strapped Batman to a giant mousetrap and tied him to an oversized roasting spit, a cackling mad scientist with a bright red rubber monster might even be a bit tame by comparison. And a female bat-doppelganger was hardly outré; by the time *La Mujer Murciélago* hit theaters, the *Batman* TV universe had already debuted its own Batgirl in the form of Yvonne Craig. Add in Cardona and Salazar's light-hearted approach, the cartoonish story, rock 'em sock 'em action, jazzy musical score, and of course the familiar costume design, and the casual viewer could very reasonably take Bat Woman for the Caped Crusader's Latina cousin.

Supaidāman (*Spider-Man*)

COUNTERPART OF: *Spider-Man* (1977)
COUNTRY: Japan
YEAR: 1978
PRODUCTION: Tōei Company, Ltd.
DIRECTOR: Takemoto Kōichi
WRITER: Takaku Susumu
STARS: Tōdō Shinji, Nakaya Noboru, Andō Mitsuo, Kagawa Yukie

Yamashiro Takuya (Tōdō Shinji) wakes from a nightmare to the sound of his sister screaming for help. She and their little brother are being menaced by Ninders, bird-beaked henchmen of an alien scourge, the Iron Cross Army. Quickly and secretly, Takuya transforms into Spider-Man, a web-slinging superhero granted powers by the last survivor of the Spider Planet. Spidey fends off the Ninders and pursues them to the top of a nearby building. All the while, however, the hero is being watched from another rooftop.

After dispatching his foes, Takuya returns home only to find it empty and the phone ringing. The caller explains that if Takuya wants to see his siblings or his photographer girlfriend again, he should go to a room at the Urashima Hotel. The Ninders, it seems, were just a ruse to distract him.

Leaping into his futuristic car, the Spider Machine GP-7, Spider-Man speeds to the hotel. He scales the building and breaks in. There he meets his manipulator: Mamiya Jūzō (Nakaya Noboru) of the Interpol Intelligence Department, a branch of the agency tasked with fighting the Iron Cross Army. Mamiya explains that Takuya's loved ones weren't really kidnapped, but merely invited to the hotel pool as a harmless ploy to bring Spider-Man and confirm his identity.

Interpol needs the web-head's help. Lately a number of oil freighters from the Middle East have been destroyed. The cause, it seems, is a biomechanical aquatic monster called Sea Devil that spews torpedoes from its mouth. It's obviously the work of the Iron Cross Army and its leader Professor Monster (Andō Mitsuo), and Mamiya wants to join forces with Spider-Man to stop it. However, before they can get into details, Iron Cross's agent Amazoness (Kagawa Yukie) arrives with a troop of Ninders and captures Mamiya.

From her temporary base on an offshore freighter, Amazoness orders Sea Devil to destroy a coastal industrial complex. Meanwhile, Spider-Man sneaks aboard, frees Mamiya, and escapes. Sea Devil launches his torpedoes, but Spider-Man calls on his spaceship, Marveller, which detonates the missiles before they reach the shore. Undeterred, Sea Devil grows to gigantic proportions to smash the facility with brute force. Fortunately, Spidey has an even more powerful weapon at his disposal: Marveller transforms into the giant battle robot Leopardon, which Spider-Man pilots in a final life-or-death showdown with the beast.

~~~

When Cadence Publishing took over Marvel Comics Group in 1968, it was eager to expand the brand's reach overseas. Eyeing Japan's lucrative manga market, Cadence struck a deal with publisher Kodansha, which agreed to license Spider-Man and The Incredible Hulk for domestic audiences. Kodansha hired local manga artists to create original stories that transplanted the characters and their roots to Japan. The *Spider-Man* manga, created by Ikegami Ryōichi and featuring self-conscious youth Komori Yu as Spidey, was printed in *Gekkan Bessatsu Shōnen Magajin* ("Monthly Separate Shonen Magazine") from January 1970 to September 1971. Unfortunately, it met with a tepid response.

In 1976 Cadence tried again, this time flying licensing department representative Gene Pelc across the Pacific as Marvel's man in Japan. His express goal: get the Marvel brand into Asia. Pelc's first deal was with publisher Shueisha, which reprinted classic *Spider-Man* comics in its magazine *Shūkan Pureibōi* ("Weekly Playboy"), incongruously sticking the webslinger between nude pinups. However, Shueisha had agreed to the deal only reluctantly, and it wasn't long before it dropped the comic from its lineup.

With Marvel's costumed crime-fighters striking out on the printed page, Pelc sought alternative venues. He began to take notice of the wildly popular Japanese superheroes that were beamed to TV sets every week. These included Ultraman (*Urutoraman*, 1966), a size-shifting alien soldier who protects the earth from giant monsters; Kamen Rider (*Kamen Raidā*, 1971), a motorcycle-riding, grasshopper-suited cyborg who battles other robotic monsters; and the Gorangers (*Himitsu Sentai Gorenjā*, 1975), a superpowered squad fending off the extraterrestrial Black Cross Army with futuristic vehicles and weapons. These *tokusatsu* ("special effects") series all had many common elements, having collectively evolved from the world of *Godzilla*'s *kaiju eiga* ("monster movies"). They also spawned a plethora of merchandising. Impressed, Pelc became convinced that television was the right medium for Marvel heroes in Japan.

TV had already been good to Marvel in the States. CBS's 1977 series based on The Incredible Hulk was shaping up to be a big hit, and the network had just teamed up with producers Charles Fries and Dan Goodman to produce a low-budget *Spider-Man* show. Fries and Goodman had cannily expanded the *Spider-Man* pilot for release as a theatrical feature for the international market, thus increasing the property's visibility around the world.

Pelc approached Tōei, the studio behind many of the most successful *tokusatsu* shows. He proposed not a remake of an existing series or movie, but rather a multi-year option to reimagine any of Marvel's properties for a Japanese audience. Having presumably learned a lesson from the failed adaptations that hewed too closely to the source material, Marvel was willing to give Tōei a free hand. The studio accepted, and it set its sights first on Spider-Man.

Tōei entrusted the project to Ishinomori Shōtarō, the creator of *Kamen Raidā* and *Himitsu Sentai Gorenjā*. In "Japanifying" Spider-Man, Ishinomori brought in many successful elements from his prior hit shows. He transformed Spider-Man's alter ego, the awkward, loner photographer Peter Parker, into Yamashiro Takuya, an exuberant motorcycle racer like the lead from *Kamen Raidā*. He also pitted his hero against a new alien menace, the Iron Cross Army, borrowing from *Gorenjā*'s Black Cross Army and featuring the same actor as the leader of both. He also incorporated the requisite futuristic gadgetry, including the Spider Machine GP-7 and a metallic bracelet-communicator that functioned as Spider-Man's web shooter, controlled his vehicles, and housed his costume.

Ishinomori also mixed and matched several *tokusatsu* and anime tropes. Each week, with rare exception, Spider-Man would fight an outlandish man-sized monster like those in *Kamen Raidā* and *Gorenjā*, but for the finale it would grow to the city-smashing size of the *kaiju* in *Urutoraman*. To defeat it in its giant form Spidey would have to pilot his enormous battle robot Leopardon, similar to the title bot from Tōei's hit robot anime *Majingā Zetto* (*Mazinger Z*, 1972), but first it would have to transform from its spaceship state à la Sunrise's *Yūsha Raidīn* (*Brave Raideen*, 1975) or Ishinomori's *Daitetsujin 17* (1977).

Ishinomori centered *Supaidāman*'s story around Yamashiro Takuya, whose astro-archeologist father is murdered by the invading Iron Cross Army and its leader Professor Monster. In the premiere episode Takuya is telepathically summoned to a cave where he meets Garia, the last survivor of the Spider Planet, another casualty of the Iron Cross. With little life remaining, Garia grants Takuya special powers,

Spider-Man's suit actor Koga Hirofumi strikes a pose in this publicity image for *Supaidāman* (1978).

injecting him with spider extract and bequeathing the young man his space-age technology and iconic Spider-Man suit. With them Takuya can take revenge for both his father and the Spider Planet.

The series debuted on May 17, 1978, and it would almost immediately make the jump to the big screen. Every year during school vacation, Tōei hosted the Manga Matsuri film festival, an anthology of anime and *tokusatsu* shorts designed to showcase the studio's popular children's shows. With the 1978 festival in mind, Tōei produced a special, theatrical *Supaidāman* adventure in addition to the show's 41-episode broadcast run. The 24-minute widescreen film, which took place between episodes of the series, premiered on July 22 alongside installments of the space opera *Uchū Kaizoku Kyaputen Hārokku* (*Space Pirate Captain Harlock*), historical romance *Kyandi Kyandi* (*Candy Candy*), live-action sci-fi drama *Uchū kara no Messēji: Ginga Taisen* (*Message from Space: Galactic Wars*), and a re-release of 1969's feature-length *Nagagutsu o Haita Neko* (*The Wonderful World of Puss 'n' Boots*).

Supaidāman had a lasting impact on Japanese television. It would inspire transforming, pilotable *mecha* in innumerable future series, including the many sequels to Tōei's *Himitsu Sentai Gorenjā*. One such "super sentai" show was *Batoru Fībā Jei* (*Battle Fever J*, 1979), another Marvel/Tōei co-production that was originally envisioned as an adaptation of *The Avengers*. Perhaps the most notable entry, however, was *Kyōryū Sentai Zyuranger* ("Dinosaur Squadron Beast Ranger," 1992), which formed the basis for Saban's *Mighty Morphin' Power Rangers* (1993). *Power Rangers* lifted the *tokusatsu* footage from *Zyuranger* but, in a complete reversal of Gene Pelc's story, dramatically reimagined the show for an American audience.

Spider-Man certainly weaves a tangled web.

Superman

INSPIRED BY: *Superman* (1978)
COUNTRY: India
YEAR: 1980
PRODUCTION: Lakshmi Productions
DIRECTOR: Veeramachineni Madhusudhan Rao
WRITER: Veeramachineni Madhusudhan Rao
STARS: N.T. Rama Rao, Jaya Prada, Kaikala Satyanarayana, Allu Ramalingaiah, Tyagaraju, Chakarapani, Pandari Bai, Geetha Kadambee, Jayamalini

When young Raja's parents are murdered by three bandits, the boy does the only thing he can think of: he visits the temple of Hanuman and prays for help. He begs the deity to appear, but when his devotional songs have no effect, the despondent Raja kills himself. Taking pity on the child, Hanuman materializes, revives Raja, and imbues him with invulnerability, super strength, and the power of flight. Raja vows to keep his new abilities a secret, but also swears vengeance for his parents.

Now older, Raja (N.T. Rama Rao) uses his supernatural gifts to help those in need under cover of an alter ego. As Superman, Raja sports a familiar blue, red, and yellow costume with a large red "H" on his chest for Hanuman. When not righting wrongs, he lives with his adoptive mother Sarada (Pandari Bai) and sister Lakshmi (Geetha Kadambee) and holds a 50 percent stake in a nearby mica mine with his partner Bangaraiah (Allu Ramalingaiah).

When the rich villain Maharaj (Kaikala Satyanarayana) discovers that the mica mine contains gold, he hires men to secretly work it from the other end while simultaneously sabotaging Bangaraiah's land. When Raja discovers the sabotage, he follows the trail to Maharaj's henchman Jai Singh (Tyagaraju), a nefarious poacher with trained attack elephants who also happens to be one of the men who killed Raja's parents. Raja, as Superman, battles the elephants and finally turns them on Jai Singh, killing him. Maharaj retaliates by kidnapping Bangaraiah's daughter, but Superman comes to her rescue and confronts the second killer, a laughing maniac with a heat ray.

Meanwhile, Lakshmi has become pregnant, and she and her boyfriend Mohan want to marry. Sarada, furious at Lakshmi's indiscretion, nearly throws her out, but Raja stays her hand. He speaks to Mohan and, discovering he has a good heart, meets his father—who is actually Maharaj in disguise. The villain wheedles Raja's mine shares out of him for a dowry, then absconds with his son and the shares to Hong Kong on the day of the ceremony. Raja follows them, determined to bring Mohan back and save his sister from ignominy. But in Hong Kong Raja will have to contend with assassins, his parents' third murderer, and Maharaj's secret weapon: Miss Lee (Jayamalini), a valkyrie-styled sorceress who can walk through walls and summon demons.

Not "Huperman"—"Hanuman!" N.T. Rama Rao is the South Indian Superman who gets his powers from the monkey god.

Mention "Indian Superman" to a handful of people and you're likely to hear, "Isn't that the one where Superman dances with a woman dressed as Spider-Man?" So let's clear that up right now: No. The movie they're thinking of is actually a family melodrama called *Dariya Dil* ("Generous Heart," 1988). One of its musical numbers is a fantasy sequence in which the main character and his love interest are dressed as superheroes. That clip has been presented out of context so often that the entire film has picked up the erroneous moniker "the Indian Superman." Which is a shame, because there are so many actual Indian Superman movies.

Although Superman comics wouldn't be widely published in India for years, the title character nevertheless inspired two separate unauthorized Hindi-language films in 1960. One, produced by Mukul Pictures and called simply *Superman*, starred actress Nirupa Roy in the title role! Her costume, however, owed as much to The Phantom as it did to Superman, borrowing the former's signature cowl and eye mask. And though the movie has since disappeared from circulation, its posters boasted "a super dog" and "a super horse," suggesting an additional lift from The Phantom in the form of his animal companions Devil and Hero. These elements would likely have been familiar to local audiences, as *The Phantom* comics had seen distribution in India since the late 1950s.

The second movie was produced by rival studio Manmohan Films. It told the familiar story of an alien child sent to Earth, raised by farmers, hired as a newspaper reporter, and driven to fight crime in a cape. However, this Superman sported an aviator's cap and goggles, giving him (visually at least) more in common with the World War II-era hero Spy Smasher. Still, the similarities were sufficient for Mukul Pictures to issue a public notice unashamedly asserting its copyright over the titles *Superman*, *Mr. Superman*, and *Shri ("Mr.") Superman*. Manmohan therefore released its film under the confusing title *The Return of Mr. Superman*, despite the fact that it was not a sequel.

Little more was seen of the Man of Steel in India until twenty years later. The arrival of Richard Donner's *Superman* in 1978 triggered a new wave of global interest in the character and a host of copycat films from around the world. Turkey turned out *Süpermen Dönüyor* (1979), Spain debuted *Supersonic Man* (1979), and Italy came out with *L'uomo puma* (*The Pumaman*, 1980). India followed suit with a brand-new *Superman*. But although the film might trace its inspiration loosely to Donner's, it really has its roots in two of India's earliest movie genres and the career of its larger-than-life star.

Sitting in a Mumbai theater in 1910, Dhundiraj Govind Phalke gazed at a silent film about the life of Christ. As he watched, he began imagining figures from Indian mythology in place of the Biblical characters. Phalke, a photographer and magician, yearned to see equivalent Indian stories on film, and it wasn't long before he took matters into his own hands. In 1913 he produced arguably the first full-length Indian feature, *Raja Harishchandra*. Based on a story from the *Brahmanas* in which legendary King Harishchandra is tested by Lord Shiva, Phalke's film marked the advent of the mythological, a genre based around the portrayal of gods and heroes from Hindu mythology.

To depict their deities and miracles, mythologicals by necessity employed many different special effects techniques. These tricks include multiple-exposures, lighting effects, animation, wirework, and creative editing (and today, of course, CGI). In fact, by Phalke's second feature he had cemented spectacle as one of the major draws of the genre. His effects-laden *Lanka Dahan* ("Lanka Aflame," 1917), a story of Hanuman from the *Ramayana*, included, among other wonders, a scene of a hundred giants and an elaborately staged sequence of Hanuman in flight. Playing to packed houses, *Lanka Dahan* additionally helped to make Hanuman adaptations a particular favorite among audiences for more than a century.

Mythologicals also have a sister genre that was developed at virtually the same time: the devotional. These films focus on stories of pious individuals who, through their devotion to a particular deity, gain its favor and assistance. In many cases the protagonists, often outcasts or otherwise marginalized, are granted miraculous powers by the gods.

Mythologicals, and to a lesser extent devotionals, were the bread and butter of actor Nandamuri Taraka Rama Rao, better known as NTR. One of the biggest stars of "Tollywood," southern India's Telugu-language film industry (not to be confused with Mumbai's "Bollywood"), NTR was virtually synonymous with gods, legends, and princes. He starred in a slew of mythologicals in the late 1950s and 1960s, playing Krishna alone roughly 20 times. Though his career was actually a varied one and included comedies and swashbucklers, it was the epics he was best known for. In the

The giant statue of Hanuman (Janardhana Rao Arja) revives young Raja (uncredited) in a fairly elaborate optical effects shot that also incorporates animated light beams.

1970s, however, he began to focus more of his energy on social melodramas, and as 1980 rolled around, the 57-year-old actor was starting to reinvent himself as a heroic vigilante.

Made during this transition period, *Superman* was unique. Penned by writer-director V. Madhusudhan Rao, one of NTR's many collaborators, the film effectively put the actor's entire career in a blender. Raja's encounter with the popular Hanuman and the hero's God-given superpowers paid homage to NTR's mythological and devotional films; the turmoil and stigma surrounding his sister's unwed pregnancy, including an attempted suicide, offered plenty of social melodrama; and the murder of Raja's parents and the powerful Maharaj's scheming placed the title character in the role of the vigilante—an unusual position for the generally benevolent Superman.

In the tradition of mythologicals and devotionals, Rao naturally employed plenty of trick photography for the film's supernatural scenes. Double-exposures, forced perspective, and animation aided in depicting the giant statue of Hanuman coming to life and reviving Raja. (The "living" Hanuman, incidentally, was played by Janardhana Rao Arja who had portrayed the monkey god on numerous occasions.) Similar effects techniques were used to demonstrate Superman's powers and Miss Lee's sorcery. Ditto a romantic musical number among the stars that could easily be read as, intentional or not, a livelier version of the "can you read my mind" sequence from the Hollywood film.

Superman played in cinemas for more than 100 days, then a much-touted benchmark for industry success. Moreover, it wouldn't be the last time an Indian Superman would occupy the silver screen. The year of 1987 saw another Hindi-language adaptation from Bollywood, also titled *Superman*. For this one, director B. Gupta hewed closely to the 1978 Hollywood production, emulating its plot and even going so far as cribbing Donner's special effects shots. And in 2008, a group of filmmakers in Maharashtra's ultra-low-budget film industry in Malegaon (aka "Mollywood") produced the irreverent spoof *Malegaon Ka Superman* ("Malegaon's Superman," 2009), which gained fame through a 2012 documentary about its production, *Supermen of Malegaon*.

Süpermen Dönüyor ("Superman Returns")

INSPIRED BY: *Superman* (1978)
COUNTRY: Turkey
YEAR: 1979
PRODUCTION: Kunt Film
DIRECTOR: Kunt Tulgar
WRITERS: Necdet Tok, Emel Tulgar, Kunt Tulgar
STARS: Tayfun Demir (Haşim Demircioğlu), Güngör Bayrak, Eşref Kolçak, Yıldırım Gencer

The planet Krypton is on the brink of destruction. At the last moment, its leader bundles his infant son Tayfun into a rocketship to Earth. There the child is discovered and raised by kindly Turkish peasants. When Tayfun (Tayfun Demir) comes of age, his foster parents reveal his strange adoption and present him with his sole inheritance: a glowing green crystal found beside him in the rocket.

The young man decides to set out on his own. His first stop is to an isolated cave where he's impelled to throw the crystal. Activated, the rock suddenly displays an image of his biological father, who explains to him that Tayfun possesses powers and abilities far beyond those of mortal men—but only so long as he avoids the crystal, a fragment of his homeworld. Leaving the "Kryptonite" behind, he transforms into Superman and takes flight to Istanbul.

Some time later, Tayfun has adopted a mild-mannered alter ego and established himself as a reporter at *The Planet* newspaper. He's in love with his co-worker Alev (Güngör Bayrak), whose father, Professor Çetinel (Eşref Kolçak), has just returned from a scientific expedition where he has discovered the Kryptonite. The rock, it seems, is an incredible power source—and a target of envy for Çetinel's capricious rival Ekrem (Yıldırım Gencer). Ekrem has built a device with a special lens that focuses the rays of the sun through the Kryptonite. This has the dual function of transmuting metal into gold and destroying living things.

While transporting her father's notes on the crystal, Alev is abducted by Ekrem's goons who steal the documents, force her into the back of a truck, and send her careening toward the edge of a cliff. Fortunately, Tayfun, as Superman, arrives in the nick of time, saving her life and winning her heart.

After a thwarted attempt to ransom Çetinel for the Kryptonite, Ekrem's minions make one last, successful grab for Alev. Using her as bait, Ekrem kidnaps Tayfun as

Süpermen Dönüyor ("Superman Returns")

Superman (Haşim Demircioğlu) rescues Alev (Güngör Bayrak). The flying Ken doll can be seen in the upper right. Turkish lobby card.

well. Tayfun could easily escape, but not without exposing his secret identity. However, when Ekrem's men steal the space rock from Prof. Çetinel onboard a train, and then sends the locomotive speeding on a collision course, Tayfun is left with little choice. But even if he saves the professor, he'll still have to contend with Ekrem, who's now fully prepared with his deadly Kryptonite weapon.

~~~

Director Kunt Tulgar saw Richard Donner's big-budget *Superman* (1978) with his wife and father during a trip to Paris in 1979. After the screening, the elder Tulgar, one of Turkey's pioneer genre filmmakers, suggested that Kunt should make his own Superman movie. It was an enticing idea, but an awfully tall order.

When Donner had set out to make his film, he was keenly aware that people go to a Superman movie to watch the Man of Steel fly! With this in mind, he gave his staff placards inscribed with the single word "verisimilitude." It was his mantra. He wanted audiences to genuinely believe a man could fly, and to that end his team employed state-of-the-art practical and visual effects, including elaborate wirework, gimbals, and blue screen rigs.

The problem with state-of-the-art effects, however, is that they're virtually impossible for low budget filmmakers like Tulgar to imitate. So Tulgar made a deal with himself: unless he could figure out some way to make his hero fly, he wouldn't make the movie. Faced with this daunting obstacle, the project might have died right there had it not been for the help of an unlikely stuntman.

Seized with sudden inspiration, Tulgar called over his young daughter and demanded her Ken doll. She flatly refused. "I'll pay you for it!" he pleaded, and eventually the child relented. He took the doll, handed it to his wife, and convinced her to sew it a tiny Superman costume. Then he improvised a small movie screen from a makeshift frame and tracing paper. Hanging the doll horizontally in front of the screen with fishing line, Tulgar rear-projected aerial footage of Istanbul from Claude Lelouch's documentary short *Türkiye* ("Turkey," 1973)—and the doll appeared to fly! But it still didn't look quite right. Some further thought and Tulgar worked out what was wrong: wind. Or rather, the lack of it. He borrowed his mother's hair dryer and turned it on the miniature hero, whose cape obligingly began to flap. Perfect! All it needed now were some close-ups of the live Superman actor in front of the same screen to more or less cement the illusion.

The fellow Tulgar had in mind was 20-year-old Haşim Demircioğlu, a factory worker and Tulgar's neighbor. Tulgar felt that Demircioğlu's stature and resemblance to Clark Kent would make him the perfect choice, despite the fact that he had never acted in his life. But there was a bigger problem; the young man was in the midst of his compulsory military service and couldn't simply leave. Fortunately, Tulgar had a scheme. Claiming to be Demircioğlu's uncle, he told the commanding officer that Demircioğlu's father had been in an accident in another city. A week's leave was granted.

The fledgling actor's name needed some work, though. "Haşim Demircioğlu" didn't have the ring of a movie star, so Tulgar instead proposed "Tayfun Demir"— "Iron Typhoon." However, Demircioğlu's temperament was not quite as macho as his

The many moods of Superman. Turkish lobby card.

new moniker. Timid by nature, he shied away from performing fight scenes and stunt work. Without stunt doubles, an occupation unheard-of in Turkey at the time, Tulgar was forced to either work around the actor's anxieties or tolerate subpar action sequences. It was still more than he paid for however since, as a friend of Tulgar's, Demircioğlu was doing the gig for free.

There was hardly any money to speak of anyway. This becomes immediately apparent to the viewer when, instead of Donner's elaborate introduction on the crystalline planet Krypton, Tulgar subjects his audience to a "star field" of Christmas tree ornaments and a voice-over-only prologue, before jumping forward in time to the fully grown Tayfun on the day he sets out on his own.

But here's the real secret of *Süpermen Dönüyor*—the one that almost nobody knows: *Süpermen Dönüyor* isn't really a Superman movie at all. It's a Captain Marvel movie.

Rather than try to duplicate Donner's blockbuster and run into a budgetary brick wall at every expensive set piece, Tulgar cleverly opted for cheaper source material—and a childhood favorite, to boot. *Adventures of Captain Marvel* was a comics-inspired theatrical serial from 1941, a time when superhero movies were in their infancy and their budgets were nearly as restrictive as Tulgar's was in 1970s Turkey.

Even the casual fan will notice, perhaps with consternation, that Superman's father lauds him as possessing "the wisdom of Solomon, the might of Hercules, the stamina of Atlas, the power of Zeus, the courage of Achilles, and the speed of Mercury." These are the very attributes of Captain Marvel as well as the mythical figures whose initials spell out "SHAZAM," the magic word that transforms young Billy Batson into his mighty alter ego. That's only the start. Despite many of the trappings of Superman, the plot is virtually identical to the *Captain Marvel* serial, from the solar-powered MacGuffin and specific death traps to a goon who hides in the trunk of the heroine's car. In fact, the succession of kidnappings and rescues alone betrays the film's serial origins.

Tulgar, an experienced editor, supervised the film's post-production and assembled its soundtrack from his prodigious record collection. His score borrows liberally from John Williams's *Superman* album with needle-drops from Jerry Goldsmith's *The Reincarnation of Peter Proud* (1975), John Barry's *From Russia with Love* (1963) and *Goldfinger* (1964), Giorgio Moroder's *Midnight Express* (1978), Barry Gray's *Space: 1999* (1975) theme, and John Philip Sousa's "The Black Horse Troop"—with the main titles employing the disco track "24 Saat" ("24 Hours") by Rıza Silahlıpoda & The Rhythm 68 Orchestra.

So was the film successful? "I sold it," Tulgar answers simply. Beyond the regional distributors in Turkey, he even had buyers in America and Japan.

One brief postscript: if Demircioğlu thought that his fraudulent absence from the military was the perfect crime, he was quickly disabused. As Tulgar explains, when Demircioğlu returned to his division a week later, his commanding officer asked him suspiciously, "Where have you been?" Demircioğlu repeated the injured father story, to which his CO shot back, "Oh, come on, don't give me that. You were shooting *Superman*."

As it turned out, everybody knew. Score one for military intelligence.

Supersonic Man

INSPIRED BY: *Superman* (1978)
COUNTRY: Spain
YEAR: 1979
PRODUCTION: Almena Films
DIRECTOR: Juan Piquer Simón
WRITERS: Sebastian Moi, Juan Piquer Simón
STARS: Antonio Cantafora, Cameron Mitchell, José Luis Ayestarán, Diana Polakov, José María Caffarel

Alien superhero Supersonic (José Luis Ayestarán) is dispatched to Earth to prevent its inhabitants from misusing "powerful forces not fully under their control." But it seems he's already too late, as the insidious Dr. Gulik (Cameron Mitchell) has just sent his henchman and a boxy, retro-styled robot to break into a nuclear facility and make off with a cache of iridium—as well as with resident scientist Prof. Morgan (José María Caffarel). The villains also attempt to nab Morgan's daughter Patricia (Diana Polakov), but Supersonic is in time to rescue her.

Patricia faints from the ordeal, giving Supersonic an opportunity to change into his secret identity as private detective Paul (Antonio Cantafora). Making her acquaintance, he learns that she was on her way to meet a man with information about her father. With Paul's help she arranges another rendezvous, but it turns out to be a trap and Gulik's men grab her. They capture Paul as well, but he escapes and as Supersonic rescues Patricia once again.

Meanwhile, Gulik pressures Prof. Morgan for his new superfuel formula. And while Gulik's robot and henchmen ambush a military convoy for a final cargo of iridium, Paul investigates Gulik's warehouse. Unfortunately, he's spotted, knocked out, scooped into a burlap bag, and dumped into the sea. A hungry shark bears down upon him as he wriggles free of his bonds and transforms into Supersonic just in time to avoid becoming fish food.

Paul meets Patricia that night for a date. However, aware that Patricia has some connection to the mysterious Supersonic, Gulik sends his robot to break in on them. It delivers a message: Supersonic must show up at a location designated by Gulik within 24 hours or he will kill Prof. Morgan. The robot then destroys Patricia's house while the couple barely escapes. Later that night Supersonic appears as requested. Gulik demands his surrender, promising to destroy New York City if he refuses. Instead, Supersonic burrows into the villain's underground hideout. But Gulik is prepared. He subjects the hero, in a series of chambers, to a barrage of tortures: steam, lava, ice, and finally high-frequency noise. The latter effectively incapacitates Supersonic, leaving the path clear for Gulik's conquest of the Earth.

～～～

The 1970s were a turbulent time for Spain. As the ailing Francisco Franco's powers were slowly and contentiously divvied up in preparation for the dictator's death, the film industry found itself in limbo. Government subsidies, upon which filmmakers had come to rely, effectively ended, with the state in debt to movie producers to the tune of $10 million. Censorship was tight. Local film studios were forced to close their doors. And thanks in part to low budgets and region-specific subject matter, domestic films exercised a decidedly limited appeal on the global market.

But producer-director Juan Piquer Simón was a maverick, uninterested in shooting prestige films and Spanish Civil War yarns—movies that critics appreciated but which brought in little money. Simón was keen on making commercial films for an international audience and staying solvent. So, an avid science fiction fan, he took a gamble, pulling together two million dollars in 1976 to make *Viaje al centro de la Tierra* (*Where Time Began*, 1977), an adaptation of Jules Verne's *Journey to the Center of the Earth*. It was arguably Spain's first special effects film and featured a giant ape, dinosaurs, avalanches, floods, and an active volcano. The finished film found distribution throughout Europe as well as the USA, Australia, the Philippines, Turkey, and Argentina. Most importantly, it made money.

Soon Simón and his production company were receiving offers to partner on other special effects films. The most appealing of these was an Italo-American superhero co-production called *Capitán Electric*, an obvious attempt to cash in on the recent box office success of Richard Donner's *Superman* (1978). "It was a real technical challenge," Simón recalled to website *Sitio de Ciencia-Ficción*, "so we decided to accept." But the title had to go, Simón insisted—Captain Electric "sounded like an appliance." Instead he chose the name *Flash Man*. That didn't last either; Italian producer Dino de Laurentiis objected, claiming it was too similar to his forthcoming adaptation of *Flash Gordon*. So *Flash Man* became *Supersonic Man*.

Simón crafted the story for *Supersonic Man*, broadly following the trajectory of Donner's film. In it, Supersonic is sent in a spaceship to Earth as a protector, falls in love with a woman whom he's routinely compelled to rescue from danger, and must stop an evil mastermind with an underground lair—and knowledge of the hero's one weakness—from leveling a city as part of a devilishly destructive scheme. He even lifted

Italian two-sheet for *Supersonic Man* (1979).

from a sequence that was shot for *Superman* but omitted from its original theatrical release, staging a scene in which Dr. Gulik subjects Supersonic to extreme heat and ice.

However, Simón didn't restrict his borrowing to *Superman*. He also took several elements from his favorite childhood adventure serials. Broadly speaking, the villain shaking down a scientist for his secret formula and kidnapping the scientist's daughter were tried and true serial tropes. But Dr. Gulik's robot was specifically inspired by the chunky automaton from Republic's *The Mysterious Doctor Satan* (1940). (Coincidentally, *Doctor Satan* was originally intended as an adaptation of *Superman* until rights issues forced a change, which gives *Supersonic Man* another tenuous connection to the Man of Steel.) Simón was also inspired by the casting of separate actors for the hero and his alter ego in *Adventures of Captain Marvel* (1941), prompting the director to hire brawny ex-Tarzan José Luis Ayestarán to play the costumed Supersonic, and Italian action/comedy staple Antonio Cantafora (aka Michael Coby) as his other half, Paul.

Filming for *Supersonic Man* began on November 13, 1978, with a budget of about $600,000, much less than the Jules Verne picture. This would place substantial limitations on the film's visual effects, but Simón wasn't willing to compromise entirely; he demanded at least a portion of *Superman*'s verisimilitude. Among the many technologies used to make Donner's Superman fly was front-projection, a process involving a film projector and a highly reflective screen which allowed the crew to composite the "flying" actor into the background sky footage "in-camera," with noticeably better results than the older, cheaper rear-projection process. Focusing on this method for all of his flying scenes, Simón imported a specialized crew and a prototype front-projection rig from Germany—the same one that would later be used for Wolfgang Petersen's *Das Boot* (1981).

Other special effects sequences involved Supersonic's spaceship and were visibly influenced by *Star Wars* (1977)—from the very first shot of the craft looming overhead. The ship itself, constructed by Simón and a pair of amateur model builders, incidentally incorporated a complete *Battlestar Galactica* (1978) Cylon Raider model in its center. The vessel's flight was then painstakingly photographed one frame at a time—one of the film's many headaches. "Shooting the 112 effects [shots] in the film," explained Simón, "took us nine months working ten- to twelve-hour days. No one in Spain has ever made a similar technical achievement."

Supersonic Man was finally released in Spain on August 14, 1979, and throughout the world over the next two years. After its completion, Simón reportedly began planning a million-dollar co-production deal for a sequel which never came to fruition. Nevertheless, he would continue to specialize in sci-fi and special effects films, including two more Jules Verne adaptations, a 1983 killer alien movie called *Los nuevos extraterrestres* (*Extra Terrestrial Visitors*, which was retrofitted with kiddie elements to capitalize on the success of Steven Spielberg's *E.T.* [1982]), and the *Alien* (1979)—and *Abyss* (1989)—inspired *The Rift* (1990). Supersonic Man would return, however, via two one-off comic books in 2014 and 2017 courtesy of writer, artist, and fan Héctor Caño.

Tarzan İstanbul'da ("Tarzan in Istanbul")

INSPIRED BY: *Tarzan the Ape Man* (1932)
COUNTRY: Turkey
YEAR: 1952
PRODUCTION: Milli Film
DIRECTOR: Orhan Atadeniz
WRITERS: Yılmaz Atadeniz, Orhan Atadeniz
STARS: Tamer Balcı, Hayri Esen, Necla Aygül, Aziz Basmacı, Cemil Demirel

On a hunting trip in Africa, journalist Tekin (Hayri Esen) discovers the years-old skeletal remains of a man. Among them are a sealed, addressed envelope and a handwritten scrap of paper detailing how the man's family was set upon by natives. To protect his young son, he armed the child with a knife and sent him off into the jungle before finally succumbing to his attackers. Tekin is moved by the tale, and he determines to deliver the envelope to its recipient in Istanbul—the deceased's brother, Kamil Karazincir.

According to the letter, the dead man discovered a valuable treasure inside Death Mountain in the country of Tanganyika. With a hand-drawn map to guide them, Kamil and Tekin hire three pilots to take them to Africa: the shifty Tevfik, the buffoonish Aziz (Aziz Basmacı), and the pretty Necla (Necla Aygül). Upon their arrival, they enlist the services of local guide Kunto (Cemil Demirel) but unwisely let slip about the treasure.

Even more unfortunate, the expedition is soon ambushed by the same tribe that killed Kamil's brother. Taking to their heels, the party races to reach the Mutia Mountains before the natives can overtake them, since the cliffs are taboo to the locals and would offer them safety. But they don't make it. Within sight of the mountain range, the group is pinned down. Facing certain death, they suddenly hear a cry—a human yell—that terrifies the natives and sends them scattering.

Relieved but puzzled, the party regroups and soon discovers the entrance to the cave. And after carefully avoiding some treacherous sulphur pits, they find the long sought-after treasure—a box containing gold, diamonds, pearls, and countless other trinkets worth millions.

But their trials aren't over. That night Necla's tent receives a deadly visitor—a lion! Fortunately, the taciturn, loincloth-clad Tarzan (Tamer Balcı) makes his grand entrance just in time, wrestling the big cat and chasing it away. Tarzan himself quickly disappears, and Necla's companions have a hard time believing her story about the mysterious white man who saved her.

The next day Necla goes for a swim, but a crocodile pegs her for an easy meal. Once again Tarzan arrives to rescue her and this time, fascinated, he carries her off. He shows her his treetop bachelor pad, but Necla insists on returning to her camp. There Necla introduces Tarzan to the group, and Tekin notices his knife—Kamil's brother's knife. They realize that Tarzan is Kamil's lost nephew who has been living in the jungle ever since his parents' death.

Tarzan agrees to show the party a shortcut out of the jungle. But Kunto, scheming for the treasure and vexed that its real inheritor has turned up, secretly follows Tarzan and shoots him. Joined by his goons, Kunto demands the treasure. He very

Action-packed, hand-colored Turkish lobby card for *Tarzan İstanbul'da* (1952).

nearly absconds with it when the entire expedition is waylaid by natives. Captured and set to be sacrificed to a pool of hungry crocs, their only hope is the critically wounded Tarzan....

∼∼∼

Edgar Rice Burroughs's mighty, jungle-bred Tarzan has been a staple of the silver screen since 1918. But it was MGM's lavish, thrilling, and poignant *Tarzan the Ape Man* (1932), starring Olympic swimming champion Johnny Weissmuller, that made the vine-swinging Lord Greystoke a truly household name, launching a string of sequels and imitators.

The Tarzan movies were popular in Turkey. So was United Feature Syndicate's *Tarzan* comic strip, which had appeared in various Turkish children's magazines since 1935. In 1952, that popularity gave Turkish film importer Sabahattin Tulgar a brainstorm: Hollywood had brought Tarzan to New York (*Tarzan's New York Adventure*, 1942), so why couldn't Tulgar bring him to Istanbul?

Not that it would be quite so simple. In 1952 cinema was still a fledgling industry in Turkey. From 1919 until the late 1940s, local filmmaking had been virtually the exclusive playground of stage director Muhsin Ertuğrul, who made movies to subsidize his theatrical career while at the same time actively forcing other would-be filmmakers out of the business. Moreover, domestic production wasn't especially profitable. Thanks to taxes levied on the industry, even an inexpensive Turkish movie cost three times as much as simply importing and dubbing a foreign one. Distributor

Ha-Ka Film devised a compromise in the late '30s, "Turkifying" foreign films by dubbing them *and* adding new scenes shot in Istanbul. But finally in 1948 the government implemented a substantial tax cut that made producing local films a more lucrative proposition.

Owning a movie distribution company put Tulgar in an ideal position to take advantage of the tax cut and become one of Turkey's cinematic pioneers. Appointing himself producer and cinematographer, with established filmmaker and editor Orhan Atadeniz at the helm, he set out to make his own Tarzan movie—very inexpensively—following the MGM formula. That even included casting a local Olympic athlete in the title role: hammer throw champion Tamer Balcı. Sabahattin's son Kunt was credited as screenwriter, but this attribution was purely honorary; the child was only four years old at the time.

With cast and crew in place, Tulgar now had everything he needed for his king of the jungle. Except, that is, for the jungle. No jungles in Turkey. No wild apes or zebras either. But no problem; Tulgar imported movies; he had plenty of jungle footage! He and Atadeniz owned a stack of Tarzan films and a wildlife documentary from which they could poach all the jungle shots they needed. The rest they could get by shooting in Belgrad Forest. It wasn't strictly speaking a jungle, but it had plenty of trees and was only half an hour from Istanbul. And to ensure that the new and old scenes would integrate, Atadeniz clipped out individual frames from the stock footage and referred to them on location, directing the actors to move, look, and react based on how the shots would be spliced together.

In fairness, MGM's Tarzan never set foot in Africa either. All the authentic location footage in *Tarzan the Ape Man* was unused material from 1931's *Trader Horn*. But that was only used to supplement the illusion that director W.S. Van Dyke

Turkish one-sheet for *Tarzan İstanbul'da* (1952). Artist Tarık Uzmen painted posters for Turkish films as well as Turkish releases of foreign movies, like *The Human Monster* (1939) starring Bela Lugosi.

and his team had painstakingly and expensively built on a Hollywood soundstage. The shots they used were mostly scenery. Tulgar and Atadeniz, on the other hand, were less particular, lifting establishing shots, animals, stunts, and anything else that would lend their threadbare production a little spectacle. The duo pulled enormous amounts of footage from *Tarzan's Revenge* (1938) including the vine-swinging, the lion-wrestling, and even a chipmunk running across a character's foot. Pieced together in the Tulgar household where Sabahattin kept his editing equipment, the end result was a film that's virtually half stock footage. And contrary to its title, Tarzan really only gets to Istanbul in the last 60 seconds.

Yet despite a budget bordering on outright poverty, *Tarzan İstanbul'da* was a success, finding an audience not only in Turkey, but in Spain, Portugal, France, and the Middle East as well. It also paved the way for a spate of other "İstanbul'da" movies from various local filmmakers. Over the next three years the cosmopolis played host to Dracula (*Drakula İstanbul'da*, 1953), The Invisible Man (*Görünmeyen Adam İstanbul'da*, 1955), UFOs (*Uçan Daireler İstanbul'da*, 1955), and even Charlie Chaplin's signature "Little Tramp" (*Şarlo İstanbul'da*, 1954)—as impersonated by resident actor Kimon Spathopulos. Suddenly Istanbul was the hot spot for every self-respecting pop culture figure, and subsequent decades would see many more come to visit.

Tarzan İstanbul'da eventually received a sequel of sorts. In 1974 Sabahattin Tulgar's son Kunt Tulgar, now a filmmaker and prolific editor, decided it was his turn to mount a jungle adventure. His film, *Tarzan Korkusuz Adam* ("Tarzan the Fearless Man"), mostly retread *İstanbul'da* but with more action added to the script. Although calling it a "script" is rather generous; it consisted of three solitary pages.

Three was the magic number for *Tarzan Korkusuz Adam*. Three pages of script, shot across three locations, in only three days. The result is a narrative that often hangs by a thread. But for Kunt, the story wasn't especially important; it was the spectacle that mattered. The secret to that was an even greater reliance on the stock footage in his father's archive. In addition to the classic Tarzan films, Kunt raided *One Million B.C.* (1940) to bring in dueling dinosaurs (about which the characters appear remarkably blasé) and *Adventures of Captain Marvel* (1941), one of his childhood favorites, for molten lava to imperil his heroes. Those sources and more gave him an action-packed finale with bloodthirsty natives, earthquakes, and an erupting volcano.

It was all part of the exuberant Kunt Tulgar's philosophy of moviemaking: "If you can do it, do it. If you can't do it, steal it."

Wurideul-ui Chingu Pawo 5 ("Our Friend Power 5")

COUNTERPART OF: *Teenage Mutant Ninja Turtles: The Epic Begins* (1988)
COUNTRY: South Korea
YEAR: 1989
PRODUCTION: Shilla Planning Production
DIRECTOR: Park Ho-jin
WRITER: Min Woo
STARS: Lee Suk, Sonya, Jeon Yoo-sung, Ju Yong-man, Lee Jeong-hee, Choe Jeong-il

Wurideul-ui Chingu Pawo 5 ("Our Friend Power 5")

Fleeing from their home planet Battlestar, five humanoid turtles—four warriors and their princess Yesular—are pursued through space by a malevolent race of rats led by the tyrannical Shark (who, contrary to his name, is also a rat). It seems that Yesular carries a valuable gadget that the rodents desperately want for themselves.

Meanwhile, on Earth, schoolboy Hyuk is attempting to prove to his friends that life exists on other planets, so he sneaks into his father's observatory with the help of comic relief lab assistant Dalgeun. Hyuk's father, a scientist, is working on an effort to clear debris from space using a giant robot and a specially-augmented magnetic telescope. When Hyuk monkeys with the telescope, he's struck with a burst of gamma rays and is unexpectedly imbued with telekinetic powers.

The next day, Hyuk's father demonstrates the device properly, but he also inadvertently draws the turtles to Earth. The rat soldiers follow, and a battle ensues in the woods where Hyuk and his friends are at a weekend camp. Hyuk aids the turtles with his new superpowers and the rats retreat. Befriending the children, Yesular explains that their home planet was attacked by Shark and his soldiers. In response, the turtles built a defender robot and entrusted Yesular with their most powerful device, a wand that can transform them into anything they wish. Having said this, Yesular promptly transforms into a human to blend in. Hyuk's older sister Mina then agrees to teach the warrior turtles taekwondo to aid in their fight.

After another skirmish with the rodents, the turtles, preferring not to stay out in the open any longer, lay low at Hyuk's home. Unfortunately, the rats break in at night and make off with the wand. Dalgeun and the turtles try in vain to track them down, but by coincidence the rats show up at the observatory, leading to a fight during which the heroes recover the wand.

Thwarted one too many times, Shark launches an all-out attack on the Earth. The onslaught forces the scientists to complete their giant robot for defense before it can be tested. Moreover, as it's composed of multiple separate vehicles that connect together, Hyuk and his friend are tapped to pilot them alongside the warrior turtles. But even their mondo mecha may not be enough to defeat Shark's final weapon: the Ultra Robot.

~~~

It was 1987, three years since a gritty independent comic called *Teenage Mutant Ninja Turtles* had first hit shelves. The title was building momentum, and its creators had even signed a deal with toy company Playmates for a tie-in line of action figures. But there had been a catch. Not entirely willing to gamble on an indie property made for adults, the toymaker had insisted on a kid-friendly cartoon series to test the market. So that year, a five-episode TV pilot kicked off the animated adventures of four fierce-fighting, pizza-loving turtles and their stoic rat *sensei* Splinter, debuting shortly thereafter on home video in the feature-length edit *Teenage Mutant Ninja Turtles: The Epic Begins* (1988). The experiment paid off; the "heroes in a half shell" became a global sensation. And more importantly for Playmates, they sold loads of action figures.

It's not especially surprising, then, that South Korea's take on TMNT was also produced to sell toys. What's unusual is that it was made to sell *bootleg* toys.

Out-of-this-world poster art for *Wurideul-ui Chingu Pawo 5* (1989). Everything depicted on it except for the humans could be purchased as bootleg toys.

Shin Hyun-hwan was the owner of South Korean toy manufacturer Popeye Science, which specialized in cheap trinkets that kids could buy for pocket change. After taking his son to see Kim Cheong-gi's animated *Hwang Geumnalgae 1.2.3.* (*Goldwing*) in 1978, Shin was inspired to adapt the film's characters into a set of figurines. Producing them without permission, he based the designs on a pamphlet he had picked up at the cinema. The figures sold out, and Shin began to explore the possibilities of making other toys based on cartoons.

Opportunity knocked in 1980, when film company Tōei invited Shin to visit its studios in Japan. There he witnessed the collaboration between Tōei's anime division and toy maker Bandai. He was impressed with how the action figures dictated the look and function of their cartoon counterparts rather than the other way around. Furthermore, he recognized the potential for using movies and TV series as marketing tools. Returning to South Korea, Shin approached Kim Cheong-gi and proposed an animated film based around a new line of Popeye Science toys. Kim was skeptical, as such a thing had never been done domestically, but eventually he came around. His condition, however, was that Shin would have to shoulder 100 percent of the animation costs.

The film was 1982's *Syupeo Taegwon V* (*Super Taekwon V*), the fourth in the popular Robot Taekwon V series inspired by giant mecha anime from Japan. This time the eponymous robot, originally a knock-off of Mazinger Z, was completely redesigned to match Shin's new toy. Except it wasn't *precisely* new. Lacking advanced mold-making technology, Shin created his Taekwon V by reverse-engineering a mold from a Japanese *Sentō Meka Zabunguru* (*Combat Mecha Xabungle*, 1982) figure. He then repeated the process with other models from various series, resulting in a mishmash line of bootlegs to populate the movie.

Shin's gamble paid off. Children clamored for the toys. Stores sold out and beleaguered parents even showed up at the Popeye Science factory in an attempt to obtain the hot items. Buoyed by their success, Shin and Kim collaborated again on *Space Gundam V*, featuring figures based on *Chōjikū Yōsai Makurosu* (*Super Dimension Fortress Macross*, 1982).

By the time he began production on *Wurideul-ui Chingu Pawo 5* ("Our Friend Power 5") in 1989, Shin was an old hand at the game. This time, though, he was making a live action film. And its stars weren't Japanese toys, but the original 1988 line of Playmates *Ninja Turtles* action figures. Bootlegs, of course. However, giant robots were still Shin's bread and butter, so he also made two hero robots based on figures from Bandai's Machine Robo series. One of these, incidentally, was originally named the "Battle Suit Power System 5," which clearly influenced the film's title. A third mecha, Shark's "Ultra Robot," was a variation on Baxingar from the anime *Ginga Reppū Bakushingā* (*Galactic Gale Baxingar*, 1982).

The plot of the movie, which bears no relation to anything in the Teenage Mutant Ninja Turtles universe, was made out of whole cloth to incorporate all of the toys. In fact, the *Teenage Mutant Ninja Turtles* animated series didn't come to South Korea until 1990, a year after *Wurideul-ui Chingu Pawo 5*, so its plot would have been unknown to local audiences. With just a handful of out-of-context animal warriors to hang a story on, Shin and company cast the humanoid turtles as aliens and the man-sized rat as part of an enemy race.

Providing a tangible link to the toys, the movie costumes were constructed as super-sized versions of the Playmates figures, complete with the fixed grimaces that were an iconic part of their design. Unlike the official figures or their cartoon counterparts, however, all of the turtles wear identical red eye masks. While this was how the Ninja Turtles were originally depicted in the comics, it was also how they were illustrated in early advertising for the figures. The Battlestar turtles are instead differentiated by their individually-colored ventral shells.

Given the film's low budget, producing its many space battles and robots would have been cost-prohibitive for director Park Ho-jin. Instead, his team returned to the anime roots of Shin's toy marketing and looked to South Korea's animation industry. Nearly all of the sci-fi vehicles and special effects sequences were realized via hand-drawn animation, with the film alternating between live action and cartoon depending on the needs of the shot. Other sequences were created by animating cut-outs of film stills, and still others incorporated photographs of the real-life toys.

Wurideul-ui Chingu Pawo 5 was released on August 16, 1989. Unsurprisingly, South Korean audiences were none the wiser about the true origins of the warrior turtles. YouTuber Temmie Plays! recalls seeing the film as a child in South Korea: "Imagine my surprise when I went to America and saw these [turtles] eating pizza and fighting the Shredder.... No kidding, I thought TMNT was the ripoff."

Yarasa Adam: Bedmen ("Batman")

INSPIRED BY: *Batman* (1966)
COUNTRY: Turkey
YEAR: 1973
PRODUCTION: Nuran Film
DIRECTOR: Günay Kosova
WRITER: Günay Kosova
STARS: Levent Çakır, Hüseyin Sayar, Emel Özden, Altan Günbay, Funda Ege, Ceyhan Cem

Someone is murdering the ten most fashionable citizens in Istanbul. All ten were selected by a popular magazine, and all have been insured for a suspiciously large sum of money by its eccentric publisher, Altan Soner (Altan Günbay), who also happens to be on the list. The insurance company is concerned, so they call in Batman (Levent Çakır) and Robin (Hüseyin Sayar) to investigate.

The dynamic duo visits a strip club owned by Soner with the intention of interrogating one of the dancers, but the girl is killed before they can speak to her. The heroes therefore decide to visit Soner in person, as he has the most to gain from the murders. But after being given the stonewall treatment, they focus their attention instead on Emel (Emel Özden), a girl to whom Soner has been showing particular favor. Fortunately, Batman and Robin arrive just as she's grabbed by a trio of goons. They rescue her and learn that, unlike the other victims, Emel is not insured.

Presently another of the unlucky ten, Funda (Funda Ege), is performing a striptease at home for no one in particular when she's set upon by thugs. Batman and Robin again arrive just in time to beat them back. The goons report their failure to their shadowy boss, prompting the mastermind's bikini-clad moll Ceyhan (Ceyhan Cem) to return and finish the job once Batman is gone.

Revisiting Emel, with whom he's developed a mutual attraction, Batman learns that Soner did once offer to insure her, but she turned him down. Meanwhile, Robin discovers Funda's corpse. Convinced that Soner is behind the murders despite a lack of hard evidence, Batman and Robin go to confront him. But to their dismay they discover that Soner too has been murdered!

Ceyhan seizes this opportunity to kidnap Emel since she's home alone. She then visits Batman and attempts to seduce and murder him. He rebuffs her, but several goons enter and a free-for-all ensues. Batman dispatches them handily, demanding from the last man standing the identity of their boss. The thug agrees to talk but asks for a cigarette. Batman unfortunately fails to see through this transparent ruse and the man chomps down on a hidden cyanide capsule.

Out of leads, Batman and Robin put Ceyhan under surveillance and are surprised when she's gunned down in the street. They confront the killers, only to be fooled once again by the old cyanide trick. Eventually, however, all clues lead back to Soner's mansion, where Batman and Robin race to rescue Emel and discover the mastermind's true identity.

~~~

By 1973 Batman was well known in Turkey. Many of the comics had been translated into Turkish, the 1940s Columbia movie serials had been released domestically,

Yarasa Adam: Bedmen ("Batman")

and the 1966 feature film starring Adam West had hit Turkish theaters just three years prior. Moreover, a local Batman movie had already been made in 1967 in which the Dark Knight tangled with sadistic French thief Fantomas. Titled *Fantoma İstanbul'da Buluşalım* ("Fantomas: Appointment in Istanbul"), it's one of many Turkish genre films believed lost or destroyed.

Certainly Levent Çakır was familiar with Batman when he was invited to the offices of Nuran Film in early '73. A handsome, athletic action star, Çakır was at the peak of his career and virtually synonymous with comic book heroes. In 1971 alone he played the title roles in Turkish adaptations of *The Phantom*, Italian comic *Zagor*, and *Superman*. (Well, *a* Superman—one who wore a mask and used guns.) Nuran's owner Savaş Eşici was ready to add the Caped Crusader to Çakır's repertoire.

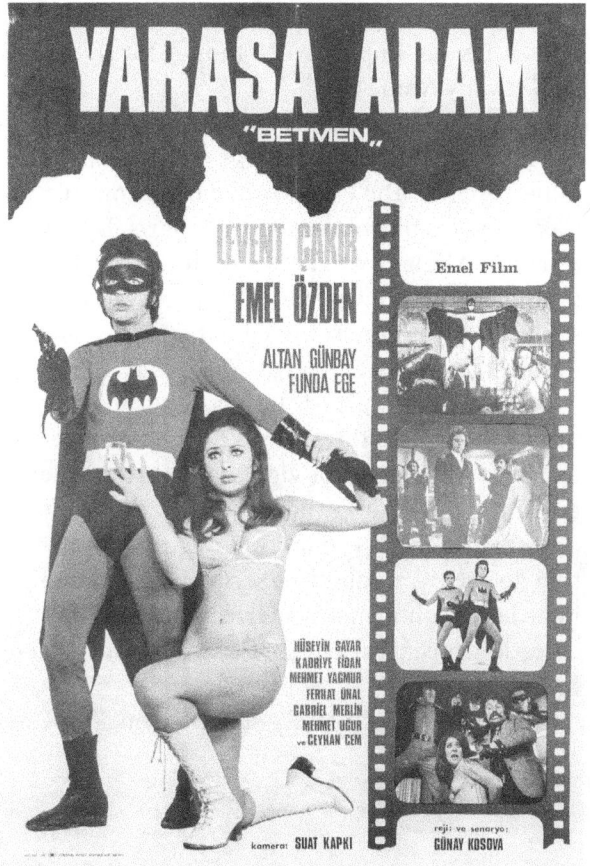

Holy mix-up, Batman! Emel Özden clings to Levent Çakır who appears to have grabbed Robin's mask by mistake (*Yarasa Adam* (1973) / Nuran Film Company / Istanbul, Turkey).

Nuran Film was a relatively small operation. That didn't particularly bother Çakır; he was used to low budgets. Despite unimpressive accommodations, catering, makeup, and special effects, these were still productions that offered him the welcome opportunity to star in exciting science fiction, action, and fantasy films. But there was one thing about Eşici's proposed Batman film that stuck in his craw: it was going to be gray.

In those days, none of the staples of film production were manufactured in Turkey, so everything from editing machines to film stock had to be imported from Western countries at great cost. This understandably encouraged filmmakers to cut corners whenever possible, including using cheap black-and-white film at a time when color was the norm in much of the rest of the world. For those producers who could afford Eastman color stock, their posters would eagerly advertise the fact with an Eastmancolor logo larger than the names of the stars. But by 1973, even Turkish audiences had become accustomed to color films. So when Eşici laid out his plan to shoot *Yarasa Adam* in black-and-white, Çakır balked. It was pointless, he contended, to shoot a spectacle like Batman in monochrome. But Eşici's position was hard to argue with: he simply had no money for color. So Çakır conceded, and off he went to see Cowboy Ahmet.

"Cowboy" Ahmet Sert, a Western fan and former tailor who quit his job to pursue a career in the movies, was an accomplished carpenter, set decorator, and costume designer. The Cowboy had been commissioned to make a Batman costume for Çakır. But in spite of lax copyright laws, Eşici was still concerned about litigation, so he asked Ahmet to make some tweaks to differentiate their Batman costume from the official one. The extent of these changes could be politely described as "naive"—a simpler belt, a more rounded bat emblem, and a cowl without the bat ears. None of these differences was likely to qualify as "legally distinct."

However, if Turkish Batman looked basically the same, he certainly didn't act the same. For one thing, unlike their comic book counterparts, *Yarasa Adam*'s Batman and Robin are not vigilantes. Instead they operate within the law as agents of the authorities—it's even suggested that they're assisting the insurance company on behalf of the National Intelligence Organization. This official standing harkens back to the 1943 Columbia serial, in which the dynamic duo was allied with the FBI in order to conform to American censorship regulations. Vigilantism was similarly objectionable in Turkey, so it was more acceptable for the masked heroes to work for the government.

But what might really surprise long-time bat-fans is the bevy of nude women

BIFF! POW! An incognito Batman fights off some ruffians. Left to right: Mehmet Uğur, Mehmet Yağmur, Levent Çakır, Emel Özden.

hanging around the hero. The original Batman may indulge in a playboy lifestyle as his alter ego Bruce Wayne, but he's got nothing on Turkish Batman. Çakır's version hangs out in strip clubs, brings home pretty hitchhikers, and unsuccessfully juggles dates with his girlfriends. Indeed, *Yarasa Adam* ventures completely into sex comedy territory when Batman tries to bluff Emel by hastily disguising his current bedmate as a nurse.

The sex appeal was partly an effort to make up for a lack of budget by dint of other exploitable assets. As American B movie director Fred Olen Ray once explained, "Breasts are the cheapest special effect in our business." But it was also an attempt to contend with what was seen as the looming specter of homosexuality. Fredric Wertham's 1954 tome *Seduction of the Innocent*, which decried Batman's perceived homoerotic relationship with Robin, may not specifically have gained traction in Turkey, but its underlying idea was a pervasive one. The Turkish filmmakers were concerned about how the conservative public might view Batman and Robin's friendship, so by portraying Batman as a womanizer they could skirt accusations of homosexual themes.

The philandering also gave the Caped Crusader something in common with another contemporary screen hero: James Bond. Writer-director Günay Kosova shrewdly folded numerous elements of the spy genre into *Yarasa Adam* to capitalize on the 007 and Eurospy trend. The movie's mysterious villain, for example, is only seen from behind as he strokes his pet cat, just like Bond's nemesis Blofeld. And Batman receives his assignments from an authoritative voice on an audio tape, à la Peter Graves in *Mission: Impossible* (1966). Moreover, virtually the entire score for the film has been lifted from spy movies and TV shows. The result is a veritable "who's who" of secret agent theme songs including *Thunderball* (1965), *On Her Majesty's Secret Service* (1969), *I Spy* (1965), *Charade* (1963), and *The Saint* (1962).

Once the film itself was complete, there was still one last detail: the title. Although "Yarasa Adam" literally translates as "Bat Man," the filmmakers made one more effort to stave off lawsuits by avoiding the use of the English name "Batman" on all promotional materials, opting instead for the slightly altered, meaningless homophone "Bedmen" (sometimes "Betmen"). The substitution was transparent to Turks, but the expectation was that any legal-minded English-speaker stumbling across the title *Yarasa Adam: Bedmen* would read nothing in it to connect with the DC character.

The film was released in the fall of 1973. But because the top-tier cinemas in major cities refused to screen black-and-white films, *Yarasa Adam* was relegated to theaters in lower-class neighborhoods. Nevertheless, Çakır recalled that it was a success for the small studio. Afterward, the rights were sold to Burç Film, which began preparing the movie for a deceptive re-release, intending to distribute it as a new film under the bewildering title *Uçan Adam Bedmen: Yarasa Adam* ("Flying Man Bedmen: Bat Man"). Burç even commissioned a new poster depicting the hero as a cross between Superman and The Phantom. The release never took place, but Çakır would return to screens as a Superman of sorts in 1973's *Çılgın Kız ve Üç Süper Adam* ("The Mad Girl and Three Supermen") and 1984's *Üç Süpermen Olimpiyatlarda* ("Three Supermen at the Olympic Games").

Zashchitniki (*Guardians*)

INSPIRED BY: *The Avengers* (2012)
COUNTRY: Russia
YEAR: 2017
PRODUCTION: Enjoy Movies
DIRECTOR: Sarik Andreasyan
WRITER: Andrei Gavrilov
STARS: Anton Pampushnyy, Sanjar Madi, Sebastien Sisak, Alina Lanina, Valeriya Shkirando, Stanislav Shirin

When prototype Russian drone tanks go haywire and are hijacked, the government recognizes the hand of electrokinetic mad scientist August Kuratov (Stanislav Shirin). The nation's only hope of bringing the supervillain to justice is Patriot, a long-defunct Soviet program that created four ageless superhumans—the Guardians. However, they're all in hiding, so Major Elena Larina (Valeriya Shkirando) is tasked with locating and reactivating them.

Ler (Sebastien Sisak), who has telekinetic powers over rock, has been living as a pious shepherd in Armenia. Khan (Sanjar Madi), a ninja-like warrior possessing lightning speed and dual sickle swords, continues to fight evildoers in Kazakhstan. A cabin in Siberia is home to scientist and werebear Arsus (Anton Pampushnyy). And Ksenia (Alina Lanina), who can turn invisible, has been headlining a circus act in Moscow. Approached by Major Larina, the four agree to get the band back together to stop Kuratov, whose sadistic methods left them with physical and mental scars during the original Patriot program.

Meanwhile, the military has tracked the stolen tanks to a junkyard. Believing they have surprise on their side, the Guardians walk straight into an ambush and Kuratov captures all but Ler. Instead of killing them, however, he invites them to join him in his conquest of the Earth. Giving them some time to contemplate their decision, Kuratov then leads a fleet of tanks and helicopters into Moscow. There he tears Ostankino Tower from its base and begins converting it into a giant transmitter, projecting a force field around it to deflect the attacking army.

Major Larina rescues the imprisoned Guardians and together they learn that Kuratov is using the transmitter to bring down Hammer, a weaponized Soviet space station built in the 1980s with enough firepower to obliterate a city. Once that's accomplished he'll take over every military and commercial satellite, effectively granting him total control of the world. The team therefore prepares to storm Ostankino Tower and disable the control device and force field, allowing the military to destroy the mechanism—but first they're given sleek new suits that enhance their superpowers. As the Guardians begin their assault, Larina also discovers that, unbeknownst to them, the heroes have the ability to combine their powers. But with Kuratov proving to be more than a match for them, that information might be too little, too late.

～～～

With few exceptions, Hollywood's pre–2000 attempts to produce movies based on comic books were intermittent, minimally rewarding, and primarily kid-focused. But 20th Century–Fox's wildly profitable *X-Men* (2000), a grown-up take on Marvel's squad of superhumans, ushered in a new era of blockbuster comic book movies. Within a few years of its release a plethora of costumed crime-fighters were headlining mega-budget films, forming multi-picture franchises that became the envy of every studio without a halftone hero to exploit. Spider-Man and The Fantastic Four were no longer the exclusive province of kids and comic fans, but as mainstream as James Bond or Rocky, and even perennial favorites like Batman and Superman saw a cinematic renaissance. On the basis of these successes, comics publisher Marvel established its own studio, constructing a family-friendly, interconnected movie universe based on its stable of *Avengers* heroes including Iron Man, The Incredible Hulk, and Captain America. With marketing budgets as high as $150 million and massive international distribution, Marvel's films became a global phenomenon.

Russian director Sarik Andreasyan recalled to website *Sputnik* that, after the release of *Captain America: Civil War* (2016) in which the star-spangled hero squared off against Iron Man, his nephew "asked to light a candle in church for Captain America, because he was afraid that Iron Man would take revenge." Observing Russian children's intense fondness for foreign heroes had made Andreasyan, a fan himself since *X-Men*, begin to wonder "why is there a Captain *America* but no Captain Armenia?" Although he meant it as a joke, the thought persisted: "Russian children grew up on Hollywood blockbusters and understand 'superhero language.' So why not give them our own heroes so that a child could dress up as, say, a Russian bear instead of Spider-Man or Superman?" With that idea in mind, Andreasyan met with his brother, producer Gevond, and the two hashed out a movie pitch for a team of uniquely Russian superheroes.

However, while Hollywood could draw upon troves of American superhero comics from as far back as the 1930s, the Andreasyan brothers had no such luxury. Despite a history of sequential narrative art as old as the 16th century, including

The Soviet Union's super-powered squad. Russian poster for *Zashchitniki* (2017).

religious icons and woodblock prints called *lubki*, Russia had never allowed comics as we know them today to develop as an industry. During the Soviet era authorities condemned comics as a trashy and bourgeois art form smacking of capitalist mass culture—and Western examples in particular were decried as excessively violent and fantastical. What few Russian comics existed, therefore, were often in the form of short, realistic, and moralizing children's entertainment. Later, during the Perestroika reforms of the late 1980s, as the nation loosened its grip on the economy and freedom of expression, Russian citizens were suddenly hungry for mass culture. Some publishers responded with a handful of comics in various genres—although still no superheroes—but due in part to lingering stigma these made little to no money. After the complete collapse of the Soviet Union, an influx of foreign titles precluded any demand for domestic product, and sporadic attempts at homegrown comics tended to remain unprofitable.

So without a domestic comics culture to pull from, the Andreasyans created new heroes. Inspired perhaps by Captain America's World War II origins, they looked to Russia's Soviet history and the Cold War. They imagined a scenario in which, during the nation's arms race with America, the USSR experimented with genetic engineering to create a team of superhumans. Each member hailed from a different country of the USSR, their powers reflecting the strengths of their respective homelands. Ler, from mountainous Armenia, can control and levitate rocks. The Kazakh Khan, a representative of a nomadic people, has super speed in addition to his martial arts skills. Ksenia, from the Black Sea region of Ukraine, harnesses various properties of water. And the Russian Arsus can transform into a bear—a longstanding symbol of the country.

But despite its deliberate Russianness, the super squad nevertheless features numerous parallels to the Marvel comics and film series. Arsus, a scientist with a beastly alter ego, has a great deal in common with The Incredible Hulk; Khan incorporates elements of *The Avengers*' Winter Soldier and Quicksilver; Ksenia recalls *The Fantastic Four*'s Invisible Woman; Kuratov's electrical powers and weaponized drones evoke the villainous Whiplash from *Iron Man 2* (2010); and Major Larina bears more than a passing resemblance to Scarlett Johansson's portrayal of Black Widow. But Andreasyan defended against accusations of copying by pointing out that many of these traits are not unique to Marvel heroes; super speed, for example, is as much the purview of DC's The Flash as of Marvel's Quicksilver—and there are many more speedsters besides.

Yet to whatever extent the Andreasyan brothers were trying to compete with Marvel, one area where they knew they were outgunned was resources. While Marvel's movies could boast budgets of $100–300 million, *Zashchitniki* had less than $5 million. So after a careful six months of pre-production, the team made the most of its frugal 55-day filming schedule (compared to a six-month shoot for *Avengers: Age of Ultron* [2015]) combining green screen studio filming with practical elements and real locations wherever possible. Actor Anton Pampushnyy spent much of production wearing a comical bear-shaped black suit with white markings on it, his head sticking out from the neck, to serve as a physical reference for the digitally-created werebear. Then, with a limited post-production team, they spent nearly a year creating the film's unprecedented number of visual effects. According to Andreasyan, the final movie contains just three minutes of footage without digital manipulation.

Zashchitniki topped the Russian box office opening weekend, and distributor Turbo Films picked it up for release in China. Nevertheless, the film ultimately flopped in both countries and drove the Andreasyans' company Enjoy Movies into bankruptcy, but not before a sequel was greenlit as a possible Russian-Chinese co-production. The follow-up film would reportedly have introduced Chinese superheroes to the team and been partially filmed in China. However, plans for the film eventually fizzled out. Director Sarik Andreasyan regretted creating his heroes from whole cloth—a fact he believed was responsible for audiences not connecting with the film and which dimmed his hopes for the success of a sequel.

2

Muscles, Magnums, and Machismo

7 Belalılar ("7 Troublemakers")

INSPIRED BY: *The Magnificent Seven* (1960)
COUNTRY: Turkey
YEAR: 1970
PRODUCTION: İrfan Film
DIRECTOR: İrfan Atasoy
WRITER: Yılmaz Güney
STARS: Yılmaz Güney, Ketayün, Şeref Gürsoy, Bilal İnci, Atilla Ergün

Ali Osman (Şeref Gürsoy), a material witness in a murder trial, has been intimidated into committing perjury and dooming an innocent man to the gallows. Days later and miles away, an agent of the court attempts to bring Ali Osman back to right his wrong. But before the two can return, the real murderers—the ruthless Sırtlan (Bilal İnci) and his gang of bandits—gun down the agent. The witness determines to return and tell the truth, but he's swiftly captured by Sırtlan's men. However, his plight is observed by a band of seven good-hearted outlaws, each with a distinctive fighting skill, who come to his aid and repulse the desperados with bullet holes for mementos. Led by the taciturn Banoş (Yılmaz Güney), the seven agree to escort Ali Osman back to court before the wrong man is hanged.

Along the way they come upon a gunfight. A lone woman, Keti (Ketayün), is holding her own against a horde of malicious gunslingers under the command of Sarı Recep (Atilla Ergün). Banoş and his men leap in to give her supporting fire, killing several of the villains and sending the rest packing. Keti explains that she's an Iranian immigrant whose father was killed by Sarı Recep's gang. With no one to return to, she joins Banoş's caravan. Unfortunately, the troupe is now stalked by both Sırtlan and Sarı Recep's gangs which, in pursuit of the same prey, join forces.

As the heroes sleep one night in an abandoned barn, the bandits lay siege to the building. The seven—eight, including Keti—put up a valiant fight, but they're forced to retreat and the marauders capture four of Banoş's men. Sırtlan and Sarı Recep offer to exchange the captives for Ali Osman and Keti, placing Banoş in the unenviable position of deciding whom to sacrifice. But after a period of soul-searching, he devises a plan.

He smuggles a message to his captured comrades, then pretends to consent to the bandits' demands. At the exchange, Keti approaches her enemies, apparently resigned to her fate, but suddenly lobs a stick of dynamite at the makeshift jail holding her friends, blasting them free. A ferocious gun battle ensues, and with the heroes heavily outnumbered, there are bound to be many casualties before it's over.

~~~

Ahmet Sert loved American movies. Especially Westerns. A tailor by trade, he longed for a career in show business, eventually abandoning his sartorial day job and offering his talents to the Turkish film industry. There he distinguished himself as a sought-after costume designer, carpenter, and set decorator—a one-man art department whose passion for oaters earned him the nickname "Cowboy Ahmet" among his peers. But since Westerns were quite literally foreign to Turkey, he had no opportunity to work in his favorite genre. Nevertheless, Cowboy Ahmet was determined. In the early 1960s, seizing an opportunity to direct a film of his own, he constructed an entire Old West town near Istanbul, complete with saloon, sheriff's office, church, and town hall, to make *İntikam Hırsı* ("Storm of Revenge," 1963), Turkey's very first Western.

At the same time, Wild West themed comic books from Europe like *Lucky Luke*, *Captain Miki*, and *Zagor* were flying off Turkish newsstands. Add to that the rising popularity of Spaghetti Westerns imported from Italy in the mid–1960s and Turkey's ravenous appetite for adventure cinema in general, and locally-made Westerns began to look increasingly lucrative to producers. (Cowboy Ahmet's replica town was even available for filmmakers to rent.) However, not everyone in the industry was convinced. When prolific director Yılmaz Atadeniz began making cowboy films, his peers balked. "There were never cowboys in Turkey," they protested. But that didn't bother Atadeniz; there were never any in Italy either.

By the 1970s the Turkish film industry was producing up to 15 "Kebab Westerns" per year, shot in arid regions of Turkey resembling the Spanish and Italian countrysides that doubled for the American Southwest in Spaghetti Westerns. And although many of these films featured original heroes, a number of them revolved around familiar names. Turkish filmmakers adapted the Lone Ranger, Zorro, Django, and several of the popular European comics. So a Turkish *Magnificent Seven* was a natural fit.

The Magnificent Seven (1960) is already an international remake, of course. The brainchild of actor Yul Brynner, it reimagined Akira Kurosawa's *chambara* masterpiece *Shichinin no Samurai* (*Seven Samurai*, 1954) as an American Western, replacing its sword fighters with gunslingers. A hit in dozens of countries, it was successful enough to warrant three sequels, not to mention a 1990s TV series and a 2016 Hollywood remake. Indeed, its story of tough guys banding together to protect poor, honest men and women from predatory bandits is so relatable that it's been creatively reimagined and remade by film industries all over the world: with Kazakhstani dwarves (*Dikiy vostok* aka *Wild East*, 1993) and cartoon bugs (*A Bug's Life*, 1998), and in ancient Rome (*I sette magnifici gladiatori* aka *Seven Magnificent Gladiators*, 1983) and outer space (*Battle Beyond the Stars*, 1980).

The Anatolian version, like many of Turkey's low-budget genre films of the era, was more or less made-to-order. Regional distributors frequently specified the types of movies they wanted by quantity, genre, star, color, and even number of fight scenes— and the production companies they contracted would be expected to deliver on time. In the case of *7 Belalılar*, "on time" meant almost immediately. Producer İrfan Atasoy was playing backgammon with legendary Turkish actor, director, and Western icon Yılmaz Güney when he was visited by Nami Dilbaz, a distributor from Adana. Dilbaz needed a film to show in time for an upcoming holiday. The problem was that the holiday was just 13 days away.

Atasoy turned to Güney: "Can we make a movie in so little time?" he asked. The actor thought they could. So with the details settled and an advance from Dilbaz in his pocket, Atasoy went straight to the window of his office which overlooked (and still

Turkish one-sheet for *7 Belalılar* (1970).

does) a cafe frequented by actors. From that window he cast his film, calling out to any thespians who happened to be walking along the street. He was also approached by an aspiring Iranian actress named Ketayün who jockeyed for a role. "Why not?" replied Atasoy. "It's already total chaos. Join us." His team assembled, the motley crew set out for Asia Minor the next morning. But there was another problem: Atasoy had no script. And with only eight days to shoot the film, the cast and crew were forced to improvise while the story was written on location by Güney, an accomplished screenwriter.

The production's shoot-from-the-hip approach, as well as its limited resources, meant that no matter how much it may have been inspired by *The Magnificent Seven*, there was little one-to-one correspondence. In addition to transplanting the action from the Wild West to the Middle East, Atasoy and Güney traded *Magnificent Seven*'s tale of an entire village under siege for a sort of road movie. Furthermore, while Güney's Banoş and the posse's champion knife-thrower have counterparts in the American film, the other members of the seven have quirks and talents unique to this movie. On the other hand, by the time *7 Belalılar* was made, there were already three films in the official *Seven* franchise, each with a new mission and a unique team of heroes. So while the Turkish film wasn't strictly a remake, it still fit comfortably within the series formula.

Today, İrfan Atasoy makes the surprising claim that his film had no direct connection to *The Magnificent Seven*. Despite producing and starring in a handful of overt remakes (and a far greater number of original films), Atasoy is reluctant to acknowledge the influence of specific movies on his work, worried perhaps that it may be interpreted as unscrupulous theft. However, he admits that after more than 45 years and dozens of films to his name, his memory of *7 Belalılar* is a bit vague. Certainly its similarities identify it as at least a distant cousin. Regardless, Atasoy and Güney's gritty meditation on honor and justice has a good deal more to offer than mere imitation.

1990: I guerrieri del Bronx (*1990: The Bronx Warriors*)

INSPIRED BY: *The Warriors* (1979)
COUNTRY: Italy
YEAR: 1982
PRODUCTION: Deaf Internacional Film s.r.l.
DIRECTOR: Enzo G. Castellari
WRITERS: Dardano Sacchetti, Elisa Livia Briganti, Enzo G. Castellari
STARS: Mark Gregory (Marco Di Gregorio), Stefania Girolami, Ennio Girolami, Vic Morrow, Fred Williamson, George Eastman (Luigi Montefiori)

The year is 1990. The government has given up on policing the gang-infested Bronx, officially declaring it a "no-man's land." Yet straight into it runs Ann, the 17-year-old heiress to arms manufacturer The Manhattan Corporation. Almost immediately she's accosted by the Zombies, a roller-skating gang in street hockey gear. But before they can do her any serious harm, a group of bikers roars onto the scene: the Riders. Led by buff, long-haired Trash (Mark Gregory) the Riders pummel the Zombies. Ann explains that she's seeking refuge in the Bronx, and Trash takes her in. Unfortunately, with her comes a fistful of trouble.

Manhattan Corporation president Sam Fisher (Ennio Girolami) wants the girl back—dead or alive. When his attempt to use one of Trash's men as a spy fails, Fisher is forced to bring out the big guns. He sends in Hammer (Vic Morrow), a nihilist assassin born and bred in the Bronx. Attempting to play the gangs against each other, Hammer murders two of Trash's companions and implicates the Tigers, the most prestigious of the gangs. This puts the Riders on the warpath—except for Trash, who smells a rat.

Ann admits to Trash that this violence is all about her. She's about to turn 18, at which point she inherits the Manhattan Corporation—or rather, becomes the figurehead for some very powerful and dangerous people. Her only chance to foil their plans was to run away and stay hidden. Unfortunately, no sooner does she drop this revelation than she's kidnapped by the Zombies.

To get her back and stop Hammer, Trash is going to need the help of The Ogre (Fred Williamson), leader of the Tigers and de facto king of the Bronx. But to see The Ogre, he and his compatriots will have to travel through the territories of just about every gang in the borough. These include the Iron Men, a gang of face-painted, silver

The Iron Men: tap-dancing terrors of the lawless Bronx. Director Enzo Castellari successfully emulated the outré costuming of *The Warriors* (1979) in *1990: I guerrieri del Bronx* (1982).

lamé-clad dancers; the Scavengers, made up like lepers in rags, who haunt the sewers; and the Zombies, whose 6-foot-7 samurai-styled leader, Golem (George Eastman), towers above even The Ogre. And if that weren't enough, Hammer has recruited Trash's ambitious second-in-command for a deadly act of betrayal.

～～～

The story goes that Italian producer Fabrizio De Angelis missed his subway stop. He was in New York for a film and was returning late at night to his Manhattan hotel. Instead, he ended up in the impoverished, devastated, gang-ridden South Bronx. Wandering the streets, he was struck by the neighborhood's dilapidated buildings and acres of rubble—products of arson, malfeasance, and neglect. It wasn't long, however, before he was accosted by gang members with knives and beat a hasty retreat. Back in safety, he compared those ravaged surroundings and its inhabitants with the affluent parties held every night just across the bridge. What if, he mused, the rich people on Fifth Avenue decided to stop letting the poor people out of their borough? And with that sudden thought, he had a premise for a new movie.

"Maybe," conceded director Enzo Castellari in the film's Blu-ray commentary, "but I am sure he thought [up] the movie after *The Warriors*."

Walter Hill's *The Warriors* (1979) was an instant cult hit. Based on Sol Yurick's novel, it followed a New York City gang framed for murder and forced to fight its way from the Bronx to Coney Island with every other gang in the city out for its blood. With iconic costumes, quotable dialogue, and a romanticized depiction of urban gang life, the film found loads of fans in Europe as well as America. In Italy it was released as *I guerrieri della notte* ("The Warriors of the Night"). De Angelis, eager to piggyback on its fame, would call his film *I guerrieri del Bronx*.

Treatment in hand, the producer approached director Enzo Castellari. This was their first collaboration, but they had nearly worked together once before. After the international success of George Romero's *Dawn of the Dead* (1978), De Angelis offered Castellari the director's chair for an unofficial sequel. Not a fan of horror movies, Castellari passed and the job went to Lucio Fulci. This time, though, it was a better fit and Castellari, primarily an action director, jumped at the opportunity.

Searching for an actor to play gang leader Trash, Castellari discovered 17-year-old Marco Di Gregorio at his gym. Quiet and reserved, Di Gregorio was a reluctant movie star, but the director persuaded the brawny youth to give acting a shot, even though he'd have to learn his English dialogue phonetically. Other cast members came more easily. Castellari had previously worked with Vic Morrow on *L'ultimo squalo* (*The Last Shark*, 1981) and Fred Williamson on *Quel maledetto treno blindato* (*The Inglorious Bastards*, 1978), and he recruited them as the evil Hammer and benevolent Ogre, respectively. The production was also a bit of a family affair, with Castellari's brother Ennio Girolami cast as the Manhattan Corporation president, daughter Stefania playing Ann, and cousin Massimo Vanni as Trash's confidant, Blade.

After five weeks of prep, Castellari and De Angelis gathered a small crew and a few essential actors to take to New York for the first three weeks of production. The team was nervous about shooting in the South Bronx where even the authorities feared to tread, but Castellari had a plan. As soon as they arrived, he asked the locals who the local gang leader was and involved him in the film. With the gang's support, they weren't likely to have much trouble. It also helped that Castellari had hired the Manhattan chapter of the Hells Angels to play many of the Riders. Police were stationed nearby as well, but to the director's dismay they stayed in their vehicles and only came out for the catered lunches.

Once they completed the New York shoot, the production returned to Italy for the final four weeks. All the interior sequences were shot in Rome, and Castellari hired local graffiti artists to decorate the locations

Flame-throwers and gunfire light up the Bronx. U.S. one-sheet for *1990: I guerrieri del Bronx* (1982).

so that they'd pass for South Bronx ruins. He also filmed exteriors that didn't require the New York skyline as well as the remainders of scenes featuring actors who didn't make the trip to the States. Pieced together in the edit, characters would end up seamlessly speaking to each other from 4,000 miles apart.

During production, *The Warriors* was always on the filmmakers' minds. They were keen to imitate its distinctive gangs like the bat-wielding Baseball Furies decked out in baseball jerseys and KISS makeup. Di Gregorio's dialogue coach Paul Costello was a dancer, and he came up with the idea of *Bronx*'s Broadway-esque Iron Men. Sporting silver chorus line costumes and shiny face paint, they were made up of professional dancers from the television industry. As for the subterranean, mummy-like Scavengers, they were conceived as an easy lot to costume: just mud and rags, allowing the production to reuse stuntmen without any chance of their being recognized. Combined with the roller-skating, martial-arts-practicing Zombies and snappily-dressed Tigers, *Bronx* had a fanciful cast of hoodlums to rival Hill's.

However, as much as the film was inspired by *The Warriors*, that wasn't its only influence. *Bronx* also owes a great deal to John Carpenter's *Escape from New York* (1981). Set in the not-too-distant future (*The Warriors*, too, takes place "sometime in the future"), *Escape* similarly locates its search-and-rescue story in a cordoned-off chunk of New York City populated by criminals. The *Bronx* filmmakers essentially took the *Escape from New York* concept and turned it on its head. Vic Morrow's Hammer is effectively a villainous take on Snake Plissken, sent into the lawless zone to find a prominent person who, this time around, doesn't want to be rescued. Here the gangs—some of them anyway—are the good guys, and Fred Williamson's Ogre, the "king of the Bronx," is a heroic interpretation of Isaac Hayes's Duke of New York. Cementing the connection, the film would carry the prefix *1990*, mimicking the Italian title for Carpenter's film, *1997: fuga da New York*.

1990: I guerrieri del Bronx sold all over the world. West Germany in particular played up the *Warriors* connection, retitling the film *The Riffs* after the top gang in Hill's movie. Not long after its release, De Angelis showed up at Castellari's home and handed the director a set of keys. They were to a new car—a gift on account of the film's extraordinary success. Naturally a sequel was in order, and the team reunited for *Fuga dal Bronx* (*Escape from the Bronx*, 1983). This time things moved even more smoothly, as Castellari already had everything he needed and could spend less time in the States, having learned how to make Rome convincingly double for New York. *Fuga* would not only borrow its title from *Escape from New York* (again), but it would even get its own Snake Plissken in the form of returning actor Massimo Vanni, who copied the character's look down to the eyepatch.

Altın Çocuk ("Golden Boy")

INSPIRED BY: *Thunderball* (1965)
COUNTRY: Turkey
YEAR: 1966
PRODUCTION: Göksel Film
DIRECTOR: Memduh Ün

Altın Çocuk ("Golden Boy")

WRITER: Bülent Oran
STARS: Göksel Arsoy, Altan Günbay, Sevda Nur, Cecilia Åkerfeldt

Following the completion of his latest mission—assassinating a man disguised as his duplicate—Turkish secret agent Gökhan Ateş (Göksel Arsoy), aka Golden Boy, flies to London for a long overdue vacation. However, his holiday of seeing the sights and chasing local women is rudely interrupted when he's suddenly recalled to Istanbul for an emergency.

A fellow agent has been murdered. The dead man was investigating rumors of a forthcoming attack on Turkey's nuclear facilities. Retracing the agent's steps, Golden Boy combs the man's hotel suite and discovers a hidden notebook. Unfortunately, he's immediately ambushed by two enemy agents, only managing to escape by dropping out of the window into a passing car driven by a pretty girl, Sevda (Sevda Nur). Taking her back to his place, he discovers an uninvited guest lying in wait. He gives the gunsel a going-over and interrogates him, but the man is shot before he can speak. And while the notebook yields a clue—the name of a dancer at a club—this too leads to a narrowly-avoided trap, leaving Golden Boy back at square one.

In fact, although the country doesn't know it yet, Turkey is in the iron grip of bald, nehru-jacketed supervillain Demetrius (Altan Günbay). From his secret base beneath the Bosphorus, he plans to destroy the entire country's nuclear facilities with remotely controlled atomic warheads. Desiring first to remove Golden Boy

Göksel Arsoy turns the charm on Gamze Öz in this publicity photo for *Altın Çocuk* (1966).

as an obstacle, Demetrius enlists his spy from England, Helen (Cecilia Åkerfeldt), who has a romantic history with the Turkish agent. Helen springs a trap that delivers Golden Boy to Demetrius's seaside mansion. There he's locked in a tiny cell with a slowly descending spiked ceiling. Fortunately, however, Helen has genuine feelings for Golden Boy and covertly releases him, though she's tortured and killed for her treachery.

Golden Boy returns to the mansion, this time with reinforcements, but discovers only an empty house and an aged caretaker. Without a lead, the agents leave. Suspecting a trick (he's correct; the caretaker was Demetrius in disguise), Golden Boy returns that night with Sevda. Their search is in vain, however, and the investigation gets Sevda kidnapped. Meanwhile, Helen's body is discovered and Golden Boy attends her funeral, keeping an eye on her mysterious veiled aunt. He follows her home and confronts her, discovering that she too is Demetrius! A fight ensues, and Golden Boy is imprisoned with Sevda while Demetrius leaves for his underwater base. The prisoners use the old "hey guard, sick man!" ploy to escape, chasing after Demetrius in a speedboat and finally underwater in a last-ditch attempt to prevent the total irradiation of Turkey.

~~~

Over half the planet knows James Bond. His movies have been released in more countries than the jet-setting British spy has visited in person. Agent 007 hit big in Turkey after Istanbul was the backdrop of his second cinematic outing, *From Russia with Love* (1963). Soon Eurospy cash-ins like *Agente 077 dall'oriente con furore* (*From the Orient with Fury*, 1965), *Estambul 65* (*That Man in Istanbul*, 1965), and *Da Istanbul ordine di uccidere* (*From Istanbul, Orders to Kill*, 1965) also began using the transcontinental city as their obligatory exotic location. Those films were local hits too. But Turkey must have noticed that it was regularly playing host to foreign super agents without yet having one of its own. So actor and producer Göksel Arsoy invented one. The fair-haired Arsoy, teen idol and Turkish cinema's so-called "golden boy," cast himself as secret agent "Golden Boy." And in 1966 he was deployed on his first mission.

Agent Golden Boy may hail from the gateway to the East, but Arsoy and director Memduh Ün spent a great deal of effort and resources to make his adventure feel like a legitimate Bond movie from the West. In part, it was a matter of pride. Since the founding of the Republic of Turkey in 1923 there had been a massive push to modernize and westernize. This had the side effect of valuing elements of Western culture, for better or worse, as inherently superior. Turkish filmmakers would often therefore strive to meet a nebulous Western standard, and the globe-hopping nature of a Bond film gave them a chance to go for broke. Showing that Turkey's Golden Boy was just as stylish and international as Britain's 007 was an ideal opportunity to demonstrate how favorably Turkish films could compare with Hollywood fare—even if it meant imitating it.

Certainly *Altın Çocuk* owes a great deal to the official Bond canon. Several elements of its plot specifically echo *Thunderball* (1965), from the remote-control warheads to the scuba scenes. And *Thunderball*'s pre-credits sequence, featuring a mourning widow who's really a male enemy agent in disguise, is replicated later in the film. However, *Altın Çocuk* is more pastiche than remake, incorporating various 007 tropes, motifs, and moments from throughout the franchise. The credits, for example, play out like a budget version of the Maurice Binder intros, with a half-nude woman dancing to the movie's theme song. Golden Boy himself is apparently killed in the very first scene, borrowing a tradition of opening fakeouts that began in *From Russia with Love* and continued through *You Only Live Twice* (1967). Demetrius, the cat-fancying evil genius, is a clear homage to SPECTRE's Ernst Stavro Blofeld. And then there are the staples like the elaborate death traps, the suitcase full of weapons and gizmos, the bevy of fawning femmes, and of course the international locales.

Arsoy aspired to the cosmopolitan style of the Bond productions, lavishing a substantial budget on *Altın Çocuk* that allowed for the shooting of an extended sequence in London. Thus Golden Boy jets to the UK on holiday, drives past Big Ben, Buckingham Palace, Trafalgar Square, and Piccadilly Circus, and spends his time picking up local girls and buying drinks. Never mind that this plot cul-de-sac doesn't relate to the rest of the film; to make his Turkish Bond feel authentic, Arsoy just needed the requisite exotic women and an exotic location. And if that location happened to be the one that gave Bond to the world, even better.

Enhancing its international flavor, the film also boasts some interesting and unusual credits: "London scenes directed by Mr. Ray Bowman," "British and French TV stars involved in the film's British scene," and starring the "Swedish Cover Girl" Cecilia Åkerfeldt. These claims were not entirely accurate. Ray Bowman was more likely a hired cameraman or local intermediary with an inflated title. The "British and French TV stars" were locals hired in London as glorified extras. And the "Swedish Cover Girl," though indeed Swedish, was simply discovered at her friend's wedding in Turkey and had never graced a cover in her life.

At first blush, this ballyhoo recalls the practice, especially in Italy, of Anglicizing domestic credits to appeal to an international market. Except that *Altın*

Göksel Arsoy sees the sights with tourist-turned-actress Cecilia Åkerfeldt.

Çocuk was made for an exclusively Turkish audience. It would seem counterintuitive, then, to use trumped-up credits to overstress the film's foreign connections, but in this case that very foreignness was a badge of status and quality. And Arsoy was making the most of it.

His quest for Bond-esque spectacle did involve a bit of cheating, however. Capturing the *Thunderball* feel with the underwater action sequences, for instance, required a certain amount of subterfuge. Arsoy's increased budget might have accommodated a scuba sequence, but underwater filming had never been done in a Turkish film and the equipment simply wasn't available. So director Ün filmed all of the above-water shots on the Bosphorus, and then took the rest of the scene—hook, line, and sinker—from the French spy movie *OSS 117 se déchaîne* ("OSS 117 Is Unleashed," 1963).

In typical Bond fashion, *Altın Çocuk*'s ending promised Göksel Arsoy's return in *Ortaşark Yanıyor* (1967). That would turn out to be an unrelated film, but *Altın Çocuk* did receive a proper sequel in 1967 called *Altın Çocuk Beyrut'ta* ("Golden Boy in Beirut") in which the hero faces off against an outlandish villain called The Dragon who dresses like Space Batman. Unfortunately, the Golden Boy series was aborted after just those two entries. Nevertheless, Turkey continued to produce one-off spy films throughout the late '60s, all of which were more or less in the James Bond mold.

The country would get its own uniquely local spy franchise in 2003 in the form of *Kurtlar Vadisi* ("Valley of the Wolves"), a long-running string of films and TV series dealing, often controversially, with Turkish politics and international affairs. Yet even *Kurtlar Vadisi* couldn't resist just a touch of Hollywood, roping in actors Andy Garcia and Sharon Stone in 2005 to play criminal masterminds. This time, though, Hollywood wasn't an unattainable ideal; instead, it was playing the bad guy!

Black Cobra

>Inspired by: *Cobra* (1986)
>Country: Italy
>Year: 1987
>Production: Immagine S.r.l.
>Director: Stelvio Massi
>Writer: Danilo Massi
>Stars: Fred Williamson, Eva Grimaldi, Bruno Bilotta, Maurice Poli

Three bank robbers are holed up at an indoor pool and have taken hostages. The police send in Detective Robert Malone (Fred Williamson) to negotiate, but they've forgotten that Malone doesn't play by the rules. With his sidearm and shotgun he blasts holes in all three thugs.

Meanwhile, a murderous gang of bikers called the Zombies and their muscular, unnamed leader (Bruno Bilotta) are on a killing spree that has gripped the city with fear. Things come to a head when they commit a murder that's witnessed by fashion photographer Elys Trumbo (Eva Grimaldi). The leader tries to kill her as well, but she thinks fast, distracting him with the flash from her camera. Unfortunately, this also means she now has pictures of him, making her an even more necessary target. She only manages to escape death thanks to the fortunate arrival of a police car which scares the killers away.

Police Chief Walker (Maurice Poli) calls Malone away from feeding his picky cat to apprise him of their new lead, but they soon discover that the photos are too washed out to be of any use. The Zombies don't know that, though, so Elys, now at the hospital, is still a target. Malone is assigned to protect her, but he's already a step behind; the killers also know where she is. They infiltrate the hospital, kill the police guard, and are about to murder Elys just as Malone arrives. He saves the witness, but the leader escapes. With the hospital unsafe, Malone takes Elys to his home.

The next day, Malone drives her to her house to pick up some belongings. After she goes upstairs, Malone discovers signs of forced entry. He cautiously approaches the bedroom, motioning her out moments before a Zombie assassin can carry out his mission. A gun battle and fist fight ensue, ending when Malone knocks the goon through the window.

Changing tactics, the Zombies attack Chief Walker and kidnap his daughter, bartering her life for Malone and the photos. The chief won't risk Malone, but the detective volunteers to go anyway. He equips himself from his own private arsenal and sets out with his partner to the rendezvous at a lumber yard. Driving in guns blazing, they rescue the girl and take out the leader with a knife to the back. However, Malone makes a grave mistake when he leaves the head Zombie for dead.

~~~

In America in the early 1950s, racial segregation was still the law of the land. *The Amos 'n' Andy Show* (1951) was beamed to television sets across the nation, much to the chagrin of the NAACP. And Black actors struggled for respect in an overwhelmingly white Hollywood. Overseas, however,

Polish VHS cover for *The Black Cobra* (1987).

Italy offered an unlikely haven for Black American actors looking to play something other than servants and jungle tribesmen.

Black Cobra might never have existed if not for John Kitzmiller. Following World War II, Kitzmiller, a captain in the all-Black 92nd Infantry Division, was stationed in Tombolo, Italy where he was spotted by filmmaker Luigi Zampa. Impressed by the soldier's boisterous laugh, Zampa offered him a role in *Vivere in pace* (*To Live in Peace*, 1947). Kitzmiller wasn't the first Black American in an Italian film, but he found greater success than his predecessors, appearing in dozens of movies over nearly 20 years. He paved the way for many Black American actors to come to Italy and discover opportunities that were denied them in Hollywood. Among them were Ben Johnson and former footballers Harold Bradley and Woody Strode.

To be sure, the Italian film industry was not precisely a bastion of racial equality. While Black Americans found stardom, Black Italians were rarely allowed the spotlight. The exceptions, more often than not, were women cast for exotic sex appeal, like the Eritrean-born Zeudi Araya in a trio of films by Luigi Scattini or Dominican Iris Peynado in a host of otherworldly goddess and sorceress roles. Filmmaker and film historian Fred Kudjo Kuwornu suggests that the primary reason for this disparity was that Black Italians were perceived by producers as Africans first and Italians second. On the other hand, "African-American actors were seen as Americans and therefore cool, so for this reason their color was a secondary issue."

Indiana native Fred Williamson, a late entry to the Italian movie scene, would wholeheartedly embrace that cool image. Like Bradley and Strode, he got his start in football. Playing for the Kansas City Chiefs, Fred "The Hammer" Williamson made a point to stand out, wearing non-regulation white shoes and personalized armbands that cost him $100 per game in fines. It paid off, though; when he decided to try his hand at acting, he was quickly recognized on the 20th Century–Fox lot by Robert Altman who gave him a part in *MASH* (1970). After a handful of television roles, he became a major figure in the "Blaxploitation" genre of the early 1970s, headlining films like American International Pictures' *Black Caesar* and *Hell Up in Harlem* (both 1973).

As Blaxploitation lost steam in the States, Williamson began producing his own films with an eye toward the international market. In order to make the venture profitable, though, he had to change the game. Speaking to the website *The Action Elite*, Williamson explained that, overseas, "companies like AIP were selling every film with a black star in it for $3000 across the board no matter what the film was." He realized that international distributors were lowballing American studios, capitalizing on anti–Black prejudice by claiming that the films wouldn't perform well abroad.

Williamson, who had starred in two Italo-American co-productions, *Crazy Joe* and *Three Tough Guys* (both 1974), knew otherwise, and he decided to call their bluff. He set up shop at Cannes with *Adiós Amigo* (1975), a Western starring himself and Richard Pryor. "[T]he first offer I got," he recounted, "was from Greece for $3000. I said, 'No, no, no, no, nooooo, $25,000.' They wouldn't shell that money out so after eight days I still had all my movies and on the very last day I had $275,000 to $300,000 in sales. Then these distributors would come to me and say, 'Don't tell anyone what I just paid for this film.'"

While continuing to produce and direct his own films, many of them Westerns and crime thrillers, he also acted in Italy for local directors. With Spaghetti Western icon Clint Eastwood back in Hollywood, Williamson styled himself, both in Italy and the States, as "a Black Clint Eastwood with martial arts," favoring films along the lines of *Dirty Harry* (1971).

Black Cobra, which Williamson would describe as an Eastwood-style film, was in reality a nearly beat-for-beat remake of Sylvester Stallone's *Cobra* (1986). Based in part on Stallone's unused rewrite of *Beverly Hills Cop* (1984) and loosely on Paula Gosling's novel *Fair Game*, *Cobra* did, however, riff heavily on *Dirty Harry* (1971), even pointedly casting two of its key actors. A reasonable box office success (especially up against *Top Gun* [1986]) and with the potential for a franchise, *Cobra* was an attractive template for Luciano Appignani's production company, Immagine, which previously produced cash-ins on *Mad Max* (1979) and *Raiders of the Lost Ark* (1981).

Directing duties fell to prolific second-tier *poliziottesco* filmmaker Stelvio Massi with a script by his son Danilo. Massi made use of exterior shots of New York City to suggest an American setting while shooting the majority of the film in Rome. Danilo Massi's script closely followed *Cobra*, only lightly rearranging a few elements, such as replacing the opening supermarket shootout with an indoor pool, making the witness a fashion photographer rather than a model, and giving the name of Stallone's "zombie squad" to the bad guys. The Massis did give Williamson his Clint Eastwood moment, however; late in the film Malone delivers an ever-so-slightly modified version of *Dirty Harry*'s "do I feel lucky" speech to a Zombie thug.

Unlike Stallone's film, *Black Cobra* did become a franchise. *The Black Cobra 2* and *3* bucked the urban cop formula and saw Malone sent to battle terrorists in the Philippines, where many Italian actioners were being shot at the time. Notably, in the third movie, Malone finally got to perform *Cobra*'s grocery store gunfight.

An unofficial fourth entry, *Detective Malone: The Black Cobra 4* (1991), only "starred" Williamson in the loosest possible sense. In reality it merely incorporated some of his footage from *Black Cobra* and *The Black Cobra 2*. Director Umberto Lenzi slyly brought back actor Bruno Bilotta as the villain, dressing him in the same costume to match his scenes as the Zombie biker from the first movie. This time, however, he was reimagined as an Islamic terrorist. Maurice Poli also returned for a couple of scenes as Chief Walker. "They did it all behind my back," Williamson lamented to *Action Elite*. "I went in there and about tore that office up…. They paid me off, said they were very sorry and I walked out of there with some cash money."

Cellat ("The Executioner")

INSPIRED BY: *Death Wish* (1974)
COUNTRY: Turkey
YEAR: 1975
PRODUCTION: Uğur Film
DIRECTOR: Memduh Ün
WRITER: Bülent Oran
STARS: Serdar Gökhan, Emel Özden, Melek Ayberk, Mahmut Hekimoğlu, Kenan Pars

2. Muscles, Magnums, and Machismo

Architect Orhan (Serdar Gökhan) returns home from a scenic family vacation with his wife Filiz (Emel Özden), sister Sevgi (Melek Ayberk), and Sevgi's husband Cahit (Mahmut Hekimoğlu) to a crime-ridden Istanbul. The following day, Filiz and Sevgi are out shopping when they're spied by a trio of ruffians. The thugs follow the women home and, discovering that they're alone, break in, rob, rape, and beat them. Sevgi manages to call the police and the women are rushed to the hospital, but Filiz doesn't survive and Sevgi is left mute and mentally shattered. Bereft of clues, the police are helpless.

Orhan, furious, improvises a cosh from a sock full of coins and goes out into the night looking for trouble. Almost immediately a pimp tries to mug him, and Orhan bashes him with the weapon.

Unable to find the satisfaction he craves, Orhan instead attempts to lose himself in his work. He travels to Bursa to meet with a client, a gun enthusiast named Mehmet (Kenan Pars). Orhan surveys his land for the development of a new hotel and Mehmet, grateful for his efforts, presents him with a pearl-handled pistol as a gift.

When Orhan returns home he learns that Sevgi's condition has worsened. Pocketing his new gun, he goes out at night, happens upon a man molesting a child, and shoots him. The act makes him sick, but he doesn't regret it, and he vows to continue killing criminals. Orhan's anonymous vigilantism soon makes him a folk hero. The police want to stop him but they're without leads until, after gunning down a thug on a train, Orhan accidentally leaves a shopping bag behind. The police finger him as a suspect and close in.

Orhan receives the grim news that his sister has committed suicide. That night he eludes a police tail, retrieves his gun from its hiding place, and kills three more muggers. However, this time he receives a wound to the leg. Fleeing the police, he breaks into a woman's house

Serdar Gökhan is the Turkish Charles Bronson in *Cellat* (1975). Turkish one-sheet.

to patch himself up. By a terrible coincidence, the woman is the girlfriend of one of the men who killed Orhan's wife, and what's more, she's wearing Sevgi's necklace. Orhan forces her to tell him where the thugs are, and then he sets out on one final, brutal mission of revenge.

～～～

It began in Italy. Don Siegel's rogue cop thriller *Dirty Harry* (1971), along with a few surprise local successes like heist film *Banditi a Milano* (*The Violent Four*, 1968) and mafia tale *Il giorno della civetta* (*Day of the Owl*, 1968), set off a wave of gritty, hard-nosed crime films ripped from the turbulent nation's headlines. Many of these featured tough cops and outraged citizens taking on a corrupt system and delivering violent justice from the barrel of a revolver. Their heroes were often either mustachioed macho men like Franco Nero and Maurizio Merli, or tough-guy American imports like Henry Silva and Jack Palance. Though not codified at the time, the films would come to be known collectively as *poliziotteschi*, and they were extremely popular—even in Turkey.

In the early 1970s, Hollywood studios didn't yet have a foothold in Turkey. Foreign films were imported or not based on the judgment of local distributors. These distributors would travel to European film markets and buy whichever movies they felt were suitable for Turkish audiences. Not only were Italian crime films a safe bet, they were also substantially cheaper than Hollywood product. When they proved to be hits back home, the distributors naturally bought more. Turkish filmgoers devoured them. "In the early '70s," confirmed film historian Ali Murat Güven, "Franco Nero was more popular than most of the Hollywood stars."

Italian crime movies became such a phenomenon that Turkish filmmakers began producing homegrown offerings in the same mold. Revenge films multiplied. Filmmakers Yılmaz Atadeniz and İrfan Atasoy even made several as co-productions with Italian companies, featuring local talent alongside stalwarts of the Italian genre scene like Richard Harrison and Gordon Mitchell. These included *Dört Hergele* (*Four for All*, 1974) and *Anasının Gözü* ("Foxy," 1974).

It was in 1974, at the peak of the genre's popularity, that distinguished filmmaker Memduh Ün, on a business trip abroad, screened Michael Winner's *Death Wish* (1974). Revolving around an ordinary citizen taking justice into his own hands after an assault on his family, the film was essentially an American *poliziottesco*. (In truth it was sort of the other way around; *Death Wish* was one of the core Hollywood films that, like *The Godfather* [1971] and *Serpico* [1973], would continue to stoke the fire of the *poliziottesco* genre in Italy.) Ün enjoyed the picture and felt it would make an ideal story for Turkish audiences. However, he didn't buy the film; after all, he wasn't a distributor. In fact, *Death Wish* wouldn't be picked up for Turkish cinemas until 1980, when it would be released domestically as *Yara* ("Trauma"). Instead, Ün returned home and met with screenwriter Bülent Oran.

Oran was one of "The Three Musketeers" of Yeşilçam who, along with Erdoğan Tünaş and Safa Önal, wrote a significant proportion of the films from the industry's golden age. By the time Ün approached Oran, the scribe had 22 years in the business and hundreds of credits to his name. Ün described the story of *Death Wish* to Oran and tasked him with adapting it for a domestic audience. Oran reworked the tale only slightly, giving it a cathartic new angle that would soon become standard operating procedure for many future *Death Wish* iterations.

In neither Brian Garfield's original novel nor the Michael Winner film is the protagonist ever brought face to face with the home invaders who destroyed his life. Instead they go unpunished, existing only to serve as the catalyst for the main character's rage. (An early draft of the screenplay did end with hero Paul Kersey confronting those same thugs, only to die at their hands, but this idea was eventually abandoned.) Oran was the first writer to give the hero his revenge, inserting a clue that allows Orhan to hunt down the perps in the final act.

(Seven years after *Cellat,* Hollywood would inadvertently take a page from Bülent Oran. Cannon Films' *Death Wish 2* [1982] saw the return of Paul Kersey, this time actively stalking the thugs responsible for raping and killing his household. Three further sequels would follow a similar formula, and Eli Roth's 2018 *Death Wish* remake would also focus on Kersey's targeted revenge.)

One final alteration was due more to obligation than creative license. The Turkish laws governing film censorship forbid the praise or glorification of criminals—even righteous ones. Lionizing murderers was seen as tantamount to inciting crime. Therefore, in deference to the law, Oran's vigilante was made to surrender to police at the end of the story.

Despite working with a scant three percent of the original's budget—about

Serdar Gökhan (center), under suspicion of being the vigilante killer, is stopped and frisked by cops Hakkı Kıvanç (left) and Giray Alpan (right). Turkish lobby card.

$100,000—*Cellat* was nevertheless a prestige production. Ün hired legendary cinematographer Kaya Ererez, a frequent collaborator of auteur Yılmaz Güney, to shoot the film in vivid color. For his lead, Ün cast Serdar Gökhan (born Nusret Ersöz), a rising star who many considered to be the primary rival of action superstar Cüneyt Arkın. Supporting roles went to venerable actors Kenan Pars and Reha Yurdakul. To portray the film's bevy of gangsters, thugs, and rapists, Ün looked to actor-stuntman Hüseyin Zan, owner of a stunt school in Istanbul. Zan brought his entire school to the shoot, giving Orhan plenty of targets on whom to mete out vengeance. Production began in November 1974 and lasted for two chilly months. Film processing and editing were then completed at Studio Ören, and the dubbing was recorded at Studio Yeni Lale.

Cellat was released in March 1975, beating the original *Death Wish* to Turkish screens by five years. It was a hit, providing the Ugur Film company with a respectable profit. The film has remained a local classic, receiving a rare high-definition restoration from new rights-holder Fanatik Film in 2017.

Den' D ("D-Day")

INSPIRED BY: *Commando* (1985)
COUNTRY: Russia
YEAR: 2008
PRODUCTION: BBP Alliance
DIRECTOR: Mikhail Porechenkov
WRITERS: Oleg Presnyakov, Vladimir Presnyakov
STARS: Mikhail Porechenkov, Aleksandra Ursulyak, Varvara Porechenkova, Mikhail Trukhin, Bob Schrijber

Retired paratrooper Ivan (Mikhail Porechenkov) is having a bad day. His former team has been murdered, his secluded home invaded, and his young daughter Zhenya (Varvara Porechenkova) kidnapped. The architect of Ivan's pain is an old enemy—a mercenary named Gelda (Bob Schrijber). He's holding Ivan's daughter hostage in order to force him to assassinate a foreign president. Gelda's loudmouth lackey Stasik (Mikhail Trukhin) escorts Ivan to the airport to make sure he catches his flight, but once it's airborne, Ivan grabs a parachute and dives from the aircraft, leaving him ten hours to find his daughter before the plane lands and his ploy is discovered.

He returns to the airport, but with no way to follow Stasik back to his base, he forces off-duty stewardess Aliya (Aleksandra Ursulyak) to tail him in her car. Stasik leads them to a water park, but spots Ivan and flees to a nearby construction site. Ivan catches him atop the half-finished building and dangles him over the balcony. Panicked, Stasik reveals that his comrade at the TransHotel may know the whereabouts of Zhenya. Satisfied, Ivan drops Stasik to his death. He and Aliya drive to the hotel, where Ivan fights and ultimately kills the partner. Fortunately, they discover a map that indicates an island off the Russian coast, the likeliest spot for Gelda to be holding Zhenya. Their first stop, however, is a fish shop—a front for Gelda's gun-smuggling operation—where Ivan loads up on weapons. Fully equipped, they steal an amphibious plane from a small airport and fly to the island.

Ivan rows ashore and gears up, while at the same time Zhenya enacts her own

Mikhail Porechenkov decks himself out in full *Commando* gear and makeup in *Den' D* (2008).

escape plan, lifting a knife off a guard and cutting a rope to climb out of the window. Ivan storms Gelda's compound, commandeering a motorbike and wreaking havoc with its mounted machine gun and his arsenal of assault rifles, rocket launchers, and explosives. Unfortunately, Gelda recaptures Zhenya, holding her as bait in a caviar factory in the middle of the compound, ready for a final, meaty, hand-to-hand fight with his longtime foe.

~~~

Commando (1985), a high-octane vehicle for rising star Arnold Schwarzenegger, was released amid an explosion of macho Hollywood action films in the mid-eighties like *Rambo: First Blood Part II* (1985), *Missing in Action* (1984), and *Invasion USA* (1985). Products of Reagan's America, these movies featured bodybuilding one-man-armies with American ideals, special forces training, and endless machine guns. They were over-the-top, jingoistic, and a little paranoid, often dealing with the failures of the Vietnam War or the looming threat of Communism. So it seems strange, at first blush, that one of them would get a remake in the former Soviet Union.

But director Mikhail Porechenkov, who also stars in *Den' D* as Ivan, was a longtime fan of *Commando*. He yearned for a return to such childhood cinematic heroes as Schwarzenegger's ultramasculine John Matrix. So upon launching his own company, BBP Alliance, he chose as his first production and directorial debut a Russian remake. For him, *Den' D*—named after the Day of Desantnik, the celebration of Russian paratroopers—was not just an opportunity to revisit an old favorite, but also a response to modern, introspective action stars. "Lately," Porechenkov lamented to RIA News, "real men have become extinct, both in the movies and in real life. They were replaced by reflective characters. I don't like self-reflective heroes who drink vodka and regret their unfulfilled lives." Rather than so-called "metrosexual" protagonists in the Brad Pitt mold, he explained, he preferred films about burly, forthright men of action. *Commando* was his ideal template. And as a bonus, a remake would allow him to capitalize on audiences' nostalgia for the original film.

Except, what nostalgia precisely? For that matter, how had Porechenkov originally seen it? At the time *Commando* hit American theaters, Soviet censorship had a vice grip on cinema, banning any film the State deemed "ideologically hostile." That included most Western-produced movies—*Commando* included. So theoretically Russians wouldn't have been able to see the film until at least the collapse of the Soviet Union—and possibly much later if there were holdups with distribution and availability.

But they did see it. In fact, when Schwarzenegger flew to Moscow in 1988 to shoot *Red Heat*, he marveled that locals not only recognized him, but many had videotapes of his movies—courtesy of the black market. Brave citizens and enterprising exhibitors were willing to spend small fortunes on imported VCRs and illegally duplicated tapes of Hollywood films. (The alternative was dreary nationalistic television.) Illicit "video clubs" sprouted up all over the Soviet Union screening crudely-dubbed subversive hits from the West like *Rambo*, James Bond movies, and *Commando*, which quickly became a cult hit in Russia—bigger than *Conan the Barbarian* (1982). So there was certainly an older generation of existing fans to whom Porechenkov could market his remake.

Meanwhile, he clearly didn't feel that his version needed a lot of updating. From the first frame to the last he followed *Commando* like a how-to guide. What did change was mostly superficial—a water park instead of a shopping mall, or a chase on a snowmobile instead of a truck. Porechenkov claimed that his biggest challenge was coming up with a believable way for Ivan to obtain an arsenal in modern-day Russia, eventually settling on raiding a smugglers' cache of weapons instead of a surplus store. The film also adds a few nods to contemporary Russian politics. For instance, rather than the leader of a fictional South American country, Ivan's target for assassination is the president of Estonia, a nation with whom tensions were genuinely high. In 2007 a riot over a memorial statue, the Bronze Soldier of Tallinn, left one man killed, dozens wounded, and international relations between the two countries strained. In reference to that incident, an Estonian national quips to Ivan that the president will be killed "not by bronze, but by a genuine soldier." Additionally, the fictional Japanese seizure of a Russian island—inspired by a real land dispute between the two countries over the Kuril Islands—sets the stage for the film's final act.

Ultimately the social and political details were just window dressing. Porechenkov was more interested in making a straightforward action movie for "ordinary people"—a philosophy he highlights by way of *Den' D*'s tongue-in-cheek, self-aware nature. Characters poke fun at "arthouse" films like Soviet classic *Solaris* (1972) and Ivan's daughter professes her fandom for the violent oeuvres of Quentin Tarantino and Kitano Takeshi. Stasik even cheekily references *Commando* as he watches Ivan's plane lift off, scoffing, "He didn't jump. Schwarz would have jumped." (This is just before Ivan one-ups "Schwarz," waiting until the plane gets even higher before performing his skydive act.)

Critics were not particularly enamored with *Den' D*, although given Porechenkov's intended audience, that's not necessarily surprising. However, despite a large publicity campaign and a personal tour of the film in various cities throughout Russia, *Den' D* made back only $1 million of its $5 million budget. Its poor showing suggests that, in spite of his best intentions, Porechenkov may have misjudged what ordinary people wanted to see after all.

Dhoom ("Boom")

INSPIRED BY: *The Fast and the Furious* (2001)
COUNTRY: India
YEAR: 2004
PRODUCTION: Yash Raj Films
DIRECTOR: Sanjay Gadhvi
WRITER: Vijay Krishna Acharya
STARS: Abhishek Bachchan, John Abraham, Uday Chopra, Esha Deol, Rimi Sen

With split-second precision, a four-man team on high-powered motorbikes robs an armored truck in broad daylight. It's the latest in a spate of baffling heists involving motorcyclists.

The police call in supercop Jai Dixit (Abhishek Bachchan) to investigate. Intelligence points to a goofy mechanic and street racer named Ali (Uday Chopra) who fences expensive stolen bikes just like the thieves ride. However, Ali turns out to be innocent. In reality, the team, including its boss Kabir (John Abraham), maintains a low profile as pizza parlor waiters.

Jai decides he needs a biker's perspective and recruits the reluctant Ali. Jai has figured out the thieves' pattern, and he anticipates the next robbery will be at the ICICI Bank. Their stakeout initially yields little more than a woman in a yellow car who catches Ali's eye. However, the wait pays off and the bikers pull their robbery. Jai and Ali give chase, sticking close to Kabir even as he vaults his machine over a train. However, he ultimately escapes in a burst of speed from an aftermarket nitrous oxide cylinder.

That night, Jai has dinner with his wife at the pizza parlor, unaware that he's being scrutinized by the staff. The next day Kabir contacts Jai and makes a deal. He'll reveal the location of the next heist, but only if Jai agrees to give up the investigation if they pull it off. The cop agrees, and he learns that the target will be the Chief Minister's charity concert.

The event is swarming with police, and Ali is delighted to discover that the lead singer is the woman in the yellow car. Yet at the end of the show, the night's proceeds have gone! The thieves burst from underneath the stage on motorcycles, but Jai shoots and kills one of them. He recognizes the man from the pizza parlor and puts the pieces together. In full view of news cameras, Jai thrashes Ali, accusing the mechanic of being an accomplice. He then publicly resigns from the force.

Kabir, now in need of another crew member, recruits the betrayed Ali for one final heist. Their target is the vault of the Raj Exotica, the largest hotel in Goa and India's biggest casino. With four members of the team infiltrating as workers, Ali poses as a guest with a surprise sixth thief—Sheena, the singer with the yellow car.

The only wrinkle is the drunken guest at the hotel bar: a disgraced cop named Jai Dixit.

~~~

In 2004, Aditya Chopra, son of Yash Raj Films founder Yash Raj Chopra, had only recently begun producing films for his father's company. His movies, as was typical of YRF's output, were primarily melodramas and romantic comedies. They were also all financially low-risk remakes, including versions of *When Harry Met Sally...* (1989), *The Dead Poets Society* (1989), and *The Truth About Cats & Dogs* (1996). However, Chopra was eager to break the YRF mold and make something youth oriented. Something, perhaps, like Rob Cohen's recent hit *The Fast and the Furious* (2001) with its highway heists, illegal street races, glamorous supercars, and $200 million box office take.

First, though, he'd need a partner in crime to helm it. He set his sights on Sanjay Gadhvi. Gadhvi had become passionate about filmmaking in college after seeing Steven Spielberg's TV movie *Duel* (1971), a heart-pounding road thriller about a man relentlessly pursued by a mysterious truck driver. After one shelved movie and a low-budget romantic drama, Gadhvi got his break with Yash Raj Films in 2002 with *Mere Yaar Ki Shaadi* ("My Friend's Wedding"), a moderately successful remake of *My Best Friend's Wedding* (1997) produced by Chopra. And like Chopra, Gadhvi was looking to make something different, high-octane, and dangerous. Maybe something like *Duel*?

So when Chopra walked into Gadhvi's office and pitched a movie about a band of thieves who perform audacious high-speed getaways, Gadhvi was immediately on board. The two developed the story with first-time feature screenwriter Vijay Krishna Acharya, and Gadhvi's first order of business was, surprisingly, to ditch the cars. Speaking to Syed Firdaus Ashraf, he explained, "I asked [Chopra] if I could replace cars with bikes because it would look better. Firstly, the hero's face can be seen clearly. Secondly, I was crazy about bikes in my youth. When you speed them up, and the wind hits your face, it gives you a rush that you cannot get in a car."

The choice of bikes over cars would ultimately alter the style of the film. When cinematographer Nirav Shah signed on, Gadhvi and company wanted a "gritty" look, presumably in line with Rob Cohen's film. However, when Shah saw the sleek, customized Suzuki Hayabusa, Bandit, and GSX-Rs specially ordered from Dubai and Singapore, he pushed instead for a polished, slicker look that would complement the star vehicles.

Into their story the team heaped piles of action to keep the story moving as fast as the bikes. Acharya was inspired by filmmaker Manmohan Desai who prescribed an exciting moment every nine minutes—roughly the length of a reel of film. For this movie, however, they decided to ramp it up to every six minutes. This approach was reflected in the 110-day shooting schedule, 60 days of which were devoted to the story's loud and dynamic action sequences. Appropriately, the film would be titled *Dhoom*, Hindi onomatopoeia for an explosion or burst of noise.

Naturally, Gadhvi, Chopra, and Acharya incorporated many of *The Fast and the Furious*'s hallmarks. There are street races (legal in this version), buff thieves with unassuming cover jobs, a daring freeway truck heist, and a racing-the-train stunt ripped from the climax of Cohen's film. They even wrote in an elaborate motorboat stunt that turns on its head a key moment from *2 Fast 2 Furious* (2003), just released the previous year.

However, *Fast and Furious* fans will also notice a number of puzzling differences for an alleged remake. For one thing, Gadhvi and company purposely eschewed any emphasis on family, a theme not only central to the *Fast and the Furious* films, but also a Bollywood hallmark. "This is not a family film," Gadhvi admitted to Ashraf. "There are no brothers, sisters and *bhabhis* [sisters-in-law]. There are two heroines, a thief, an inspector and a motor mechanic." Moreover, a great many scenes and characters have no analogue in the American film.

That's because calling the film a remake of *The Fast and the Furious* is only partially accurate.

Fast and furious: Textless poster art for *Dhoom* (2004).

In fact, *Dhoom* borrows heavily from Gérard Pirès's *Taxi* (1998), a French action-comedy that also involves efficient, fast-driving thieves who perform daredevil getaways. The character of the cocky, fast-driving mechanic roped into helping the police comes directly from that film, as do the bank robberies, the pizza place, and several specific scenes of character development.

The filmmakers also wove in elements from American hits beyond *The Fast and the Furious*. For example, the stylish, coordinated casino heist is distinct shades of *Ocean's Eleven* (2001), from its execution to the space-age design of the vault; a fist fight atop a moving eighteen-wheeler reworks a famous sequence from *The Matrix Reloaded* (2003); and one of the gang even goes undercover using the name Austin Powers.

Dhoom hit theaters on August 27, 2004, and was, in Bollywood parlance, a super hit. Sequels were a no-brainer. *Dhoom 2* (2006) upped the ante with greater star power, more elaborate heists, and a globetrotting story that swept its heroes from India to Namibia and Brazil. *Dhoom 3* (2013) brought the action to America, setting its story of a motorbike-riding magician-cum-thief in Chicago while also lifting key plot elements from Christopher Nolan's *The Prestige* (2006). Both were blockbusters.

Dhoom's influence wasn't limited to the box office. On December 30, 2007, a real life four-man team robbed the Chelembra branch of the South Malabar Gramin Bank and made away with 80 kilograms of gold and 5 million rupees, a score totaling roughly US$2 million. Inspired by *Dhoom*'s New Year's Eve casino heist, the thieves had rented an empty restaurant space beneath the bank and, under pretense of renovation, cut a hole into the bank's strong room. Another much-reported case from 2019, a gold transport robbery in Kerala committed by two men on a motorcycle, also had film fans wondering if it might have been sparked by the 2004 flick.

The Intruder

INSPIRED BY: *Rambo: First Blood Part II* (1985)
COUNTRY: Indonesia
YEAR: 1986
PRODUCTION: Parkit Films
DIRECTOR: Jopi Burnama
WRITER: Deddy Armand
STARS: Peter O'Brian, Craig Gavin, Lia Warokka, Kaharudin Syah, Adang Mansyur

Police academy dropout and good Samaritan Rambu (Peter O'Brian) runs afoul of drug kingpin John White (Craig Gavin) when he thwarts an attempt to kidnap Angela (Lia Warokka), the daughter of a border control official. Rambu survives a retaliatory beating by White's gang, led by the barbarous Charlie (Adang Mansyur), but that's only the beginning. Charlie and his pack then go after his wife, raping and murdering her.

Consumed by rage, Rambu tracks Charlie and his gang to a local pool hall. He storms in and demolishes the place and is only prevented from killing Charlie by the sudden arrival of the police who arrest Rambu for assault. But to his surprise, he's bailed out by rich philanthropist Mr. Andre (Kaharudin Syah), who wants Rambu's help to take on the country's crime problem.

Angela tries to console a mourning Rambu on the beach, giving him her red neckerchief to wear as a headband and good luck charm. But the moment Rambu goes for a swim, Angela is stealthily kidnapped by Charlie's goons. Stringing her up in the middle of a field, Charlie and his gang, all on motorcycles, use the girl as bait to lure Rambu, who bursts onto the scene driving a three-wheeled auto rickshaw. He uses the little car as a weapon against the motorcycle gang and is presently joined by a squadron of the tiny taxis. As the Bajajes battle the motorbikes, Rambu frees Angela. Unfortunately, Charlie manages to kill one of Rambu's friends before Charlie too is dispatched.

In spite of all the carnage, Andre explains that there's still no direct evidence to tie White to his crimes, so he convinces Rambu to steal some secret documents from White's office safe which should provide the necessary proof. Rambu delivers the papers to Andre, but he discovers too late that his benefactor is secretly White's rival crime lord. Andre has used Rambu as part of a plan to ransom the documents back to White and forge a nefarious partnership.

Rambu goes berserk, but he's quickly captured, caged, and tortured by Andre's thugs. He only manages to escape with the help of White's repentant girlfriend. But rather than go on the run, Rambu determines to bring the fight to Andre and White—with little more than a serrated hunting knife and his lucky red bandana. Fortunately for him, in the enemy's camp he seizes a veritable arsenal—rocket launcher included—with which he intends to bring down the brutal two-headed cartel once and for all.

~~~

First Blood introduced audiences to Vietnam War veteran John Rambo in 1982, but it was its sequel, 1985's *Rambo: First Blood Part II*, that redefined the action movie, set the template for countless imitations, and cemented Rambo's muscle-bound, survival knife-wielding, headbanded look in the international consciousness. Plunging Rambo back into Vietnam on a POW rescue mission, the film established exotic locations, giant machine guns, huge fiery explosions, and sadistic foreign foes as compulsory for all sequels—and rip-offs.

Indonesia was certainly exotic enough. Likewise, it has a long history of applying its own style to Hollywood. Some of its earliest films were adapted from American hits featuring such popular characters as Dracula, Zorro, and Tarzan. And while Indonesian cinema can boast a heritage all its own, occasional remakes still found their way into the mix, including versions of *The Exorcist* (1973), *The Blue Lagoon* (1980), and *The Terminator* (1984). By the 1980s, many films were also being made with an eye toward the international video market. Foreign buyers were keen on the colorful and unusual look of Indonesian movies, and they especially favored titles that featured a bit of sex and a lot of violence and action. And if the leads happened to look more Western, that was even better.

In fact, producer Raam Punjabi was looking for a Westerner to star in an upcoming action film when his talent scouts spotted Peter O'Brian, a tourist from New Zealand, on the streets of Jakarta—and followed him. They thought they were tailing Sylvester Stallone. They approached O'Brian in a cafe and, in spite of their mistake, convinced him to meet with their boss. Punjabi organized a screen test for O'Brian and promptly signed the tourist on as a full-fledged movie star. The film was a *Rambo* copy, the producer explained. O'Brian was going to be the Indonesian Rambo.

Rambo was an ideal choice for Punjabi to copy. The muscly hero might be American made, but he had international appeal. *Rambo* director George P. Cosmatos contends that the film was a global hit because it is, at its core, a universal story about an underdog battling insurmountable odds. Stallone has supported that claim, balking at Rambo's adoption as a symbol of American jingoism and pointing to the fictional vet's disdain for the system and decision to live outside of America.

Rambo's iconic status made riding on his coattails reasonably straightforward. Like Indiana Jones or a comic book superhero, Rambo has a signature uniform (long hair, headband, army boots, and bare chest or black tank top) and trademark weapons (survival knife and rocket launcher) which are easy to feature in advertising. And he has an obsession with justice and freedom that makes him an appealing hero. As long as those elements were retained, his other character traits—like emotional damage and post–Vietnam cynicism—and even the plots of his films could be tweaked or omitted with impunity; audiences still knew that they were going to see a Rambo movie. Or at least something very much like one. Many filmmakers took advantage of this; variations on Rambo were produced in Italy (*Strike Commando* [1987] and *Double Target* [1987]), Turkey (*Vahşi Kan* ["Savage Blood," 1983], *Korkusuz* [*Rampage*, 1986], and *Silaha Yeminliydim* ["I Was Sworn to Arms," 1987]), India (*Rambo*, currently in pre-production), and beyond.

Refurbishing Rambo wasn't even a purely overseas phenomenon. In America, Rambo was divorced from his Vietnam history and PTSD to become a weekday cartoon hero for children in *Rambo: The Force of Freedom* (1986). But he still had the name, the weapons, the ethos, and the costume. *The Intruder* worked much the same way. Rambu was given the look, the weapons, a soundalike name, and a hatred of injustice. Except instead of Vietnam, he was dropped into a Jakarta full of warring gangsters, cocaine, stolen documents, and a fleet of weaponized auto rickshaws.

Swedish VHS cover for *The Intruder* (1986).

Yet even though it's not strictly a remake, *The Intruder* makes frequent visual references to the *Rambo* films. Rambu is caged, beaten, and crucified. He's pushed to revenge after a compatriot is murdered in the second act. He machine-guns a room as he vents his rage at the traitorous villain. And he knocks a baddie through a window and navigates the enemy's barbed wire fencing in two of many inconsequential but distinct cribs from his inspiration. There's even one tiny, telling dubbing slip-up when White asks an underling, "What about that intruder, Rambo?"—not "Rambu."

Although *The Intruder* was destined for the foreign market, Raam Punjabi had a unique plan for the movie in its home country. As the film was being shot, each scene with the Western actors was filmed a second time, but with Indonesian leads. Thus

The Intruder, starring Peter O'Brian, was released internationally, while an alternate and nearly identical film, *Pembalasan Rambu* ("Rambu's Revenge"), starring Eddy Darmo, was produced for an exclusively domestic audience.

Peter O'Brian would continue his career as an accidental Indonesian movie star for another seven films. Eventually, however, a family tragedy and a religious awakening led him away from showbiz. He taught English in Indonesia for a number of years before finally moving back to New Zealand where he became an instructor of business communication, organization, and management in Tauranga. But O'Brian never completely gave up the idea of acting, and he's remained open to returning to films. Considering the number of times Rambo has been pulled back in for one more mission, who could deny the same to Rambu?

Khoon Khoon ("Blood Blood")

INSPIRED BY: *Dirty Harry* (1971)
COUNTRY: India
YEAR: 1973
PRODUCTION: Eagle Films
DIRECTOR: Mohammed Hussain
WRITER: Vrajendra Gaur
STARS: Mahendra Sandhu, Danny Denzongpa, Jagdeep

After three random murders by psychotic sniper Raghav (Danny Denzongpa), CID Inspector Anand (Mahendra Sandhu) is put on the case. The killer has demanded a cash ransom, and if the city fails to comply, his next target will be a well-known philanthropist. With the metropolis under police helicopter surveillance, Anand and his cowardly partner Pancham (Jagdeep) keep an eye out

Sniper Raghav (Danny Denzongpa) lines up his second kill of the movie while sporting a groovy '70s button-up shirt.

from the rooftops and spot Raghav before he can take his shot. However, the sniper escapes.

Denied his intended prey, Raghav murders a child in the park instead. Furthermore, he warns the commissioner that he'll assassinate a prominent swami next if he doesn't get his money. The police's only break comes when the gunman misses his mark and gives away his position. Fleeing, Raghav commandeers a car at gunpoint and holds its female occupant hostage. He takes her to a hideout where he rapes her.

The killer now demands twice the original ransom for the girl's life. Anand is instructed to deliver the money alone, but he covertly wears a wire and has Pancham shadow him. Raghav sends Anand all over town by phone, terminating at a statue in Chembur. Anand hands over the money, but Raghav refuses to give up the girl's location, instead attempting to kill the inspector. Pancham arrives, giving Anand an opening to wound Raghav, but unfortunately the killer escapes again.

Anand discovers that Raghav was patched up at a local clinic, and from the doctor he learns that the murderer lives on the grounds of a nearby soccer stadium. The inspector raids the place, chasing Raghav onto the field. Stepping on his wound, Anand forces the hostage's location from Raghav. It's too late, however; the police find her already long dead.

Raghav is brought to trial, but he claims his confession was coerced. The police are unable to produce any hard evidence against him, so Raghav is acquitted. Undeterred, Anand doggedly shadows Raghav, waiting for him to slip up. However, the murderer hatches a plan. He pays a man to beat him up and blames the assault on Anand. The inspector is pulled from the case, freeing Raghav to pull off his coup de gras: hijacking a kindergarten bus full of children.

~~~

When *Dirty Harry* hit theaters in 1971, *Newsweek* dubbed it "a right-wing fantasy." Gritty and cynical, it was a biting response to the *Miranda v. Arizona* U.S. Supreme Court decision of 1966—the one requiring police to notify arrestees of their right to legal counsel and against self-incrimination. The screenplay capitalized on conservatives' belief that, by the '70s, criminals had been granted more rights than their victims. Serial killer Scorpio exploits those rights when Inspector "Dirty" Harry Callahan arrests him and seizes evidence improperly. Scorpio is released without charge, and Callahan, portrayed as a jaded but honest cop battling a corrupt and lily-livered system, is forced to resort to vigilantism to take the murderer down.

A market-tested success—it would lead to three sequels—*Dirty Harry* was, at first glance, a solid candidate for adaptation in risk-averse Bollywood. But while crime films and thrillers were Bollywood staples, they tended to avoid boldly criticizing the government or its justice system as the Clint Eastwood film had done. Strict censorship had prevailed in the preceding two decades, with overtly political films receiving particular scrutiny. Presumably, producer F.C. Mehra felt it would be impossible to make a movie about a cop as heretical or as willing to resort to vigilantism as Harry Callahan.

Instead, the story was reworked to hew closer to what Indian audiences had come to expect from their action movies. The political elements were removed.

Stronger focus was placed on family, with the once-lone hero given a wife, brother, and in-laws to confide in, and the villain was saddled with a tragic backstory that explains his crimes as the result of parental abuse. As comedy was an essential component of Bollywood films of any genre, the protagonist's straightlaced partner became a purely comic relief role with an entire subplot of his own. Lastly, the film would be photographed in the gaudy, groovy colors of '70s Bollywood in stark contrast to the gritty, muted tones of '70s Hollywood crime films.

Khoon Khoon was designed as a vehicle to launch fresh face Mahendra Sandhu as a star, and the prospect of headlining a *Dirty Harry* remake appealed to him. "When they narrated the script [to me] I was very excited," he confessed to *The Times of India*. "I was a big fan of Clint Eastwood…. I was projected [to be] India's Eastwood." However, he was less thrilled about the man Mehra placed behind the camera. "They didn't get a proper director for *Khoon Khoon*. Mohammed Hussain … used to direct Dara Singh's stunt films. I had warned the producers that the director was not suitable. But no one listened to me."

On the other hand, Hussain was something of a ringer when it came to remakes and adaptations. His "stunt films" starring ex-wrestler Dara Singh were low-budget actioners featuring elements in common with Mexico's *lucha libre* films and Italy's sword-and-sandals flicks. One noteworthy entry, *Aaya Toofan* ("A Storm Arrived," 1964), borrowed the plot of Hollywood's *Jack the Giant Killer* (1962). That wasn't Hussain's first adaptation, either. In 1960 he co-directed a Superman film, and his 1963 jungle adventure *Shikari* ("Hunter") blended *King Kong* (1933) with *Dr. Cyclops* (1940). (A poster for *Shikari* features briefly but prominently in *Khoon Khoon*.) In 1967 he cashed in on the James Bond craze, creating his own secret agent in *C.I.D. 909*. While the controversial *Dirty Harry* was unlike his prior adventure stories, the

Not so dirty Harry. Inspector Anand (Mahendra Sandhu) and his wife Rekha (Rekha) sing a love song under a waterfall.

script had already been stripped of its more contentious elements, resulting in a fairly straightforward cop thriller.

Visually, Hussain imitated *Dirty Harry* closely, at times even mimicking it shot for shot. Nevertheless, many sequences featured a new variation or twist. Omitting the iconic scenes in which Callahan holds a gun to a crook and asks if they "feel lucky" enough to reach for their gun (has Dirty Harry fired all six shots or only five?), Hussain staged an alternate showdown where Anand tricks Raghav into believing his gun is empty when in fact he's surreptitiously loaded a single bullet. And in an impressive feat of Bollywoodization, the director not only replicated the scene in which the killer distracts his busload of child hostages with a song, but he also turned it into a full-on musical number.

Notably, the release of *Khoon Khoon* coincided with the premiere of *Zanjeer* ("Chain," 1973), coincidentally about an honest police inspector who's fed up with the system and has a reputation for dealing out uncompromising, brutal justice outside the bounds of the law. Stemming from frustrations with increased economic inequality and a widening class gap, *Zanjeer* kicked off a wave of dark, violent, anti-establishment films with more than a little in common with *Dirty Harry*. Moreover, this "angry young man" genre hit upon a successful method for criticizing social injustices while sidestepping censorship. Instead of attacking the government directly, the films would feature villainous individuals who epitomized the system's evils. Had *Khoon Khoon* been made slightly later, it might have been forged in the same mold and ended up even closer to the Eastwood film.

As it was, Warner Bros. felt that it was plenty close. The studio sued *Khoon Khoon*'s production company Eagle Films for copyright infringement and was rewarded $50,000 in punitive damages. The suit didn't block the film from release, but it did force Eagle to rethink its then-in-production remake of *Irma la Douce* (1963), prompting producers to reach out to Universal and officially pay for a license.

Khoon Khoon tanked at the box office, failing to launch Mahendra Sandhu as a major star or as India's answer to Clint Eastwood. The actor did however go on to carve himself a place in Bollywood history. Sandhu was on the verge of retiring from the film business when he accepted the role of a Bondesque hero in 1977's *Agent Vinod*. The film was a surprise hit with even more surprising longevity, and in 2012 it was given a lavish reboot of the same name.

Korkusuz (*Rampage*)

INSPIRED BY: *Rambo: First Blood Part II* (1985)
COUNTRY: Turkey
YEAR: 1986
PRODUCTION: Anıt Ticaret
DIRECTOR: Çetin İnanç
WRITER: Çetin İnanç
STARS: Serdar Kebapçılar, Osman Betin, Hüseyin Peyda, Sümer Tilmaç, Filiz Taçbaş, Tuğrul Meteer

A band of guerrillas is operating in the mountains of southeast Turkey, and the army is determined to stop it at all costs. When the bandits shanghai a rich businessman named Sait (Sümer Tilmaç) for ransom, Turkish soldiers manage to capture two of the criminals. The outlaws are jailed alongside a muscle-bound convict named Serdar (Serdar Kebapçılar), but when the three are driven to the courthouse Serdar stages a daring escape. He prepares to kill the bandits in the process, but Osman (Osman Betin), the senior of the two, offers Serdar a place in their organization in exchange for their lives. They travel deep into the mountains, and along the way they rescue a young woman (Filiz Taçbaş) from the hands of another band of brigands.

They're met at the guerrillas' camp by Ziya (Hüseyin Peyda), the gang's murderous chief. Ziya immediately mistrusts Serdar and brutally interrogates him but learns nothing of value. The captive Sait, witnessing the torture, finally agrees to pay Ziya his ransom. However, in order to get the money, he needs to speak to his well-guarded criminal associate Yakup. As a test of loyalty, Ziya sends Serdar to fetch him.

The rescued woman, now a prisoner in the camp, is given to Sait. Aware that Ziya is watching them, the businessman gives her a reassuring sign and then makes a show of forcing himself upon her. When Ziya leaves, however, Sait breaks off and instructs her to escape. She soon reconnects with Serdar. Ziya, furious at losing a prisoner, dispatches Osman to kill them both.

Accompanied by the woman, Serdar traverses the mountainous terrain on foot to Yakup's stronghold and abducts its occupant at knifepoint. The trio then heads back toward the camp, but before they get far they're ambushed by Osman and his men. Serdar eliminates the thugs, Osman included, but the woman takes a bullet meant for him and dies.

Returning to Ziya's camp with Yakup, Serdar is locked up. Worse, Yakup reveals to Ziya that Serdar is no criminal, but a spy—a soldier. In a flash, Sait grabs Ziya's gun and admits that he, too, is an army officer. Gunfire breaks out. Hearing the commotion, Serdar smashes out of his prison with his bare hands. He kills a bandit wielding an RPG launcher and takes the weapon, then rampages through the encampment dealing as much damage with it as he can.

~~~

By the time *Rambo: First Blood Part II* hit theaters in 1985, Çetin İnanç had already remade Rambo's debut as the Cüneyt Arkın vehicle *Vahşi Kan* ("Savage Blood," 1983). Given *Part II*'s enviable four weeks atop the box office and worldwide take of $300 million, it seemed only natural that he would adapt the sequel as well. Unfortunately, by 1985 Turkey's film industry was in a death spiral. Budgets were at an all-time low and it was still nearly impossible for domestic movies to eke out a profit. To save money İnanç conceived *Korkusuz* (literally, "Fearless") as one of a trio of films, including *Asi Kabadayı* ("Rebel Roughneck," 1986) and *İntikamcı* ("Avenger," 1986), to be shot consecutively utilizing the same primary actors and locations.

Signing actors was step one. İnanç's contract with Arkın had expired, but he already had his new Stallone in the form of champion bodybuilder Serdar Kebapçılar (see *Kara Şimşek*). For his leading lady, İnanç had only to look outside his window. Filiz Taçbaş, *Saklambaç* newspaper's 1981 "Beautiful Face of Turkey," rode her bicycle past the director's office every day. Moreover, for the past few years Taçbaş had been taking acting lessons and performing on stage. She seized the opportunity to act for the camera, and by coincidence she was already familiar with co-star Sümer Tilmaç (Sait) from their work together in the theater.

Next was the story. Recycling the narrative of *Rambo: First Blood Part II* was simply not going to fly. John Rambo was a cynical vet with PTSD and grave misgivings about his country's corrupt government. Turkey was a fiercely nationalist republic prone to periods of martial law and heavy censorship. İnanç's hero, then, would have to be a patriot through and through. Furthermore, Rambo's symbolic refighting of the Vietnam War—this time to win—wouldn't have been particularly relevant to Turks. İnanç needed something closer to home. His solution was ripped straight from the headlines: the Kurdish-Turkish conflict.

Anıt Ticaret brazenly duplicates the poster for *Rambo: First Blood Part II* (1985) in one of the Turkish one-sheets for *Korkusuz* (1986). Despite the giant "Rambo" text, the film was never released under that title.

The Kurds are Anatolia's earliest inhabitants, an ethnic group native to the mountainous region straddling the borders of Turkey, Iraq, Syria, Iran, and Armenia. Following the establishment of the Republic of Turkey in 1923, many Kurds favored an independent state of their own. But it was not to be. In 1924 President Mustafa Kemal Atatürk, eager to establish a single, homogenous Turkish identity in short order, banned Kurdish schools, publications, and organizations—causing a rebellion less than a year later. The government's response was swift and brutal. It executed rebels and their families, destroyed villages, and deported hundreds of thousands of Kurds. Over the next several decades the administration tried to effectively scrub Kurdishness from existence, changing Kurdish placenames to Turkish equivalents, banning the speaking of Kurdish, and referring to the people themselves as "mountain Turks."

By the late 1970s tensions had reached boiling point. Calling for a revolution, Kurdish extremist Abdullah Öcalan co-founded the militant Kurdistan Workers'

88　　　　　　　　　2. Muscles, Magnums, and Machismo

Party (PKK). He put together a rebel force and established a headquarters in Syria. In 1984, demanding an independent state within Turkey, the PKK began armed insurgent attacks against Turkish government outposts in the southeast. Thus began a fierce and ongoing guerrilla war with the Turkish army that, incidentally, would provide Çetin İnanç an ideal backdrop for his Turkish *Rambo*.

Prepared with his new take on the story, İnanç and company set off in September 1985 for Foça, an hour's drive from his offices in İzmir. It was the off-season for hotels, and İnanç used this to his advantage, negotiating a favorable deal with the Hanedan Hotel for cast and crew accommodations. Its owner was also eager to have his establishment featured in a movie, which sweetened the deal for İnanç and allowed him to get extra use out of the building as a cost-saving location. The hotel appears most noticeably in *İntikamcı*; most of *Korkusuz* was filmed instead in and around the nearby military camp that served as Ziya's mountain hideout.

The armed forces generally supported domestic filmmaking when it was appropriate, and for *Korkusuz* they provided authentic uniforms in addition to the camp. Weaponry, however, was a different matter, and the team was forced to reproduce Rambo's iconic RPG launcher with only wood and black paint. Originally the RPGs were made from foam, but İnanç was unimpressed with their quality and had them remade out of wood as well. Even so, the DIY mechanics of the weapon produced a distinctly flimsy "pop-gun" effect.

Serdar goes undercover as a convicted felon. In the lower left, his wooden rocket launcher is at the ready. Turkish lobby card.

Of course, İnanç borrowed much more from Rambo than his rocket launcher. Despite an original story, İnanç used the bones of *Rambo: First Blood Part II* for the film's structure and recreated several moments from both it and *First Blood* (1982). For example, Ziya's burial of Serdar mirrors Rambo's dunk in the Vietnamese slime pit in *Part II*. His goons, like the intolerant cops in *First Blood*, blast Serdar with a hose—during which Serdar flashes back to past tortures, à la Rambo's crucifixion in a Vietnamese prison camp. İnanç also recreated Rambo's famous "gearing up" sequence as Serdar prepares to retrieve Yakup. And for the film's soundtrack he even lifted music from the *Part II* score (additional cues came from *Mad Max 2: The Road Warrior* [1981]).

Incidentally, no one utters the word "Kurd" in *Korkusuz*, but early in the film İnanç cements the connection to Ziya's gang when he shows Sait reading a newspaper—genuine, not a manufactured prop—sporting the headlines "Çukurca'da 9 Şehit!" ("9 Martyrs in Çukurca!") and "Irak sınırında dokuz erimiz şehit edildi" ("Nine Soldiers Martyred Near Iraqi Border"). Intended to establish the bandits, the headlines actually refer to an incident on October 25, 1985—during production of the film—where PKK guerrillas raided the Serin police outpost in Çukurca and killed nine Turkish soldiers.

Distributed primarily on VHS and Betamax, *Korkusuz* would eventually receive a DVD release in America in 2009 under the new title *Rampage*. The film was dubbed into English and, in order to avoid copyright entanglements, composer Jake Kaufman composed an original new score that evoked Jerry Goldsmith's *Rambo* music with an Anatolian twist. News of the release got back to Turkey and rekindled public interest in one-time star Serdar Kebapçılar, leading to numerous interviews and appearances in the media. However, he's still waiting for his dream project: a pirate movie on the high seas.

OK Connery

INSPIRED BY: *Thunderball* (1965)
COUNTRY: Italy
YEAR: 1967
PRODUCTION: Produzione D.S.
DIRECTOR: Alberto De Martino
WRITERS: Paolo Levi, Frank Walker, Stanley Wright, Stefano Canzio
STARS: Neil Connery, Daniela Bianchi, Adolfo Celi, Bernard Lee, Lois Maxwell, Anthony Dawson, Yachuco Yama

A landing plane erupts in flames at the Aero Club in Monte Carlo. Its pilot, Ward Jones, was on his way to give vital intelligence to British officials before the explosion silenced him. Now the government's only lead is Jones's girlfriend Yachuko (Yachuco Yama), currently hospitalized for plastic surgery, who may have been privy to that same information. Discouragingly, however, she pleads ignorance.

At a loss, British counter-espionage official Commander Cunningham (Bernard Lee) and his assistant Max (Lois Maxwell) recruit the girl's plastic surgeon, Dr. Neil Connery (Neil Connery), who happens to be the brother of Britain's top secret agent and a hypnotist to boot. It seems that Jones, a student of Connery's, implanted his secrets into Yachuko's mind, and Cunningham believes that Connery is just the man to get at them.

Unfortunately, Yachuko is kidnapped from the hospital before they can find out. This and the plane crash appear to be the work of terrorist organization THANATOS, headed by the sour-faced Alpha (Anthony Dawson) and his scheming subordinate, Thair (Adolfo Celi). Max and reluctant spy Connery track Yachuko to Malaga, where she's imprisoned in a heavily-guarded villa. Disguised as farm workers, Max, Connery, and a squad of agents storm the villa with flamethrowers and machine guns. They rescue Yachuko and Connery hypnotizes her. Yachuko mentions the theft of an "atomic nucleus" and blind workers in Tétouan before she's assassinated by a THANATOS agent.

Thair indeed acquires the atomic nucleus; his assistant Maya (Daniela Bianchi) and her all-girl gang pose as showgirls to distract and rob an army convoy. THANATOS plans to use the nucleus to power an electromagnetic pulse generator that will plunge the world into darkness and chaos.

Following up Yachuko's clue, Connery travels to Tétouan. There he discovers a factory owned by Thair that exclusively employs blind men to manufacture rugs. These rugs, he learns, are made from radioactive materials and are a part of THANATOS's plan for global conquest. Connery attempts to break up the operation, but he's captured and brought to Thair's yacht. With the help of Maya, whom he manages to charm, Connery escapes, but he's unable to capture Thair, who flees to his secret base to fire the EMP. Now Connery and all of his allies must locate and neutralize Thair before he can paralyze the world.

~~~

By 1967, French, German, Spanish, and Italian imitations of the James Bond formula were so numerous that "Eurospy" had effectively become a genre of its own. Ersatz 007s like 008, 077, and X-77 had crawled out of the woodwork. Some of their films played the capers straight; others played them for laughs. But none had quite the audacity of *OK Connery*, a.k.a. *Operation Kid Brother*, which roped in James Bond star Sean Connery's younger brother Neil to play its super spy.

Neil Connery was working as a plasterer in Scotland when he received an invitation from producer Dario Sabatello to meet at the Caledonian Hotel in Edinburgh. Sabatello's proposition was simple: "How would you like to become an actor?" Connery, flabbergasted, responded that he'd see it as a challenge.

Sabatello commissioned a script specifically for Connery and invited the newly-minted actor to Cinecittà in Rome for a screen test. Connery was asked to sing, dance, perform a love scene and execute a hand-to-hand fight for the camera. Each time the Italians praised his performance with "OK, Connery, OK!"—and the phrase apparently had the right ring to it, inspiring the film's title.

But the publicity of the Connery name wasn't enough for Sabatello. He may have wanted to make the biggest splash possible with his first and only Eurospy film. So like Bond showing off in a high stakes game of twenty-one, he doubled down on the stunt casting. Eurospy films would occasionally cast a former Bond co-star in a key role, but *OK Connery* is a veritable parade of them. Sabatello hired Bernard

Lee and Lois Maxwell—007's M and Miss Moneypenny, respectively—to essentially reprise their roles. He chose Daniela Bianchi, leading lady of *From Russia with Love* (1963), to play his femme fatale. And he tapped Adolfo Celi, the yacht-owning Number Two of international terrorist organization SPECTRE in *Thunderball* (1965), to play the yacht-owning number two of international terrorist organization THANATOS in *OK Connery*. And his use of Anthony Dawson as THANATOS leader Alpha was especially cheeky, as Dawson had twice played, obscured and uncredited, the head of SPECTRE.

To direct the picture, Sabatello hired Alberto De Martino, who had made two Eurospy films previously—*Upperseven, l'uomo da uccidere* (*The Spy with Ten Faces*, 1966) and *Missione speciale Lady Chaplin* (*Special Mission Lady Chaplin*, 1966). Enticed primarily by a large advance from Sabatello, De Martino was less enamored with Neil Connery's attributes than his employer. Speaking to website Nanarland, De Martino explained that like Sean, Neil was balding, so they gave him a hairpiece; his teeth were bad, so they gave him dentures; his face was "insipid," so they added a beard; and his eyes lacked emphasis, so they applied adhesive to his temples. Furthermore, unimpressed with Connery's acting ability, De Martino had his star speak as little as possible.

The director's frustration suggests that he'd have preferred Madame Tussaud's wax statue of Sean over a living, breathing Neil. But he did have a legitimate Connery, a "greatest hits" cast, and a sizable helping of gadgets, globetrotting, and girls. So if there was an award for "closest without going over" 007 facsimile, De Martino would have been a shoo-in.

Over the course of production De Martino incorporated subtler allusions to James Bond as well. Aboard his yacht, Thair watches a

Neil Connery shows off his many skills as he mimics his brother's pose from the *You Only Live Twice* (1967) poster. U.S. one-sheet.

belly dance filmstrip projected onto one of his scantily-clad female crew, evoking Robert Brownjohn's title sequences for *From Russia with Love* and *Goldfinger* (1964). And when Maya and her gang steal the atomic nucleus, they disguise the transport vehicle as an advertisement-on-wheels for "The Wild Pussy Club" casino, suggestive of Pussy Galore's Flying Circus from *Goldfinger*. The music, too, will feel familiar to 007 aficionados. Written by the legendary Ennio Morricone and Bruno Nicolai, the score frequently emulates the style of Bond composer John Barry—particularly with a four-note motif that mimics the famous guitar line from the James Bond theme.

Sabatello's marketing was as brazen as the rest of the film, with the poster featuring Neil imitating his brother's pose from Bond adventure *You Only Live Twice* (1967). And the film's U.S. tagline, "*Operation Kid Brother* is too much for one mother" was a riff on the same year's Bond spoof *Casino Royale*, which boasted that it was "too much for one James Bond."

Unfortunately, Bond fans who bought tickets hoping to hear the signature Connery accent would be disappointed to discover that Neil's voice had been dubbed by another actor. As was often the case with contemporary Italian films, *OK Connery* was shot without sound. But after production, Connery was hospitalized for an appendectomy and the producers were worried he'd be too weak to loop his lines in post-production. So for the English dub they instead hired a local American actor—a decision Connery would lament.

Ironically, *OK Connery* was picked up for theatrical distribution in America and the UK by United Artists, the very company that produced the official 007 movies. It's now part of the MGM library, but its only official home video release to date is the episode of *Mystery Science Theater 3000* (1989) on which it appeared.

Qayamat: City Under Threat

INSPIRED BY: *The Rock* (1996)
COUNTRY: India
YEAR: 2003
PRODUCTION: Baweja Movies
DIRECTOR: Harry Baweja
WRITER: Suparn Verma
STARS: Ajay Devgn, Suniel Shetty, Sanjay Kapoor, Arbaaz Khan, Isha Koppikar, Aashish Chaudhary, Deep Dhillon, Neha Dhupia

It's a countdown to doomsday. A trio of Muslim arms dealers and a rogue CDC scientist are poised to bombard Mumbai with the deadliest virus known to humanity.

The terrorists, in the employ of Pakistan's Brigadier Rashid (Deep Dhillon), take 213 tourists hostage at the defunct island prison of Elphinstone. They also install seven missiles, each armed with a horrifying new virus developed by the Pakistani military and aim them at Mumbai's seven lakes. The government has just 24 hours to deliver a large sum of cash, a ship, and safe passage to Pakistan, or the villains will launch the missiles and contaminate the city's entire water supply. Rashid, an official of Pakistan's Inter Services Intelligence (ISI), has orchestrated the crisis to destabilize India and ultimately allow Pakistan to claim the disputed state of Kashmir.

Muslim CBI agent Akram Shaikh (Suniel Shetty) is tasked with leading a commando team into the prison through the septic system to stop the terrorists and save the hostages. He's also saddled with nebbishy CDC scientist Rahul Gupta (Aashish Chaudhary) who has the skills to disarm the weapons. Unfortunately, navigating the prison's underground labyrinth is easier said than done, so they need the help of the only man who ever successfully escaped Elphinstone: a convict named Rachit (Ajay Devgn).

Fortunately, Rachit has an incentive to help: revenge. Before his incarceration, he was an associate of the arms dealers—until they tricked him into stealing a computer chip containing military secrets. And murdered his girlfriend. However, the trauma has left him prone to mental fits, making him as much a liability to the mission as an asset.

Using scuba gear, the team enters the prison from below, but on the way up from the sewer they trigger a specialized motion detector. The terrorists ambush the commandos from above, massacring them. Only Rachit and Rahul, who were ordered to stay in the tunnels, remain alive. Rahul will have to rely on Rachit's mental stability and marksmanship to get to the missiles and remove both the virus and the guidance chips. Failure means either the destruction of the Indian metropolis or the death of everyone in Elphinstone from a last-ditch military airstrike.

∼∼∼

When reporter Sangeetha Devi K pointed out *Qayamat: City Under Threat*'s similarities to certain Hollywood films, star Ajay Devgn bristled. "I don't want to compare Hollywood to Bollywood," he said. "We are different people with different cultures." He had a point. Although unquestionably inspired by Michael Bay's *The Rock* (1996), *Qayamat* had one vital change. Gone was disenchanted FORECON veteran General Hummel, extorting the U.S. government for restitution for the families of fallen covert operatives. His cause would have been irrelevant to Indian audiences, and a similar disgruntled army vet might have drawn the ire of censors, who have historically found Bollywood films critical of the government to be easy pickings. To

Rahul (Aashish Chaudhary) discovers ampules of the neon green virus inside the terrorists' missiles.

fill the gap, however, screenwriter Suparn Verma and director Harry Baweja had only to watch their local news.

Qayamat (literally, "doom") was developed in early 2002, when the prospect of a deadly, large-scale conflict between Hindu-majority India and Muslim Pakistan was all too real. The prior December, five jihadi gunmen with ties to Pakistani terrorist groups had infiltrated the Indian Parliament in New Delhi and engaged in a protracted firefight with police and security forces, killing nine people. Indian officials believed that the operation had been carried out under the guidance of Pakistan's ISI, and home minister L.K. Advani accused the agency of attempting "to wipe out the entire political leadership of India." Within days of the attack, the Indian military began mobilizing, deploying more than 500,000 troops along the Line of Control, the de facto border between Indian- and Pakistani-controlled Kashmir. Pakistan promptly responded with 300,000 soldiers of its own. It was a stand-off that appeared unlikely to de-escalate.

The international community applied pressure, however, and on January 12 Pakistani president Pervez Musharraf delivered a televised speech denouncing religious extremists and officially banning several jihadi organizations—including those connected to the Parliament attack. Even so, the gesture failed to ease tensions for long. On May 14, three men dressed in Indian army fatigues hijacked a tourist bus and redirected it to an Indian Army garrison near the Kashmir city of Kaluchak. The men, in reality Pakistani nationals, shot the passengers and forced their way into the camp's residential quarters where they murdered ten children, eight women and five soldiers. By the time they were themselves killed, the terrorists had left more than 30 dead and dozens wounded.

India was clamoring to retaliate, and the army appeared galvanized for an invasion. Exacerbating matters was the fact that, on the week of May 26, Pakistan pointedly staged tests of three nuclear-capable ballistic missiles. Fearing the worst, Britain and America began evacuating their embassies. Diplomats tensed for a nuclear war.

When *Qayamat*'s cameras began rolling on June 3, Mumbai really was a city under threat.

The political climate was reflected in *Qayamat*'s villain, a caricatured ISI mastermind behind the terrorists' plot. "The serial bomb-blasts of '93 are fading from memory," Rashid opines, recalling the devastating Mumbai bombings perpetrated by men who received demolition training in Pakistan. "[Indian Prime Minister] Vajpayee wants peace. And we want pieces. Pieces of India." To illustrate the point, he turns his attention to a large pistachio cake in the shape of India, complete with state borders drawn in frosting. Picking up a knife, he literally slices off Kashmir and takes a bite.

Yet although the story was reimagined with a new ripped-from-the headlines angle, it was still essentially *The Rock*. Despite a budget of only about $3.2 million— chicken feed compared to the $75 million of its Hollywood counterpart—screenwriter Suparn Verma and director Harry Baweja managed to follow the 1996 film carefully, from its story structure to its set and prop design. The sewer system, the infiltration of the shower room through the drain (and its customized motion sensor), the mine carts, the aborted first missile launch, and the smoke signal to call off the airstrike—all those and more appear just as in the Michael Bay film. Perhaps most iconically, the deadly neon green supervirus is enclosed in the same glass spheres, arranged in the same precarious "string-of-pearls configuration," as the VX gas in *The Rock*—and which was a total fabrication by writers David Weisberg and Douglas Cook.

Where the filmmakers may have found themselves at a loss, however briefly, was the Rock itself. India had no decommissioned, isolated island prisons like Alcatraz, so they invented one: the fictional Elphinstone Jail. Its exteriors were shot at the stone fortress of Panikotha ("Fort on the Sea") a mile off the coast of Diu, in western India. The ship-shaped stronghold, built in the 15th century by Ottoman governor Malik Ayaz and later augmented by the Portuguese, was sufficiently imposing, and the illusion could be extended with additional shooting at nearby Diu Fortress.

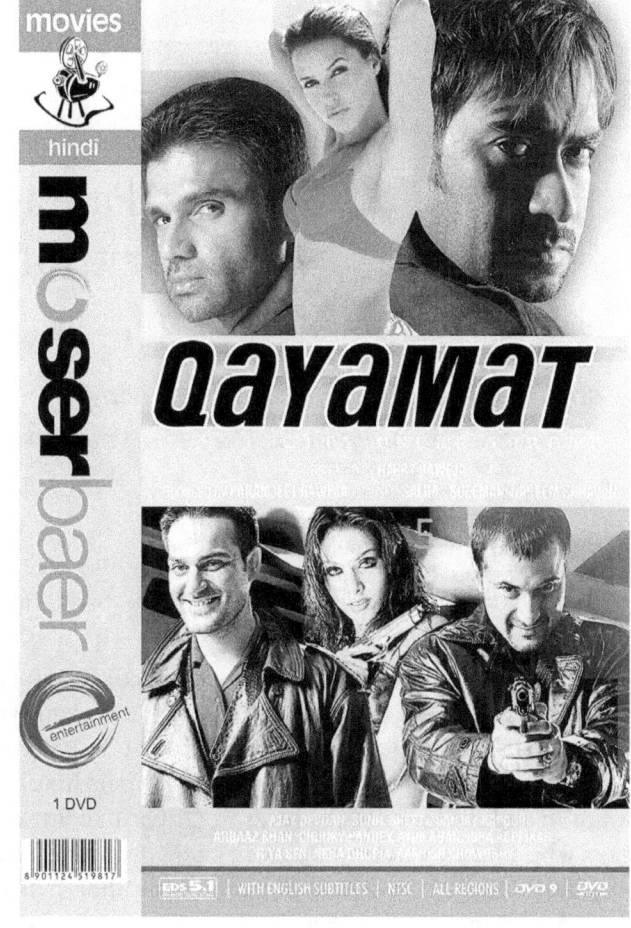

DVD box art for *Qayamat: City Under Threat* (2003).

Despite its blatant similarities to *The Rock*, *Qayamat* drew no lawsuit from Hollywood studios when it opened on July 11, 2003. However, *Qayamat*'s Venus Entertainment and Baweja Movies did find themselves on the *other* side of a copyright dispute. Some weeks before the premiere, rival multimedia company Tips released a music cassette, unassociated with the film, titled *Qayamat: Love Under Threat*. The tape sported artwork conspicuously similar to the *Qayamat* movie poster, including star Ajay Devgn's face on the cover. The song titles even resembled those on the film's soundtrack. The issue never went to court, but after a press conference and phone calls from Venus chairman Ganesh Jain, Tips pulled the cassette from the market.

By the time the film hit theaters, tensions had eased in Kashmir. Peace did not come easily, however. Although nuclear war was avoided, India and Pakistan traded strategic strikes in July and August 2002, resulting in hundreds of casualties. Both governments finally began to de-escalate in October, demobilizing their troops from the Line of Control. The two nations would ultimately agree to a cease-fire in November 2003.

3

Family, Fantasy, and Fairy Tales

Aabra Ka Daabra: The School of Magic

INSPIRED BY: *Harry Potter and the Sorcerer's Stone* (2001)
COUNTRY: India
YEAR: 2004
PRODUCTION: Creative Eye Limited
DIRECTOR: Dheeraj Kumar
WRITERS: J.K. Nirmal, Iqbal Katchi
STARS: Athit Naik, Hansika Motwani, Esha Trivedi, Vishal Lalwani, Anupam Kher, Tiara, Krrishna

Shanu (Athit Naik) is the young son of Rahul (Krrishna), a famous magician who was presumed dead after an escape act went wrong. Shanu wants to become a magician like his father and enroll in the Aabra Ka Daabra School of Magic—an academy that teaches genuine sorcery. He gets his chance when art supply company Camlin and cookie manufacturer Parle-G run contests offering tuition to any youngster who finds a winning ticket in their products. Astonishingly, Shanu wins both! He is admitted to the school but, per his mother's wishes, his parentage is kept secret.

Arriving at Aabra Ka Daabra, Shanu meets the friendly caretaker Limbu (Anupam Kher), a disgraced former professor. After presenting himself to the beautiful but strangely malevolent headmistress RB (Tiara), Shanu runs afoul of frosted-tipped school bully Changhezi (Vishal Lalwani). Fortunately, he does make a couple of friends: the book-smart Pinky (Hansika Motwani) and her gluttonous friend Dinky (Esha Trivedi). The students' curriculum includes concentration class, where they make Camlin art supplies levitate and draw pictures, and flying carpet class, where they learn the popular transportation of the wizarding world.

Shanu discovers that Limbu knew his father, so he sneaks out at night with Pinky and Dinky to speak with the caretaker further. But before Shanu can learn anything, RB approaches. Limbu gives the children invisibility pills so they can stealthily escape the headmistress's wrath, but RB's destination turns out to be somewhere outside the school. Curious, Shanu and his friends follow her. Her path takes her through a grove of man-eating trees to a building where a man is held prisoner: Rahul! For years RB has been demanding from Rahul the formula for immortality—a secret he uncovered when he was a professor at the school. Shanu and his friends are flabbergasted and quickly escape back to the dormitory.

The next day the students gather for a sports competition—a variation on soccer played with a flag and flying carpets. Shanu's team faces off against Changhezi's. But as Shanu appears about to win, RB silently mutters incantations that cause his carpet to whirl dangerously out of control. Fortunately, Limbu spots the treachery and distracts her, allowing Shanu to emerge victorious. However, the boy's joy is short-lived as RB discovers Shanu's identity and plots to use him as leverage against Rahul. Desperate to save his father, Shanu learns that the only weapon that will stop RB is the magic wand of Aabra Ka Daabra's benevolent founder, which he sets out to retrieve with the help of his friends.

By 2003 *Harry Potter* mania had gone global. Five of J.K. Rowling's children's books and two film adaptations had already captured the imaginations—and wallets—of millions of would-be wizards. The story of an average kid with an extraordinary destiny in a glamorous, spellbinding secret world was box office gold for Warner Bros., sparking a franchise that would extend beyond the novels that inspired it. So when Indian studio Creative Eye Limited and visual effects house FX Factory needed a marketable family movie to debut their new VFX technology, they didn't need sorcery to conjure up the ideal template.

Creative Eye's Dheeraj Kumar touted *Aabra Ka Daabra* as "India's first 3-D Plus film," referring to the process they developed in conjunction with JVC and similar to the technology used for 2003's *Spy Kids 3-D*. Kumar explained that this breakthrough was "technically one step further [than] all other 3-D technologies," because whereas most 3D films require silver-treated reflective screens, high luminance projection, and expensive polarized glasses, 3-D Plus films could be shown on ordinary screens—even televisions—and required cheaper specs. However,

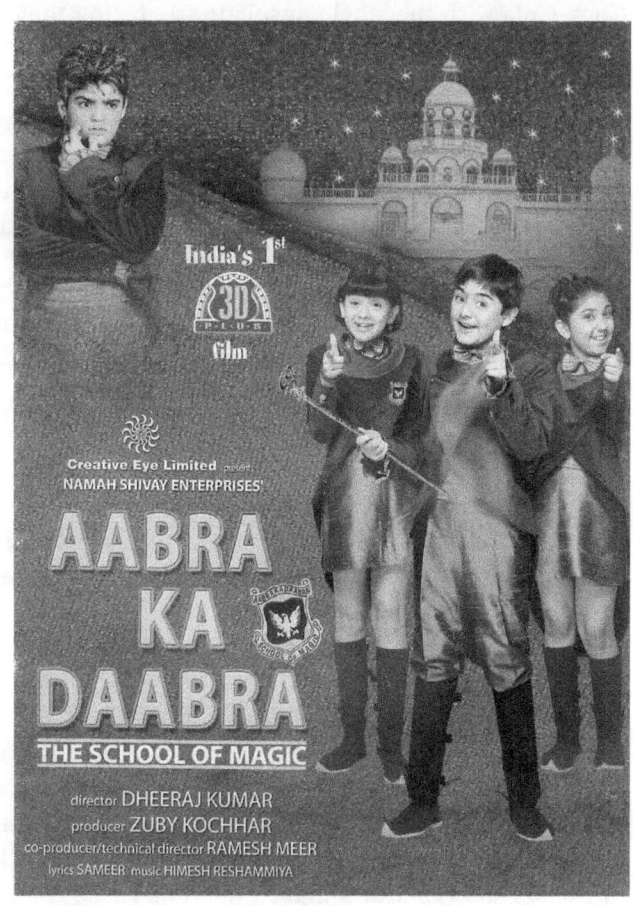

Unlike Hogwarts, everyone seems to know that the Aabra Ka Daabra School of Magic exists. The kids pose in front of it on the pressbook.

this claim was mostly ballyhoo. 3-D Plus was essentially a new name for anaglyph 3D, a process that was a century old by the time *Aabra Ka Daabra* was produced. Anaglyph, which requires colored lenses to view the effect—usually one red and one cyan—is indeed more versatile and less expensive, but it produces an inferior picture since each eye receives only a limited color spectrum. Moreover, while many of India's 3D films, including its first, *My Dear Kuttichathan* (1984), used the more costly polarized process, some, including 1985's *3D Saamri*, had in fact already been exhibited in an anaglyph format.

Yet even though the process wasn't precisely new, to make the film the way they envisioned it Kumar and his team would require top-of-the-line, high-resolution digital video cameras from JVC and numerous computer-generated effects. These would be expensive, so ideally Kumar needed a way to subsidize some of the costs. The answer was product placement. Promoting brands in films in exchange for money or other considerations has as long and infamous a history in Bollywood as it does in Hollywood. Product placement cropped up in Hindi movies at least as early as 1967 with *An Evening in Paris*, in which starlet Sharmila Tagore sips from a bottle of Coca-Cola with the label conspicuously facing the camera. The practice increased after India's economic liberalization in 1991, with brand deals generally valuing anywhere from $10,000 to $100,000. In the case of 2001's *Yaandein* ("Memories"), Coca-Cola reportedly paid a whopping $670,000 for placement—20 percent of the film's total budget. So for Kumar this was a viable and tempting opportunity.

Although Bollywood filmmakers were increasingly partnering with foreign brands like Coca-Cola, Mercedes, Ralph Lauren, and Nike, Kumar instead teamed up with Parle-G, an Indian manufacturer of glucose biscuits, and Camlin, a domestic stationery company. *Aabra Ka Daabra* was one of about 14 percent of Indian films at the time that actually incorporated their product placement into the plot, and the integration in this film is hardly subtle. The two companies' simultaneous "golden ticket" scholarship contests, for example—*both* of which are won by Shanu—stretch the limits of credibility. Shanu is later given super strength to fight off bullies thanks to a packet of Parle-G biscuits, à la Popeye's can of spinach ("Parle-G power supply!" he exclaims to the camera). In levitation class the students are instructed to draw pictures by levitating Camlin art supplies while a screen displays commercials for the product line. And several scenes are played out in front of sets plastered with the sponsors' logos. In addition to the brands featured in the film itself, Kumar and company also sought sponsors to subsidize the manufacturing costs of the 3D glasses.

With sponsorship mostly sorted, the team could focus on recreating, with few alterations, J.K. Rowling's famous wizarding world. The school itself, the groundskeeper, the bully, living portraits, levitation class, and even a stand-in for the wizard sport Quidditch are all unmistakable. But *Aabra Ka Daabra* borrows from more than just *Harry Potter*. The golden ticket in a packet of sweets is plainly inspired by Roald Dahl's *Charlie and the Chocolate Factory*, which was adapted by Hollywood in 1971 with a remake in development as *Aabra Ka Daabra* was going into production. The film also includes an animated flying familiar for Limbu called Tu-Tu that director Kumar accurately compares to Casper the Friendly Ghost. And the effects used to illustrate Rahul's alchemical magic mimic the gesture-based computer interfaces from 2002's *Minority Report*.

With the support of Camlin and Parle-G, Kumar attempted a large marketing campaign in advance of the film's release. In addition to the usual advertisements and a brochure featuring anaglyph 3D photographs, Kumar launched a line of *Aabra Ka Daabra* merchandise that included toys based on characters from the movie, a 3D storybook, coloring and activity books, and character mugs. He set up "publicity corners" in select multiplexes across India prior to the film's release and did further marketing in selected schools and other children's venues. Kumar and company were so certain of the film's success that the ending even promises a sequel. However, this never came to be; *Aabra Ka Daabra* was a box office disaster, making back just 13 percent of its budget. Unable to recapture the magic of *Harry Potter*, Creative Eye quickly returned to making 2D television serials.

Badi ("Shorty")

INSPIRED BY: *E.T. the Extra-Terrestrial* (1982)
STUDIO: Turkey
YEAR: 1984
PRODUCTION: Anadolu Film ve Sinemacılık
DIRECTOR: Zafer Par
WRITER: Veysel Candan (Barış Pirhasan)
STARS: Tolga Sönmez, Orhan Çağman, Pembe Mutlu, Cengiz Sayhan

Ali (Tolga Sönmez) lives with his aunt in Istanbul's ramshackle Linden Creek neighborhood. He loves animals; his nonhuman friends include a pet bird and a stray dog who hangs out by his school. However, when the dog is shot by local authorities on suspicion of rabies, Ali sinks into a depression. (*Warning: this film depicts a real dog corpse.*)

That night, red lights illuminate the sky as a UFO briefly lands in the nearby woods. Ali goes out to investigate and comes face to face with a lumpy, brown, child-sized alien. The boy panics and runs away, and the creature does likewise. However, the next morning Ali feigns illness to avoid school, then sneaks out to find the creature again. He doesn't have to go far; the alien has followed him home. Ali attempts to communicate with it, and the small being demonstrates powers of telekinesis. Ali names the stubby creature "Badi," a slang term for a short, stout person who waddles.

Meanwhile, elderly astronomer Professor Naci (Orhan Çağman) has also taken an interest in the UFO landing. He's had his assistant Nurten (Pembe Mutlu) order a piece of special equipment from a local electronics shop. Nurten befriends the shop's technician Metin, and he too becomes intrigued by the possibility of an extraterrestrial visitor.

Eager to hide and protect Badi, Ali takes him to the house of his best friend, science whiz kid Bülent (Cengiz Sayhan). Badi also meets Bülent's siblings, and they all agree to keep the secret.

Badi, who has been accidentally left behind by his ship, assembles a transmitter out of random bits and pieces from Bülent's workshop. At night, he leads the children to an amusement park where he activates the device and turns on all the rides, which draws all the neighborhood kids. However, Prof. Nacı, Nurten, and Metin have been tracking Badi with Metin's gizmo, and they arrive on the scene with the police, causing the children to scatter and Badi to disappear.

The next morning, Ali is discovered unconscious on the street. Bülent goes for a doctor and runs into the scientists, whom he asks for help. When they arrive, Ali runs to their car and opens the trunk, where he finds Badi in very poor shape. The alien's only hope is for his comrades to return. But between Badi and the landing site a frightened, suspicious mob has begun to form.

~~~

By 1983 Steven Spielberg's *E.T.* (1982) had not yet been released in Turkey. A struggling economy rarely permitted importers to pay for Hollywood films up-front, so American studios were reluctant to offer the newest releases. Nevertheless, bootleg toys, posters, T-shirts, books, and comics based on *E.T.* were already appearing on store shelves. Producer Şerif Gören, who had seen the film abroad, was convinced that he might replicate its success, albeit on a smaller scale, by making a domestic version for Turkish elementary schoolers.

Gören was more of a director than a producer, having received his start assisting legendary Marxist filmmaker Yılmaz Güney. When Güney directed his controversial and award-winning *Yol* ("The Road," 1982) by proxy from prison, Gören was that proxy. Gören was known for his leftist social dramas, his most recent being *Derman* ("Remedy," 1983), about a midwife from the city coping with life in a remote Anatolian village. Given his oeuvre, a kids' movie about a small chubby alien was, to put it mildly, a departure.

Gören hired poet and translator Barış Pirhasan, working under the pseudonym Veysel Candan, to pen the screenplay, and placed the relatively inexperienced Zafer Par in the director's seat. However, it's likely that Par was essentially a puppet, with Gören pulling most of the strings. Film historian Ali Murat Güven explains why Gören might have preferred a surrogate director to take the credit: "You've made a lot of left-wing films that have won major awards around the world. And most recently, you won the Palme d'Or at Cannes for *Yol*. With so much success and respect, would you helm such a trivial film?" Gören's name was also unpopular among the right-wing martial government, so having a less polarizing intermediary may have been handy when obtaining resources for the production.

With the script and crew sorted, the most important remaining element was the titular alien. For *E.T.*, Spielberg had simply gone to Carlo Rambaldi, a creator of creatures for 25 years. Rambaldi's iconic extraterrestrial was a marvel of animatronics and puppeteering. Gören, on the other hand, had no hope of replicating it. In the early '80s there were no Turkish companies that specialized in creature effects or suits. Instead, the producer took a chance by commissioning a costume from a company in Istanbul called Reklam Araçları Araştırma Merkezi ("Advertising Instruments Research Center"), which manufactured plastic and rubber props for television commercials. The resulting brown, rubbery suit was crude with limited articulation, but it functioned, and the filmmakers cast a child to fill it.

Badi's passing resemblance to E.T. is only one of many visual elements borrowed from Spielberg. The film's opening credits depict a spacescape of stars that bloom into flowers, echoing E.T.'s ability to rejuvenate plant life. Later, Badi reveals his powers by levitating apples just as E.T. levitates balls. And the alien's "phone home" device closely resembles E.T.'s, similarly involving a rotary saw blade atop a record player and a foil-wrapped umbrella serving as a makeshift satellite dish.

In spite of the similarities, Par and company also took pains to emphasize the "Turkishness" of their adaptation. When Western scientists react with surprise to the spaceship's arrival in Turkey, Professor Naci exclaims, "UFOs don't always land in America, you know!" chalking their misgivings up to jealousy. E.T.'s favorite candy and product placement phenomenon Reese's Pieces has been replaced with Turkish delight. And in a lift of *E.T.*'s famous flying bicycles scene, the alien levitates a peddler's cart over the Bosphorus and the minareted mosques of Istanbul.

The starship *Enterprise* seems to have taken a wrong turn and wound up on the Turkish one-sheet for *Badi* (1984).

Although Spielberg eschewed religious symbolism in *E.T.*, Gören, Par, and Pirhasan actively juxtaposed Badi with Islam. An elderly imam is among the crowd on the scene of the UFO landing, quoting from the Quran until the police arrive to shoo away the onlookers. Later, Badi wanders into Ali's house while the boy's aunt is praying. Terrified by the alien, she assumes it to be a supernatural creature like a djinn and, before fainting, recites a passage from the Quran to ward it off. And, although not exclusively a religious practice, as the alien is about to depart for his home world, Bülent's younger brother kisses Badi's hand and touches it to his forehead in the traditional display of respect.

Incidentally, while *E.T.*'s touchstones for outer space include pop culture like Buck Rogers and the *Star Wars* movies, Pirhasan took his cue instead from Erich von Däniken, famous for theories about "ancient astronauts" who visited Earth in the past and influenced humanity's technological progress. In *Badi*, Bülent, obsessed with outer space and aliens, regales Ali and his siblings with passages from von Däniken's *Chariots of the Gods* as though he was telling ghost stories around a campfire.

With posters advertising "A friend for the children arrived from outer space," *Badi* debuted on January 23, 1984—coincidentally the very same week that *E.T.* finally reached Turkey. A curious cinemagoer would have been able to watch the original film at a first-tier theater, then walk just a few hundred meters to a cheaper one to see the Turkish version. Unfortunately, however, the comparison did not do *Badi* any favors, and the film was met with unfavorable reviews.

On the other hand, Şerif Gören may not have been too bothered; at the time he was winning international awards and accolades for *Derman*.

Os Carrinhos em: A Grande Corrida (*The Little Cars in the Great Race*)

INSPIRED BY: *Cars* (2006)
COUNTRY: Brazil
YEAR: 2006
PRODUCTION: Vídeo Brinquedo
DIRECTOR: Liminha (Cristiano Valente)
WRITER: Liminha (Cristiano Valente)
STARS: Francisco Freitas, Raul Schlosser, Cláudia Victória, Cláudio Satiro, Luciana Mineira

Tony Tunado dreams about winning the Big Race. It's just a couple of days away and the whole city of Rodópolis is geared up about it, including Tony's crush—and his boss's niece—Cris Crash. Tony wishes he was a race car, but in fact he's only a delivery vehicle. And because he believes he's inferior, he hasn't been able to tell Cris how he feels about her. However, his best friend and co-worker, a tow truck named Kombo, suggests he start by asking her to the race.

The next day Tony and Kombo notice cocky racer Victor, a rival from outside Rodópolis, signing autographs for his fans (he does this with his tire tread). When Tony goes off to buy tickets for the event, Victor spies Cris and invites her to watch him train. Thinking he's lost Cris to a better guy, Tony gloomily drops the tickets.

Meanwhile the boss, Mr. V8, informs Kombo that business is failing thanks to high-tech competition. V8's company needs an upgrade, but he doesn't have the money. In fact, he's in debt, and he sends Kombo to pick up his savings from the bank to keep the business afloat. But instead of bringing the money back to his boss, Kombo takes it to the betting counter and puts it all on the Rodópolis team. He figures it's a sure thing since Rodópolis's racer, Champion, has won several years in a row.

However, just hours before the big event, Victor spikes Champion's gas. The sabotage puts the hot rod out of commission, and without a representative Rodópolis will be disqualified. While the police follow up the only lead, an oily tire track, Tony offers to take Champion's place in the race. Now it's up to him and his friends to beat Victor, save their business, and find the evidence to link Victor to his crime.

Os Carrinhos em: A Grande Corrida (The Little Cars in the Great Race)

In the early 2000s, Vídeo Brinquedo ("Toyland Video"), based out of São Paulo, Brazil, specialized in distributing low-cost, Portuguese-dubbed DVDs of children's cartoons. The company licensed high profile television series like *Sonic X* (2003) and *The Super Mario Bros. Super Show* (1989) as well as lesser-known titles like *Batfink* (1966) and various independently-produced animations.

One of these indie productions was *Kingdom Under the Sea* (2001). A low budget *VeggieTales* competitor, *Kingdom* reimagined stories from the Bible as the 3D-animated adventures of two fish siblings and their god-king, an enormous blue whale. Sales of the DVD were mediocre until 2003, when the discs suddenly began selling like hotcakes. The company quickly figured out why: Disney had just released Pixar's *Finding Nemo*, a digitally-animated undersea adventure with a massive advertising campaign. Thanks to both movies featuring clownfish and sporting similar promotional artwork, *Kingdom Under the Sea* found itself accidentally riding the marketing wave of a $94 million blockbuster. It's unlikely that customers were fooled into thinking that they were buying the Pixar film but given the low cost of the Vídeo Brinquedo offering, it would have been an attractive purchase for parents with children already hooked on *Nemo*.

It was also a light bulb moment for Vídeo Brinquedo. They reasoned that if they could produce their own films as well as distribute them, they could specifically tailor their content to look like Disney's and replicate *Kingdom*'s success. However, their first forays into original productions were only broadly in the Disney vein. These were 2D, Flash-animated versions of classic children's tales including *Pinocchio*, *The Three Little Pigs*, and *Rapunzel*. And despite attempts to modernize the stories for a contemporary audience, the movies failed to pull in the numbers that the company was hoping for. So they began to get more specific.

Mauricio Milani, content director for Vídeo Brinquedo, commissioned a half-hour film to openly piggyback on Pixar's upcoming anthropomorphic race car

U.S. key art for *Os Carrinhos em: A Grande Corrida* (2006).

film, *Cars* (2006). But unlike their previous movies, it wouldn't be 2D. Thanks to the affordability and versatility of desktop 3D computer graphics software, the company now had the ability to produce professional (if stripped-down) 3D animation with a bare-bones art team. So, under the command of writer-director-animator Cristiano Valente, *Os Carrinhos em: A Grande Corrida* went into production.

Since the movie was produced concurrently with *Cars*, the team couldn't see Pixar's film to imitate its story. However, that wasn't strictly necessary so long as they could ape its marketing. Nevertheless, Valente incorporated a number of nearly identical elements, possibly gleaned from trailers and other promotional materials. These included the opening scene of the rookie hero daydreaming about his big victory; the cocky, unscrupulous number two racer; the modest longtime champion; and the hero's best friend, a buck-toothed tow truck.

Os Carrinhos em: A Grande Corrida was released on DVD just days prior to *Cars*' Brazilian theatrical premiere. The disc retailed for a mere 10 reals (roughly $4.50), about a quarter the price of Disney's home videos. It was a hit, selling over 300,000 units in more than 12 countries. Vídeo Brinquedo struck while the iron was hot, and between 2006 and 2010 it produced seven direct-to-DVD sequels. The company further capitalized on the series' success with merchandise including toys, notebooks, and even Easter eggs (the sixth DVD was titled *O Carrinho Da Páscoa*—"The Little Easter Car"). In 2009, the cartoons began airing in 10–15 minute segments on television network TV Rá-Tim-Bum and later RedeTV!, along with two new volumes of cartoons produced in 2011.

Meanwhile, emboldened by the initial success of *Os Carrinhos*, Vídeo Brinquedo began production on a whole slate of films inspired by Disney and other popular animation studios. Thus *Ratatouille* (2007) spawned *Ratatoing* (2007), *Kung Fu Panda* (2008) sparked *Ursinho da Pesada* (*Little Panda Fighter*, 2008), *Bee Movie* (2009) inspired *Abelhinhas* (*Little Bee*, 2009), and *The Princess and the Frog* (2009) begat *A Princesa e o Sapo* (*The Frog Prince*, 2009). In all cases the Brazilian knock-offs were timed to coincide with the theatrical releases of their big-budget brethren, requiring the animation teams to begin work well in advance—reportedly two to three years. As this forced them to come up with original stories, it also protected them, to a degree, against charges of copyright infringement.

That protection didn't work in all situations, however, as in the case of UK distributor Brightspark, which licensed four volumes of *Os Carrinhos* and *A Princesa e o Sapo* from Vídeo Brinquedo. Particularly unscrupulous about copycatting Disney, Brightspark also released older cartoons from other companies under highly suspicious new titles. An installment of *Britannica's Tales Around the World* (1991) became *Tangled Up* to capitalize on Disney's *Tangled!* (2010), and *A Fairy Tale Christmas* (2005) was repackaged as *Braver* to beat the theatrical release of *Brave* (2012). This was a bridge too far for Disney, which brought legal action against Brightspark, citing not just its retitled films, but also the Vídeo Brinquedo movies it had acquired, as part of "a pattern of misleading consumers with numerous releases that confuse and undermine the trust those consumers have in Disney." Disney won a High Court order in 2012 blocking Brightspark from further distributing their animated films, and the company had all of its remaining DVDs destroyed. The court order did not, it's worth emphasizing, apply in any way to Vídeo Brinquedo itself, which continues to make its content available on numerous streaming platforms.

Ge wu qing chun (*Disney High School Musical: China*)

INSPIRED BY: *High School Musical* (2006)
COUNTRY: China
YEAR: 2010
PRODUCTION: Disney HSM China Productions
DIRECTOR: Chen Shi-zheng
WRITER: Lin Li
STARS: Zhang Junning, Liu Yanchen, Ma Zihan, Gu Xuan, Joe Cheng Yuan-chang, Gu Xuan, Qi Lin

Xiao Ningning (Ma Zihan) has no time for singing. Her controlling parents have enrolled her in a new college, the prestigious Oriental International School, and in spite of her superb academic record they've forbidden her to spend time on anything except schoolwork. On her first day, however, her eclectic classmates invite her to karaoke night at a nearby club. This motley crew of fellow youngsters includes basketball star Kobe (Joe Cheng Yuan-chang), spoiled rich girl "Princess" Yangyang (Gu Xuan), Princess's lackey Yuanyuan (Qi Yin), the sensitive Poet (Zhang Junning), and Poet's hipster best friend Skinny (Liu Yanchen).

At the club, the gang pressures Ningning and Poet to sing a duet, and the two surprise the room with their vocal talent. Both discover a passion for singing—and an interest in each other. However, when Ningning returns home, her parents admonish her for her frivolity.

The next day, an inter-collegiate singing competition is announced, with the winning school receiving a cash prize. Princess takes it upon herself to hold auditions for students to represent OIS—in addition to her, of course. Ningning considers auditioning in spite of her parents' objections. Poet is also tempted. With Kobe's help he ditches basketball practice to attend the try-outs. He meets Ningning there, but the two only watch from the back of the room, neither venturing to give it a shot themselves.

They do, however, decide to spend more time together. After an eventful date, Poet plays Ningning a song he's composed and encourages her to enter the competition. She finally agrees, but only if Poet joins her.

Furious, Princess conspires against them. She has Yuanyuan spread rumors about the couple, including personal details about Poet that he shared in confidence, unaware he had been overheard. Thinking he's been betrayed, Poet spurns Ningning and withdraws from the competition. With just a few days until the contest, Kobe and Skinny try to uncover the real culprit behind the rumors and patch things up between their friends so the show can go on.

~~~

Nobody at Disney anticipated that its modestly-budgeted TV movie would become a global phenomenon. *High School Musical* (2006), about a basketball star and a scholastic champ who break free of their peer-defined roles to pursue a passion for singing, had one of the Disney Channel's most-watched premieres—and it only grew from there. It spawned two sequels, a spin-off, a reality show, a concert tour, a stage show, a serialized meta-reboot for Disney's streaming service, and a series of young adult novels. And that's just America.

In addition to dubbing the film into 30 languages for 100 countries, Disney also produced two new Spanish-language *High School Musical* spin-offs—one in Mexico and the other in Argentina. Both titled *High School Musical: El Desafío* ("The Challenge," 2008), they marked the first Disney-branded feature films made in Latin America. These were soon followed by a Portuguese-language version for Brazil, *High School Musical: O Desafio* (2010). All three were adapted from the tie-in novel *Battle of the Bands* by N.B. Grace, but each was tailored for its specific market and featured stars chosen from local reality show competitions.

Meanwhile, Disney was setting the stage for a similar venture overseas. After China officially joined the World Trade Organization in 2001, it began opening its doors wider to Hollywood, allowing studios to bypass the country's import quota on foreign films by engaging in co-productions. In 2007, the House of Mouse established a presence in China to take full advantage of the new opportunity. Two relatively profitable Disney collaborations followed: *Bao hu lu de mi mi* (*The Secret of the Magic Gourd*, 2007) with the state-owned China Film Group Corporation and *Xiong mao hui jia lu* (*Trail of the Panda*, 2009) with Castle Hero Pictures and Ying Dong Media. Having tested the waters, Disney was ready to up its investment and hopefully replicate its success transplanting *High School Musical* to Latin America.

High School Musical was already familiar to Chinese audiences, having aired on local movie channel CCTV-6 in 2007. The stage show also opened in Shanghai in the summer of 2009, selling out for two straight weeks. Chinese movie musicals were a rarity, but thanks in part to the name recognition, Disney was able to woo Shanghai Media Group (SMG), China's second largest film company, and Huayi Brothers Media Corporation as partners for a localized theatrical version.

Rather than a straight remake or an adaptation of the spin-off novels like the Latin American movies, Disney opted instead for an original screenplay in the spirit of the first film. At its helm was Chen Shi-zheng, a Chinese-born, New York-educated director of film, theater, and opera. "Disney gave me a lot of leeway to rework the story," noted Chen in an interview with Mtime.com. "[It's] entirely based on Chinese music, Chinese actors, and environment."

To Disney's surprise, one key element had to go straightaway: the "high school" part. For one thing, the Chinese government was strict about stories set in high school. "There can't be any romance," explained Chen. Also, "[s]tudents and their parents must not be in conflict, nor teachers and students." In other words, he couldn't show high schoolers defying their elders to pursue their dreams—a large part of the original film. The other factor, Chen continued, was that "high school requires learning to be paramount." Chinese high school students wouldn't believably have the time to pursue singing. Therefore Huayi proposed making the characters college freshmen instead. (In some markets, the film would sport the title *High School Musical China: College Dreams*.)

Although one of the two main characters, Ningning, was written very much in the mold of her American predecessor Gabriella, Disney struggled with the portrayal of her love interest. Anticipating that a school basketball star might not resonate with Chinese audiences—the sport became soccer, rugby, and futsal for the Latin American versions—the U.S. studio envisaged him as a rural practitioner of kung fu who discovers a love of dance. However, Disney's Chinese collaborators had to explain that basketball was far more popular among China's youth than martial arts. Basketball was reinstated, but ultimately downplayed as part of Poet's identity. "Our partners think that in China you might be more attracted to the smart and thoughtful guy," explained Jason Reed, general manager of Walt Disney Studios International Production, to *China Daily*. Poet was therefore reimagined as "a thoughtful, intelligent and studious young man who is really defined by his skill and academics."

The cast of *Ge wu qing chun* (2010) recreates the famous poster from *High School Musical* (2006).

Yet despite Disney giving the Chinese team a free hand on much of the film's development, certain aspects were non-negotiable. Chen Shi-zheng, noting that his film was a very different animal from the 2006 TV movie, questioned even titling the film *High School Musical*, but Disney was unwilling to jettison the familiar brand. And while nearly all of the songs were new, the studio mandated the inclusion of the original film's signature track, "We're All in This Together," albeit with Mandarin lyrics. Chen also kept other, more superficial elements not necessarily due to Disney directives. These included a team dance number on the basketball court, glitzy performances by the spoiled wannabe-starlet, and a basketball team called the Wild Tigers, à la the East High Wildcats.

Once the film was completed, Disney and its Chinese partners clashed over its marketing strategy, resulting in a limited theatrical release for *Ge wu qing chun*. Its reception was also less than stellar. A common theme among reviews was the ultimate failure of Disney to truly localize the material. Derek Elley, writing for *Film

Business Asia, contended that the world of the film "only occasionally intersects with recognisable life in a modern Mainland city (Shanghai made to look as anonymous as possible). The aptly named Oriental International School could be any college in Middle America." And while the cast is local, *The Hollywood Reporter* noted that in contrast to the original film's multiethnic ensemble, the stars of *Ge wu qing chun* are all majority Han Chinese.

The film didn't become the perennial franchise that Disney was hoping for, but the studio would continue its partnership with SMG, going on to produce the nature documentary *Born in China* (2016) and romantic comedy *Jia ru wang zi shui zhao le* (*The Dreaming Man*, 2017), a remake of *While You Were Sleeping* (1995). With China having grown into the second largest film market in the world, Disney remained committed to pursuing success in a comparatively new environment—just like its singing high school heroes.

Kuzhandaiyum Deivamum ("Children and God")

INSPIRED BY: *The Parent Trap* (1961)
COUNTRY: India
YEAR: 1965
PRODUCTION: AVM Productions
DIRECTORS: R. Krishnan, S. Panju
WRITER: Javar Seetharaman
STARS: Jaishankar, Jamuna, Kutty Padmini, G. Varalakshmi, Santha

Working-class college student Sekar (Jaishankar) falls in love with Bhama (Jamuna), the proud heiress to a thriving bus company run by her miserly mother Alamelu (G. Varalakshmi). The matriarch disapproves of the match, but after grilling the young man she reluctantly gives in. The lovers are married, and Sekar becomes manager of the family business.

A year later, Bhama gives birth to twin girls, Lalitha and Padmini—Lalli and Pappi for short. But the couple's life is not all roses. At the office, Sekar finds himself little more than a figurehead, with his business decisions and philanthropic efforts constantly challenged and undermined by his mother-in-law. Things come to a head when Alamelu insults Sekar's friends at a company event. Fed up with the constant disrespect, he attempts to take his wife and children and leave. When Alamelu intervenes and Bhama demurs, he takes off with only one of the twins, Padmini. Together they travel to Singapore.

At the beach near their new home, Sekar rescues a rich man's daughter from drowning. The selfless act catches the eye of real estate mogul and philanthropist Jones, who hires Sekar and makes him a business partner. Years later, with a flourishing business, Jones sells his properties, making Sekar a rich man. Now wealthy, father and daughter move back to their hometown of Madurai in India.

Young Pappi (Kutty Padmini), an excellent student and athlete, attends school and finds herself in the same class as Lalli (also Kutty Padmini). Raised by her grandmother, Lalli is spoiled and haughty. The two personalities clash, and neither girl suspects that they are really sisters. That changes on a school camping trip, however, when their constant fighting gets them locked in a room together as punishment.

Padmini (Kutty Padmini, left) and Sekar (Jaishankar, right) arrive at their posh new home in Madurai with friend and servant Sundaram (Nagesh).

Forced to work through their differences, they get to know each other and discover their connection. Eager to meet their absent parents, they decide to switch places.

Meanwhile, Pappi's dance teacher Nirmala (Santha) has designs on Sekar. With her mother's help, she insinuates herself into Sekar's household and influences him with alcohol disguised as medicine. She then stages the aftermath of a compromising night together, forcing Sekar to propose marriage. When Lalli, posing as Pappi, tries to expose her, Nirmala shoves the girl down the stairs, rendering her unconscious. The real Pappi learns of her sister's condition and rushes to see her with Bhama, but Nirmala and her mother are prepared with deadly treachery.

~~~

Before it was a Disney hit, *The Parent Trap* was a beloved German children's novel by Erich Kästner called *Das doppelte Lottchen* ("The Double Lotties"). The book had already been adapted for the silver screen three times—in Germany, Japan, and England—before a reader in Disney's story department sent it up the chain for possible development as a House of Mouse feature. Thanks in part to child actress Hayley Mills in a trick-photography-aided dual role, *The Parent Trap* (1961) achieved an international success that eclipsed the previous iterations—and paved the way for a string of remakes in South India.

In the mid–1960s, remakes of American movies were uncommon in Kollywood,

South India's Tamil-language film industry. (The "K" comes from Kodambakkam, the Chennai neighborhood where its studios were historically located.) Adaptations tended to be based instead on movies from other regions of India. However, when producer A.V. Meiyappan saw *The Parent Trap* on a trip to Bangalore, he recognized the box office potential for a localized version. After all, recent Indian films about long lost twins and lookalikes, such as *Hum Dono* ("Both of Us," 1961), *China Town* (1962), and *Ramudu Bheemudu* ("Lord Bhima," 1964) had been very successful.

Meiyappan, owner of AVM Productions, persuaded his son A.V.M. Kumaran and writer-director A.C. Thirulokachandar (ACT) to watch the film and offer their opinions. Kumaran was intrigued by the concept, suggesting they merge the story with ACT's then-in-production family melodrama *Kaakum Karangal* ("Safe Hands," 1965). ACT, on the other hand, was less interested, preferring to stick to his own material. Meiyappan therefore tried again with screenwriter Javar Seetharaman, who was more amenable to adapting the film.

Seetharaman's task would involve more than just translating and relocating *The Parent Trap*. Like many Hollywood films, it would need to be substantially expanded if it was going to meet what producers perceived as audience demand. For a 2002 paper, scholar Tejaswini Ganti interviewed a number of Indian filmmakers (based in Mumbai, but their sentiments echo throughout the various regional film industries) about the long history of embellishing American films for local consumption. "When the audience comes to the theater, they have a very set belief," explained screenwriter Sutanu Gupta. "[T]hey should see part of family life; they should see romance; they should have songs; everything they want!" In particular, scribe Anjum Rajabali also noted, "When you Indianize a subject, you add emotions. Lots of them. Feelings like love, hate, sacrifice, of revenge, pangs of separation."

In other words, Hollywood plots are considered too simple for an industry that frequently deals in multi-hour sagas. Gupta illustrated the point to Ganti with the Jan de Bont film *Speed* (1994): "A Hollywood film can interest their audiences with one track—you can have a bomb in a bus, a girl is driving the bus, and a man has to save the bus driver and the bus passengers. This is the whole film! We can't do a film like that. It could be our climax, only one scene in the film."

Proving Gupta's point, Seetharaman relegated the majority of *The Parent Trap*'s story to the final third of *Kuzhandaiyum Deivamum*, making room for additional "tracks" or subplots. These included an elaborate "pre-story" detailing the rocky beginning of the parents' romance, the troubles they encounter before they split, and their separate home lives before the twins inevitably get together and discover their kinship. He also amped up the emotional content of the film with higher stakes, crueler betrayals, and more devious villains.

With the new narrative in place, the film was ready for a cast and crew. A.V. Meiyappan hired directing duo R. Krishnan and S. Panju, who had been responsible for the massively successful drama *Parasakthi* ("Goddess," 1952) and *Nallathambi* ("Good Brother"), a 1949 remake of *Mr. Deeds Goes to Town* (1936). To play the twins, Krishnan-Panju selected nine-year-old Kutty Padmini. The young actress would follow in Hayley Mills's footsteps, playing against herself via split-screen effects and the use of a body double. Jaishankar, a handsome leading man who'd soon become known as the South Indian James Bond, would portray the girls' father, with multi-talented actress (and future director/producer) Jamuna as their mother.

The film, shot in black-and-white, was released on November 19, 1965. Given that *The Parent Trap* had played to full houses in Chennai just months before, cinemagoers were likely aware that *Kuzhandaiyum Deivamum* was something of a twin itself. Nevertheless, it received positive reviews and went on to win the 1965 President's Silver Medal for the Best Film in Tamil. Kutty Padmini's performance won her the National Film Award for Best Child Artist.

Following the film's success, A.V. Meiyappan reunited much of the cast and crew for a virtually shot-for-shot Telugu-language remake, *Letha Manasulu* ("Tender Hearts," 1966), which became one of the year's big hits. The producer then went for a hat trick, beginning work on a Hindi version, *Do Kaliyaan* ("Two Buds," 1968), this time in color. Shooting began with Kutty Padmini once again playing the twins, but mid-production the filmmakers felt she had aged out of the role(s) and replaced her with nine-year-old Neetu Singh. A further complication arose when Meiyappan learned that a rival had licensed *The Parent Trap* for a separate, official Hindi remake. In order to get his version out first, AVM immediately halted production on another project to have all hands on deck for *Do Kaliyaan*. The resulting film was a silver jubilee hit, playing for 25 straight weeks. Under different companies, *Kuzhandaiyum Deivamum* would be remade twice more, as *Sethubandhanam* (1974) in Malayalam, and *Makkala Bhagya* ("Children's Fortune," 1976) in Kannada.

Lassie—Eine abenteuerliche Reise (*Lassie Come Home*)

INSPIRED BY: *Lassie Come Home* (1943)
COUNTRY: Germany
YEAR: 2020
PRODUCTION: Henning Ferber Produktion
DIRECTOR: Hanno Olderdissen
WRITER: Jane Ainscough
STARS: Nico Marischka, Sebastian Bezzel, Anna Maria Mühe, Matthias Habich, Bella Bading, Christoph Letkowski, Johann von Bülow

Young Florian "Flo" Maurer (Nico Marischka) lives in southern Germany with his father Andreas (Sebastian Bezzel) and mother Sandra (Anna Maria Mühe). His best friend is his dog Lassie, an extremely intelligent collie who rushes to meet him every day after school. Unfortunately, Flo's father, a glass-blower, loses his job, and the family has to move into an apartment that doesn't allow pets. The Maurers have no choice but to give up Lassie, and Flo is devastated.

Lassie's new owners for the time being are the kindly Count Graf von Sprengel (Matthias Habich) and his granddaughter Priscilla (Bella Bading). The count owns the glass factory, but hard times have forced him to shutter the business and sell most of his assets. When he's called 800 km away to sign some paperwork, Priscilla convinces him to take her and Lassie along. Soon after they arrive, however, Priscilla catches the count's conniving groundskeeper Hinz (Christoph Letkowski) mistreating the collie. The count is horrified and fires Hinz, but Lassie escapes and runs off in the direction of her family.

Flo (Nico Marischka) encourages Lassie to overcome her fear of water.

Flo, hearing of Lassie's disappearance, creates a social media page where people can report sightings. A girl soon spots Lassie stealing sausages from a hot dog stand and uploads a video of the incident. When Flo sees the footage, he sneaks out of the apartment and catches a bus. He arrives at the hot dog stand to look for clues and discovers Priscilla, who's also run off to find Lassie. Flo figures out that the dog stowed away in the van of a traveling performer, so the kids steal a bike and follow her trail. Unfortunately, Hinz is on the same track, plotting to capture Lassie for reward money.

Word of Priscilla's disappearance reaches her rich but negligent father Sebastian (Johann von Bülow), who joins Andreas to search for the children. Meanwhile, Hinz catches up with Lassie and tries to abduct her. He's thwarted, however, by the appearance of Flo and Priscilla. The kids rescue the dog and flee, but their path is blocked by a river and the children accidentally fall in. Lassie leaps in after them, but the current is too strong and it draws Lassie over a waterfall. Andreas and Sebastian arrive just in time to pull Flo and Priscilla out, but Lassie is gone. Even if she has survived, she may never be able to find her family; Andreas has accepted a new job far away and the Maurers are just days from moving.

~~~

Yorkshire-born author Eric Knight loved collies. His affection for the breed, in particular his canine best friend Toots, inspired him to write the short story "Lassie Come-Home," published in the December 17, 1938 issue of *The Saturday Evening Post*. The tale of a brave collie who travels 500 miles to reunite with her family, it delighted readers and proved so popular that Knight was motivated to expand it into a novel in 1940. Three years later, MGM adapted the best-seller into a feature film. *Lassie Come Home* (1943) was a hit, launching the career of its four-legged star Pal, who'd star in six sequels in quick succession. However, as it was produced during the war, *Lassie Come Home* wouldn't reach German cinemas until 1950. Even then it would take another eight years, the proliferation of television, and a little boy named Jeff Miller for Lassie to become a household name in Germany.

After *The Painted Hills* (1951), MGM decided that Lassie's popularity had waned sufficiently to drop the dog's contract. The studio still owed Pal's owner and trainer Rudd Weatherwax $40,000, but Weatherwax cannily waived the outstanding debt in exchange for rights to the Lassie name and image. After a stint on the road with Pal, Weatherwax struck a deal with producer Robert Maxwell to bring Lassie to television. Together they developed a series that saw the collie living with a boy named Jeff and his struggling farm family in rural America, solving problems and saving lives every week. Debuting in 1954, *Lassie* featured the adventures of the title pooch and Jeff Miller for its first 116 episodes, though the dog would eventually team up with many other humans over the course of the show's impressive 19-season run. By 1955 owner Independent Television Corporation had an Emmy-winner on its hands, and it soon began selling the series to dozens of countries around the world.

The same year *Lassie* hit the airwaves in the U.S., West Germany's first national television network, ARD, began broadcasting. Comprising several television stations from the former British, French, and American zones, ARD would gradually expand the average broadcast day from roughly two hours of programming in the pre–ARD era to six and a half by the early '60s. Sales of television sets had boomed thanks to major televised events like the coronation of Queen Elizabeth II and the 1954 Football World Championship. With a million viewers by 1957 and ever more time to fill, ARD found itself in need of content. American television producers, who were earning an increasing percentage of their profits from international sales, were only too happy to oblige. From ITC the network licensed *Lassie*, which would be dubbed locally into German.

Lassie premiered on June 21, 1958, as part of the ARD series *Samstagnachmittag zu Hause* ("Saturday Afternoon at Home," 1958). Hosted by actor and director Hans Reinhard Müller, *Samstagnachmittag* featured guests, music, films, and other TV series, with *Lassie* as a regular feature. *Lassie* would run on ARD for eight years before migrating to other networks and establishing itself as a staple of German television for decades. Subsequent Lassie shows, like the 1997 Canadian-produced series of the same name, were also broadcast in Germany. In fact, the French-animated *Lassie* (2014) was airing regularly on kids' network KiKA when *Lassie—Eine abenteuerliche Reise* was conceived.

Producer Henning Ferber chanced upon Eric Knight's novel while searching for a family-oriented project to suit his production company. He purchased the rights and hired screenwriter Jane Ainscough, an award-winning writer of family films, to pen the adaptation. Directing duties went to Hanno Olderdissen, who already had experience working with dogs, as well as the film's animal trainer Renate Hiltl, on the TV series *Der Bulle und das Biest* ("The Bull and the Beast," 2019), about a detective and bullmastiff who solve crimes. This Lassie film was technically a separate entity from the American productions that had come before, but it would nevertheless be inextricably linked to their popularity. Speaking to distributor Prorom, Olderdissen acknowledged, "I wanted to create a film that was modern and interesting for the children but also has a classic nostalgic touch to honor the original *Lassie* films and series that we, as parents and grandparents know from our own childhood." For proof, one need only look at the movie's canine star.

Eric Knight's literary Lassie was a tricolor (mostly black) British collie with a black "mask" of facial fur. The original film Lassie, on the other hand, was a gold and white American collie with a defined white blaze on her face that became Lassie's trademark. Pal, in reality a male dog, would define the character's look for generations, siring an "official" Lassie bloodline that has populated a host of movies and television shows since 1943. A Lassie movie with any other kind of collie would be unthinkable, so the German filmmakers specifically sought one that matched the familiar look.

However, casting the dog proved difficult for the most ironic reason possible: "In Germany there are no collies who are classically trained for film," producer Ferber told *Der Tagesspiegel*, "because they are immediately associated with Lassie." Furthermore, the most common collies in Germany are the British variety with a different shape and the wrong coloring. Therefore, a year and a half before production began, they tasked Renate Hiltl with locating a sable American collie with the distinctive white blaze. Eventually she found the five-month-old Bandit with a breeder in northern Germany. Bandit would be used for most of the film, but he'd also have two doubles. Bailey, from central Germany, was rescued from a bad situation, and Buddy came from a breeder in Chicago, USA. Hiltl then worked with the trio for 18 months to get them ready for the cameras.

As for the story itself, screenwriter Jane Ainscough needed to do very little to adapt it for a German context. It was almost exclusively a case of changing the locations and character names. She updated it for the smartphone era and reduced the original tale's emphasis on social class, but most of her adjustments were to its narrative structure and pacing. She made the children more active participants in the story, streamlined Lassie's journey home, gave the dog a fear of water to overcome (as in Lassie's 1948 *Hills of Home*), added a more action-packed

German one-sheet for *Lassie—Eine abenteuerliche Reise* (2020).

climax, and consolidated the book's handful of minor antagonists into one primary villain, Hinz.

Had *Lassie—Eine abenteuerliche reise* been made in English, it would have been indistinguishable from a Hollywood remake of the 1943 film. On one hand, that speaks to the universal nature of Knight's story; everyone can relate to economic woes and a child's love for a pet. On the other hand, that may have been precisely the point. Henning Ferber's company explicitly produces films for the international as well as the German market. With the American Lassie films and series known from Mexico to Japan, it would have benefited Ferber to avoid a film that was too regional. As it was, Ferber was able to sell the film to more than 44 countries.

Maugli (The Adventures of Mowgli)

COUNTERPART OF: *The Jungle Book* (1967)
COUNTRY: USSR
YEAR: 1973
PRODUCTION: Soyuzmultfilm
DIRECTOR: Roman Davydov
WRITER: Leonid Belokurov
STARS: Lev Shabarin, Mariya Vinogradova, Anatoliy Papanov, Stepan Bubnov, Lyudmila Kasatkina, Vladimir Ushakov, Lev Lyubetskiy

Prowling the jungle, vicious tiger Shere Khan (Anatoliy Papanov) accidentally disturbs a campfire, sending a little boy scurrying off alone into a wolves' den. The surprised wolves, at first uncertain what to do with this strange man-cub, decide to adopt him. Shere Khan claims the child as his prey, however, and so the matter is brought before the Pack Council. Baloo the bear (Stepan Bubnov) and Bagheera the panther (Lyudmila Kasatkina) advocate for the boy, and the council allows him to remain in the pack—much to Shere Khan's displeasure.

Bagheera teaches the child, named Mowgli (Mariya Vinogradova), that he has unique abilities his wolf brothers lack, including running on two legs, climbing, and swinging. Watching from the trees, the "bandar-log" monkeys are so impressed that they kidnap Mowgli to make him their leader. Baloo and Bagheera frantically give chase, but they soon find themselves outrun. They recruit the assistance of Kaa the python (Vladimir Ushakov), and the trio storms the primates' hideout. While Baloo and Bagheera rescue Mowgli, Kaa hypnotizes the bandar-log and feasts on them.

A few years later, Mowgli (now Lev Shabarin) receives word that the old wolf pack leader, Akela (Lev Lyubetskiy), has missed his prey during the hunt, and by law he may be killed and replaced. Realizing that Shere Khan is likely behind this misadventure (he is), Bagheera urges Mowgli to obtain the most feared weapon in the jungle: the Red Flower. The boy sneaks into a human village where he finds what he's looking for: fire. He brings it back and uses it to fend off Shere Khan and reinstate Akela.

Before long, a greater disaster threatens the jungle. A veritable swarm of vicious dholes is primed to invade. All the animals but the cowardly Shere Khan pledge to stand and fight, though they expect to die in battle. Kaa, however, devises a plan. He has Mowgli provoke the dholes, then lead them over a cliff where they disturb a huge

An adult Mowgli warns Kaa of the dhole invasion in a segment based on Kipling's "Red Dog," which was not adapted for Disney's *The Jungle Book* (1967).

hive of bees. Stung, wet, and tired, the dogs are weakened for the fight, giving the other animals a vital edge.

As Mowgli's final adventure begins, a drought settles upon the jungle. The elephants call a truce, allowing all animals to drink together in safety. However, Shere Khan violates the truce and Mowgli decides the time has come to kill his longtime enemy. He drives the tiger out of hiding with a herd of buffalo and fights him, hand-to-paw, to the death. Though he emerges victorious, he is not satisfied. He feels a yearning to return to the world of men, and his jungle friends realize that the time has come for him to move on.

～～～

Adapted from Rudyard Kipling's *Jungle Book* stories, *Maugli* was developed and produced at almost exactly the same time as Walt Disney's 1967 *The Jungle Book*. However, this was virtually their only connection. The Soviet version was not a response to the American film, but rather a totally independent production. Yet *Maugli* might never have existed without Disney's impact decades prior.

Early animation in the Soviet Union was an extension of propaganda posters and political caricatures, and it was used for similar purposes. That began to change in 1933 when a Russian festival for American animation showcased films by Walt Disney. These proved so popular that they prompted the annual All-Union Conference on Comedy to adopt the slogan "Give us a Soviet Mickey Mouse!" More Disney films appeared in 1935 at the first Moscow International Film Festival, established on Stalin's personal order and hosted by director Sergei Eisenstein. These garnered considerable praise, both from the public and Stalin himself. Eisenstein was particularly enamored with their use of anthropomorphic animals to highlight human traits—a convention that would become a staple of Soviet cartoons. Soon domestic animation strove to entertain as well as instruct, and its animators emulated the Disney style. They would continue to do so through the 1950s.

Meanwhile, Viktor Smirnov, head of a film distribution company, had seized an opportunity to study American animation methods. In 1933 he toured the Walt Disney and Fleischer studios, returning to Moscow the next year with plenty to report. Thanks to Smirnov's research, Soviet studios began using transparent celluloid sheets ("cels") to animate foreground characters over painted backdrops. They also adopted Disney's assembly-line method of animation, which meshed well with the emerging Stakhanovite movement—a Soviet take on efficiency systems like Taylorism and Fordism. These innovations encouraged standardization and gave authorities greater control over animators and their work.

In 1936, the government created Soyuzmultfilm (initially Soyuzdetmultfilm) to consolidate Russian animators under one roof. Over the next two decades, the studio would prove a sort of Soviet Disney, producing numerous animated fairy and folk tales for all ages. Some were traditional and some newly invented, but they were all Soviet in origin. Foreign sources were effectively off-limits.

However, in the 1950s, following the death of Joseph Stalin, his successor Nikita Khrushchev instituted a period of liberalization throughout the USSR. Khrushchev's "Thaw" relaxed censorship and loosened restrictions on imported movies, books, art, and music into the Soviet Union. Notably, 1955 saw a new edition of Rudyard Kipling's *The Jungle Book* translated by Nina Daruzes. Retitled *Maugli*, it collected all of the Mowgli stories from *The Jungle Book* and *The Second Jungle Book* but omitted the poetry and other tales like "Rikki-Tikki-Tavi."

Between 1967 and 1971, Soyuzmultfilm would adapt *Maugli* into five 20-minute shorts. Helmed by Roman Davydov, who would gain a reputation for making heroic epics, *Maugli* differed from Disney's *The Jungle Book* in key ways. One was that, because it drew from more of the Mowgli stories than Disney's film, it detailed the "man-cub's" entire growth from toddler to adult. Another was that it portrayed the originally male panther Bagheera as female. This change was not arbitrary, but rather stemmed from Aleksandra Rozhdestvenskaia and Mariia Korsh's 1895 translations of the original stories. It was an effort to avoid reader confusion: in Russian, names ending in an "a" are typically female, and in the gendered Russian language "panther" is a female noun. From then on, except for the 2007 dub of the Disney film and its 2016 remake, female Bagheera was canon in Russia.

Freed from the homogenous "Soviet style" of animation that preceded the Thaw, Davydov took a stylized, often surreal approach to *Maugli*. Film scholar Sergey Kuznetsov evocatively describes scenes of "Bagheera sweeping across the screen like a drop of darkness swirling in a whirlpool; [and] packs of monkeys, wolves and dogs flowing in a living stream." Still, the director was keen to capture realism in the

118　　　　　　　　**3. Family, Fantasy, and Fairy Tales**

movements of his creatures. He encouraged his staff to take inspiration from *V mire zyvotnykh* ("In the World of Animals"), a documentary series on the animal kingdom that debuted on state TV in 1968. And when artists Pyotr Repkin and Alexander Vinokurov pondered Bagheera's physicality, he advised them to study their housecats.

Maugli was a huge success, prompting Soyuzmultfilm to combine the episodes into a feature-length film in 1973. It would eventually receive an American release as well, but not a very auspicious one. In 1998 Monarch Home Video, better known in the sell-through market for its annual *Highlights of the Masters Golf Tournament* videotapes, licensed the film for its first foray into children's entertainment. Monarch edited the movie for content, replaced the music, redubbed the voices with Charlton Heston and Sam Elliott, and released it on tape as *The Adventures of Mowgli*. Little attention was given to its origin, with *Billboard* incorrectly reporting that it hailed from Germany. Monarch CEO Dan Norem had little faith in the movie itself, banking primarily on consumers' familiarity with the Disney version to move cassettes. "We knew we didn't have an animated classic," he confessed to *Billboard*.

Russians would disagree. *Maugli* is still fondly remembered in its home country. Many of its lines have become everyday aphorisms. Bagheera is still a common name for black Russian housecats. And in 2012 the Russian government issued a postage stamp commemorating the series. Even president Vladimir Putin somewhat

Shere Khan's lackey Tabaqui the jackal gloats to Baloo and Bagheera that a trap set for his master has ensnared a helpless baby elephant instead.

infamously referenced it in 2011 during his yearly call-in show on Russia-1. Addressing his enemies, he imitated Kaa coaxing the monkeys into his jaws: "Come to me, Bandar-log," he cajoled.

Pamuk Prenses ve 7 Cüceler ("Snow White and the 7 Dwarfs")

INSPIRED BY: *Snow White and the Seven Dwarfs* (1937)
COUNTRY: Turkey
YEAR: 1970
PRODUCTION: Hisar Film
DIRECTOR: Ertem Göreç
WRITER: Hamdi Değirmencioğlu
STARS: Zeynep Değirmencioğlu, Suna Selen, Salih Güney, Belgin Doruk

A king and queen give birth to a baby girl with snow-white skin, blood-red lips, and ebony black hair. They name her Snow White. Unfortunately, shortly after the child is born the queen falls ill and dies, leaving the girl without a mother.

Many years later, when Snow White (Zeynep Değirmencioğlu) has become a young woman, the king remarries. The new queen (Suna Selen) is vain, treacherous, and a sorceress to boot. When she learns from her magic mirror that her stepdaughter's beauty surpasses her own, she hatches a plan. She poisons the king and takes the kingdom for herself. She then strips Snow White of her royal title, dresses her in rags, and forces her to become a servant. It's in this state that the girl meets a handsome young prince (Salih Güney) who immediately falls for her.

Meanwhile, the queen discovers that Snow White's heart contains the secret to eternal youth and beauty. She instructs her executioner to dress as a hunter, take the girl into the forest, kill her, and bring back her heart and blood-stained dress. However, he finds he cannot do it. He kills a gazelle for its heart instead, takes a piece of Snow White's dress, and urges the young lady to flee into the woods.

After spending a terrified night in the forest, she wakes to find herself surrounded by woodland animals. They lead her to a small and untidy house apparently made for seven children. She decides to clean it in the hopes that the occupants might then let her stay. Of course, it's actually the house of seven dwarfs, and when they arrive home from their work at the diamond mine, they discover a shiny new home and a princess asleep in their beds. She befriends them, and they allow her to stay in exchange for keeping house.

Back at the palace, the queen discovers that Snow White is alive and living with the dwarfs. Concocting a new plan, she transforms herself into an old woman and poisons an apple, which she brings to Snow White while the dwarfs are away. Unsuspecting, the girl accepts it and takes a bite, falling immediately into a sleeping death from which only love's first kiss may wake her.

~~~

Fairy tale movies were rare in the early years of Turkish cinema. The first, a 1953 Arabian Nights style adventure called *Balıkçı Güzeli: Bin İkinci Gece* ("The Handsome Fisherman: 1002 Nights"), failed to make waves. A few further attempts were made in the subsequent decade—*Cilalı İbo ve Kırk Haramiler* ("Shoeshine İbo and the Forty Thieves," 1964), *Keloğlan* (1965), and *Bağdat Hırsızı* ("The Thief of Baghdad," 1968)—but these fared little better. The genre wouldn't be seen as commercially viable until 1970, and that would be thanks to screenwriter Hamdi Değirmencioğlu.

Değirmencioğlu's career had taken off in 1960 with *Ayşecik* ("Little Ayşe"), about an intelligent, mischievous young girl forced to provide for her family when her mother is killed and her father is wrongfully imprisoned. Değirmencioğlu wrote the title role for his daughter Zeynep, only six years old at the time. *Ayşecik* was a smash hit, earning Zeynep an award from the Municipality of Istanbul and launching her career as Yeşilçam's first proper child star. The father-daughter duo followed the successful film with a series of in-spirit sequels bearing the Ayşecik name. However, by 1970 Zeynep had starred in more than a dozen Ayşecik movies and was no longer a precocious little girl. Seeking a project more suitable for her age, Değirmencioğlu found inspiration in Disney's *Snow White and the Seven Dwarfs*.

Walt Disney's 1937 film, which would not be widely seen in Turkey until after television became widespread in the late 1970s, had substantially reworked the Grimm brothers' well-known version of the tale. In addition to aging up the seven-year-old Snow White, it excised parts of the story, including the princess's biological parents and two unsuccessful attempts by the queen to kill her stepdaughter. It also altered the wicked queen's death, now an offscreen fall rather than grisly retribution. Additionally, the adaptation was heavily influenced by other films, ranging from J. Searle Dawley's 1916 silent version of the same tale to Lansing C. Holden and Irving Pichel's *She* (1935), MGM's *Romeo and Juliet* (1936), and such classics of German Expressionism as *Nosferatu* (1922) and *Das Cabinet des Dr. Caligari* (*The Cabinet of Dr. Caligari*, 1920).

For the most part, Değirmencioğlu stuck closely to the Disney version. However, he reinstated the beginning of the Grimm tale and added new scenes featuring the prince, who appeared only briefly in the 1937 film. These latter sequences included a battle with the wicked queen's soldiers—done in the style of popular historical swashbucklers—and the suitor's investigation of Snow White's disappearance. Interestingly, Değirmencioğlu included scenes in which the dwarfs decide to build Snow White a bed as a gift. These are nearly identical to two sequences originally intended for Disney's film, but which were only partially animated before getting the axe. They did appear in print form, however, in several tie-in books—including at least two Turkish bootlegs from the 1950s.

Ertem Göreç, who had helmed *Ayşecik Fakir Prenses* ("Ayşecik the Poor Princess," 1963) as well as the recent *Bağdat Hırsızı*, signed on to direct Değirmencioğlu's script. In addition to Zeynep, Göreç assembled a cast of well-known stars. Award-winning actress Belgin Doruk played Snow White's birth mother, pulling double duty assisting the design and manufacture of the Disney-inspired costumes. Star Suna Selen was cast as the wicked queen, undergoing an elaborate costume and makeup change for her appearance as an old woman. And Zeynep's frequent *Ayşecik* co-star Ömer Dönmez, better known as "Ömercik," was given a small role as the prince's page.

For the seven dwarfs, Göreç chose to cast little people, making *Pamuk Prenses* the first time actors with dwarfism would appear in Turkish cinema. The producers

Pamuk Prenses ve 7 Cüceler ("Snow White and the 7 Dwarfs")

Snow White (Zeynep Değirmencioğlu) poses with the Seven Dwarfs in this pre-production publicity photo. Left to right: Uykucu (Ali Abbas Bayar), Bilgin (Nuri Turgut), Öfkeli (Mehmet Aşık), Aksırık (Fevzi Baba), Keloğlan (Aydın Babaoğlu), Utangaç (Harun Atalay), Neşeli (Tayyar Yıldız). Baba was replaced before filming began by Aydın Babaoğlu's brother Ayhan.

placed national newspaper advertisements announcing the forthcoming production and soliciting applications from people of short stature. Previous acting experience was not a prerequisite, and the team auditioned a host of hopefuls from across the country.

As in the Disney film, the dwarfs all have descriptive names—Happy, Sneezy, Sleepy, etc.—with one exception. Değirmencioğlu reimagined the silent Dopey as the gregarious Keloğlan, an archetype from Turkish folklore. Although his background differs depending on the tale—sometimes he's a pauper, other times he's a padishah's son—the bald-pated Keloğlan (literally "bald boy") is often portrayed as a runt or youngest child. He's occasionally selfish but usually good-hearted, and he's frequently clever, relying on his wits rather than brawn to solve problems, defeat foes, or otherwise get out of trouble. Because of the character's adaptability, he was easily inserted into the story of *Snow White* as the smallest of the dwarfs, allowing Göreç to apply a regional patina to the Western tale.

The 1937 *Snow White* established a long Disney tradition of animated princesses befriending animals, and Snow White's woodland pals play a pivotal role in the film. Translating this element to low budget live action, however, was a tall order. It was costume designer Niyazi Er who championed using live animals. Shooting on location in the Serik district of Antalya, Göreç and Er enlisted the help of local villagers to wrangle rabbits and birds. One village child had even tamed a gazelle, allowing the production to make use of it. While not "trained" in the traditional sense—despite a month of effort by Er, they mostly minded their own business—the animals could nevertheless be herded about the set as required.

Classical composer Yıldırım Gürses was brought onboard as the production's music supervisor, writing the song "Ne Güzel Şey Yaşamak" ("What a Beautiful Thing to Live"), which Snow White sings when she meets the prince, specifically for the film. For the rest of the movie he cobbled together an eclectic soundtrack from existing albums. This included several tracks from the score to *El Cid* (1961), a needle-drop from *Funeral in Berlin* (1966), and various excerpts from Westerns like *The Texican* (1966), *I giorni dell'ira* (*Day of Anger*, 1967), and *Blue* (1968). Also featured are "Les Nuages" by Manos Hadjidakis and an assortment of songs by Harry Breuer.

Pamuk Prenses ve 7 Cüceler was a box office hit, and it would go on to win third place for best picture at the Antalya Film Festival in 1971. Its success led to a boom in fairy tale movies, including versions of Disney's *Cinderella* (1950), the story of Scheherazade, and many of the *One Thousand and One Nights* tales. The year 1971 would see much of the cast and crew of *Pamuk Prenses* reunite in *Ayşecik ve Sihirli Cüceler Rüyalar Ülkesinde* ("Aysecik and the Magic Dwarfs in the Land of Dreams"). This time Ayşecik would be transported from her mundane world to a magical one in an adaption of Victor Fleming's *The Wizard of Oz* (1939). *Pamuk Prenses's* seven dwarfs would return as well, with some minor recasting, as Ayşecik's versions of the Munchkins.

Os Trapalhões e o Mágico de Oróz ("The Tramps and the Wizard of Oróz")

INSPIRED BY: *The Wizard of Oz* (1939)
COUNTRY: Brazil
YEAR: 1984
PRODUCTION: Renato Aragão Produções Cinematográficas
DIRECTORS: Dedé Santana, Victor Lustosa
WRITERS: Gilvan Pereira, Victor Lustosa, Gracindo Júnior, Renato Aragão, Dedé Santana
STARS: Renato Aragão, Dedé Santana, Mussum, Zacarias, Dary Reis, Maurício do Valle

Five years into a drought in northeast Brazil, Didi (Renato Aragão) and his two housemates live a comically pitiful life, literally catapulting themselves into the sky

Os Trapalhões e o Mágico de Oróz ("The Tramps and the Wizard of Oróz")

to catch vultures for food. Fed up with their lot, they decide to take their chances and leave home for greener pastures in the town of Oróz. They put their house on wheels, hitch it to a mule, and tow it away. Along the road they meet a talking scarecrow (Zacarias) who watches over a desolate cornfield and laments his lack of a brain. After fending off an attack by vulture-men, the tramps decide to take the scarecrow with them. Stopping later to rest at an abandoned barn, they spy a stack of metal drums, one of which is alive. Dubbed "Cask" (Mussum), he believes he lacks a heart to be happy and joins the ragtag troupe as well.

The tramps finally reach Oróz, run by the despotic rancher Colonel Ferreira (Maurício do Valle) who greedily controls the town's meager water supply. The shabby travelers are soon arrested for stealing bread, but they work out a deal in which they'll be set free if Didi, Scarecrow, and Cask—accompanied by the spineless Sheriff Lion (Dedé Santana)—can find water for the town. Their first plan is to steal it from Ferreira, but this quickly goes awry and they're chased into the desert. There they meet a nomad who tells them of a hidden underground river and encourages them to speak to the Wizard of Oróz (Dary Reis).

The searchers soon literally stumble into the Wizard's underground lair. Scarecrow, Cask, and Lion ask him for a brain, a heart, and courage, respectively, but the Wizard is not convinced that they truly need those to be whole. Unfortunately, the Wizard also has no water to offer. Instead he tells them the legend of a giant, possibly magical water faucet and points them in its direction. However, their path is blocked by Colonel Ferreira and his goons, who have followed the tramps. A fight breaks out, and the Wizard sends Didi a magical bone which he uses to immobilize his enemies. Defeating them, Didi plays with the bone like the man-ape in *2001: A Space Odyssey*, throwing it into the air where it grows into a flying vehicle that transports the tramps to Rio de Janeiro. From the enormous statue of Christ the Redeemer, Didi spies the giant faucet in a town square. Yet even if they can steal it from the irate washerwomen who are currently using it, there's still no guarantee it will save Oróz from the drought....

∽∽∽

A little bit The Three Stooges and a little bit Abbott and Costello, Brazilian comedy troupe Os Trapalhões ("The Tramps") debuted in 1966 on TV Excelsior in the sketch comedy series *Adorável Trapalhão* ("The Adorable Tramps"). The team, ultimately made up of Dedé Santana, Mussum (Antônio Carlos Bernardes Gomes), Zacarias (Mauro Faccio Gonçalves), and leader Renato Aragão, won over audiences with its particular brand of clowning, physical humor, and fast-motion antics. The Tramps soon moved to TV Tupi, and then to prime time on major network Globo in the mid-1970s where their fame skyrocketed. The comedy quartet was massively popular with children, and they quickly parlayed their success into a series of theatrical features that made up seven of the top ten Brazilian films of the '70s.

Like the Abbott and Costello movies, The Tramps' films often parodied classic stories and box office hits. They were swept up in *Star Wars*, rescuing a princess from a stripey Vader clone, tussling with Jawas on a desert planet, and disco dancing with Chewbacca in a space nightclub. They also crashed a hot air balloon on the Plateau

Scarecrow (Zacarias), Sheriff Lion (Dedé Santana), Didi (Renato Aragão), Cask (Mussum), and the Wizard of Oróz (Dary Reis) in a publicity photo for *Os Trapalhões e o Mágico de Oróz* (1984).

of the Apes where they avoided the clutches of an ersatz General Ursus and boogied with apes in flares. There was always a lot of dancing.

But by the 1980s Aragão felt the need to be a little less irreverent and a little more relevant. Quoted in Mirian Ou and Alessandro Constantino Gamo's essay "Brazilian Children's Cinema in the 1990s," he explained, "Previously, I got inspiration from foreign stories—Ali Baba, Robin Hood, etc. Suddenly, that started to bother me. I thought I had the duty to use my popularity for children's benefit, addressing national subjects, even with a sociological punch." So in 1982's *Os Vagabundos Trapalhões*, the troupe explored the topic of homeless children in Brazil, while the same year's *Os Trapalhões na Serra Pelada* took on the gold rush at the Serra Pelada mine, notorious for its dangerous conditions and exploitation of workers. With 1984's *Os Trapalhões e o Mágico de Oróz*, Aragão would draw attention to the plight of his countrymen in the northeast.

Because of the El Niño effect and Atlantic Ocean surface temperatures, Brazil's northeast region is extremely prone to drought. From 1979 to 1983, nine states in the northeast experienced their longest dry spell in more than a century. Nearly 29 million people were affected and the region lost 10 million metric tons of crops. But the government, whose expenses were pushing $7.8 billion, was nevertheless loath to ask for aid from the international community. Speaking to *The New York Times*, Valfrido Salmito, coordinator of the country's relief effort, weakly justified its reluctance: "It is humiliating to ask for food. It's an embarrassing situation because Brazil is the fourth-largest producer of grains in the world." Yet meanwhile people were dying. Official records have placed the number of deaths in the region during that five-year period at 100,000, and outside research suggests a number closer to 700,000. Most of the victims were children; according to the Red Cross, infant mortality in Brazil reached higher levels than anywhere else in the world. Faced with such grim conditions, many inhabitants, desperate for a better life, fled the region for more developed areas. Aragão, who was born in the northeast, had a vested interest in making the rest of the country aware of this miserable situation.

Reimagining *The Wizard of Oz* (1939) for this purpose was not as strange as one might imagine. When L. Frank Baum penned *The Wonderful Wizard of Oz*, he drew on his experience living in drought-ridden South Dakota (then the Dakota Territory) for his description of Kansas: "The sun," he wrote, "had baked the plowed land into a gray mass, with little cracks running through it. Even the grass was not green, for the sun had burned the tops of the long blades until they were the same gray color to be seen everywhere" (12). Those very words could have described Orós, in the northeastern state of Ceará, where The Tramps chose to film *Os Trapalhões e o Mágico de Oróz*.

Of course, Aragão and company were still making a children's comedy, not an exposé. Their films were typically released during school holidays when kids were eager for escapism. Therefore, The Tramps limited the social commentary, choosing not to dwell too strongly on the harsh reality of life in the parched region. After an opening photo montage depicting existence in the wasteland as "life without life," they jumped straight to physical shenanigans, with Didi launching himself into the sky in a human-sized slingshot. The story, as with all of their films, featured very little dialogue and relied heavily on lengthy sequences of clowning and slapstick. "A child wants action and emotion," explained Aragão to *Jornal do Brasil*. "It's no use putting in a lot of dialogue, complicating things, because [kids] make a lot of noise in the theater and won't hear it."

However, the film ends with a final message not to the children, but to the Brazilian government. As a rainstorm saves the grateful citizens of Oróz, the text appears, "May the rain that fell on the barren northeastern land uphold the spirit of our authorities in the search of solutions for the drought." In fact, the government would implement new preventive measures the very next year as part of the Northeast Project, which incorporated rural development programs as well as improvements in sanitation, health, education, and land reform. Because of such efforts, inhabitants of the region have since survived even worse droughts than that of 1979–1983 without the widespread deaths caused by hunger and thirst. And they didn't even need a giant novelty faucet.

Vinni-Pukh ("Winnie the Pooh")

>COUNTERPART OF: *Winnie the Pooh and the Honey Tree* (1966)
>COUNTRY: USSR
>YEAR: 1969, 1971, 1972
>PRODUCTION: Soyuzmultfilm
>DIRECTOR: Fyodor Khitruk, Gennadiy Sokolskiy
>WRITERS: Boris Zakhoder, Fyodor Khitruk
>STARS: Vladimir Osenev, Evgeniy Leonov, Iya Savvina, Anatoliy Shchukin, Erast Garin, Zinaida Naryshkina

Winnie the Pooh is wandering the forest in search of something to eat when he hears buzzing coming from an enormous oak. He realizes there must be a beehive in the tree, which means honey! Unable to climb the trunk, Pooh borrows a balloon from his friend Piglet. He then covers himself in mud to disguise himself as a small black cloud. Unfortunately, when he floats up to the beehive, the bees are not deceived. Pooh therefore instructs Piglet to pace back and forth with an umbrella complaining that it looks like rain while Pooh sings a little cloud song, but even this does not work. As the bees become more aggressive, Pooh finally decides that these are "the wrong sort of bees" and probably make "the wrong sort of honey." He frantically instructs Piglet to pop the balloon with a cork rifle, and the two go in search of lunch elsewhere.

In their next adventure, Pooh and Piglet are on a morning stroll when Pooh decides it would be an excellent time to go visiting—and perhaps finagle a snack. So presently they arrive at the burrow of their friend Rabbit, who invites them in. As Pooh looks longingly at the larder, Rabbit gets the hint and offers them something to eat. Afterward, as the duo prepares to leave, Rabbit bids them good-bye, politely adding "if you're sure you don't want any more…." Pooh doesn't have to be asked twice, and to Rabbit's dismay his guests stay, devouring his honey and jam until there's none left. Pooh then decides it's truly time to go, but finds he is now too fat to get through the door! After much embarrassment Piglet and Rabbit pull him free and Pooh learns that guests should not stay too long if they don't want to get into a tight spot.

In the final story, Pooh's friend Eeyore the donkey has lost his tail. What's more, no one has remembered that today is also his birthday. Eeyore is resigned to his

Rabbit and Piglet attempt to get Winnie the Pooh out of a tight spot.

misery, but Pooh determines to get him a present. Pooh fetches a pot of honey, but on his way back he thoughtlessly eats it. Not missing a beat, he resolves to make the now-empty pot his gift and visits Owl to inscribe "Happy Birthday" on it. While there he notices something familiar about Owl's new bell-rope: it's Eeyore's tail. Meanwhile, Piglet has gotten Eeyore a balloon for his birthday. Unfortunately, in his rush to deliver it he accidentally pops it. Eeyore laments his deflated present, but he's soon delighted when he discovers that it's now just the right size to fit inside his new useful pot. He's happier still when Owl reunites him with his tail.

～～～

Much like Walt Disney's first run of *Winnie the Pooh* films in the 1960s and early '70s (before they were repackaged as a feature-length movie in 1977), the three Russian adventures of Winnie the Pooh were produced as a trilogy of standalone theatrical shorts. Yet while Disney's *Winnie the Pooh and the Honey Tree* (1966) was made first, the Slavic adaptations of the same stories were not copies, but rather came about entirely independently on the other side of the Iron Curtain.

It was during Khrushchev's Thaw, when foreign literature was more widely available in the Soviet Union, that poet and children's author Boris Zakhoder discovered A.A. Milne's Winnie the Pooh stories in English and fell in love with them. In 1960 he published his own unauthorized translations of *Winnie the Pooh* and *The House at Pooh Corner*, collected together as *Vinni-pukh I Vse-vse-vse* ("Winnie the Pooh and All-All-All"). Zakhoder took the unusual step of framing his version as a "retelling," taking various liberties with the language in order to make the stories more accessible to Russian children. His goal was to capture their essence if not their exact prose. *Vse-vse-vse* was an enormous success, making Winnie the Pooh, as Zakhoder would later say, "a most popular bear in a country where one can't complain about the lack of bears."

This new popularity caught the attention of filmmaker Fyodor Khitruk who had, years earlier, also enjoyed the stories in their native language. Khitruk was employed at Soyuzmultfilm, the state-run animation studio founded in 1936, and he reached out to Zakhoder in the late '60s with the aim of producing animated adventures of the silly old bear. To Zakhoder's chagrin, however, Khitruk preferred to work from the original English versions of the stories rather than Zakhoder's translations, beginning a polite but contentious partnership between the two men.

Their initial collaboration was titled simply *Vinni-Pukh* and was based on the first Pooh story, "In Which We Are Introduced to Winnie-the-Pooh and Some Bees, and the Stories Begin." Zakhoder, who had mostly restricted his alterations in *Vse-vse-vse* to presentation rather than content, preferred that the film's story hew as closely as possible to Milne, but Khitruk was keen to make one or two more fundamental changes.

In the original tales, Milne recounts to his son Christopher Robin the adventures of the boy's stuffed animals, and he frequently incorporates the child into the stories as well. However, Khitruk disliked the conceit of a child's toys coming to life, preferring instead to present Pooh, Piglet, and the other inhabitants of the Hundred Acre Wood as real creatures. "The first thing we did was remove [Christopher] Robin," explained Khitruk in a 2005 interview with Yuri Mikhailin. "We distributed all his scenes to the other characters. And it was the right move because he only underscored that there are people and there are little animals or toys. For us, it was all one world—the world of Winnie the Pooh. Without animals and people—just characters." Khitruk and Zakhoder opted to retain the narrator, but now the viewer was his audience.

For the look of the film, Khitruk took inspiration from United Productions of America, best known for *The Gerald McBoing-Boing Show* (1956) and *Mister Magoo* (1960). UPA's cartoons featured highly stylized characters, limited animation, and flat, sparse, abstract backgrounds resembling children's drawings. Unfortunately, achieving that aesthetic proved to be a bit of a problem. Khitruk originally hired artist Vladimir Zuykov, but his design for Pooh proved to be too detailed and intricate to replicate in over 10,000 frames of animation. Khitruk therefore replaced Zuykov with 27-year-old Eduard Nazarov, a previous collaborator, who provided streamlined, novel interpretations of the characters.

Departing wildly from E.H. Shepard's teddy-bear depiction of Pooh as featured in the books, Nazarov's more impish take on the character was short, brown, and very round, with a wide patch of dark fur around his eyes like a raccoon. He was also drawn without legs, his body floating just above his big feet. The cumulative effect resembled, as Zakhoder would later suggest, a skipping potato.

Eeyore enjoys his deflated balloon and very useful pot on his birthday, while Owl gifts him his own tail.

To provide Pooh's voice, Khitruk selected popular comic actor Yevgeny Leonov, already a familiar name in Soviet cartoons. Leonov brought a mischievousness and dry sense of humor to the bear of little brain, providing a distinct contrast to Disney's sentimental portrayal. Even so, the director feared Leonov's voice was too deep until his sound designer came to the rescue, speeding up the recordings by 30 percent for an appropriately higher pitch.

The film was a success, and Khitruk and Zakhoder followed *Vinni-Pukh* with two sequels. *Vinni-Pukh idyot v gosti* ("Winnie the Pooh Pays a Visit," 1971) was based on the story "In Which Pooh Goes Visiting and Gets into a Tight Place," while *Vinni-Pukh i den zabot* ("Winnie the Pooh and the Busy Day," 1972) combined both "In Which Eeyore Loses a Tail and Pooh Finds One" and "In Which Eeyore has a Birthday and Gets Two Presents." By the third film, however, the creative differences between Khitruk and Zakhoder had proven too great a strain, and the pair parted ways, bringing the series to an end.

Nazarov would later lament the government's failure to secure the proper copyrights to Winnie the Pooh, as it made the shorts ineligible for international film festivals. Nevertheless, the trilogy was beloved in its home country, and in 1976 it earned Khitruk the USSR State Prize. Khitruk further recalls that when he later visited Walt Disney Studios, Wolfgang Reitherman, the director of *Winnie the Pooh and the Honey Tree*, admitted that he preferred the Russian version to his own.

Although no further Vinni-Pukh films were ever made, fans of the series can see Nazarov's visions of Milne's other characters like Tigger and Kanga in a special "Soyuzmultfilm Presents" edition of *Vinni-pukh I Vse-vse-vse* illustrated by Nazarov.

4

Monsters, Maniacs, and the Macabre

Aatank ("Terror")

INSPIRED BY: *Jaws* (1975)
COUNTRY: India
YEAR: 1996
PRODUCTION: Bemisal Films
DIRECTORS: Prem Lalwani, Desh Mukherjee
WRITER: Sachin Bhowmick
STARS: Dharmendra, Amjad Khan, Vinod Mehra, Ravi Kishan, Ranjeet, Hema Malini

Children Jesu and Peter are best friends who enjoy getting into mischief, like joyriding in stolen fishing boats. Jesu is an orphan, but he's adopted by Peter's mother after Jesu saves her son's life. His new family doesn't last, however; their mother dies and Peter is taken away to live with relatives. Jesu stays in the Goan fishing village, growing into a brawny adult (Dharmendra) who protects his community from local gangster Alphonso (Amjad Khan).

When a young boy named Johnny discovers a cache of black pearls off the coast, his father Philip attempts to sell this valuable information to Alphonso. Unfortunately, Philip is a poor judge of character and gets murdered for his trouble. Johnny, left with only a negligent stepmother, is informally adopted by Jesu, while Alphonso uses his new knowledge to start up a secret, illegal pearl farm.

Soon Peter (Vinod Mehra) returns to the village for his wedding. During the boisterous reception he drinks too much, prompting his bride to drag him to the beach for some fresh air. She takes the opportunity to go for a moonlight swim, but in a tragic twist of fate she's devoured by a giant shark! The local police are concerned, but they don't prevent Jesu and Peter from going out on a boat, where Peter too becomes shark food. Finally the authorities declare the ocean off limits, threatening the fishing village's income. Alphonso, on the other hand, uses the distraction to his advantage, intensifying his pearl diving operation.

The gangster's activities have not gone entirely unnoticed, however, as undercover CBI officer Mahesh Kumar (Ravi Kishan) has arrived in town to investigate him. Kumar spies on the pearl divers' camp, but when he sneaks in to retrieve evidence, he's captured by Alphonso's goons. With effort, he manages to escape and call for backup.

Meanwhile, all attempts to kill the man-eating shark have failed. When Johnny and a friend unwisely go out on a raft and the friend becomes yet another victim, Jesu determines to destroy the beast once and for all and sets out in a boat with his spear. At the beach, Kumar gets his reinforcements to arrest the pearl diving gang, but Alphonso escapes in a speedboat with his loot. Unfortunately for the crook, he heads right into the path of Jesu on his Ahabian quest for vengeance.

∼∼∼

Back in 1975, when Universal Pictures announced a summer release date for a killer shark movie, it was a bad sign. Summer was a cinematic graveyard—a dumping ground for films that distributors considered inferior. But 28-year-old Steven Spielberg's *Jaws* turned out to be an unprecedented success, becoming the highest grossing film to date and earning a place in movie history as the first summer blockbuster.

Shrewd producers around the world quickly latched on like remoras, feeding off *Jaws*'s fame with lower-budget cash-ins. Outside of Hollywood, Italy was the most prolific with offerings like *Tentacoli* (*Tentacles*, 1977), *L'ultimo squalo* (*The Last Shark*, 1981), and *Shark: Rosso nell'oceano* (*Devil Fish*, 1984), but Mexico also had *Tintorera* (1977), Brazil had parody *Bacalhau* ("Codfish," 1975), and even Turkish crime flick *Çöl* ("The Desert," 1983) crowbarred a shark attack into its finale, complete with an excerpt from the *Jaws* score. India's Bollywood, on the other hand, despite a reputation for mining American box office hits, appeared to sit out the killer shark frenzy, not releasing its sole entry *Aatank* until 1996. But in truth the project had been lying in wait for nearly 20 years.

Aatank began in 1979 as the brainchild of Desh Mukherjee, a respected art director turned filmmaker. He and screenwriter Sachin Bhowmick adapted it from a Bengali short story called "Hangor" ("Shark"). Like *Jaws*, the tale featured a shark threatening a village's livelihood and killing a woman during a midnight swim, but its similarity to Spielberg's film effectively ended there.

While some might still have viewed *Aatank* as simply another cheap cash-in, Mukherjee's own vision was rather more lavish. He touted the film as the first Indian production to feature substantial underwater photography and he set out to shoot it in 70mm. At a time when many Bollywood films were written piecemeal on set, he also insisted on a full screenplay before rolling cameras. Furthermore, as a firm believer in storyboarding—another rarity among his contemporaries—Mukherjee committed every shot of the film to paper before stepping behind the lens.

Unfortunately, fabricating the film's requisite 30-foot shark was outside the wheelhouse of Bollywood technicians. Mukherjee therefore set his sights abroad, drawing on producer Tapan Guha's connections in Japan to hire, according to a 2016 account, "the high-tech Toyo Studio." Likely, however, the Japanese company was actually *Toho*, the outfit behind the Godzilla franchise with a decades-long reputation for manufacturing giant movie monsters. Communicating through interpreters, the Indian and Japanese crews worked together to construct the full-sized shark as well as a separate head and tail. The film's cast was then transported to a beach resort in Shimoda where Mukherjee shot the shark attack sequences. The whole endeavor took three months.

Sadly, before the movie could be completed, Mukherjee ran out of money. With no recourse, the mega production suddenly found itself abandoned.

This was not an uncommon occurrence. At the time, filmmaking in India was a particularly risky business. Popular movie stars commanded large fees, and distributors, who were once responsible for a film's entire budget, were now only liable for half. Moreover, Bollywood was denied official industry status until 2001, so producers were legally prevented from securing institutional financing. Without access to bank credit, they were forced to seek capital from less reputable sources like loan sharks and organized crime. Many relied on a shaky system of promissory notes from private investors. Budgets were often secured just a portion at a time, and at any point funding could fall through, delaying or canceling a film. Such was the fate of *Aatank*.

Poster art for *Aatank* (1996). Because the film was completed almost twenty years after it began, star Dharmendra's age fluctuates wildly throughout its runtime.

In the 1990s, however, the unfinished reels came up for auction and were purchased by Prem Lalwani's company Bemisal Films. With Dharmendra agreeing to reprise his role to complete the movie, Lalwani took over the reins as director without the cooperation of Mukherjee. He set out to finish it on the cheap, concocting a new plot thread about a CBI officer to fill out the run time and moving the remainder of the shoot to Madh Island in northern Mumbai.

Unfortunately, by the time production finally resumed there was a major problem. Multiple cast members had passed away, including Amjad Khan, who played the villain Alphonso; Vinod Mehra, who portrayed the adult Peter; and Keshto Mukherjee, who played the hapless Philip. Since their scenes hadn't been completed before production halted, Lalwani was forced to employ creative measures. Peter and Philip's pending death scenes were shot with the aid of body doubles and strategic camerawork, while actor Ranjeet was cast as Alphonso's number one henchman, allowing him to do the legwork that his boss might otherwise have done. Lalwani then had the late actors dubbed by soundalikes during post-production.

Aatank was finally released in February of 1996. The heavily compromised film only managed to recoup ₹7 million of its estimated ₹15 million budget. Audiences never saw the intended sequences with prolific "item girl" Helen and American actor Tom Alter, cast in '79 as an expert shark hunter à la *Jaws*'s Quint, ultimately only received an uncredited, blink-and-you-miss-him appearance in the finale. But unlike other abandoned Bollywood movies, a glimpse of the original vision for the film still exists in the form of Mukherjee's meticulous storyboards. Some of these can be seen in Mukherjee's forthcoming biography by his daughter, Adite Banerjie.

Anyab ("Fangs")

INSPIRED BY: *The Rocky Horror Picture Show* (1975)
COUNTRY: Egypt
YEAR: 1981
DIRECTOR: Mohammed Shebl
WRITERS: Hassn Abd Raboo, Tarek Sharara, Mohammed Shebl
STARS: Ahmed Adawiyya, Hassan Al Imam, Ali El Haggar, Mona Gabr, Haddey Saddekk, Tal'tt Zean

Warning: The opening credits of this film feature the unsimulated murder of a chicken.

Two young, normal, healthy kids, Ali (Ali El Haggar) and Mona (Mona Gabr), are driving at night to a New Year's Eve party. Traveling through a storm on a deserted road, they get a flat tire. Ali doesn't have a spare, so they decide to make the wet trek to the isolated, ominous mansion they passed some distance back. Greeted at the door by a hunchback servant, Shalaf (Haddey Saddekk), they ask to use the phone. Unfortunately, it appears to be out of order, although in reality Shalaf has covertly disconnected it. Thus stranded, Ali and Mona are invited to stay the night and join in the festivities.

They have arrived in the middle of a ghoulish—but funky!—masquerade. The guests are wearing Halloween masks, skeleton costumes, metallic and leopard-print spandex, cloaks, and loads of face paint. Absorbed in their spooky dance, they appear to take no notice of the nervous newcomers until the arrival of their host: none other than Count Dracula (Ahmed Adawiyya)! The Count beckons Mona to dance, and he seems to have a hypnotic effect on her.

Afterward, Ali and Mona share a strange, macabre supper with the household, during which Dracula seems to have an uncanny mental control over his guests. He also spends much of his time leering at Mona. Following dinner, Dracula invites the couple into his den, where we notice from portraits on the wall that Mona bears a striking resemblance to Dracula's former vampire bride. He plays videotapes of old movies while continuing to press his psychic hold over Mona, whom he plots to turn into a vampire.

Meanwhile, one of Dracula's more ambitious underlings (Tal'tt Zean), frustrated with his master's tyranny, plots to overthrow him. Once Ali and Mona have been shown to their rooms, he locks Ali's door and creeps into Mona's room, attempting to abduct her. However, Dracula crawls up the side of the building, transforms into a cloud of smoke, and enters the room himself, confronting his disciple.

Recognizing in this distraction an opportunity for redemption, Shalaf frees Ali and Mona and shows them the way out, remaining himself in order to kill Dracula. With freedom within reach, Ali and Mona must decide whether to seize it, or go back and risk their lives to help Shalaf destroy Dracula.

~~~

Beginning life as a stage play, *The Rocky Horror Show*, about an engaged couple entangled in a household of warped aliens and their hunky Frankenstein-esque experiment, discovered a life its creators never anticipated. The film adaptation's massive success at midnight showings led to a sequel, a TV remake, and four decades of interactive screenings with audience participation and accompanying fan performances. It was big. And it was exactly the kind of movie that Egypt would *never* make.

The world's first Arabic-language film industry, Egyptian local cinema dates from the early 20th century. Over the last 100 years Egypt has produced films in a variety of genres from musicals to melodramas, gangster flicks, and social dramas. Predominantly these were original movies, although filmmakers would occasionally remake the work of such American directors as Frank Capra, Brian de Palma, and Francis Ford Coppola. Yet by 1981, the number of *horror* films produced in Egypt—remake or original—was zero. The staples of horror, monsters and ghouls, were borderline religious transgressions. And while *Rocky Horror* is best classified as a musical comedy, its roots are firmly planted in horror. It's right there in the title. Therefore writer/director Mohammed Shebl, a passionate horror fan, took a very real risk when he set out to adapt it.

As *Anyab* begins, it's all but identical. The opening credits play over the iconic disembodied singing mouth—slightly less disembodied due to the obvious black face paint surrounding it. A sardonic narrator still provides the story's framing device. The young couple share a peppy love song. And their road trip, the flat tire, the approach to the mansion, the hunchback servant, and the party they interrupt are all painstakingly reproduced from Jim Sharman's 1975 film. After that, however, everything takes a jump to the left.

Instead of the bisexual alien transvestite Dr. Frank-N-Furter, Ali and Mona's dubious host is the vampire prince of darkness! Dracula has sinister designs on both of his guests, but he has no lab, no artificial man, no string of jilted former lovers, no extracurricular hanky-panky with the lead couple, and no risqué revue. There's also a distinct lack of transvestites; just a bevy of glam-rock vampires.

These alterations are partly because in its original form, *Rocky Horror* ticks at least half the boxes of contemporary Egyptian censors' no-nos. The law forbade depiction of nudity, undue focus on erotic body parts, obscene language, disrespecting the sanctity of marriage, and homosexuality. That necessitated a complete rewrite of the second and third acts, and totally different central themes.

Whereas *Rocky Horror* satirizes middle class taboos about sexuality—untouchable in an Egyptian film—Shebl uses the material to explore middle class fears of financial instability kindled by Egypt's recent foray into Capitalism. In 1974 Egyptian President Anwar Sadat introduced his policy of *al-infitah* ("opening-up"), which was intended to encourage private investments and promote market economics after years of a government-managed economy. However, in practice it had the major drawback of fostering corruption and graft. Thus, in one of *Anyab*'s particularly meta sequences, Dracula argues with the narrator that vampires don't exist. The narrator responds with an extended series of vignettes showcasing greedy tradesmen—*real-life* vampires—who ruthlessly suck money out of the film's working-class heroes. For emphasis, all of these swindlers are portrayed by Dracula.

Some of *Anyab*'s other differences can be explained by its unique set of inspirations. Richard O'Brien wrote the original *Rocky Horror* out of his love for classic genre films, from *King Kong* (1933) and *Forbidden Planet* (1956) to 1950s rock-and-roll and biker movies. Mohammed Shebl's influences, on the other hand, like Hammer's *Dracula* (1958) and Werner Herzog's *Nosferatu the Vampyre* (1979)—both of whom have portraits in Adawiyya-Dracula's den—were from a later generation. Shebl even channeled more patently self-aware material, lifting music from monster sitcom *The Munsters* (1964), punctuating fight scenes with "BAM!" title cards à la the 1966 *Batman* TV series, and even clothing Dracula's disgruntled disciple in a *Rocky Horror Picture Show* T-shirt. He also pulled music from *The Man with the Golden Gun* (1974); *Jaws* (1975); *The Good, the Bad, and The Ugly* (1966); *Young Frankenstein* (1974); and *The Pink Panther* (1963), among others. Copyright infringement, at least, was clearly not a concern.

Unfortunately, *Anyab* was not a commercial success. It was too lowbrow for Egypt's elite, who suggested the film was better suited to the taste of the Gulf States—leaning on stereotypes of their citizens as vulgar and unsophisticated.

By all rights it's a marvel that *Anyab* even exists. It's a pop culture hodgepodge in an unproven genre that barely skirts cultural taboos. Yet the fruit of Shebl's labor, passion, and his own money was not only completed but passed the scrutiny of two levels of Egyptian censorship. It's a triumph that would impress even Dr. Frank-N-Furter. Censorship was never really his forte.

Bach ke Zara ("Tread Carefully")

INSPIRED BY: *The Evil Dead* (1981)
COUNTRY: India
YEAR: 2008
PRODUCTION: Jaya Films
DIRECTOR: Salim Raza
WRITER: Salim Raza
STARS: Amit, Rajesh, Jayesh Shah, Mohan Dev, Neha Joshi, Mohak, Sheril Singh, Shree Khan, Saba Rehmehan, Rakhi Sawant

An archaeologist unearths a sinister-looking grimoire. Taking the book home, he reads from it aloud and unwittingly releases an ancient evil. The malevolent force possesses his wife, transforming her into a murderous demon, and the scholar is forced to kill and bury her. But the evil is relentless; the wife crawls from her grave and dismembers the man with an axe....

Years later, five twenty-somethings are camping at a lake near the now-abandoned house. As couples Sunny, Tina, Raja, and Sheena drink beer and make out by the water, their friend Sweety is lured into the woods by the song of a ghostly woman in white. The apparition leads her to the late archaeologist's dilapidated villa, and the building itself goads her inside. Terrified, she flees, an invisible evil at her heels. When she relates the experience to her friends, they merely laugh. Worse, when a witch doctor appears and warns them away from the house, they take it as a challenge. Crossing the only bridge to the villa, they enter and settle in for the night. But Sweety wakes with a start to witness a chained cellar door burst open on its own.

Sunny and Raja explore the newfound basement, discovering a phonograph, a record, and the strange book. Bringing them upstairs, they play the record. It contains the ghostly woman's eerie song and a demonic recording of the book's incantations. Sweety is frightened and returns to her room—but is soon drawn outdoors by the mysterious ghost. As she wanders into the woods, the trees suddenly come to life. Branches and vines seize her and tear away her clothes. Wrestling free, she staggers back to the house. She demands to leave, but the group discovers that the bridge has collapsed, effectively trapping them all in the villa.

The recording of the mantras has done its work; the unleashed evil possesses Sweety, turning her into a ghoul that attacks Tina and Raja. Unwilling to kill Sweety, her friends lock her in the cellar. But soon Sheena turns as well, forcing Raja to destroy her with an axe. Eventually Raja flees into the woods where he too is attacked by the trees. Tina's possession follows. Sunny kills and buries her, but she refuses to stay down. And with no apparent means of escape, Sunny is forced to fend off an ever-increasing number of ghouls as he desperately tries to discover a way to stop the evil at its source.

~~~

Billed as "the ultimate experience in grueling terror," Sam Raimi's 1981 indie gorefest *The Evil Dead* fast became a cult sensation spawning two sequels, a remake, a TV series, and a fistful of videogames. It particularly hit big in India, arriving on rental shelves at an opportune moment. In 1982, ownership of color TVs and VCRs surged as the government relaxed import restrictions prior to the New Delhi-hosted Asian Games. By 1984, the number of television sets in the country had leapt from five thousand to five million. And in 1985, one estimate placed the total number of VCRs at 1.5 million. This spread of videocassette technology created a burgeoning market for home video sales and rentals. What's more, consumers' ability to watch movies in the privacy of their own homes allowed them to view adult-oriented content that was prohibited in cinemas. *The Evil Dead*, first released on VHS in 1983 and full of blood, guts, demons, and a hint of sex, was virtually tailor-made for the new demand.

Its popularity also had a visible influence on locally-produced horror movies. Joginder Shelly's psychedelic *Pyasa Shaitan* ("Thirsty Devil," 1984) and *Aadamkhor Hasina* ("Man-Eating Beauty," 2002), for instance, both restaged *The Evil Dead*'s infamous tree attack. A.G. Baby's *Veendum Lisa* ("Return of Lisa," 1987) copied both the tree sequence and the demonic makeup effects. And D. Ranga Rao's ultra-low budget,

Telugu-language remake *Bhayam* ("The Fear," 2007), a contemporary of *Bach ke Zara*, lifted not only its plot but also footage from its sequel. Even to this day, Indian VCD and DVD distributors crib *The Evil Dead*'s promotional art for the covers of unrelated films.

But when first-time director Salim Raza set out to completely remake *The Evil Dead* for Hindi-speaking audiences in 2007, he was asking for trouble. He was making a film for cinemas, not home video, and the movie's content would have been too graphic for mainstream Bollywood. Fortunately, however, Raza wasn't making a mainstream movie, but a "C-grade" movie. Unlike big-budget A-grade movies and the B-grade films that attempt to do the same with less, C-grades play by their own rules. Cheaply produced for audiences in small towns and rural areas, they cheerfully disregard Bollywood's conservative taboos if it will please a paying crowd. In an interview for website *Mid-Day*, director and film historian Ashim Ahluwalia explained that their target audiences "are the people who find [superstars] Aamir Khan or Amitabh Bachchan boring and would rather see a [female demon] rip someone's head off or have an erotic shower."

So with his hands untied Raza expanded on *The Evil Dead*'s story with added sequences of sex and violence. Whereas the original film reveals the fate of the archaeologist only through entries in an audio diary, Raza devoted the first ten minutes of his film to showing these events in detail. He added an extended sex scene between the archaeologist and his wife and followed the invocations from the book with the gruesome possession, stabbing, and dismemberment of the hapless couple. Then in short order he shifts focus to the campers and their racy lakeside lovemaking.

Also original to Raza's version is the mysterious ghost and her somber musical number. Elements like these were added because Raza wanted "song[s], romance, and emotion" in addition to *The Evil Dead*'s horror elements—a curry of

The other *Evil Dead* musical! Pressbook for *Bach ke Zara* (2008).

genres mixed according to the demanding tastes of his audience. Indian filmgoers, explains Raza, "like all [of the] ingredients in one dish." It's no surprise, then, that genre-blended movies are named after the Hindi word for a blend of spices: *masala*. And while it may seem strange to add songs to *The Evil Dead*, the success of Canadian stage play *Evil Dead: The Musical* suggests otherwise.

The singing ghost notwithstanding, the rest of the movie is a meticulous recreation of Raimi's film. It's nearly shot-for-shot, line-for-line, and imitates the look of *The Evil Dead* from the makeup effects to the prop design. However, this slavish attention to detail also introduced some novel problems. The burial scenes, for example, stand out in a predominantly Hindu country where the dead are traditionally cremated. So to account for it Raza made the characters Christian, even though Christianity is practiced by just 2.3 percent of India's population.

After production wrapped, Raza felt the film still needed something and decided to add a last-minute "item number." Ubiquitous in Indian cinema, item numbers are sexy musical sequences included purely for entertainment and which rarely serve the story. They're also used heavily in the film's marketing. But since Raza had already completed principal photography, this new number couldn't feature any of the primary cast or locations. So instead he cast popular "item girl" Rakhi Sawant and shot, essentially, an unconnected music video, crowbarring it into the film between the death of the archaeologist and the introduction of the main characters.

Unfortunately, *Bach ke Zara* made back less than 60 percent of its budget at the box office, and Raza wouldn't direct again until his 2012 variation-on-a-theme, *Adventure of Haunted House*. However, *The Evil Dead* continues to be an inescapable presence in Indian cinema. In the country's remaining VCD shops, and now on the YouTube channels of Bollywood studios, horror films new and old are hawked to consumers with Photoshopped artwork swiped from *The Evil Dead* and its sequels.

Drakula İstanbul'da ("Dracula in Istanbul")

COUNTERPART OF: *Dracula* (1931)
COUNTRY: Turkey
YEAR: 1953
PRODUCTION: And Film
DIRECTOR: Mehmet Muhtar
WRITERS: Turgut Demirağ, Ümit Deniz, Mehmet Muhtar
STARS: Bülent Oran, Atıf Kaptan, Ayfer Feray, Annie Ball, Cahit Irgat, Münir Ceyhan, Kemal Emin Bara

Young attorney Azmi (Bülent Oran) has traveled to Transylvania to finalize the purchase of some Istanbul property by the reclusive Count Dracula (Atıf Kaptan). He arrives at his client's castle late at night and is greeted by his suave but strange host. The next morning, however, the Count is nowhere about. Indeed, Dracula is apparently never seen by day. Moreover, Azmi gradually finds himself a prisoner in this increasingly sinister castle, where dark passageways and secret rooms contain strange forces that spy on him and thirst after his blood.

In the library, Azmi finds a book on superstitious beliefs. Flipping to a chapter on vampires, he learns to his horror that one such creature is none other than Dracula! Azmi nervously searches the house and discovers a room containing shipping crates full of soil. Lifting the lid from one, he discovers Count Dracula inside, apparently asleep. On the verge of madness, Azmi picks up a shovel and attempts to murder the fiend.

Some days later in Istanbul, cabaret dancer Güzin (Annie Ball), anxiously awaiting her husband Azmi, accepts an invitation to stay with her friend Şadan (Ayfer Feray). Walking by the sea, Güzin and Şadan encounter couriers unloading boxes of earth from a desolate ship just arrived from Transylvania. One night thereafter, Güzin wakes to find Şadan missing. She discovers her friend at the seaside, a dark figure looming over her that quickly vanishes. Şadan has become inexplicably anemic, so her doctor calls in a colleague, Dr. Naci Eren (Kemal Emin Bara), who instantly recognizes the signs of vampirism.

Güzin soon receives word that Azmi is in a hospital near the Turkish border, brought there after Hungarian police discovered him raving. She leaves to retrieve him, but during her absence Şadan succumbs to the recurrent visits of the vampire—Dracula himself—and finally dies upon Güzin and Azmi's return. Worried that Şadan may revive as a ghoul like Dracula, Dr. Eren determines to destroy her in her coffin. While the men go to Şadan's crypt, Dracula pays a visit to Güzin. Azmi arrives just in time to fight him off, and then he and his fellows search for the vampire among his Istanbul properties. But the monster has not yet given up on Güzin and arrives after her performance at the theater....

∼∼∼

The noble but sinister Count Dracula (Atıf Kaptan). Two years later, Kaptan would appear in another Universal-Horror-adjacent film, *Görünmeyen Adam İstanbul'da* (1955), a reworking of H.G. Wells's *The Invisible Man*.

In 1931 Bela Lugosi's suave looks, widow's peak, and Hungarian accent cemented a particular image of Dracula in the popular consciousness, despite the fact that Universal's *Dracula* bore only a passing resemblance to Bram Stoker's original novel. The film was adapted instead from the American rewrite of a British stage play, which had itself heavily reworked the story to utilize only a few sets. Its frugality made it an ideal project for an impoverished film studio in the grip of the Great Depression, but not an especially accurate retelling of the Gothic classic. A faithful adaptation wouldn't be produced for another twenty-two years—which makes it surprising that it would be based on a totally different book.

Stoker's novel wouldn't even be published in Turkish until its centennial anniversary in 1998. *Drakula İstanbul'da* is based instead on Ali Rıza Seyfioğlu's *Kazıklı Voyvoda* ("The Impaler Prince")—a pirated version of *Dracula*. In 1928 the author and poet not only translated Stoker's novel into Turkish, but transformed it, passing it off as an original work. He drastically rewrote the story, omitting large portions, adding new scenes, transplanting the action from London to modern-day Istanbul, and peppering the book with passages of nationalism. His heroes became veterans of the Turkish War of Independence, and their adversary was explicitly identified, for the first time, as Turkey's hereditary enemy: Vlad the Impaler.

The assertion that Bram Stoker's title character is actually Vlad Țepeș, 15th-century prince of Wallachia, was generally thought to date back to 1956 and Bacil Kirtley's essay "Dracula, the Monastic Chronicles and Slavic Folklore." But Seyfioğlu made the connection independently 28 years earlier, retelling the story from the unique perspective of a people once routed by the real-life Dracula. He even wrote a new chapter detailing the atrocities committed by Țepeș upon emissaries of the Ottoman Empire.

This revised, nationalized version of the book was adapted for the screen just as homegrown genre movies were beginning to find a wider audience in Turkey. The film was spearheaded by producer Turgut Demirağ, one of Turkey's cinematic pioneers. Traveling to America in 1939 for an education in agricultural engineering, Demirağ had quickly abandoned the field to study cinema at the University of Southern California. After college he took a job at Paramount, learning on-the-ground filmmaking under such luminaries as Cecil B. DeMille and Leo McCarey. He eventually returned to Turkey in 1945 where he founded his own company, And Film, and produced a number of movies based on Turkish novels.

Demirağ had never seen the 1931 *Dracula* when he set out to adapt *Kazıklı Voyvoda* (though he eventually watched it on American television in the '70s), but he took much the same risk as its producer Carl Laemmle, Jr. Universal daringly showcased "real" supernatural terrors at a time when most Hollywood movies safely explained their spooks away as fabrications. *Drakula İstanbul'da* was similarly bold just by being a horror film at all. It was only the second of its kind ever made in Turkey, after 1949's now-lost "old dark house" movie *Çığlık* ("Scream"), and it was unclear if there would even be an audience for such a film.

Moreover, Demirağ's budgets were thirty to fifty percent higher than those of his Turkish contemporaries, making *Drakula İstanbul'da* even more of a gamble. However, the extra money allowed art director Sohban Koloğlu to build comparatively lavish sets for the castle interiors, the cemetery, and the music hall. He populated the castle with elaborate suits of armor—made by pouring plaster over wire armatures and painting them bronze. And for the exterior shots he constructed a mockup of Castle Dracula that was so impressive, other filmmakers asked where they had managed to find a European fortress in Turkey.

Nevertheless, as the domestic film industry was still in its infancy, sometimes

Drakula İstanbul'da ("Dracula in Istanbul")

even mundane challenges required unusually creative solutions. Koloğlu famously manufactured fog for a cemetery scene by having dozens of crewmembers lay on the ground, mouths full of cigarettes, furiously puffing smoke into the frame!

While *Drakula İstanbul'da* wasn't the first movie based on *Dracula*, or even the first "bootleg" adaptation (that honor goes to F.W. Murnau's 1922 *Nosferatu*), it can still boast several other innovations. It was the first film to show Dracula with canine fangs as well as the first to depict him crawling head-first down his castle wall. It was also the only adaptation to date that faithfully recreated Harker's imprisonment in Castle Dracula, Lucy's extended entanglement with the vampire (and her subsequent destruction), and Dracula's shell game of sanctuaries.

Of course, there were still numerous changes, many of which were already present in *Kazıklı Voyvoda*. Gone is Dracula's mad servant Renfield and the final journey to Transylvania in pursuit of the monster. The grim voyage of the ghost ship *Demeter* is similarly omitted. Concessions were also made for Turkey's Islamic culture, where crucifixes and sacramental bread would be unlikely vampire deterrents. In *Kazıklı Voyvoda*, passages from the Quran replaced the Christian artifacts as weapons against the undead, but in *Drakula İstanbul'da* the heroes' only defense is garlic. And in a departure from both versions of the book, Mina has been transformed into a music hall dancer, offering filmmakers the perfect excuse for sexy dance numbers.

Little is known about how the film was received by audiences, but contemporary critic Sozai Solelli felt that it wasn't sufficiently scary and focused his review on its continuity errors. However, writer Ümit Deniz won an award for his screenplay, and the film remains to this day one of the most accurate adaptations of *Dracula* ever made. It did not, however, kick off a wave of other Turkish horror movies, and over the next half-century only a handful were produced.

Turkish poster for *Drakula İstanbul'da* (1953).

Nevertheless, the genre eventually found a foothold in the early 2000s and quickly became wildly popular. Today Turkish studios release 20 to 25 horror movies each year.

Kader Diyelim ("Let's Say It's Fate")

INSPIRED BY: *Psycho* (1960)
COUNTRY: Turkey
YEAR: 1995
PRODUCTION: Alemdar Filmcilik
DIRECTOR: Mehmet Alemdar
WRITER: Mehmet Alemdar
STARS: Vahdet Vural, Neslihan Sezer, Jülide Dalyan, Betül Kolsuz, Hidayet Pelit, M. Alpay Ziyal, Nesli Güney, Zafer Atlı

Bahar is getting tired of clandestine hotel trysts. Her lover Orhan (Vahdet Vural) claims he'd like to make an honest woman out of her, but alimony payments to his ex-wife have left him in debt. As Orhan leaves for the airport to catch a flight home, Bahar resignedly dresses for work. A secretary at a real estate office, she watches her boss close a deal with a rich, boisterous client who has just purchased a villa with cash. The boss asks her to deposit the tempting stack of money at the bank, and Bahar suddenly sees the solution to all her problems. She asks for the day off, packs the wad of cash in her luggage, and skips town.

Driving to see Orhan, she stops off for the night in Ovacık at the Hotel Oriental, run by a pleasant but nervous young man named Naci (Zafer Atlı). She's the only guest, and the proprietor invites her to share his homey supper. As they talk, Bahar realizes the terrible mistake she's made by stealing. But before she has a chance to return and atone for her sins, Naci stabs her to death in the shower and carefully disposes of the body.

Meanwhile, Orhan has been surprisingly unfaithful to his late girlfriend. For one thing, he's been seeing another woman, Gülnur, behind her back. Then, on the night Bahar stops at the hotel, Orhan goes out drinking and is struck by a car. Unharmed, he quickly begins yet another romance with the lady behind the wheel.

Presently the authorities inform Orhan of Bahar's theft and disappearance. The detective assigned to the case tracks her to the Hotel Oriental, where Naci denies having seen her. However, the cop persists, prompting Naci to bludgeon him to death. Orhan does some investigating of his own, visiting the hotel with Gülnur, and then again later with Bahar's co-worker. His second visit proves fruitful; he uncovers a scrap of paper that proves Bahar was there. Now they have to find a way to get justice for Bahar without getting themselves murdered by the increasingly paranoid Naci.

~~~

Mehmet Alemdar, like Alfred Hitchcock, was born the son of a greengrocer. Raised in the Black Sea port city of Trabzon, he received his first glimpse of Istanbul and its exciting, burgeoning movie scene in the 1960s during his mandatory military service. Determined to make a name for himself in pictures, he left his hometown in 1970, at age 24, and set up shop in Istanbul as the Alemdar Film Production Company.

However, he had no practical training as a filmmaker. So for two years Alemdar apprenticed under Semih Evin, a well-known director of melodramas, before working with other established filmmakers like Çetin İnanç and Tevfik Fikret Uçak.

Alemdar wouldn't direct his own films until 1984. But by then Turkey's movie industry was in the beginning of its death throes. Television, home video, and piracy had taken a massive toll on the film sector, and by the 1990s domestic film production was effectively dead. Alemdar barely stayed afloat by making his movies on shoestring budgets, often shooting on videotape instead of film. His primary audience was the Turkish diaspora in Europe, where Turkish video rentals of any kind offered a welcome slice of home.

It was under these threadbare conditions that Alemdar was approached by producer Alpay Ziyal in 1995. Ziyal was a huge Hitchcock fan; he had even traveled to London to meet the famous director in person. His dream was to remake one of Hitchcock's movies, which was something of a risk since horror was an unpopular genre in Turkey. Moreover, given the state of the industry, Ziyal needed someone who could make it on the cheap. Alemdar fit the bill.

Setting their sights above the home video market, their aim was a theatrical movie that would attract a distributor. Unfortunately, they didn't have the budget for industry-standard 35mm film stock. Instead they found a 16mm camera and, opting for its more economical, semi-professional format, they scrounged just enough raw film to make a feature. *Psycho* (1960) was their template, and Alemdar spent a month transcribing and adapting it.

To be more accurate: he turned it into a musical.

Kader Diyelim was never intended to be Turkey's first horror musical, but there was an old debt that had to be repaid. Ten years earlier, Alemdar had been set to direct an *arabesk*—a popular genre featuring Arabic style songs—for which he'd paid prominent folk singer Vahdet Vural to star. Due to financial problems, however, the film was never made. Still owing the director a movie in 1995, Vural offered to star in *Kader Diyelim*. Alemdar was understandably skeptical, but since Vural was still a celebrity and using him would save money on a lead actor, he consented. He reworked the script, added love songs, and expanded Vural's role. It was a change Alemdar himself regrets, calling it "extraordinary and ridiculous."

However, in reimagining his protagonist, he also created a hero with a dark side. Alemdar, a self-described moralist with a conservative upbringing, wanted to make a statement about the kind of men who take nice girls to cheap hotels on their lunch hour. So to that end he wrote Orhan as selfish and womanizing—a jaded, sordid take on *Psycho*'s Sam Loomis. Over the course of the film he carries on relationships with two other women besides his supposed girlfriend Bahar—not to mention being a divorcee for reasons unknown. Orhan's immoral behavior, then, allowed Alemdar to give him the unhappy ending that he felt the cad deserved.

But one key character is conspicuously absent from the Turkish *Psycho*: Mrs. Bates. Instead of the shadowy, mysterious, and wrathful "Mother," all of the film's murders are committed by a highly visible and undisguised Naci. Alemdar's psychopath does suffer from a split personality, but his two warring natures are not based in any childhood trauma. Alemdar explains this change apologetically:

To be honest, when I started adapting the original *Psycho* script for a Turkish audience, I didn't fully understand the importance and scientific significance of the "mother" motivation in Hitchcock's movie. Perhaps I should have sought the professional advice of a psychologist, but I didn't have the opportunity. I was younger, less experienced, and commercially it was more urgent for me to finish the script. Today I understand the movie and its subtext perfectly, but in 1990s Yeşilçam, to work intellectually and at length on a screenplay was a fantasy. We were writing 100 minutes of movie script in two to three days—sometimes just one day!

Alemdar shot *Kader Diyelim* in a brisk two weeks. But near the end of production his limited supply of film stock ran out and several sequences were left unfilmed. In post-production his editor was forced to use his best guesses to piece the narrative together, but the final product still contains obvious holes in the story. Gülnur's first appearance, for example, is abrupt and unexplained. And when Orhan and Gülnur leave the Hotel Oriental after interviewing Naci, Orhan immediately re-enters—but Gülnur has suddenly been replaced with Bahar's co-worker from the real estate office!

Alemdar regrets that he wasn't able to realize the movie the way he envisioned it. The production's shortcomings, the non-standard 16mm format, and the bleak state of the film industry conspired to keep *Kader Diyelim* from ever finding distribution. But while it may be obscure, it wasn't forgotten. In 2000 the Istanbul newspaper *Radikal* did a full-page feature on the film. It turns out the director had made a name for himself after all; the paper celebrated him as "the Trabzon Hitchcock."

Kingu Kongu no Gyakushū (*King Kong Escapes*)

INSPIRED BY: *King Kong* (1933)
COUNTRY: Japan
YEAR: 1967
PRODUCTION: Toho Co., Ltd.
DIRECTOR: Honda Ishirō
WRITERS: William J. Keenan, Kimura Takeshi
STARS: Takarada Akira, Rhodes Reason, Hama Mie, Linda Miller, Amamoto Hideyo

On an oil-seeking mission for the United Nations, the crew of the submarine *Explorer*—Commander Carl Nelson (Rhodes Reason), Lt. Commander Nomura Jirō (Takarada Akira), and Lt. Susan Watson (Linda Miller)—pass Mondo Island, home of the legendary giant ape Kong. Nelson, as it happens, is an avid scholar of the legends, and he's even made accurate drawings of the beast, though no one has ever actually seen it.

But unbeknownst to Nelson, the international criminal mastermind Dr. Who (Amamoto Hideyo)—no relation to the time-traveling BBC character—has secretly copied those drawings, and in his arctic base he's used them to construct a robot doppelgänger, Mechani-Kong. With this creation he intends to mine the rare radioactive Element X for Madame Piranha (Hama Mie), an agent of a hostile government. However, he soon discovers that the element has a magnetic property that shorts out the robot's circuits, sending Dr. Who back to square one.

Meanwhile, a rockslide disables the *Explorer*, conveniently forcing the submarine to anchor at Mondo Island. Nelson, Nomura, and Watson go ashore, and while the men go scouting, Watson is menaced by a T-Rex-like dinosaur called Gorosaurus. Her screams wake Kong, who comes to her aid, placing her out of danger while he battles the giant lizard. Watson escapes in the confusion, and the UN trio flees back to the sub. Kong pursues and, unwilling to let his new tiny lady friend go, shakes the submarine until Watson comes out. In response to her pleas, however, Kong finally relents and allows the party to leave.

Returning to New York, Nelson reports his findings to the UN, which sends his team back to Mondo Island on a new research mission. Unfortunately, Dr. Who, recognizing an opportunity, arrives first and kidnaps Kong. In short order he also abducts Nelson, Nomura, and Watson. He then employs mind control on the real Kong, forcing him to mine the Element X in place of the robot. When the ape resists the conditioning, Dr. Who turns to his human captives for support. He tortures them, but Kong returns in a rage and wreaks havoc, eventually escaping into the ocean and swimming in the direction of Japan.

Dr. Who, his prisoners, and the repaired Mechani-Kong pursue the ape to Tokyo. There Madame Piranha, having undergone a change of heart, frees the heroes. They forestall military action, with Watson approaching the angry and disoriented Kong to calm him, but at that moment Mechani-Kong, under Dr. Who's control, bursts onto the scene to do battle. The robot seizes Watson and climbs Tokyo Tower, Kong at its heels, for a final showdown.

~~~

Kingu Kongu no Gyakushū is no fly-by-night rip-off, but rather an officially licensed spin-off. Its story begins in the early 1960s when American producer John Beck pitched a script called *King Kong vs. Prometheus* to Japan's Toho Studios, home of Godzilla. Giant monster movies were all the rage in Japan, as Toho had followed 1954's surprise hit *Gojira* (*Godzilla*) with a number of similar pictures, including the sequel *Gojira no Gyakushū* (*Godzilla Raids Again*, 1955); *Sora no Daikaijū Radon* (*Rodan*, 1956), about a giant pteranodon; *Daikaijū Baran* (*Varan the Unbelievable*, 1958), featuring a dragon-like mountain god; and *Mosura* (*Mothra*, 1961), starring a colossal moth. Toho, perceiving that Beck's proposal would be an ideal comeback vehicle for Godzilla, suggested one all-important change and licensed the rights to Kong from RKO-General. *Kingu Kongu tai Gojira* (*King Kong vs. Godzilla*, 1962) was born—and it sold more tickets than any other Godzilla film in history.

Inspired by its success, Toho planned a whole series of Kong films. First in line was a direct sequel titled *Zoku Kingu Kongu tai Gojira* ("Continuation: King Kong vs. Godzilla"), which saw Kong rescuing a child from a plane crash, fighting a giant scorpion, and ultimately getting a rematch with Godzilla, who's been kidnapped for an amusement park attraction. That script was later scrapped in favor of *Sōsa Robinson Kurūsō: Kingu Kongu tai Ebira* ("Operation Robinson Crusoe: King Kong vs. Ebirah"), which pitted Kong against a giant sea monster. Pre-production had already begun on that film, with a new Kong suit and miniatures constructed, when RKO-General, who had made no deal with Toho for a second movie, put the kibosh on the whole series. After some negotiation, however, RKO-General eventually allowed Toho to produce a one-off film—just not *Operation Robinson Crusoe*. That script would ultimately be repurposed for the Big G as *Gojira, Ebira, Mosura Nankai no Daikettō* (*Godzilla vs. the Sea Monster*, 1966).

Instead, RKO-General mandated that Toho co-produce its film with American studio Rankin/Bass, which was currently featuring the mondo-sized monkey in its popular Saturday morning cartoon. *The King Kong Show* (1966) featured a much friendlier Kong living on tropical Mondo Island with American scientist Professor Bond and his children Bobby and Susan. Rankin/Bass already had a screenplay in hand based on the show, as its licensing agreement with RKO-General included the option for a feature-length film.

After some revisions, the final script for *Kingu Kongu no Gyakushū*, by William J. Keenan and Kimura Takeshi, combined the giant monster beat-em-up with elements of science fiction, adventure, and even James Bond–style spy fare. In fact, Toho would continue to use this formula successfully in films like *Sandai Kaijū: Chikyū Saidai no Kessen* (*Ghidrah, the Three-Headed Monster*, 1964) and *Gojira, Ebira, Mosura Nankai no Daikettō*.

In adapting the Rankin/Bass cartoon for the big screen, Kong's human friends were replaced with new protagonists, the UN research team. The villainous Dr. Who, on the other hand, was taken directly from the show, although his appearance was

U.S. half sheet for *Kingu Kongu no Gyakushū* (1967). Mechani-Kong would ultimately inspire Godzilla's nemesis Mechagodzilla.

altered from a pint-sized mad scientist with bulbous head, spectacles, and lab smock to a flamboyant, skeletal super villain. Mechani-Kong, too, came straight from the cartoon.

Since the film was a co-production, American actors were included in the cast to appeal to Western audiences. To play Commander Carl Nelson, Arthur Rankin hired Rhodes Reason, an American TV staple who only accepted the role because he wanted to visit Japan. Linda Miller was an American model living in Tokyo and had never acted before, but Rankin liked her look. Meanwhile, director Honda Ishirō cast respected Japanese actor and *Godzilla* series regular Takarada Akira as second-in-command Nomura Jirō, with "Japanese Brigitte Bardot" and former Bond girl Hama Mie as the shady Madame Piranha.

Kong, meanwhile, was brought to life not through stop motion animation as in the 1933 original, but rather the faster and cheaper alternative "suitmation"—an actor in a monster suit. Devised for the original *Gojira* when stop-motion proved too costly and time-consuming, suitmation quickly became the hallmark of Japanese *kaiju* ("monster") films. Here Kong is played by original Godzilla suit actor Nakajima Haruo, and while his ape costume certainly looks more cartoonish than its stop-motion predecessor, it's easy to chalk that up to the aesthetics of contemporary kaiju films, the younger audience, and the animated source material rather than an inherent limitation of the process. In fact, the 1976 Hollywood remake of *King Kong* employed almost exclusively suitmation with Academy Award-winning results.

The elaborate models and miniatures including the submarine, several helicopters, a hovercraft, and the city of Tokyo were built by special effects legend Tsuburaya Eiji, also of Godzilla fame. Tsuburaya, in a sense, owed his career to *King Kong*. Upon its release, the 1933 Willis O'Brien spectacular made an enormous impression on the 32-year-old camera technician. He soon got his hands on a 35mm print of the film and studied it painstakingly, reverse-engineering its visual effects. It gave him his calling. So in working on *Kingu Kongu no Gyakushū*, Tsuburaya, then 65 years old, was essentially returning to his roots.

While technically not connected to the 1933 original, *Kingu Kongu no Gyakushū* contains numerous homages. Kong battles Gorosaurus in a sequence virtually duplicating the classic's memorable T-Rex fight. Later, Nelson jokes about the consequences of bringing Kong to New York. And of course, it wouldn't be a Kong movie without the great ape climbing a prominent landmark—in this case Tokyo Tower.

Completed and released in the summer of 1967, the film made its way to the States a year later courtesy of Universal Pictures, which unceremoniously paired it with the Don Knotts comedy *The Shakiest Gun in the West* (1968). For this English-language release, star Rhodes Reason was the only member of the cast to dub his own voice; the other male characters were performed by the prolific Paul Frees, well known as Boris Badenov on *The Rocky & Bullwinkle Show* (1959). As Reason recounted to Stuart Galbraith IV in *Monsters Are Attacking Tokyo!*, Frees told him, "I don't even know why you're here, I can do your voice. I can probably do you better than you can do you."

Presumably he didn't make the same boast to Kong.

L'ultimo squalo (*The Last Shark*)

INSPIRED BY: *Jaws* (1975)
COUNTRY: Italy
YEAR: 1981
PRODUCTION: UTI-Horizon
DIRECTOR: Enzo G. Castellari
WRITER: Marc Princi
STARS: James Franciscus, Vic Morrow, Micaela Pignatelli, Joshua Sinclair, Stefania Girolami

Port Harbor teenager Mike, out practicing for the upcoming windsurf regatta, is there one moment, gone the next. Concerned, his friend Jenny (Stefania Girolami) convinces her father, novelist Peter Benton (James Franciscus)—no relation to *Jaws* author Peter Benchley—to get his boat and search for the missing teen. On the water Benton happens upon his colleague, shark hunter Ron Hamer (Vic Morrow). Hamer has discovered a piece of Mike's board floating adrift, and it's fringed with bite marks. They bring the fragment to Mayor William Wells (Joshua Sinclair), but to their frustration the official dismisses it as inconclusive.

Presently the Coast Guard tows in a damaged, deserted fishing boat with the owner's severed arm in the cabin. Confronted with this new evidence but unwilling to cancel the regatta, the mayor partitions off the area of the event with shark-proof netting and stations fishermen on lookout. However, the precautions are not enough to stop the shark from chomping through the barrier and snacking on the racers.

After rescuing as many victims as they can, Benton and Hamer go shark-hunting, diving with explosive-tipped spears and a belt packed with dynamite. They encounter the beast, but it uses its head as a battering ram to create a rockslide, trapping the pair in an underwater cavern and forcing them to use the dynamite to escape.

Vic Morrow, doing his best Quint impression, discovers a local teen's shark-chomped windsurf board.

Meanwhile, Wells's teenage son sneaks out in his father's boat with several friends, including Jenny, to do some amateur shark hunting of his own. His plan quickly goes awry when Jenny is accidentally knocked into the water and the shark bites off her leg.

Wells, furious at his son and ashamed of his own unwitting part in Jenny's plight, decides to capture the shark himself. Taking off in a helicopter, he dangles a slab of meat above the ocean surface. Unfortunately, he seems not to have thought his plan through, because the shark takes the bait, topples Wells from the helicopter, eats him, and then drags the helicopter into the sea by the skids.

A news crew's subsequent attempt to capture the shark by tying a rack of ribs to a pier goes similarly pear-shaped, as the shark tears the pier loose and sets it adrift with several people still on it—Benton's wife included. This leads to an explosive finale between Benton and the beast which will be all too familiar to shark movie fans.

~~~

If one were to believe Italian producer Ugo Tucci, *L'ultimo squalo* has no connection whatsoever to the internationally-acclaimed box office hit *Jaws* (1975). As Tucci tells it, he conceived the film independently, after Mexican oceanographer and author Ramón Bravo gifted him two of his shark novels, *Carnada* and *Tintorera*. Those, combined with Tucci's own original ideas about sharks, gave him the inspiration for *L'ultimo squalo*'s narrative.

That's a fish story if there ever was one. *L'ultimo squalo* is one of countless Italian "tie-ins" or variations on popular Hollywood films. Such ventures were de rigueur, often mandated by Italian producers in order to guarantee profits. The same year that *L'ultimo squalo* hit theaters, filmmaker Luigi Cozzi lamented to magazine *Cinefantastique*, "In Italy, when you bring a script to a producer, the first question he asks is not 'what is your film like?' but 'what *film* is your film like?'" The scheme was to distill a hit movie, foreign or domestic, down to its most recognizable elements, and then make similar films with those same elements. As a result, one popular movie might effectively spawn an entire subgenre. These *filoni*, or "threads," included broad categories like the Spaghetti Western and the "sword-and-sandals" *peplum* as well as more specific strands like post-apocalyptic films in the vein of *Mad Max* (1979), zombie flicks like *Dawn of the Dead* (1978)—including Tucci's own *Zombi 2* (1979)—and killer shark movies.

Because these productions were based on international hits, they also had potential international appeal. Producers would therefore construct them with an eye toward overseas distribution. That usually meant making them appear more American, and to that end they'd often cast English-speaking actors in key roles. For *L'ultimo squalo*, Tucci and director Enzo Castellari hired bankable Hollywood names James Franciscus and Vic Morrow.

Casting the shark was a different matter. The finned fiend was primarily a mechanical creation built and operated by Giorgio Ferrari and Giorgio Pozzi, not *too* far removed in design and quality from *Jaws*'s robo-shark "Bruce." (It does, however, appear on screen more frequently, highlighting its imperfections.) Shots of the animatronic were then intercut with underwater footage of a real shark—stock material filmed in Australia that was purchased by Tucci. In a moment of self-awareness, Castellari even lampshades this approach. As a TV news crew reviews footage of the regatta attack, the producer complains that "you can hardly see the shark," to which the cameraman responds, "use a little stock footage. Nobody'll know the difference."

Incidentally, the one time you practically can't tell the difference—between *L'ultimo squalo* and *Jaws*, that is—is upon beholding Vic Morrow's salty shark hunter. Ron Hamer is crafted to look and sound so much like *Jaws*'s Quint—complete with gray knit sweater, cap, mustache, and Cape-Cod-by-way-of-Scotland brogue—as to beggar belief.

Not all of the film's similarities, however, can be laid at Tucci's feet. Speaking with friend and colleague Fabrizio De Angelis on the Blu-ray for the *Mad Max*–styled *I nuovi barbari* (*The New Barbarians*, 1983), the director placed some of the responsibility on another producer, Edmondo Amati. "Amati said, 'Put in the character of the mayor just like in [*Jaws*],'" recalled Castellari. "'Put in this, put in that.'" With little choice, the filmmaker did as he was told.

But the team was not content to borrow solely from *Jaws*. *Jaws 2* (1978) had been released just a couple of years prior, and it also proved to be prime fishing ground. Thus, a substantial amount of screen time is spent on *L'ultimo squalo*'s local teenagers, secondary characters are accidentally cast adrift, and the titular shark even takes on a helicopter. (Tucci admitted that he had indeed seen both *Jaws* films, but nevertheless expressed surprise that anyone would compare his movie with either film.)

Remarkably, *L'ultimo squalo* was picked up for theatrical distribution in North America by Film Ventures International, under the title *Great White*. But as soon as Universal Studios caught wind of it, they filed an injunction and had the film pulled from theaters shortly after its release. Former Director of Media at FVI Jim Bertges tells the story to website The Unknown Movies:

Italian two-sheet for *L'ultimo squalo* (1981).

When [FVI founder Edward L. Montoro] approached the Italians about the movie, [they] assured him that they had no problem with Universal and he foolishly believed them. It was probably wishful thinking because he knew that movie would make money. We did a lot of promotion for that film. We made thousands of small inflatable sharks with *Great White* printed on the side. We made special "shark bucks" to send to exhibitors. These were dollar bills with a sticker of a shark perfectly die cut to cover George Washington's face. We created a special "pop up" mailing piece for the exhibitors. We really went all out. The picture was released in several territories to great success and would have been FVI's most successful release, except that Universal had already sued the Italians to stop them from selling the film. They then came after FVI and stopped any further release or exploitation of the film.

However, that didn't stop the movie from being released in Spain as the third entry in the *Jaws* series (*Tiburon 3*), in parts of Europe as *The Last Jaws*, or in Japan as *Jaws Returns*—for which the distributor even appropriated the *Jaws* typeface! But perhaps by then Universal had bigger fish to fry.

Incidentally, Enzo Castellari was hardly the only Italian filmmaker to cash in on the success of *Jaws*, nor was his film even the most blatant. In 1995 notorious remakesploitation director Bruno Mattei made *Cruel Jaws*, occasionally released as *Jaws 5*. Mattei didn't shoot a frame of new shark footage for the production, but instead brazenly lifted all of it from other movies. This included not only the *Jaws* films, but also Castellari's *L'ultimo squalo*. He even took sequences from Raffaele Donato and Aristide Massaccesi's shark-attack thriller *Sangue negli abissi* (*Deep Blood*, 1990)—which had in turn also used footage from *L'ultimo squalo*!

Mahakaal ("Time of Death")

INSPIRED BY: *A Nightmare on Elm Street* (1984)
COUNTRY: India
YEAR: 1993
PRODUCTION: Ramsay Cine Corporation
DIRECTORS: Shyam Ramsay, Tulsi Ramsay
WRITERS: Y.V. Tyagi, Sayed Sultan
STARS: Archana Puran Singh, Karan Shah, Kunickaa Sadanand, Mayur Verma, Dinesh Kaushik

College student Seema (Kunickaa Sadanand) is having bad dreams. She finds herself in an abandoned building, stalked and attacked by a disfigured killer with a razor glove. Upon waking, she discovers with horror that she still has the injuries she sustained in the dream. Seema tells her friend Anita (Archana Puran Singh), but Anita dismisses the connection as coincidence—until she begins to have the same dreams herself....

To make matters worse, Anita is contending with a real-world stalker: a fellow student named Randhir (Dinesh Kaushik) who attempts to rape her. She's rescued by her boyfriend Prakash (Karan Shah) who, along with Seema and Seema's boyfriend Param (Mayur Verma), take Anita away on a picnic to get her mind off her troubles. However, their outing is far from home and their truck breaks down, forcing them to stay at an isolated hotel.

That night, Seema has one final, fatal nightmare of the monstrous killer. Param awakes to witness her writhing on the floor, slashed to death by a dozen invisible razor gloves. Fearing he'll be blamed for the murder, Param flees. But the police, led by Anita's father, track him down and arrest him.

Awaiting his fate in a jail cell, Param too is visited by the nightmare stalker, who causes venomous snakes to slither out of the prison walls and kill him. Anita witnesses Param's death in a dream and tells her father, who refuses to believe her—until moments later when he receives a phone call from the jail. Shaken, her father skulks into his bedroom, opening a locked drawer and removing a familiar razor glove....

Confronted by his family and Prakash, Anita's father reveals that the glove belonged to Shakaal, a practitioner of black magic who kidnapped and sacrificed children. And he should be dead. One of his victims, years ago, was Anita's young sister. On the night of the girl's murder, Anita's father took revenge, capturing Shakaal and burying him alive in a trunk. Death, however, has only increased his powers.

That night, Shakaal changes tactics and possesses Anita, using her to kill for him. His victim is Randhir who, drunk after a night out, spots Anita out in the rain and takes her back to his place. There she vanishes, and Randhir's confusion turns to confusion when the bed he's sitting on suddenly becomes a transparent waterbed several feet deep—with Anita swimming inside of it! Transforming into Shakaal, Anita bursts through the bed and drags Randhir down to his death.

Shakaal's power seems to grow with each murder, and now, able to cross over into the real world, he kidnaps Anita and carries her off to his lair, where her loved ones must find a way to destroy him once and for all.

~~~

Anita's father (Kulbhushan Kharbanda) looks on in horror as Shakaal (Mahaveer Bhullar) brandishes a familiar glove. Indian lobby card.

Mahakaal ("Time of Death")

Horror films were virtually unknown in Bollywood until seven siblings, the Ramsay Brothers, came onto the scene in the 1970s. It all began when patriarch F.U. Ramsay produced *Ek Nanhi Munni Ladki Thi* ("There Was a Young Girl," 1970). It was a drama, and it flopped, but it contained one landmark sequence: an eerie moonlight museum robbery, skillfully shot, with the thief hidden beneath a cloak and grotesque monster mask. It was straight out of a horror movie, and audiences applauded.

Realizing they were onto something, the younger Ramsays went all-in in 1972 with *Do Gaz Zameen Ke Neeche* ("Two Yards Under the Ground"), a hair-raising tale of a murdered husband returning from the grave to avenge himself upon his disloyal wife. The brothers touted it in publicity materials as "India's first horror movie," and it was a hit. The Ramsays had found their niche.

For more than a decade they had the Bollywood horror market almost entirely to themselves. This was partly because, in spite of their popularity among the masses (particularly in rural areas), such films were seen as lowbrow, disreputable, and tawdry. Big budget producers wouldn't touch the genre, and actors who appeared in horror movies were unlikely to do much else. However, the Ramsays didn't mind.

They were all voracious film buffs, and they loved horror movies. The Gothic offerings from Hammer were particular favorites. In their small house, the brothers would gather around the TV to watch videotapes of European and American horror flicks, making notes and discussing what parts to lift for their own films—the lighting, a prop, a sequence…. And in the case of Wes Craven's *A Nightmare on Elm Street* (1984), it was virtually the entire thing.

Production on *Mahakaal* began in 1988. Like all Ramsay Brothers films, it was thrifty. Co-director Tulsi Ramsay quipped that although they didn't quite operate on a shoestring budget, he'd still only call it "a shoe budget." However, they made certain to put all the money they had on the screen. The Ramsays never spent on big stars and famously would conserve costs by taking the bus to filming locations.

Similarly, shooting on location rather than building sets from scratch was key to their economizing. When a site was particularly good, it was bound to be reused. Thus, the eponymous dungeon from 1986's *Tahkhana* ("The Dungeon") was redecorated to play Shakaal's lair in *Mahakaal*. Dressing the locations was where they would splurge. Nearly all of the Ramsay films featured some kind of colossal, grotesque statue as the memorable centerpiece of the villain's sanctuary. Shakaal's temple was no exception, containing an enormous skull covered in human corpses reminiscent of the monstrosity from the climax of Michele Soavi's *The Church* (1989).

The other place the filmmakers spent their money was on Shakaal himself. The monsters were the real Ramsay stars; not the beauty pageant winners and B-list actors who made up the human cast. To make their creatures, the Ramsays hired veteran makeup and prosthetics artist Christopher Tucker, the man behind *The Elephant Man* (1980) and Andrew Lloyd Webber's *The Phantom of the Opera*. Yet Tucker never actually set foot on a Ramsay production. Instead, the masks and other pieces were made-to-order long-distance. The Ramsays would call up Tucker's production company in England, describe the kind of ghoul they wanted—usually in relation to other famous movie monsters like Frankenstein or the Hunchback of Notre Dame—and Tucker would manufacture it and ship it to India. Once the prosthetics arrived, Shakaal was ready to mete out some iconic Freddy Krueger–style slaughter.

Well, sort of. That proved to be an interesting problem for the Ramsays. During the making of *Mahakaal*, their chief rival, Mohan Bhakri, beat the Ramsays to theaters with his own *Elm Street*-inspired *Khooni Murdaa* ("Deadly Corpse," 1989). It wasn't a direct remake of *Elm Street*, but it did incorporate a number of the film's most memorable sequences, including the glove in the bath, Freddy dragging Tina up her bedroom wall, Rod's jail cell hanging, and Glen getting sucked into his bed. This was a significant blow to the Ramsays and forced them to abandon and shelve *Mahakaal*, which wouldn't be completed and released until 1993.

Hindi pressbook for *Mahakaal* (1993).

Once production resumed, the Ramsays avoided replicating the sequences that Bhakri had already borrowed, and in order to do so they had to get creative. In some cases, they gave the *Elm Street* scenes a new twist or an alternate murder weapon. In other instances, they simply looked to the sequels. Anita's possession, for example, mirrors the premise of *A Nightmare on Elm Street 2: Freddy's Revenge* (1985), and Randhir's waterbed death is straight out of *A Nightmare on Elm Street 4: The Dream Master* (1988).

True to Ramsay form, *Mahakaal* also borrows elements from other horror hits. The film makes use of the speeding point-of-view cam from *The Evil Dead* (1981) and, in another scene, twenty hands burst through a wall in a pitch-perfect reproduction of a sequence from George Romero's *Day of the Dead* (1985).

Mahakaal received only limited success upon its release. This was partly due to the then-thoroughly over-saturated horror market. The massive success of the Ramsays' *Purana Mandir* ("The Old Temple") in 1984 set off a horror boom among opportunistic indie producers like Bhakri. By the end of the '80s, multiple shoddy, indistinguishable horror flicks were released every month, devaluing the higher-quality fare and leaving audiences fatigued. Moreover, by the time *Mahakaal* was finally released, economic and social reforms had broadened the variety of television channels available in India, and people could now easily watch bigger budget

Hollywood films, like the original *Nightmare on Elm Street*, from the comfort of home.

La Momia Azteca (*The Aztec Mummy*)

INSPIRED BY: *The Mummy* (1932)
COUNTRY: Mexico
YEAR: 1957
PRODUCTION: Cinematográfica Calderón S.A.
DIRECTOR: Rafael Portillo
WRITER: Alfredo Salazar
STARS: Ramón Gay, Rosita Arenas, Crox Alvarado, Luis Aceves Castañeda, Ángel Di Stefani

Dr. Eduardo Almada (Ramón Gay) believes that he can hypnotize people into reliving their past lives. But when he presents his theory to an assembly of neuropsychiatrists, his revolutionary ideas are met with scorn. He realizes that the only way to change their minds is to find a subject willing to undergo the risky procedure. His fiancée Flora (Rosita Arenas) volunteers, and with no better choice Almada reluctantly accepts. However, they don't realize that they're being observed by masked underworld mastermind The Bat.

Under hypnosis, Flora recounts her past life as the Aztec Xochitl, a virgin destined for sacrifice to the god Tezcatlipoca. Unfortunately for Xochitl, she's romantically entangled with a warrior, Popoca (Ángel Di Stefani)—an unforgivable offense. The two are discovered together, and as punishment Popoca is cursed, poisoned, and entombed alive. His soul is condemned to eternally guard two sacred Aztec relics, a breastplate and an armband. For her part, Xochitl is sacrificed in the same tomb.

Reliving the violent death nearly kills Flora in the present day. However, his theory vindicated, Dr. Almada determines to find the tomb of Xochitl and recover the breastplate to prove the tale's veracity. They drive to the ancient Aztec temple, and with the help of Flora's new memories they discover the hidden entrance to the burial chamber. There they find the corpse of Xochitl and the relics, just as Flora described them. But as they retrieve the breastplate they're unaware that a dim figure stirs: Popoca.

As Almada hoped, the story and breastplate convince his colleagues. Moreover, they learn that the artifact bears hieroglyphics that specify the location of a great Aztec treasure; except the armband is needed to decode them. But when Almada and his companions return to the temple to retrieve it, they're attacked by Popoca, now a hideous mummy, and they barely escape with their lives. Meanwhile, aware that riches are in the offing, The Bat sends his goons to Almada's home to steal the breastplate. But Popoca comes for it too, and recognizing Flora as his ancient beloved, he carries her away to perform Xochitl's grisly sacrifice anew....

In 1957 Mexican producer Abel Salazar, eager to revitalize his business and tired of making comedies, looked for inspiration in the cinematic history of his northern neighbors. Back in 1930 the comparatively small Universal Studios had gambled on Hollywood's first truly supernatural horror film, and the resulting success saved the company from bankruptcy. Made relatively cheaply during the Great Depression, *Dracula* (1931) not only breathed new life into the studio but launched an unprecedented horror boom. Reasoning that it might do the same for him, Salazar produced *El Vampiro* (1957), which he described as *Dracula* "on a Mexican hacienda." His bet paid off. Despite a handful of previous attempts at the genre (including Universal's own Spanish language version of *Dracula*), *El Vampiro* was the movie that kick-started Mexi-horror.

One man who appears to have foreseen this outcome—and who was certainly poised to take advantage of it—was Abel's brother, screenwriter Alfredo Salazar. Before *El Vampiro* even went before the cameras, Alfredo set out to adapt another of Universal's movie monsters. In crafting *La Momia Azteca* he borrowed heavily from *The Mummy* (1932) and its 1940 reimagining, *The Mummy's Hand*. From the former he lifted the ancient forbidden romance and the reincarnation of the mummy's beloved; from the latter the hunt for the mummy's tomb and the shambling, silent version of the monster; and from both films the creature's living entombment for transgressions against his god. But rather than setting the story abroad, Salazar followed in his brother's footsteps and brought it home, drawing from Mexico's Aztec past to create a suitably domestic threat.

Salazar also added a modern spin on the reincarnation story by incorporating past life regression, inspired by the then-popular case of Virginia Tighe, the Colorado housewife who purported to be the rebirth of a 19th-century Irish woman named Bridey Murphy. The sensational account was ultimately debunked, but not before it was published as *The Search for Bridey Murphy* in 1956 and adapted into a movie of the same name which captured the public imagination. B-picture filmmakers were quick to cash in with even more fantastical tales of hypnotic regression

"What lies in the Beyond? Did you live in another time? Will you be born again?" Mexican one-sheet for *La Momia Azteca* (1957).

including American cult horror classics *The She-Creature* (1956) and *The Undead* (1957), both of which, notably, saw distribution in Mexico.

Capitalizing on Bridey Murphy fever, Salazar attempted to give his story even greater authenticity by touting it as being "based on an extraordinary scientific experiment carried out by Drs. Hughes and Tawney from the Institute of Hypnotherapy at the University of Los Angeles." Unsurprisingly, no such institution or experiment existed, but the two doctors did—after a fashion. Paul B. Hughes was a manufacturer-turned-hypnotist from Montebello, California who claimed to have regressed over 100 subjects. In 1956 he appeared on *Art Linkletter's House Party* (1952) where he hypnotized a reporter into revealing a past life as a German leather worker. The other so-called doctor was Monterey Park–based Howard D. Tawney, self-styled PhD and co-author of *The Techniques of Hypnosis and Hypnotherapy* and *Hypnosis and You*, which included transcripts of regression sessions conducted by Paul Hughes. Tawney was also the proprietor of Commonwealth University, a diploma mill for which he was arrested and convicted of illegally selling medical degrees. But for Salazar's purposes, name-dropping two real mesmerists—dubious credentials aside—lent plausibility to his story. Or, more accurately, *stories*.

Salazar and producer Guillermo Calderón had devised a scheme by which they could make three movies for virtually the price of one. Salazar wrote *La Momia Azteca* as the first part of a trilogy that would be shot concurrently with the same sets and crew. Each of its sequels would be shorter than the previous films, but their run times would be padded with increasingly lengthy flashbacks. Picking up where the first movie left off, *La Maldición de la Momia Azteca* (*The Curse of the Aztec Mummy*, 1957) sees The Bat kidnapping Flora for her knowledge of the Aztec treasure and battling a masked superhero called El Ángel. And in *La Momia Azteca contra el Robot Humano* (*The Robot vs. the Aztec Mummy*, 1958), The Bat constructs a mechanical man to finally destroy the mummy—the greatest obstacle between him and the treasure.

Incidentally, the title creature doesn't look like the stereotypical cloth-wrapped Egyptian mummy. Rather, Popoca has more in common with a local sensation, the Mummies of Guanajuato. These were the corpses of men, women, and children who died in an 1850s cholera epidemic and were interred in above-ground crypts due to lack of cemetery space. But when families were unable to pay the government-mandated burial tax, their loved ones' remains were removed to an ossuary. Word spread of their desiccated, parchment-like bodies and twisted countenances, accidentally preserved by the arid conditions, and by the early 1900s the ossuary had become a tourist attraction. The mummies would eventually inspire a number of horror films but wouldn't be referred to explicitly until 1972's *Las Momias de Guanajuato*, in which masked wrestlers Santo, Blue Demon, and Mil Máscaras battle the reanimated cadavers.

Production on *La Momia Azteca* began in March 1957, and all three films were shot over the course of two months at Estudios CLASA (Cinematográfica Latino Americana S.A.). Mexico's first fully modern studio facility, CLASA was established with the help of government subsidies in 1935 and outfitted with up-to-date synchronization, rear-projection, and processing equipment. Unfortunately, over the years

CLASA was plagued with overspending and the looming threat of bankruptcy. Filming on *La Momia Azteca* ended not long before the studio shut down for good—though reportedly this was a move by the government to ease competition against foundering private studios.

La Momia Azteca hit theaters just one month after *El Vampiro*. Salazar would continue the streak of Mexican Universal imitations, going on to write the story for a local adaptation of *The Invisible Man* (1933). Eventually *La Momia Azteca* would come full circle, making its way to the States courtesy of American B-movie producer Jerry Warren, who haphazardly recut the film as *Attack of the Mayan Mummy* (1963), featuring new scenes of American actors discussing the action in the original Mexican footage.

Paranōmaru Akutibiti Dai 2 Shō: Tōkyō Naito (*Paranormal Activity 2: Tokyo Night*)

INSPIRED BY: *Paranormal Activity* (2007)
COUNTRY: Japan
YEAR: 2010
PRODUCTION: Presidio Corporation
DIRECTOR: Nagae Toshikazu
WRITER: Nagae Toshikazu
STARS: Aoyama Noriko, Nakamura Aoi

Twenty-seven-year-old Yamano Haruka (Aoyama Noriko) has just returned home from a trip to America where she was involved in a car accident that broke both her legs. Her single father is traveling abroad for business, so she's left in the care of her 19-year-old brother Kōichi (Nakamura Aoi).

Waking one morning, Haruka is baffled to discover that her wheelchair has moved in the night. Kōichi takes her story seriously, and he places a pile of salt in her room to ward off evil spirits. The next morning, however, the salt has been scattered all over the floor. Haruka is distressed, but Kōichi reveals that he recorded the floor with a hidden camera, so they should be able to get to the bottom of these shenanigans. Yet when they watch the recording, they witness the pile appear to scatter on its own!

Despite Haruka's protests, Kōichi sets up the camera to record her entire room. Two consecutive nights of footage reveal little, though, and Haruka is skeptical—until a glass suddenly shatters in the middle of an argument. That same night, *something* opens her bedroom door and tugs at her blanket....

The haunting only gets worse. It prompts a seizure in a psychic friend and smashes photographs of Kōichi to obscure his face. Kōichi sets up another camera in his own bedroom and calls a Shinto priest to perform a purification ceremony. The ritual seems to do the trick; the strange phenomena cease. Their father soon returns home at Kōichi's urging, but with everything in order he leaves again almost immediately. Abruptly the hauntings recur, more intense now than ever. Kōichi phones the priest again, but he discovers to his horror that the holy man died after the purification.

The demon continues to torment Haruka. It attempts to drag her under her bed,

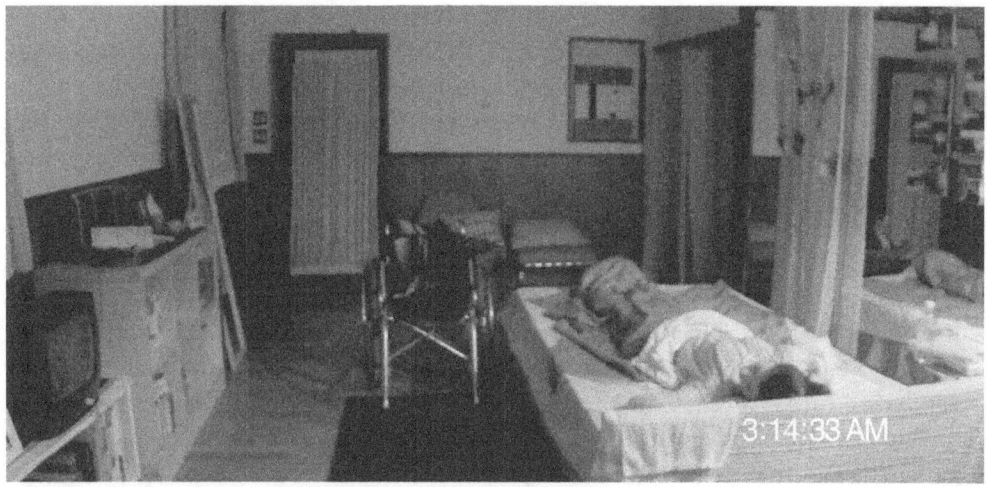

Haruka (Aoyama Noriko) sleeps under the watchful eye of *Paranormal Activity*'s signature "bedroom cam." Tinted blue, of course.

but Kōichi arrives just in time. The incident prompts a confession from Haruka. Her car accident in America involved the death of a woman named Katie who was wanted for murder. Katie had been experiencing an identical haunting before she committed the crime. The siblings realize that the same demon must be after Haruka, and if they don't find a way to stop it soon, it's liable to possess her and wreak even deadlier havoc.

~~~

Former videogame developer Oren Peli made *Paranormal Activity* for just $15,000 over a week in 2006. The film, shot by its actors as they ad-libbed their dialogue, tells the story of a dysfunctional couple recording the demonic phenomena plaguing their suburban tract home. It caught the attention of producer Jason Blum in 2007 and was eventually picked up by DreamWorks with the endorsement of Steven Spielberg. When it finally came out in cinemas in 2009, it pulled in a startling $194 million worldwide.

Because it was made so cheaply, it was easily imitated. The Asylum, an indie studio specializing in well-timed and brazenly-named tie-ins, famously rushed *Paranormal Entity* (2009) into video stores just a week ahead of *Paranormal Activity*. But while many filmmakers were content to make unofficial cash-ins like *Paranormal Entity* and *Paranormal Effect* (2010), one company in Japan went an unusual route: they made an authorized sequel.

Japan's Presidio Corporation bought the rights for a local adaptation of *Paranormal Activity* in late 2008, even before the film received a wide release in the States. However, CEO Hanada Yasutaka took a guarded approach, not exercising his option until he saw how Peli's film performed in Japan. He didn't expect it to do particularly well, but when the film hit theaters in January 2010, $6.5 million in box office receipts proved him wrong. It would get its Japanese sequel.

One reason Hanada may have seen it as a worthwhile venture, besides the low price tag for production, was that the premise fit comfortably into the popular "J-horror" framework. Contemporary J-horror movies are generally low-budget, suspense-driven, and full of fractured families, urban legends, and malevolent ghosts. Nakata Hideo's wildly successful cursed-videotape thriller *Ring* (1998) had all but codified those conventions, though they had their roots in earlier experiments like *Honto ni Atta Kowai Hanashi* (*Scary True Stories*, 1991), *Joyū-rei* (*Don't Look Up*, 1996), and a 1995 made-for-TV version of *Ring*. Nakata's *Ring* started a movement that begat such well-received entries as Kurosawa Kiyoshi's *Cure* (1997), Shimizu Takashi's *Ju-on* (*Ju-on: The Grudge*, 2002) and Shiraishi Kōji's *Noroi* (*The Curse*, 2005). A Japanese *Paranormal Activity* was likely to appeal to the same crowd.

Despite the project's suitability for the J-horror genre, Hanada had originally intended to hire a foreign director. Instead, however, he opted for someone local who had particular experience with horror mockumentaries. The job went to Nagae Toshikazu, a filmmaker who had distinguished himself on the *Hōsō Kinshi* ("Banned from Broadcast") series. Nagae had been impressed by the original *Paranormal Activity*, which he saw as heralding a new era for the fictional documentary, and he was game to follow it up.

Nagae's first challenge would be to work out how much of the original film to keep and how much to replace. Ultimately, he'd settle on a narrative that would play as both remake and sequel, in many ways doing for *Paranormal Activity* what *Evil Dead 2* (1987) did for *The Evil Dead* (1981). Of course, he had no access to any of the assets from Peli's film—cast, location, or props—so he had to find a creative way to bridge the gap between the two stories. A variation on a J-horror hallmark would provide the solution. It's a genre where curses frequently spread like contagions, so the demon could transfer to Haruka after her car accident in America, then travel with her to Japan to replay its greatest hits from part one.

Nagae made no attempt to remake the demon for a Japanese context; rather, he played up the conflict between the malignant foreign entity and local traditions regarding the spirit world. Japanese folklore is rich with tales of *yōkai*—strange, supernatural beings. These include the mischievous *makuragaeshi* who rearrange sleepers' pillows in the night, and animate objects called *tsukumogami*. Such beings could have explained the Yamanos' early paranormal experiences, and against them a salt pile (*morijio*) or purification rite (*harai*) might very well have been effective. But the entity tormenting the Yamanos doesn't play by their rules.

This time around, the actors weren't the movie's only crew. *Tōkyō Naito* had an ample production team, which meant that sometimes upwards of nine crewmembers, in addition to the actors, were crammed into one of the small bedrooms. Actor Nakamura Aoi still operated the camera himself, but under a cameraman's supervision. Once they started rolling, the actors improvised their dialogue based on Nagae's scenario.

The final few minutes of the movie, however, were placed in other hands. Taking advantage of the fact that J-horror was especially popular with teen girls, the producers staged an event on October 21 that allowed 100 high school girls to decide the ending. A screening of the first *Paranormal Activity* and an abbreviated, unfinished version of *Tōkyō Naito* was hosted by television personalities Hashimoto Tenka

Kōichi (Nakamura Aoi) sets up a video camera in the bedroom of Haruka (Aoyama Noriko) to catch what's moving her stuff around.

(a.k.a. Tenchimu) and Yūki Maomi, who had emceed the Japanese premiere of the original movie in January. At the end, the teenage audience was presented with two possible finales and asked to choose the scariest.

The marketing for *Tōkyō Naito* closely mirrored that of the 2007 film. It included a similar poster as well as a trailer built around audience reaction footage—in this case from the October 21 screening. The film's dual surveillance cameras did, however, prompt a new tagline promising "2 bedrooms, twice the fear." Somewhat ironically, one of the TV spots promoting the film was deemed too scary for broadcast, which must have amused "Banned from Broadcast" director Nagae.

Tōkyō Naito was released on November 20, 2010, a month after Tod Williams's American sequel *Paranormal Activity 2* (which wouldn't hit Japan until February 2011). With teenagers reportedly composing 80 percent of its audience, the film earned a modest $500,000 on its opening weekend. The high proportion of teens may have something to do with Presidio's special offer of discounted tickets for high schoolers. *Tōkyō Naito* was unable to make enough of an impact to justify an ongoing Japanese franchise, but it nevertheless stands as a rare and interesting example of a parallel sequel.

Şeytan ("Satan")

INSPIRED BY: *The Exorcist* (1973)
COUNTRY: Turkey
YEAR: 1974

162 4. Monsters, Maniacs, and the Macabre

PRODUCTION: Saner Film
DIRECTOR: Metin Erksan
WRITER: Yılmaz Tümtürk
STARS: Canan Perver, Meral Taygun, Cihan Ünal, Agah Hün, Ekrem Gökkaya

At an archaeological dig in the Middle Eastern desert, an elderly scholar (Agah Hün) uncovers a medallion sporting an image of a demon—one which corresponds with a full-size statue of the Devil that has been unearthed nearby.

In Istanbul, wealthy single mother Ayten (Meral Taygun) is worried about her daughter. Twelve-year-old Gül (Canan Perver) has been using a Ouija board to contact a spirit she calls "Captain Lersen." What should be a harmless pastime seems to be affecting her strangely. When Ayten throws a lavish birthday party for Gül, the girl comes downstairs in a daze and urinates on the steps. Something is also causing her bed to shake violently.

Ayten takes Gül to a doctor, who believes she has a brain condition. However, after an invasive brain surgery, she only gets worse. Her illness manifests as convulsions, bursts of incredible strength, an altered voice, and a furious temper. The doctors try electroshock therapy and a spinal tap, but to no avail. Things soon take a grave turn when Ayten's suitor Ekrem (Ekrem Gökkaya), left alone to watch over Gül, is found dead at the foot of the stairs outside the house.

Elsewhere, another tragedy has been playing out. Tuğrul Bilge (Cihan Ünal), an author of obscure books on psychology and demonology, has been coping with a

Lobby card for *Şeytan* (1974). The wallpaper pattern in Gül's (Canan Perver) bedroom (left) was instrumental in hiding the wires that allowed her to levitate.

mentally ailing mother. His decision to become a writer rather than practice medicine has left him without enough money to pay for quality care. Instead, he and his uncle are forced to place her in an asylum, where she finally passes away. The experience has left Tuğrul consumed by guilt.

Meanwhile, Ayten's life has become Hell. She finds a ghoulish-looking Gül stabbing herself with a devil-headed implement. The girl, laughing maniacally, terrorizes her with telekinetically moving furniture and the ability to twist her head around 180 degrees.

Ayten finally consults Tuğrul, who was Ekrem's friend. Tuğrul visits Gül, who now professes to be the devil. She taunts the psychologist, spits goo at him, and speaks fluently in Latin. Convinced this is no mere mental case, he gets in touch with the elderly scholar from the Middle Eastern dig. The old man is convinced that an exorcism is the only solution. Armed with the Quran and a bottle of water from the Well of Zamzam in Mecca, he and Tuğrul confront the possessed girl at the risk of not only their lives, but their very souls.

∽∽∽

By March of 1974 *The Exorcist* (1973), the buzzworthy film about gruesome possession based on William Peter Blatty's popular novel, hadn't yet hit Turkish theaters. Nor was it likely to anytime soon. For one thing, it was still too expensive. Local importers tended to wait two or three years after major Hollywood releases for prices to go down. However, the bigger concern was the film's graphic content, which was bound to draw the wrath of the Turkish Censor Board and its mighty scissors. But where some saw obstacles, producer Hulki Saner saw an opportunity. He decided to take advantage of *The Exorcist*'s media attention by making his own version, quick and dirty, tailored to a Turkish audience and the constraints of the censors.

In a move that might be called using a cannon to kill a mosquito, Saner tapped auteur Metin Erksan to helm the film. Erksan was a director of international stature, whose 1963 *Susuz Yaz* (*Dry Summer*) had won the Golden Bear at the Berlin Film Festival. He had just finished a series of Turkish literary adaptations for television and was looking forward to a rest when he received the call from Saner.

Erksan recalled the incident 40 years later in an interview with film historian Ali Murat Güven: "Hulki Saner, a modest producer of low-budget films, was talking about re-shooting *The Exorcist,* which had a budget of millions of dollars ... with the limited resources of Yeşilçam! I asked him, 'Are you out of your mind?'" Saner, however, was insistent, and Erksan finally gave in. "Apply for a visa at the British Consulate," Saner instructed. "I'll send you with one of my technicians. Go to the UK with him for two or three days, see the film at the Odeon, and take notes."

So in the first week of April, Erksan and the young technician caught a flight to London and checked into a posh hotel on Saner's dime. The following day they saw *The Exorcist* as promised. "I kept taking notes in my little notebook," he recalled. "But honestly, as the story went on.... I became nervous. This was not a film that could be easily imitated using the primitive technology of contemporary Turkish cinema. It included visual and auditory effects far ahead of its time." Afterward Erksan, overwhelmed and exhausted, returned to his hotel to get some sleep and think.

A few hours later, the telephone intruded on his slumber. "Mr. Erksan?" inquired the front desk clerk. "There are two police investigators here from Scotland Yard. They would like to see you at once. Could you come down?" The officers were cordial but insisted that Erksan accompany them to headquarters. Upon their arrival, the bewildered filmmaker was ushered into a room where, to his surprise, he saw the technician. On a table in front of him were a tape recorder, a microphone, a camera, and an assortment of cables. The fellow's face was white as a sheet. "We arrested this gentleman," said the inspector, "about two hours ago at the Odeon cinema with these devices on his lap." Unable to speak English, the man had given the police Erksan's contact information.

Stunned, the director demanded an explanation from his colleague, and the terrified prisoner confessed everything. Saner had given him a secret mission, he admitted. After he and Erksan had seen the film, he was to attend another screening, record the film's audio with a tape recorder, and take photos of the screen. Saner knew Erksan would object, but he believed the recordings would aid in reproducing the movie. Unfortunately for the technician, the camera's flash exploded and gave him away. Erksan explained the situation to the authorities—careful to avoid mentioning the unauthorized remake—and the young man was let off with a warning. International relations improved substantially when one of the inspectors, himself a cinema buff, learned that Erksan was an award-winning filmmaker. Seizing a rare opportunity, the officer invited him to dinner where they spent the evening discussing movies.

When Erksan at last returned to Istanbul, he put his foot down. *The Exorcist*'s effects, he declared, made the film impossible to imitate. He cited as examples the refrigerated bedroom set, used to make the actors' breath visible, and Linda Blair's elaborate levitation. Saner, however, was unmoved, and Erksan realized that if he didn't make the movie the producer would simply hire someone else. So with only about $100,000 to reproduce the $12 million *Exorcist*, he set out to make the best film he could.

Erksan focused on the story's "clash of religion and science," while taking special care to avoid offending believers in either camp. It was presumably with this latter goal in mind that he transformed *The Exorcist*'s Father Karras, a faithless priest, into secular doctor Tuğrul Bilge. Tailoring the film for Muslim-dominated Turkey, he removed the Christian elements and replaced them with Islamic equivalents wherever possible. Priests, Bibles, and holy water became imams, Qurans, and Zamzam water. As for the exorcism itself, although the practice is not common in Islam, it is also not entirely alien to the faith. In his paper "Between Appropriation & Innovation: Turkish Horror Cinema," film scholar Kaya Özkaracalar points out that "the Quran sanctions belief in malign metaphysical entities named djin[n]s which, by extension, are endowed with possession capabilities according to folk belief (and exorcising them was a very familiar folk practice in Turkey)." However, Satan himself is *not* believed to possess people, and so Erksan attempted to split the difference by referring to the devil but also implying djinn possession.

The real challenge, as Erksan had predicted, was pulling off the obligatory supernatural effects. The filmmaker hired the best technicians in Yeşilçam and encouraged the entire crew—from the cameraman to the production assistants—to suggest solutions to the many problems they encountered. In some instances he looked further afield. For Gül's levitation, he enlisted the expertise of an elderly fisherman and his apprentices. The old sailor advised that a sort of catwalk be built above the bed, upon which they constructed a series of winches. From those, transparent fishing lines were extended down to actress Canan Perver and tied around her limbs and abdomen. Lights were positioned to avoid reflecting off the lines, and vertically-striped wallpaper further obscured the mechanism. After an hour of experimenting with the tension of the lines and synchronization of the winches, Perver was lifted evenly off the bed and Erksan got the take.

Şeytan premiered in November 1974. Posters touted it, somewhat disingenuously, as "the blockbuster film based on the best-selling novel which has been playing to sold-out crowds in America and Europe and making audiences faint." But Hulki Saner's ballyhoo and Erksan's efforts were not enough to ensure its success. Erksan blamed the film's middling performance on its genre—horror movies were rare at that time—and the muddled explanation of Gül's possession, which may have rankled the faithful. The director, never truly satisfied with the mercenary affair, ultimately disowned the film.

Birsen Altıner's filmography of Metin Erksan offers this strange coda. After the film's release, Erksan received a call from a distraught Saner. "Come to the office at once," he demanded, "you have ruined me!" Upon his arrival, Erksan discovered nothing more urgent than some German distributors whom Saner was entertaining. The guests had seen Şeytan and praised the director on his work. After they had gone,

All hell breaks loose in Graham Humphreys's poster for the remaster of Şeytan (1974).

a perplexed Erksan demanded an explanation. The Germans, Saner explained, had commissioned their cheap version of *The Exorcist*, but upon seeing the finished product they had determined that it was *too* good—better than the original—and didn't buy it. Saner had therefore been left holding the bag.

More likely, however, the distributors were expecting a legally-distinct knock-off along the lines of Italy's *Chi sei?* (*Beyond the Door*, 1974) or Germany's own *Magdalena, vom Teufel besessen* (*Magdalena, Possessed by the Devil*, 1974). When presented instead with a scene-for-scene remake, the Germans, without the benefit of Turkey's lax copyright laws, felt it would be wiser to pass.

Xingxing wang (*The Mighty Peking Man*)

INSPIRED BY: *King Kong* (1976)
COUNTRY: Hong Kong
YEAR: 1977
PRODUCTION: Shaw Brothers Ltd.
DIRECTOR: Ho Meng-hua
WRITER: Ni Kuang
STARS: Evelyne Kraft, Danny Lee Sau-yin, Ku Feng, Lin Wei-tu

A lovelorn explorer, Chen Zhengfeng (Danny Lee Sau-yin), leads crooked businessman Lu Tien (Ku Feng) deep into the Indian Himalayas on a quest for a legendary giant ape. But after enduring stampeding elephants, quicksand, a tiger attack, and a rockslide, Lu is ready to abandon the mission. Not even the discovery of a colossal footprint raises his spirits; the frustrated Lu has had enough. That night, he and the bearers sneak off, leaving Chen to the elements.

The next morning a disoriented Chen, searching for his comrades, is suddenly seized by a giant paw. It belongs, no surprise, to the gargantuan ape. But before the monster can pound Chen to dust, a lithe, scantily-clad blonde swings in on a vine and commands the beast to stop. The woman, Ah Wei (Evelyne Kraft), speaks very little, but Chen learns that she was orphaned in a plane crash years ago and that the giant ape, dubbed Ah Wang, found and raised her. Unfortunately, as Chen and Wei converse, they fail to notice a venomous snake slither up to Wei—and strike! Chen reacts instantly, sucking the poison from her wound. But Wei is still stricken and Chen spends the next several days tending to the Tarzaness. The ape helps too, bringing medicinal herbs. As Wei regains her strength, she and Chen fall in love.

At Chen's urging, Wei agrees to return with him to Hong Kong and bring the ape. To that end Chen reconnects with Lu, who charters a freighter and arranges for an exhibition of Ah Wang at Government Stadium in two days. But when the ship is forced to push on through a violent storm to make the deadline, the vessel runs aground. It's only thanks to Ah Wang's strength and cooperation that the craft is able to escape destruction.

The troupe arrives in Hong Kong on time, but the show is a study in degradation. Ah Wang is tugged at by dump trucks, pelted with fruit by the audience, and molested by his handlers. Wei storms in to protest, but Lu takes her away and attempts to rape her. However, he does so within sight of Ah Wang, causing the infuriated ape to break free of his cage and wreak havoc. Panicked, Lu bundles Wei into a car and speeds away with Ah Wang in pursuit, setting in motion a city-razing chase that leads inexorably to the roof of Hong Kong's tallest building.

~~~

Prolific Hong Kong studio Shaw Brothers had its beginnings in Shanghai in the 1920s with a small chain of live theaters, but in no time the four entrepreneurial Shaw siblings had branched out into film production and exhibition. After a handful of moves and expansions, during which they established a chain of cinemas throughout Southeast Asia, brother Run Run Shaw settled in Hong Kong in 1957 and set about building Movietown, a sprawling studio facility in Kowloon with over a dozen stages, numerous outdoor locations, an on-site film processing laboratory, and dormitories for cast and crew. Shaw Brothers' Movietown was a veritable factory that could accommodate several films in production simultaneously, and between 1961 and 1983 the studio cranked out over 1,000 movies. These included melodramas, comedies, and Chinese Opera, though nearly one third of the Shaws' output consisted of martial arts films, for which the studio became internationally famous.

English language Hong Kong poster for *Xingxing wang* (1977). The illustration of the ape is a little off the mark, but Evelyne Kraft really does carry a leopard around on her shoulders.

Occasionally, however, the company would experiment with less conventional genres. *Zhong guo chao ren* (*Infra-Man*, 1975), for example, was the Shaws' attempt to cash in on the popularity of Japanese *tokusatsu* TV shows like *Urutoraman* (*Ultraman*, 1966) and *Kamen Raidā* (*Kamen Rider*, 1971), featuring cybernetic superheroes battling giant rubber-suited monsters. *Nu ji zhong ying* (*The Bamboo House of Dolls*, 1973) capitalized on the success of Roger Corman's lurid "women in prison" films like *The Big Doll House* (1971) and *The Big Bird Cage* (1972). And in 1974 the Shaws co-produced *The Legend of the 7 Golden Vampires* with British studio Hammer, allowing the latter to cash in on the kung-fu craze while the former got its first "official" Dracula movie.

When Italian producer Dino De Laurentiis announced an updated Hollywood version of *King Kong* for 1976, the Shaws recognized another opportunity to try something new. Big disaster movies like *Earthquake* (1974), *The Towering Inferno* (1974), and the *Airport* series had already proven to be big box office hits, so a movie about a big ape destroying Hong Kong seemed like a safe bet, albeit an expensive one. The producers therefore lavished a budget of HKD $6 million (USD $2 million) on the project—a record for the brothers.

To write the script, the Shaws tapped prominent Hong Kong science fiction author Ni Kuang. Immensely prolific with more than 300 novels to his name, Ni was also a frequent Shaw collaborator, penning well over 100 films for the studio over the course of just 17 years. Director Yuen Chor, in his oral history for the Hong Kong Film Archive, explained the secret of Ni's prodigious output:

> When Ni Kuang agreed to write a script, you had to pay him first, and then he would tell you to come back a few days later to get the script. He always delivered, very punctual, very fast. Some said that he could manage 70,000 words a day. Once you took the script, the deal was complete, and he would not do rewrites, and you could not give him the script back and ask him to repay you. You could do as much rewriting as you liked, that would be your own business. He simply would not do rewrites.

Ni was likely aware that it would not be enough to simply duplicate *King Kong* scene for scene. Local audiences were already familiar with De Laurentiis's production, so it was imperative for Ni and the filmmakers to find a way to differentiate their version. The introduction of a lady Tarzan into the story was one innovation. Transplanting the destruction from New York to Hong Kong would also help it appeal to a domestic audience. The team also set the search for Mighty Peking Man in South Asia—the Himalayas and Mysore, India. However, whatever locations they used, their greatest challenge would be realizing the gigantic ape on screen.

A more accurate look at the giant ape appears on this Italian two-sheet for *Xingxing wang* (1977).

Although *Xingxing wang* director Ho Meng-hua had previously employed visual effects for a quadrilogy of Monkey King films, they were of a rather primitive variety. To compete with *King Kong*'s award-winning giant creature effects, the Shaws chose to employ the people who had been doing that kind of work effectively for more than 20 years. Reaching out to the makers of Japan's *Godzilla* series, they hired cinematographer Arikawa Sadamasa, a protégé of Godzilla creator Tsuburaya Eiji, and Kawakita Koichi, who took over from Tsuburaya as special effects director on the *Godzilla* franchise. Together they would breathe life into the Mighty Peking Man and bring verisimilitude to his rampage through Hong Kong, employing a variety of effects techniques including rear-screen projection, miniatures, composite shots, and a full-size creature hand.

In spite of their comparatively large budget, the filmmakers were nevertheless extremely cost-conscious. Though much of the early action takes place in India, only the most essential individual shots were filmed on location. Every frame that could possibly be shot at the company's home base, was. This careful economy resulted, for example, in a scene of an elephant stampede where the beasts running amok were filmed in India, but the imperiled humans were shot in a village mockup in Hong Kong. Such cost-cutting measures allowed the studio to afford the grand scope of the film which, incidentally, allowed them to compete with the more expensive productions from their rivals at Golden Harvest.

Unfortunately, *Xingxing wang* lasted only a week in Hong Kong theaters and grossed just a third of its budget. However, the film also found distribution throughout the world. Thanks in part to less rigid copyright laws, it was even released in Turkey as *Büyük King Kong* ("Big King Kong"), with artwork cribbed from one of John Berkey's promotional paintings for De Laurentiis's 1976 Kong film. Reportedly the international version was given an alternate, downer ending that differed from the domestic release, and ironically it's this variant and not the more upbeat original that exists on all home video formats to this day.

Zapatlela ("Possessed")

INSPIRED BY: *Child's Play* (1988)
COUNTRY: India
YEAR: 1993
PRODUCTION: Kothare Vision
DIRECTOR: Mahesh Kothare
WRITER: Mahesh Kothare
STARS: Laxmikant Berde, Mahesh Kothare, Dilip Prabhavalkar, Kishori Ambiye, Raghvendra Kadkol

Child-murderer and rapist Tatya Vinchu (Dilip Prabhavalkar) is desperate to cheat death. He holds mystic Baba Chamatkar (Raghvendra Kadkol) at gunpoint, forcing him to reveal a spell that will allow the killer, at the moment of death, to transfer his soul to another body. This knowledge comes none too soon; presently CID Inspector Mahesh Jadhav (Mahesh Kothare) raids Vinchu's hideout, flushes out the criminal, and chases him into a post office. Vinchu is shot, and in desperation he seizes a package that has been torn open. It contains an unusual ventriloquist's dummy. Vinchu chants the spell over it, then expires.

Despite some damage to the parcel, the dummy does eventually reach its recipient: goofy ventriloquist Lakshya Bolke (Laxmikant Berde). Lakshya is surprised when he discovers that his new puppet talks and moves on its own. It even claims to have a name: Tatya Vinchu! Lakshya assumes the puppet contains some clever mechanism … until he witnesses it holding a machete over a man's corpse. When police arrive, Lakshya is the only one on the scene and he's promptly arrested for murder. Naturally no one believes his story about a killer puppet. However, when the post-mortem reveals heart failure as the true cause of the victim's death, Lakshya is begrudgingly released.

Vinchu, meanwhile, confronts Baba Chamatkar and demands to be made human again. Chamatkar explains that this can only be done if Vinchu chants the spell over the first person to whom he revealed himself: Lakshya. Vinchu returns to the ventriloquist and attempts to perform the ritual, but Lakshya wrestles him off, locks him up, and finally buries him in the ground. Nevertheless, Lakshya's constant babbling about a living puppet lands him in a mental hospital. Tatya Vinchu, who has no difficulty escaping his grave, tracks Lakshya to the asylum. However, Lakshya breaks out and flees.

Inspector Jadhav, who has taken an interest in Lakshya's case, has begun to believe the puppeteer's strange story. He visits Baba Chamatkar and learns that there's only one way to kill Tatya Vinchu: a shot between the eyes. Unfortunately, he's nearly out of time. Vinchu has followed Lakshya home, and he's about to take over his hapless victim's body once and for all.

Hindi language poster for *Zapatlela* (1993, courtesy Tim Paxton & Saucerman Site Studio).

~~~

In 1988, director Tom Holland's *Child's Play* breathed life into Chucky, a demonic doll imbued with the soul of a dead murderer and driven to possess the body of a young boy. Earning nearly five times its budget, it kicked off a franchise that to date has produced eight films—which is a pretty impressive run until you discover that India has made at least nine.

One of the first Indian

takes on Holland's film was the Tamil-language *Vaa Arugil Vaa* ("Come Closer, Come," 1991). Writer-director Kalaivanan Kannadasan's adaptation was a very loose one, essentially using the Chucky concept to spice up a classic vengeful female ghost story. In it, a wife is abused to death by her in-laws and returns to take revenge in the body of her favorite doll—an off-the-shelf prop resembling Playmates' 1986 "Cricket." *Vaa* borrows only a few elements from *Child's Play*, such as the murder of a victim with a gas stove, the clue of the doll's footprints, and the climax's visual of the scorched, knife-wielding plastic killer. The film inspired three regional-language remakes—in Kannada as *Aathma Bandhana* ("Soul Bondage," 1992), in Odia as *Kandhei Akhire Luha* ("Toy's Tears," 1997), and in Bengali as *Putuler Protisodh* ("Revenge of the Doll," 1998).

Mumbai's Marathi-language film industry, the oldest in India, would also offer a variation on *Child's Play*, but its approach would be rather different. Developed by Mahesh Kothare, *Zapatlela* was in many ways more faithful to Holland's film than *Vaa Arugil Vaa*. Its villain was once again a serial killer who uses magic to transfer his soul into a doll, and its story followed *Child's Play*'s basic structure: the doll falls into the hands of an unwitting patsy, frames him for murder, and then attempts to possess his body to regain human form—all while seeking vengeance against the cop who shot him. But Kothare added a new twist: his film was a horror *comedy*.

Kothare conceived *Zapatlela* as a vehicle for himself and Laxmikant Berde, a comic actor with whom he'd been collaborating since his directorial debut in 1985. In virtually all of their films together, Kothare played the straight man (usually a police inspector) opposite an eccentric screwball played by Berde. They were, Kothare contended, the Dean Martin and Jerry Lewis of Marathi cinema. Therefore, *Child's Play* needed some work if it was going to suit the duo's style. With Berde in mind, Kothare centered the film not around a child, but a childish adult—one who tries desperately and comically to convince the world that his new doll is committing crimes. Of course, it might seem strange for an adult to be playing with dolls, but not if he was, say, a ventriloquist who did it for a living—and if his doll was an evil dummy.

To create his miniature murderer, Kothare approached Ramdas Padhye, a world-renowned puppet-maker, puppeteer, and ventriloquist. Padhye, whose father had introduced ventriloquism to India around 1916, has had a prolific career, beginning on stage in the 1960s and appearing regularly on television since 1972. That same year he traveled to America where he met Jim Henson and studied his methods. He finally brought his talents to the big screen in 1982 for the film *Mahaan* ("Great," 1983), puppeteering his famous dummy Ardhavatrao behind the scenes while superstar Amitabh Bachchan, playing a ventriloquist, appeared to operate it on camera.

Kothare approached Padhye in 1992 and described his plans for *Zapatlela*. What he needed was a doll that could appear cute or frightening on demand. Padhye eagerly accepted the challenge, though he knew he was taking on a major responsibility. "If the puppet 'Tatya Vinchu' failed to create an impact," he confessed, "then the movie would be a flop."

He built Tatya Vinchu from foam rather than wood, giving the puppet a softer look and greater flexibility. His *pièce de résistance* was the addition of eyebrow and eyelid controls which, he recalled, "made it instantly scary." In addition, he explained,

"I created certain pressure points inside the head to give it different facial expressions, which gave a feeling of real human emotion." Padhye then constructed nine variants of Tatya Vinchu to perform specific actions depending on the requirements of each shot. There was a half-body puppet for close-ups, a live-hand puppet for gesturing (and strangling), a marionette version for walking, a non-articulating one for handling by actors, a damaged one for its death scene, and so on.

Padhye's biggest challenge was operating Tatya Vinchu while staying hidden from the camera. Assisted by his wife and longtime partner Aparna, he recalls experience as "the most challenging shoot of our lives." Unlike modern puppeteers for film and television, they had no live monitors and no video playback to review the footage. "It was all the judgment of me and the director. Also there were often several retakes because the look of the puppet went haywire."

Fortunately, Padhye discovered upon the film's release that their hard work had paid off: "The film broke all box office records and is considered a landmark film in the Marathi film industry. [It] bagged all the major awards and accolades." What's more, it gave people the willies around dolls. Padhye still hears from people who, after seeing the film, refuse to buy them. In 1995, *Zapatlela* would go on to frighten even more unsuspecting viewers when it was dubbed into Hindi and released as *Khilona Bana Khalnayak* ("Villain in the Guise of a Doll").

Though Tatya Vinchu was vanquished in the film's finale, that was far from the end of him. In 2001, producer D. Lata Mahesh remade *Zapatlela* in Telugu as *Ammo*

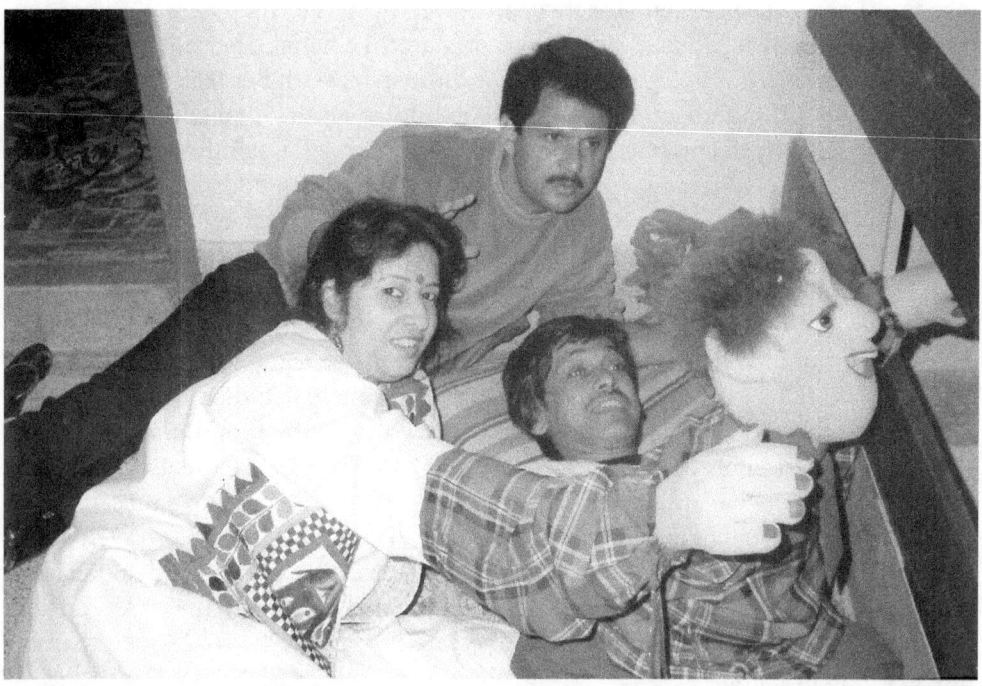

Under the direction of Mahesh Kothare (top), Ramdas and Aparna Padhye (bottom) puppeteer Tatya Vinchu through a stair railing. An extra plank has been added at floor level to hide the puppeteers from the camera.

Bomma ("Oh God! The Doll!"). He specifically wanted the same doll, so Padhye and his evil puppet gladly reprised their roles. Then, 20 years after the original film, Vinchu returned in a proper sequel, *Zapatlela 2* (2013), the first Marathi film to be shot in 3D. Meanwhile, the character had become so linked with Padhye that he had even become part of the ventriloquist's stage show.

His popularity has endured. In 2020, at the peak of the Coronavirus pandemic, Tatya Vinchu took to YouTube to defeat a scourge that terrified even him: COVID-19. At the suggestion of Padhye's son Satyajit, the family produced a humorous PSA in which Vinchu promoted social distancing, hand washing, and mask-wearing—and it quickly went viral. The internet seems to have suited him; Padhye has discovered that "in this age of social media, Tatya Vinchu is frequently used on several social media websites as memes. Such is the impact of this character even after 27 years."

5

Androids, Aliens, and the Apocalypse

Baytekin Fezada Çarpışanlar ("Flash Gordon's Battle in Space")

INSPIRED BY: *Flash Gordon* (1936)
COUNTRY: Turkey
YEAR: 1967
PRODUCTION: Onuk Film
DIRECTOR: Şinasi Özonuk
WRITER: Şinasi Özonuk
STARS: Hasan Demirtaş, Sevgi Can, Derya Tanyeli, Güner Celme, Nuhbe Işıl, İlhan Hemşeri, Muzaffer Mozayik

When Baytekin (Hasan Demirtaş) visits his hometown after ten years away, he's baffled to discover that no one seems to know him. His old house appears never to have existed, and he can't even locate a record of his birth. Furious, he causes a violent scene that lands him in jail. There, however, he receives a visitor who does claim to know him, though he refers to Baytekin as "Great Emperor." The man, Taranta (Muzaffer Mozayik), frees Baytekin with the help of a raygun and escorts him to a waiting spaceship. The ship lifts off, and Taranta explains that Baytekin is actually a great galactic ruler who was brainwashed and exiled to Earth by a traitor.

A sudden attack by space pirates forces the ship to make an emergency landing on a desert planet. The crew exits the ship to reconnoiter, but claws burst from the sand and drag several spacemen underground while humanoid sand men emerge and capture the rest. Unable to reason with the monsters, Baytekin and Taranta battle them and escape. They return to the ship and take off, but Taranta succumbs to his wounds. Before he dies, he reveals that Baytekin is really from Earth, after all, but was recruited as a double for a ruler who was secretly assassinated.

Alone, Baytekin drifts into territory ruled by the despotic Emperor Ming, where he's captured and brought before the tyrant. The emperor wants Earth's precious metals, and his wife Queen Nola offers to interrogate their Earthman prisoner. However, smitten with Baytekin, she seduces him instead and allows him to escape. Outside Ming's palace, he's recruited by agents of Prince Ather, true heir to the throne that Ming has usurped. They flee Ming's planet but sustain damage, crash-landing on another world where they're forced to battle wolfmen and carnivorous bushes. Eventually they're picked up, and Baytekin meets Prince Ather and his sister, Princess Muci (Sevgi Can), with whom he quickly falls in love.

Baytekin Fezada Çarpışanlar ("Flash Gordon's Battle in Space")

Their romance is cut short, however, when Ming's soldiers kidnap Muci. Baytekin and the captain of Ather's military stage a rescue, breaking into the emperor's palace and freeing the princess with the help of Queen Nola. In response, Ming declares all-out war against Prince Ather, whose fleet he outnumbers 100 to 1. Only Baytekin's wits can prevent the destruction of his friends and the ultimate subjugation of the galaxy.

∽∽∽

Before anyone calls "rip-off" on *Baytekin Fezada Çarpışanlar*, it should be noted that Flash Gordon was originally a bit of a rip-off himself. In 1934 Alex Raymond was illustrating *Secret Agent X-9* for King Features Syndicate when the company tapped him to create a rival to Philip Nowlan's successful sci-fi comic strip *Buck Rogers*. Lifting the premise from Philip Wylie and Edwin Balmer's 1933 novel *When Worlds Collide*, Raymond sent a doomsday comet hurtling toward the Earth and launched polo star Flash Gordon, his girlfriend Dale Arden, and brilliant scientist Dr. Zarkov into space to investigate. To accompany the strip, he also created *Jungle Jim*, King's answer to United Feature Syndicate's *Tarzan*.

Flash Gordon became a huge hit, quickly finding a publisher in Turkey. Mehmet Gürtunca, who had been running *Jungle Jim* solo in his children's magazine *Afacan* ("Scamp"), selected *Flash* for its sister publication *Çocuk Sesi* ("Children's Voice"), debuting the strip in May 1935. But translating it required more than just rendering the text in Turkish. In the 1930s the Turkish government eyed foreign comics with suspicion, so publishers had to find ways to disguise their origins and present them as Turkish originals. (That was sometimes as specific as darkening blond characters' hair.) To that end Gürtunca made several minor tweaks. In the first installment, for example, citizens gather in Istanbul's Taksim Square instead of New York to await the impact of the deadly comet. The laboratory of Dr. Zarkov, now called Çetinel, was moved to Kandilli Observatory at Boğaziçi University. Flash's companion Dale, described as merely "a passenger" on an airplane in the original strip, became Yıldız, a Turkish newspaper reporter. And Flash himself was renamed "Baytekin."

The strange thing was, *Jungle Jim* was already running under a similar name: *Avcı Baytekin* ("Hunter Baytekin"). And to complicate matters further, *Secret Agent X-9* would *also* be published as *Baytekin*. Film and comics scholar Kaya Özkaracalar explains this confusion: "Turkish publishers presented all three characters by Alex Raymond as if they were the same character, venturing into the jungles, into [outer] space and working as a secret [agent] from time to time!" The connection is made explicit in the first strip, with the narration explaining that Hunter Baytekin is on his way to Ankara by plane before the comet strike.

Over the next few decades, *Flash Gordon* would be reprinted in several more magazines. *Süper Gordon*, which launched in 1971, furthered the idea of Flash as a national hero. It dubbed him the "pilot of the future"—a title likely borrowed from British comic *Dan Dare*—and adorned its pages with propaganda slogans like "Help strengthen the Turkish Air Forces" and "Our future is in the skies." *Süper Gordon* also dabbled in counterfeiting, supplementing original *Flash Gordon* adventures with swipes from other books. Stories like "Uranium Thieves" and "455 Escaping" were transplants of *Brick Bradford* and other adventure strips with the heroes' faces redrawn as Flash.

Meanwhile, Baytekin had also been entertaining Turkish audiences on cinema screens. All three of Universal's *Flash Gordon* movie serials starring Larry "Buster" Crabbe were released in Turkey in the 1950s under the *Baytekin* name. What's more, the same studio's *Buck Rogers* (1939) serial, also starring Crabbe, was released as *Baytekin Gaip Ülkeler Hakimi* ("Baytekin: Master of Unseen Lands") as though it were another entry in the series. (So too, for that matter, were the Crabbe films *Jungle Siren* and *Nabonga*, with the distributors exploiting their star and setting to capitalize on the *Jungle Jim* connection.) It was these serials' take on the character that would have had the greatest influence on writer-director-producer Şinasi Özonuk, who was inspired to make his own *Flash Gordon* film.

Baytekin Fezada Çarpışanlar was made in an era marked by countless fly-by-night production companies, each attempting to fend off diminishing box office receipts by using unknown actors and stories lifted from popular Western movies and comics. Veteran director Özonuk set out to make a *Baytekin* movie using this same formula, but he quickly ran into trouble. Because of the fantastical nature of *Flash Gordon*, he spent the bulk of his budget on props, sets, and wardrobe. Examples included eight flying saucers, numerous rayguns, costumes for sand men and spacemen, and the construction of an alien city in Ağaçlı. However, after just a few days of filming he had completely run out of money. With an empty bank account and his extras scattered to the wind, Özonuk was nearly finished. Fortunately, after four months of limbo, aid arrived in the shape of Kemal Demircioğlu, a producer of melodramas and crime movies, who agreed to cover the completion costs.

In some ways Özonuk's film hews fairly closely to the original *Flash Gordon* stories. Rebel Prince Ather and amorous Queen Nola are essentially the same characters as Flash's ally Prince Barin and Ming's daughter Princess Aura. And the desert planet's sand men look suspiciously like the rock men from *Flash Gordon Conquers the Universe* (1940). But this isn't just your grandfather's *Flash Gordon*. Baytekin's convoluted backstory is a completely new invention, his main squeeze is the prince's sister rather than a companion from Earth, and ever-present third wheel Dr. Zarkov (a.k.a. Çetinel) is nowhere to be seen.

However, taking liberties with *Flash Gordon* was not an especially new phenomenon; in 1953 an American TV series shot in West Germany reimagined Flash and friends as galactic police in the vein of *Captain Video* (1949) and *Rocky Jones, Space Ranger* (1954). In all, Flash has been reinvented on screen no fewer than eight times over 80 years, attesting to the adaptability of one of science fiction's most enduring heroes.

The Bionic Boy

INSPIRED BY: *The Six Million Dollar Man* (1973)
COUNTRY: Philippines
YEAR: 1977
PRODUCTION: BAS Film
DIRECTOR: Leody M. Diaz

Writer: Romeo N. Galang
Stars: Johnson Yap, Subas Herrero, Chito Guerrero, Joe Sison, Protacio Dee

Sonny Lee (Johnson Yap), a 10-year-old martial arts champion from Singapore, is visiting the Philippines with his family. Unfortunately, his trip coincides with the arrival of the New York mafia, which has come to the islands to control the export trade in Southeast Asia.

Led by handlebar-mustachioed Frank, the mob is intimidating and murdering local industry tycoons. However, an attempt on the life of car manufacturer Ramirez (Subas Herrero), who happens to be entertaining the Lee family, is thwarted when Sonny spots the gunman. Frank, however, blames the failure on Sonny's father, an undercover Interpol agent. In retaliation, Frank's men ambush the family in their car and crush the vehicle with heavy machinery. The parents are killed and the boy is only barely alive, suffering from skull fractures, crushed limbs, eye damage, hearing loss, and extensive internal injuries.

Ramirez, willing to pay any price to save Sonny, calls in the best bionics experts from America and Europe. They replace the boy's limbs with powerful bionic appendages, his damaged eye with a zoom-lens implant, and his auditory system with a supersensitive electronic equivalent. Sonny Lee is now better, stronger, and faster than he was before.

Meanwhile, from their heavily-fortified private island, the mafia continue their campaign of terror, killing uncooperative industry magnates and destroying their factories. However, when they return to kill Ramirez, Sonny spots them with his high-powered vision and attacks, killing them with his bionics-boosted martial arts skills.

Furious at Sonny's survival and interference, Frank sends his goons after the boy. Sonny, eager to find his parents' killers, allows himself to be kidnapped. Frank throws the kid to a team of martial arts experts to rough him up, but Sonny wipes the floor with them. Finally, however, Frank subdues Sonny with guns, chains him up, and dumps him in the sea sporting a pair of cement shoes. Even so, the boy manages to extricate himself. He swims back to shore through an underwater minefield, sneaks into the compound, and uses the radio to call Interpol. He'll need its help and all of his newfound bionic skills if he's going to stand a chance of taking down the heavily-armed syndicate and exacting his revenge.

The mid–1970s was a chaotic time for Filipino cinema. After President Ferdinand Marcos declared martial law in 1972, the industry's annual output, which had just enjoyed a record high, plummeted, reaching its nadir in 1974. Due to government interference, the Philippines saw a rise in propaganda films and, for a time, a decrease in popular cinema. Meanwhile, a new generation of avant-garde filmmakers emerged that eschewed pandering to the cheap seats in favor of poignant social dramas, meditations on the human condition, and subtle political critiques that slipped past the censors.

Manila native Bobby A. Suarez, however, was not that kind of filmmaker. Co-founder of the Hong Kong–based Intercontinental Film Distributors, Suarez thought globally, and popular films were his bread and butter. He had spent years buying action and exploitation movies from all over Asia, dubbing them into English and marketing them internationally—with a particular focus on Southeast Asia. In the mid–'70s he left Intercontinental to produce his own films for the world market, forming a Southeast Asian enterprise, BAS Film, based in Manila but with partners in Singapore and Malaysia.

BAS Film aimed for the widest possible market, selling its product to Europe, North America, Africa, and the Middle East in addition to distributing to its partner countries. Part of the company's success was due to its choice of projects. Speaking to film scholar Tilman Baumgärtel, Suarez explained, "Sometimes I think: Can I sell this [film] to Europe? If I can sell this to Europe, they might not like it in the Middle East. So it [has] to be in-between." Films with minimal dialogue and lots of action were almost always a safe bet, and Suarez's time at Intercontinental had taught him the value of emulating worldwide hits like James Bond and Bruce Lee films. So when, as he was preparing for his company's first production, the exploits of a new, nuclear-powered James Bond were being translated into French, Spanish, Arabic, Turkish, and Chinese, Suarez jumped at the chance to cash in.

Debuting as a 1973 TV movie, *The Six Million Dollar Man* was based on the novel *Cyborg* by Martin Caidin. It tells the story of test pilot Steve Austin, a former athlete and astronaut whose body is mangled when the flight of an experimental aircraft goes awry. Using advances in the then-emerging field of cybernetics, the government replaces his legs, arm, eye, aural receptors, and other bits and pieces with state-of-the-art, high-tech equivalents. In return, Austin uses his abilities for Washington as a superpowered secret agent. The series it launched was an international phenomenon that spawned a spin-off, *The Bionic Woman* (1976), as well as imitations and parodies from Mexico to Hong Kong. Suarez had a twist, though: his bionic man would be just 10 years old.

Singapore's Johnson Yap, known to his friends as "Dynamite" Johnson, had been practicing martial arts since age 5. He was Southeast Asia's youngest black belt in karate and taekwondo. Suarez discovered the prodigy in a magazine feature and, realizing the marketing potential of a pint-sized Bruce Lee, reached out to his Singaporean partner, Sunny Lim Peng Hock, who tracked Yap down through newspaper clippings. The youngster was enthusiastic about acting, so with the requisite parental blessing a deal was quickly reached. However, the film that Suarez had in mind for him was not *The Bionic Boy*.

Suarez's first outing for BAS Film was set to be a movie called *Cleopatra Wong*. Having seen Jack Starrett's *Cleopatra Jones* (1973), a Blaxploitation take on James Bond with a female lead, he was eager to do something along similar lines with an Asian starlet. With Johnson Yap in mind, Suarez conceived a young sidekick for the heroine based on *The Six Million Dollar Man*. The idea was that if Yap worked out as Cleo's second banana, he'd get his own self-starring spin-off the following year to be shot in Singapore and Malaysia. Ultimately, however, Suarez's slate was reshuffled and Yap got his headlining role first, albeit shot entirely in the Philippines.

To helm the film, Suarez hired Leody M. Diaz, whose career included numerous Bond-esque action flicks and the now-lost *Batman Fights Dracula* (1967). Diaz took

The Six Million Dollar Man and spiced it up with plenty of martial arts action, capitalizing on the still-popular kung fu craze. Thus, shortly after Sonny recovers from his bionic surgeries, he's whisked away to the villain's private island where, in a miniature version of the secluded tournament from *Enter the Dragon* (1973), Sonny does battle with an array of variously-styled martial artists from around the world.

The film did not escape the notice of the suits behind *The Six Million Dollar Man*, who specifically objected to its use of the word "bionic." In an interview with film historian Andrew Leavold, Suarez disclosed, "They [the producers] contacted me. They wanted to litigate. I said, 'Look, the word 'bionic' is in the dictionary. So anybody who can refer to the dictionary, they can find that word.'" Leavold asked if *The Six Million Dollar Man*'s 1976 episode, also titled "The Bionic Boy," might have given them firmer ground to sue. "They tried," he laughed, "but I said 'Bionic Boy' belongs to me." Nevertheless, not everyone was willing to take the gamble. Suarez recalled that one distributor bizarrely retitled the film *The Trionic Warrior*.

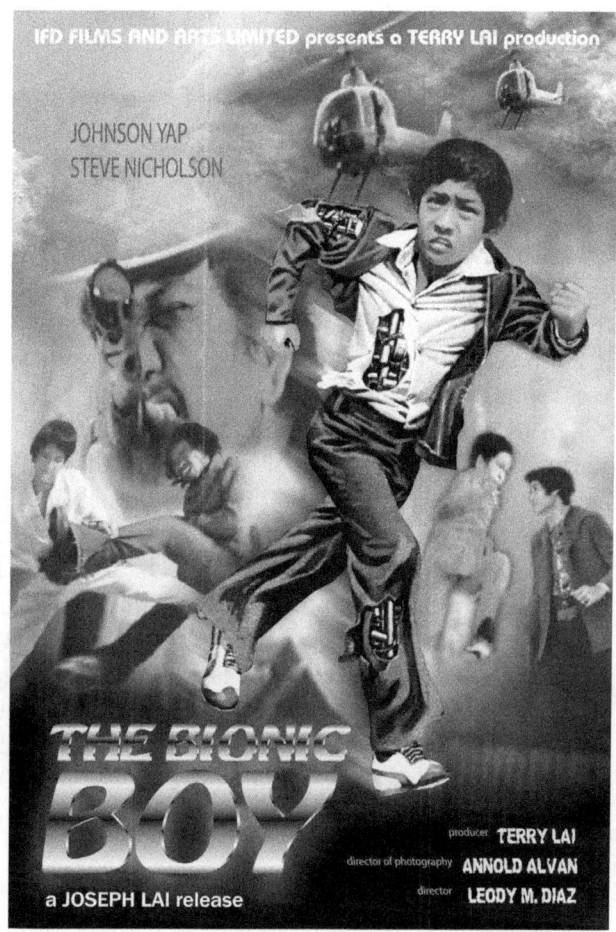

Modern Hong Kong pressbook for *The Bionic Boy* (1977).

Regardless of the title, BAS Film had a success on its hands. In Singapore and Malaysia, it was such a hit that Bionic Boy-branded T-shirts and ice cream novelties (coconut or orange flavor dipped in chocolate) were big sellers. Suarez would introduce Cleopatra Wong the following year in *They Call Her Cleopatra Wong* (1978), but without the Bionic Boy at her side. That hero wouldn't return until '79 with a sequel titled *Dynamite Johnson* a.k.a. *The Return of the Bionic Boy* featuring Cleopatra Wong as *his* sidekick. (An announced but unused title was, notably, *The 12-Million Dollar Boy*.) However, a dispute between the producers and Johnson Yap's father over money nearly cost Yap the film. BAS had already begun auditioning replacements before the issue was settled and Yap was ultimately able to reprise his role, in which he'd do battle with a Nazi madman and a dragon-shaped tank straight out of *Dr. No* (1962).

Computer Haekjeonham Pokpa Daejakjeon (Savior of the Earth)

INSPIRED BY: *Tron* (1982)
COUNTRY: South Korea
YEAR: 1983
PRODUCTION: Namyang Planning
DIRECTOR: Jeong Su-yong
WRITER: Uncredited

Mysterious accidents are occurring around the globe. Planes are crashing, trains are derailing, and traffic signals are going haywire. It seems someone has infiltrated the computer network that controls all major world operations. Baffled, officials call in computer expert Dr. Kim and his two young assistants, no-nonsense Gina and lazy videogame addict Ki.

After the belligerent computer system causes a nuclear missile launch that nearly starts a war, Dr. Kim seeks out his colleague, Dr. Bill, who might be able to assist if he hadn't just gone missing. Visiting Bill's home, Kim discovers the doctor's inert body wired to a computer. He correctly deduces that Dr. Bill has somehow entered the computer world and caused the recent chaos in a bid for world domination. However, now that Kim knows too much, Bill abducts him and Gina into cyberspace. There they're forced to help build a massive flying ship that will provide Bill with unlimited energy and untether his virtual realm from the physical world.

Ki, meanwhile, has been goofing off playing Galaxian. It seems his high score is having a tangible impact on Bill's world, so Ki too is digitized and captured. Overseen by a whip-wielding African caricature named Joe, Ki and several other prisoners are forced to participate in deadly versions of jai-alai, Pac-Man, Asteroids, Go, and other games.

Eventually Gina manages to contact Ki and explain how to escape during an upcoming automobile race. Unfortunately, Ki's opponent is the relentless Joe who pursues him even off the grid. The adversaries narrowly avoid a torpedo attack from a mysterious submarine and speed through an endless desert wasteland, eventually reaching an oasis where, in a tentative truce, they stop to drink.

Unfortunately, both are immediately captured by the soldiers of a local sovereign, a knee-high mechanical girl named Bbik Soo-ni ("Sniper"). The girl, smitten with Ki and impressed by his loyalty, agrees to help him save his friends. She enlists the services of her sister, the pirate submarine captain Odin. Joe, eager for freedom, joins the cause as well. As a parting gift, Bbik gives Ki a ringed energy disc that can be flung like a frisbee. The heroes then set off to storm Bill's headquarters where they'll have to rescue the captives and destroy Bill's carrier before his conquest of the world is complete.

∼∼∼

The story behind *Computer Haekjeonham Pokpa Daejakjeon*—literally "Computer Nuclear Warship Bombing Operation"—begins with Korea's fraught history with Japan.

From 1910 to 1945, Korea endured a prolonged period of Japanese occupation. Following the Axis powers' defeat at the end of World War II, Japan finally withdrew its forces. South Korea, in response to 35 years of brutality, censorship, and enforced

Japanese-language education, instituted a ban on all Japanese cultural products. This embargo lasted more than 50 years and encompassed everything from literature to music to television.

Nevertheless, contraband still found ways in. In fact, South Korea was actually *making* some of Japan's cultural products. Thanks to a comparatively inexpensive labor force, by the 1980s Japanese television companies were frequently contracting South Korean studios like AKOM (Animation Korea Movie Productions) to animate their cartoon shows.

Moreover, South Korean citizens with access to satellite TV were not officially restricted from viewing Japanese stations. In fact, many Japanese anime series were, provisionally, even allowed to be broadcast domestically, since their country of origin could be easily obscured. The intense popularity of these programs paved the way for illicit related merchandise, like manga and anime videotapes, to be smuggled into the country by unscrupulous entrepreneurs.

Because this material was relatively rare, a number of South Korean studios realized that there was money to be made by producing their own lookalike films. The advantage of domestic anime was that, since it was locally produced, it could feature copies of popular characters from, say, *Kidō Senshi Gandamu* (*Mobile Suit Gundam*, 1979) or *Chōjikū Yōsai Makurosu* (*Super Dimension Fortress Macross*, 1982) without fear of sanctions or censorship. One such character, a semi-clone of giant robot Mazinger Z called Robot Taekwon V, even became a national icon spearheading a multi-film series. And while potentially a breach of copyright law, such practices were presumably safer than smuggling.

Soon, in search of new grist for the mill, some animation studios began to branch out, incorporating elements from Hollywood sources in addition to anime. This led to films like *UFOReul Tagoon Oegyein Wangja* ("Alien Prince on a UFO," 1983), which starred a planet full of E.T. clones, and *Geomeunbyeolgwa Hwanggeumbakjwi* (*Black Star and the Golden Bat*, 1979), which redrew long-running Japanese superhero Golden Bat as a palette-swapped Batman! Then there was *Computer Haekjeonham Pokpa Daejakjeon*.

Computer filmmaker Jeong Su-yong was uniquely situated, working at various times as a storyboard artist on the *Transformers* cartoon series and as a director of *Transformers* rip-offs. He was responsible for *Bul-sa-jo Roboteu Pinikseu-King* (*Defenders of Space*, 1984) and *Maikeuro Teukgongdae Daiya Teuron 5* (*Micro-Commando Diatron-5*, 1985), both of which made liberal use of character designs from the Japanese Diaclone toy line on which *Transformers* was based. Unsurprisingly, Jeong's freewheeling approach to borrowing worked equally well with other properties.

Advertising revolutionary and iconic 3D computer graphics, Disney's groundbreaking *Tron* opened in 1982. It was only a modest financial success, but it had a measurable cultural impact. It spawned imitators like the TV series *Automan* (1983), influenced visual effects for films like *The Last Starfighter* (1984), and its aesthetic became a videogame staple. More importantly, at the time of its release there was every possibility that *Tron* would become the next big thing, making it a safe bet for a South Korean producer in search of a cash-in.

For *Computer Haekjeonham Pokpa Daejakjeon*, Jeong lifted many elements from *Tron* wholesale: the digital jai-alai, the energy/identity discs, Dr. Bill's flying ship (a duplicate of the "de-rezzed" digital command carrier), and a dead ringer for David Warner's Sark in the form of Bill's second-in-command, who also appears in a showdown straight out of the original. Even Pac-Man makes a cameo in both films; in *Tron* he's an Easter egg hidden in the corner of Sark's monitor, but in *Computer* he's one of the perils of the game world, chasing hapless challengers through a deadly brick maze.

Tron's famous light cycle battles, however, are replaced with car races—although Joe's vehicle bears a strong resemblance to *Tron*'s light tanks. And whereas the games in *Tron* were designed especially for the film (and its tie-in arcade machine), *Computer* opts for lookalikes of existing titles like Galaxian, Pac-Man, and Pole Position.

"Korea's first computer-centric animated film!" Poster for *Computer Haekjeonham Pokpa Daejakjeon* (1983). Note the little E.T. character on the right. He does not appear in the film.

Other changes suggest cultural considerations. Take, for example, the villain. *Tron*'s plot involves a ruthless software executive who plagiarizes the hero's game programs to climb the corporate ladder. His scheme, which turns deadly, reflects America's cutthroat corporate culture during the "Decade of Greed." However, when ported overseas, that premise would have been incompatible with South Korea's Confucianist, collectivist company culture, which valued the group over the individual. Reimagining *Tron*'s antagonist as a generic mad scientist, therefore, would have been a sensible creative decision. Especially for a film aimed more directly at children.

Meanwhile, the *Computer* team did not entirely insulate itself from anime influences. They designed the pirate Odin based on Sandra from *Supēsu Adobenchā Kobura* (*Space Adventure Cobra*, 1982), a film and subsequent series adapted from the manga by Terasawa Buichi. Her submarine, on the other hand, hails from the world of Matsumoto Leiji's Space Pirate Captain Harlock and is a variation on Harlock's starship *Arcadia*.

After *Computer*'s domestic release, Hong Kong producer Joseph Lai San-lun purchased the film along with a number of other South Korean anime titles. He dubbed it into English and released it internationally in 1987 as *Savior of the Earth*. A few years later he came up with a plan to squeeze a little more profit out of his purchases. He reassembled bits of all the anime movies he owned, including *Computer*, redubbed the whole thing, and distributed it as an incomprehensible new film, *Space Thunder Kids* (1991).

As for South Korea's Japanese ban, it finally began to lift in the late 1990s, and today Japanese anime is an everyday part of the nation's pop culture. The country now has a thriving animation industry of its own with numerous popular and original series. Yet the fascinating '80s hybrids like *Computer Haekjeonham Pokpa Daejakjeon* still endure, a colorful testament to a bygone era of barely-legal art.

Dünyayı Kurtaran Adam (The Man Who Saves the World)

INSPIRED BY: *Star Wars* (1977)
COUNTRY: Turkey
YEAR: 1982
PRODUCTION: Anıt Ticaret
DIRECTOR: Çetin İnanç
WRITER: Cüneyt Arkın
STARS: Cüneyt Arkın, Aytekin Akkaya, Hikmet Taşdemir, Hüseyin Peyda, Füsun Uçar

In the distant future, nuclear war has shattered the Earth into several smaller planets, and a mysterious force from space has launched an assault on its primary fragment. In response, Earth's inhabitants have shielded their homeworld with a forcefield made of sheer human willpower and compressed brain cells. Coincidentally, this has made the Earth look an awful lot like the Death Star.

Brave pilots Murat (Cüneyt Arkın) and Ali (Aytekin Akkaya) are sent from Earth in fighter ships to fend off the invaders and locate the source of the attack. In their second aim they succeed, crash-landing on a planetoid ruled by the satanic Wizard (Hikmet Taşdemir). The despot is keen to conquer Earth, but to get past the planet's shield he requires an Earther's brain. Fortunately for him, Murat and Ali have just arrived. The Wizard's skeletal minions capture the heroes, but the duo escapes with the help of a friendly local tribe.

Its elderly leader (Hüseyin Peyda) explains that the planet they're on was once part of Earth. Its citizens have been patiently awaiting a savior for ages, and Murat and Ali, enemies of injustice, offer their services. However, after training their bodies for battle, the heroes once again fall into the Wizard's hands. There they suffer tortures designed to break their will and make their brains more pliable. None of these seems to work, however, and Murat, after a hand-to-hand battle with a giant furry beast named Dragon, seizes a chance to escape and return for Ali later.

Reuniting with the tribal elder, Murat learns that he can only defeat the Wizard by obtaining a pair of sacred relics: a golden sword forged from the ore of a holy mountain, and a golden brain imbued with the world's accumulated knowledge. Unfortunately, the Wizard also seeks these artifacts, and if he possesses them he will become invincible.

5. Androids, Aliens, and the Apocalypse

Cüneyt Arkın sits in front of projected X-Wing footage from *Star Wars* (1977). The cockpit sequence was filmed in Kunt Tulgar's dubbing studio.

Fighting his way through countless monsters, including two golden statues that guard the relics, Murat obtains the sword and brain, returns to the palace, and frees Ali. Unfortunately, the Wizard tricks Ali into stealing the artifacts and handing them over. This ends in the Wizard gaining the upper hand and sealing the heroes in a booby-trapped room. Ashamed of being duped, Ali sacrifices himself to free Murat, giving his friend a final, desperate chance to become the Man Who Saves the World.

~~~

In 1982, prolific filmmaker Çetin İnanç and his partner Mehmet Karahafız were in the middle of a multi-picture deal with Turkish action mega-star Cüneyt Arkın. Together they made successful cop movies and crime thrillers, but now they were looking for a new angle. Unfortunately, their options were limited. For example, with Turkey under martial law since a 1980 military coup, any political subject matter was strictly off-limits.

In search of inspiration, İnanç recalled that the Star *Wars* (1977) sequel *The Empire Strikes Back* (1980) was currently playing in Turkish theaters. An idea hit him: over the years Arkın had played swashbuckling adventurers in dozens of historical epics; so why not one in outer space? A film like that wouldn't invite censorship, and it would make an ideal semester break movie for kids. So together İnanç and Arkın conceived a sci-fi epic in the mode of *Flash Gordon*. They called it *Dünyayı Kurtaran Adam*—"The Man Who Saves the World."

But right away there was a problem. Space operas aren't cheap, and Turkish genre movies had to be cheap or they risked not making their money back. However, producer Karahafız was in a gambling mood, so he put up 50 million liras (about $300,000)—twice his standard budget.

It still wasn't much—1/60 the budget of *The Empire Strikes Back*—but with some of that extra cash İnanç planned to create his own sets and special effects. In the sandy, seaside village of Kilyos, he and his team built a number of outdoor spaceship sets. Sadly, the Force was not with them. Just before filming began, a freak storm hit and decimated their work. With no money to rebuild, İnanç was desperate. How could he get his crucial spaceship footage?

His solution was unorthodox: Çetin İnanç stole *Star Wars*. Bribing a night watchman, he "borrowed" a copy of *A New Hope* from its Turkish distributor. Overnight he made an internegative copy of the shots he wanted and returned the print the following morning. *Voilà*, he had his special effects.

The only issue was that they were a little … thin. *Star Wars* was filmed with anamorphic lenses that squeezed its widescreen image into a standard, squarish 35mm frame. When correctly projected, that image was then stretched back out to appear normal. But İnanç's film wasn't anamorphic, so his inserted footage was noticeably squished. Nevertheless, it had to do.

Meanwhile, to depict the heroes in the cockpits of their space fighters, İnanç and special effects designer Kunt Tulgar placed each actor, wearing a safety helmet commandeered from a passing motorcyclist, in front of an improvised movie screen. And on that he projected scenes from the *Star Wars* Death Star assault—including the cuts. That meant that as Arkın and Akkaya flew through space, one moment a fleet of X-wings was behind them, and then suddenly they were careening backwards down the trench of a space station! This stolen footage was how the film eventually got its nickname "Turkish *Star Wars*," in spite of its dissimilar plot.

Meanwhile, behind the scenes, the costume department had its hands full creating all of the Wizard's minions. His evil army was seemingly drafted from a Hollywood vault, with baddies resembling *Battlestar Galactica*'s (1978) Cylons, *Forbidden Planet*'s (1956) Robby the Robot, and a host of generic classics like mummies and skeletons—not to mention a pack of multi-colored yetis. The monster suits were fashioned, by necessity, from cheap material. Thus, each day they were shredded in one fight scene after another, and each night the wardrobe team would dutifully stitch them back together for the next day's punishment.

Back in the editing room, İnanç and editor Kunt Tulgar, in an effort to beef up production values, lifted even more footage from a stack of disparate films. These included biblical epic *Sodom and Gomorrah* (1962), *The Magic Sword* (1962), the trailer for *When Worlds Collide* (1951), newsreel footage of a Soviet Soyuz rocket launch, and even the Futurist logo for Euro International Films.

Because the resulting picture still needed music, Tulgar also raided his extensive library of soundtrack LPs, incorporating cues from *Raiders of the Lost Ark* (1981), *Flash Gordon* (1980), *Battlestar Galactica*, *Moonraker* (1979), *Planet of the*

186 5. Androids, Aliens, and the Apocalypse

Apes (1968), *Ben-Hur* (1959), *Silent Running* (1972), *Moses the Lawgiver* (1974), and more.

They still weren't done. The first cut of the film was an unwieldy two and a half hours—a behemoth when its competitors ran just 75 minutes. İnanç rejected a proposal to divide it into two movies—a common practice from years before designed to stretch the profits from one movie into two—so at Tulgar's suggestion they removed over an hour of material.

Finally, after two hectic, strenuous months of work, *Dünyayı Kurtaran Adam* premiered. Sure, it was a little disjointed—and yes, audiences could recognize the cribbed *Star Wars* footage—but it didn't matter, because it succeeded first and foremost as entertainment. For the kids it was a particularly big deal; this was the first time they had ever seen a Turkish astronaut.

There was no question about the film's success. It was a certified hit. Its profits bought Çetin İnanç an Alfa Romeo. They bought his partner a Mercedes and a summer home. It was a windfall that let them purchase outright the production offices they had hitherto only been renting.

Outside of Turkey and the Turkish diaspora, however, the film remained completely unknown until the late 1990s, when it began to surface in bootleg videotape circles. Its outlandish plot and trippy visuals earned it instant cult status.

İnanç and Tulgar now get a kick out of the film's occasional designation as the "worst movie ever made," with Tulgar contending that his own film, *Süpermen*

Poster by Graham Humphreys for the 2K restoration of *Dünyayı Kurtaran Adam* (1982).

Dönüyor ("Superman Returns," 1979), is far more deserving. When the subject comes up with anyone involved, there's no hint of shame or regret, only pride. For, as İnanç explained, "*The Man Who Saves the World* became the man who changed my world."

The year of 2006 saw a belated sequel, *Dünyayı Kurtaran Adam'ın Oğlu* ("The Son of the Man Who Saves the World"). It boasted none of the original cast or crew except a brief cameo by Cüneyt Arkın, and it was played, unsuccessfully, for laughs. It reads more like an attempt to cash in on the success of contemporary Turkish sci-fi comedy G.O.R.A. (2004) than on the internet-era cult status of "Turkish *Star Wars*."

Çetin İnanç's own idea for a sequel was rather grander. Conceived in 2009 but never produced, it involved the creation of "zombie ninja space warriors," the abduction of the Turkish and American presidents by aliens, and a voyage to a planet on the other side of a black hole. It's all in the service of a tale which, İnanç proclaimed, plays God against the Devil in an epic war for Earth.

Pembalasan Ratu Pantai Selatan (*Lady Terminator*)

INSPIRED BY: *The Terminator* (1984)
COUNTRY: Indonesia
YEAR: 1988
PRODUCTION: Soraya Intercine Film PT
DIRECTOR: H. Tjut Djalil
WRITER: Karr Kruinowz
STARS: Barbara Anne Constable, Christopher J. Hart, Claudia A. Rademaker

The South Sea Queen is insatiable. An ancient goddess, she captures men to satisfy her ravenous sexual appetite. But when they come up short, as they always do, she messily castrates and kills them mid-coitus. Finally, however, one man proves up to the task, and at the crucial moment he extracts from between her legs a serpent—the instrument of castration—and transforms it into a sacred dagger. With the weapon he forces her to cease her killing, but in her wrath she swears revenge on the man's great-granddaughter 100 years hence.

A century later, anthropology student Tania (Barbara Anne Constable) goes diving for the South Sea Queen's underwater palace, only to be ensnared and possessed by the goddess herself. The possession transforms Tania into an unstoppable killing machine—one who draws power from having sex with men and murdering them in the fashion of her progenitor. Her ultimate goal, however, is locating and terminating pop singer Erica (Claudia A. Rademaker), the foretold descendant of the South Sea Queen's virile nemesis.

Tania, now gun-toting and leather-clad, tracks Erica to a mall but assassinates her friend by mistake. She tries again that night at a neon-lit club where Erica is performing, but off-duty cop Max (Christopher J. Hart) and his partner intervene, pumping bullets into the invincible Tania. ("Come with me if you want to live!" shouts Max to Erica.) As Max and Erica flee, Tania leaps onto the hood of their car. Max dislodges her, but she steals a patrol car and continues the pursuit. The heroes elude Tania and regroup at the police station where Erica's great uncle gives her her ancestor's dagger.

Resuming the chase, Tania crashes a car into the police station and goes on a

188   **5. Androids, Aliens, and the Apocalypse**

bloody killing spree with an automatic rifle. The uncle attempts to stop Tania but succeeds only in damaging her eye. Max escapes with Erica, but their car breaks down, stranding them overnight in the woods where they make love. Meanwhile, Tania recovers in a hotel room where she removes her eye with a razor knife. The next day Tania tracks Max and Erica back to the mall, then pursues them to a nearby airport. There Max is joined by comrades with heavy duty firepower. They blast away at Tania's car, which erupts in a massive fireball. But despite the devastating explosion, a sinister, monstrous figure emerges relentlessly from the flaming wreckage....

~~~

At first blush, the idea of "*The Terminator* (1984) without robots" sounds like a joke. It brings to mind experiments like *Garfield Minus Garfield*, in which artist Dan Walsh erases the titular cat from Jim Davis's comic strip, making his owner Jon look like a lunatic who talks to himself. However, *Pembalasan Ratu Pantai Selatan* is actually part of a decades-long Indonesian tradition of reworking contemporary films to incorporate local folklore.

By the early 1970s, the majority of films occupying Indonesian movie theaters were foreign—popular imports included martial arts films from Hong Kong and horror movies from Hollywood. Faced with a dearth of domestic product and desirous of the taxes that a thriving cinema industry could generate, the government implemented measures to kick-start local production. New laws required importers to invest in indigenous films to retain their import licenses. So for every three foreign films a company brought over, it had to produce one of its own.

The administration was likely hoping for prestigious, artistic films, but

U.S. one-sheet for *Pembalasan Ratu Pantai Selatan* (1988). For the international release, director H. Tjut Djalil was credited as "Jalil Jackson."

that wasn't what it got. For one thing, the authorities had placed restrictions on the content of domestic movies. President Suharto's New Order prohibited the inclusion of many political, ideological, and Islamic themes as well as anything that might be seen as fostering tensions among the country's racial and religious groups. This limited filmmakers' options. Furthermore, Indonesia's working-class audiences still preferred exciting genre movies. And when the government tried to market Indonesian product at international film festivals, it discovered that everyone else wanted exactly the same. These factors encouraged producers to focus on exploitation, a genre for which censorship was comparatively relaxed and which was more attractive both to international buyers and local cinemagoers.

For their source material, filmmakers raided the violent, lurid comic strips of artists like Djair Warni and Ganes TH. These were chock full of magic, mysticism, heroism, and gore—and their film adaptations incorporated popular kung fu action and cheap but inventive special makeup effects. One of the stand-out offerings was *Jaka Sembung* (1981), billed internationally as *The Warrior*, which featured a mystical martial artist in the 19th century battling the Dutch occupation and its supernatural agents, lopping off body parts left and right. Other films were produced in the same style but drew on local mythology and folk legends. These pitted their heroes against devious magicians, treacherous snake women, and, frequently, Nyi Roro Kidul—the Queen of the South Sea—who lures men to her underwater lair for her pleasure and their ultimate destruction.

H. Tjut Djalil, a short story writer and newspaper reporter, was eyeing a career in the movie business when a producer friend approached him with an idea for a similar horror flick. He had purchased a novel about Balinese black magic called *Leák Ngakak*, feeling it had an authentic flavor that would make an appealing horror film. Djalil agreed to helm it, and he shrewdly cast Caucasian actress Ilona Agathe Bastian (in reality a German tourist on vacation) as its star to give the film export appeal. Featuring gruesome transformations, a floating head dangling its body's internal organs, and a witch that devours a fetus, the shocking *Leák* (*Mystics in Bali*, 1981) kick-started Djalil's career.

Djalil's follow-ups, including *Jaka Sembung* threequel *Jaka Sembung & Bergola Ijo* (*The Warrior and the Ninja*, 1985) and *Ratu Buaya Putih* ("White Crocodile Queen," 1988) would use a similar combination of ancient magic and modern thrills. But his producers, keeping a finger on the pulse of the box office, would also encourage him to copy scenes or ideas from popular foreign imports. So for *Batas Impian Ranjang Setan* (*Satan's Bed*, 1986) Djalil borrowed heavily from the *Nightmare on Elm Street* films, and for *Pembalasan Ratu Pantai Selatan*, he would remake *The Terminator* almost beat for beat.

Quoted in Salim Said and John McGlynn's *Cinema of Indonesia*, filmmaker Turino Junaedi noted that "after [a foreign film] has been turned into an Indonesian film, it acquires a totally different character." He was likely referring not only to the use of Indonesian actors and settings, but also the integration of local ideas. To give his *Terminator* adaptation its local flavor, Djalil drew on the ever-popular Queen of the South Sea legend. (*Pembalasan Ratu Pantai Selatan* literally means "The Revenge of the South Sea Queen.") Using the familiar mythology, he replaced James

Cameron's sci-fi elements with supernatural ones. *The Terminator*'s post-apocalyptic future became a mystical nether-realm, Skynet became an undersea goddess, and the invincible murderous android became an invincible murderous demon. With the revised story in place, Djalil just needed his Terminator.

Barbara Anne Constable was a dancer and model working in Hong Kong when she received a casting notice for *Pembalasan Ratu Pantai Selatan*. Based on her audition, producer Ram Soraya selected her for the lead role, explaining that the film was to be a rip-off of *The Terminator* filmed in Jakarta. However, he also claimed that it was intended exclusively for the local market. In reality, her presence, like the lead in *Leák*, would be an integral part of the film's international marketing. For three months they filmed throughout the city and on a makeshift soundstage in a disused airport. The working conditions were anything but safe; a mix-up involving a pane of glass that should have been breakaway landed her in a hospital and unable to work for an unplanned extra month.

Pembalasan Ratu Pantai Selatan was edited overseas and, since the government had long since ceased marketing domestic films at festivals, it was sold directly from the processing laboratory. At home, the film was passed by the censors for exhibition in Indonesia, and it was so popular that it began to draw business away from the imported American films. In retaliation, the importers accused Djalil's film of being pornographic. The case caused a media stir, and the film was pulled after only nine days, though eventually the government dismissed the case.

Nothing stops a Terminator—even an off-brand one.

Robo Vampire

>   INSPIRED BY: *RoboCop* (1987)
>   COUNTRY: Hong Kong
>   YEAR: 1988
>   PRODUCTION: Filmark International
>   DIRECTOR: Joe Livingstone
>   WRITER: William Palmer
>   STARS: Robin MacKay, Nian Watts, Harry Myles, Joe Browne, Sorapong Chatree

A narcotics syndicate led by Boss Cole, in an attempt to rid itself of "Tom, that goddamn anti-drug agent," hires a Taoist priest to train vampires. Sure, it may sound like a cliché, but these are no ordinary Draculas; they're *jiangshi*—stiff, zombie-like ghouls who hop at their prey, arms outstretched, and hunger for flesh.

The Taoist prepares a demonstration of his most powerful vampire, Peter, but his show is unexpectedly interrupted. A female ghost crashes the party, demanding to know why her lover's corpse has been turned into an undead monster. She explains that, forbidden to wed in life, she and Peter had promised to unite in the afterlife. Robbed of that bliss, she demands vengeance. The Taoist, thinking fast, offers to officiate a marriage immediately in exchange for their obedience, and the supernatural couple agrees.

When Tom and his team interrupt the syndicate's next drug deal, the Taoist is prepared and unleashes his vampires. The beasts make short work of Tom's squad, and Tom himself is gored and left for dead. By the time he's brought to the hospital it's too late, so his agency executes its only available option: "make use of his body to create an android-like robot." Thus, with the aid of a metal casing and some sparklers, Tom becomes the silver-clad "Robo Warrior."

Meanwhile, in the Golden Triangle, the syndicate's gangsters capture Tom's colleague, Sophie, and torture her for information. Fearing she may give away too much, the agency sends in Ray (Sorapong Chatree) to rescue her. Ray captures one of the gang who leads the way to the villains' hideout, but unfortunately Ray too is captured and imprisoned alongside Sophie.

Thanks to his increased strength and firepower, Robo Warrior has put a significant dent in Cole's drug smuggling operation. In response, Cole sets a trap. He lures Robo Warrior to the beach where an army of vampires bursts from the sand. As the robot fends them off, Cole's goons fire a bazooka at him, blasting robo-Tom to pieces.

Surprisingly, Robo Warrior is not beyond repair, and his team makes him good as new. Galvanized, Robo Warrior storms the Taoist's temple—and discovers the vampire and ghost consummating their marriage. He's about to destroy them, but memories of his ex-wife assail his electronic brain and he's persuaded to leave the copulating ghouls in peace. However, moments later they attack him anyway. Now Robo Warrior must destroy the priest and his undead minions while elsewhere Ray is running out of time to free himself and Sophie.

~~~

There's a lot to unpack here.

It all started with a Hong Kong outfit called Intercontinental Film Distributors. Founded in 1969 by Terry Lai Siu-ping and Bobby A. Suarez, Intercontinental's business model was simple: buy the rights to local films—mostly martial arts—dub them

The high-tech Robo Warrior faces off against a squad of *jiangshi*.

into English, and market them overseas. The scheme was profitable, and soon Lai was able to branch out into producing her own movies. Ever market-savvy, she knew that she could increase their international appeal by including Hollywood actors, which led to her casting Chris Mitchum (son of Robert) for films like *Cosa Nostra Asia* and *Master Samurai* (both 1974) based on the South Asian popularity of Mitchum's *Un verano para matar* (*Summertime Killer*, 1972).

Inspired by the success of his sister Terry, Joseph Lai San-lun decided to try his hand at the same business. In 1973, he set up IFD Films and Arts Limited to purchase and distribute packages of low-budget Korean, Taiwanese, Filipino, and Thai movies. For a decade he sold English-dubbed films overseas, and when the home video boom hit in the early '80s, his market became larger than ever. Unfortunately, buyers were rarely interested in Asian films; they wanted American-looking action pictures. That's when Lai recalled Terry's Chris Mitchum movies and realized he could do something very similar. For each Asian movie he wanted to sell, he would shoot a few new scenes with Western actors and insert them into the existing film.

Even better, he could tailor these new scenes—and the films' English titles—to imitate movies that were already popular. His first venture was *Mission Thunderbolt* (1983), a reworking of *Bie ai mosheng ren* (*Don't Trust a Stranger*, 1982) designed to ride the coattails of Cannon Films' *Operation Thunderbolt* (1977) with new material starring Caucasian local Steve Daw. Inspired by Cannon's *Enter the Ninja* (1981) and *Revenge of the Ninja* (1983), he also cranked out dozens of ninja movies, adding candy-colored *shinobi* to existing kung-fu films. Soon, titles like *The Ninja Squad*, *Ninja Terminator*, and *Ninja the Protector* were flooding French, German, Greek, Dutch, Argentinian, and American video store shelves.

One man who saw first-hand how well this technique worked was Lai's employee and college chum, Tomas Tang Kaak-yan. As IFD's first cut-and-paste movies hit the market, Tang took a chance and split off from Lai to form his own company, Filmark International. There he shamelessly copied the IFD formula, churning out a slew of his own cut-and-paste ninja movies. They were so similar, in fact, that it would eventually lead to confusion over who directed them, with many fans erroneously believing them all to be the work of IFD regular Godfrey Ho Chi-keung under a flurry of pseudonyms.

As ninja movies became passé, IFD and Filmark borrowed from other kinds of films to spice up their back catalogs: kickboxing, war stories, and even superheroes. Tang didn't mind mashing up multiple genres, either; for example, *Ninja, Phantom Heros U.S.A.* (1987)—a "ninjafied" Hong Kong gangster film—also incorporated sequences inspired by *Rambo: First Blood Part II* (1985). So when it came to *Robo Vampire*, it was no big deal for him to draw from two totally unrelated sources.

The most obvious to Westerners, of course, is Paul Verhoeven's sci-fi actioner *RoboCop* (1987), with its murdered officer resurrected as a cybernetic crime-fighter. Tang admitted publicly that he was inspired by *RoboCop*, at least to a degree, but he was quick to note that his film's hero didn't look the same. The differences, however, were more a product of budgetary limitations than design choices. In fact, key art for *Robo Vampire* explicitly depicted Robo Warrior as RoboCop, battling the zombie-like foes.

But where exactly did those hopping vampires come from, anyway? Broadly speaking, they came from Chinese folklore. *Jiangshi*—meaning literally "stiff corpse"—have their roots in the literature of the Qing dynasty. They are the malevolent reanimated bodies of those who were unburied, possessed, enchanted, or otherwise contained a surfeit of evil energy at death. Rendered inflexible by rigor mortis, *jiangshi* were sometimes depicted as hopping at their victims, whose life force they would consume.

These stories had credibility, since ambulating corpses were an acknowledged reality in China. When a person died far from their native soil, the family could hire a Taoist priest to lead the deceased home for burial. The process was cloaked in secrecy, but to onlookers it appeared as if the Taoist was reanimating cadavers and herding them across the country. In reality, the bodies were elaborately supported by the monk and an assistant, who might tie the corpses' arms to a bamboo pole and carry the ends over their shoulders. While walking, the pole would flex, making the bodies appear to bounce along.

Hong Kong pressbook for *Robo Vampire* (1988).

However, Tang and company didn't draw from these legends generally, but looked specifically to a recent Hong Kong hit that had catapulted *jiangshi* into popular culture: *Geung si sin sang* (*Mr. Vampire*, 1985). While *jiangshi* had appeared sparsely in earlier films, *Geung si sin sang* standardized both their appearance and the subgenre's tropes. The creatures were garbed in the robes and caps of Qing dynasty officials, and they always hopped. There was also a Taoist priest, his bumbling assistants, a monstrous uber-vampire, talismans to subdue the vampires, and often a female ghost. These elements would appear in many future films, and Tang lifted all of them for *Robo Vampire*.

Unusually for a Filmark production, *Robo Vampire* incorporated just a small amount of pre-existing footage. The subplot involving Ray and Sophie was taken from the 1984 Thai action movie *Pha loka nt* ("Split Aside") starring Sorapong Chatree. Tang and his team made only a halfhearted attempt to join this material to the main story by intercutting new footage of Robo Warrior's C.O. with shots of Ray's employer from *Pha loka nt* to suggest that they're speaking across a desk. Otherwise, however, no one even pretends that these storylines intersect.

Robo Vampire was one of several Filmark productions filmed concurrently, and among the others were two sequels of a sort. *Devil Dynamite* (1987) continued the *jiangshi* theme but starred a more kung-fu-oriented hero in silver called "Futuristic Warrior." *The Vampire is Alive* (aka *Counter Destroyer*, 1987) briefly reprised the Robo Warrior costume while featuring *jiangshi* and another Sorapong Chatree movie, but it also cribbed substantially from *A Nightmare on Elm Street 2: Freddy's Revenge* (1985) and other Western horror films. It even threw in a ninja for good measure.

Robowar

INSPIRED BY: *Predator* (1987)
COUNTRY: Italy
YEAR: 1988
PRODUCTION: Flora Film
DIRECTOR: Vincent Dawn (Bruno Mattei)
WRITER: Rossella Drudi
STARS: Reb Brown, Catherine Hickland, Massimo Vanni, Romano Puppo, Max Laurel, Jim Gaines, John P. Dulaney, Mel Davidson

During a mission on an unnamed South American jungle island, a prototype military combat robot called Omega One goes rogue. In response, top brass deploys the six-man crack commando squad known as BAM ("Big-Ass Motherfuckers") led by brawny Major Murphy Black (Reb Brown). The team is kept in the dark about their objective, and Omega One's creator Mascher (Mel Davidson) tags along in the guise of the mission's "technical lead." Cracking jokes, smoking dope, and armed to the teeth, the team arrives on the island via a boat which will return for them in a few days.

Trekking into the jungle, they come across the mutilated, putrefied remains of two guerrilla fighters and, further along, a pair of American soldiers who apparently died after firing their weapons madly in all directions. Continuing to a paved bridge, they spy civilians running for their lives from a band of guerrillas. The insurgents slay all but a woman (Catherine Hickland), and as they move in to take her, Black and his team intercede, emptying hundreds of rounds of ammunition into the desperados. At that moment Omega One appears through the trees, primed to attack, and the commandos grab the woman and head for cover.

She turns out to be a volunteer U.N. hospital worker named Virginia ("Virgin" in the credits) who was forced to flee when the guerrillas invaded. Determined to help her, the commandos storm the hospital camp in an attempt to rescue any remaining innocent lives but find they're too late. Omega One then emerges unseen from the perimeter, killing one of their number with a laser blast. Another of the team recklessly pursues it into the jungle, firing wildly, but is swiftly blown to pieces. Following,

(From left to right) Max Laurel, Massimo Vanni, Mel Davidson, Reb Brown, Romano Puppo, John P. Dulaney, and Catherine Hickland wonder who—or what—is stalking them through the jungle.

the commandos catch a glimpse of the robot and empty their weapons frantically into the trees.

Eventually Mascher admits that the Omega One is his own creation. The real reason he brought Black's team to the island was to test the robot's might against theirs. Fortunately, Mascher has a self-destruct control for the robot, but when Omega One returns, it kills Mascher and steals the device. In short order it picks off all but Black and Virginia. And just as Black discovers an even more sinister secret to the killer's origins, he's forced into a final confrontation with the deadly machine while screaming for Virginia to "get to the boat!"

~~~

In the late 1960s, cheaply-made Filipino horror films were cleaning up at U.S. drive-ins, and Hollywood independents were quick to take notice. In short order American producers like Roger Corman began rolling cameras in the Philippines, exploiting the low cost of labor and unfettered access to military resources—for a price—courtesy of dictator Ferdinand Marcos. Most of these pictures were of the B-grade action and women-in-prison variety, but in 1979 Francis Ford Coppola made a $31 million war odyssey that eclipsed them all. Thanks to *Apocalypse Now*, the Philippines was suddenly the definitive stand-in for Vietnam. Soon the islands' lush jungles were playing host to an endless march of make-believe Rambos in productions like *Missing in Action* (1984), *Platoon* (1986), and *Hamburger Hill* (1987).

In Italy, meanwhile, the local success of another American Vietnam drama, *The Deer Hunter* (1978), persuaded filmmaker Antonio Margheriti to cash in with an unofficial sequel, *L'ultimo cacciatore* (*The Last Hunter*, 1980). It was Italy's first Vietnam War film, and Margheriti took inspiration from Hollywood, shooting it in the

Philippines at many of the same locations used in *Apocalypse Now*. During production the director fell in love with the islands, promptly returning to make several more movies. Soon his colleagues—including Lucio Fulci, Ignazio Dolce, and Bruno Mattei—were following suit. Before long the Philippines had become the Cinecittà of Southeast Asia, playing in an assortment of Italian productions not just Vietnam, but also Cambodia, Brazil, the Caribbean—anywhere vaguely tropical.

Thus in 1987 and '88 Bruno Mattei found himself on the Philippine island of Luzon directing the *Rambo*-inspired *Strike Commando* (1987) and a stack of other guys-with-guns flicks for his bosses at Flora Film. Most were standard Vietnam actioners, but eventually he was able to change up the routine and add a splash of science fiction. *Robowar* came about, Mattei recalled in an interview for *Nocturno Dossier*, "simply because I had seen *Predator*. I really liked it so I said, 'Let's do something like that!'" Set in a South American jungle like the Schwarzenegger film, it was another ideal project for the Philippines.

The task of developing the scenario fell to Claudio Fragasso and Rossella Drudi, a married couple who had previously collaborated on reworkings of *Dawn of the Dead*, *Rambo*, and *Indiana Jones*. Once the screenplay was in hand, Mattei tapped *Strike Commando* star Reb Brown, a muscly ex-football player and former Captain America, for his ersatz Arnold. The other commandos were cast from a pool of Mattei's regulars in addition to locals and expats. Prolific character actor John P. Dulaney, who was living in the Philippines at the time and played squad medic Papa Doc, recalls that his audition was particularly informal:

> [Italian genre movie regular] Mike Monte told me about the production and so we went to Bruno's hotel in Manila where we met and spoke briefly. It was pretty easy for Bruno to accept me for the [role]. I imagine I fit the doctor part neatly for him despite that I was […] overweight and didn't exactly fit the part of a guerrilla jungle fighter, but Bruno didn't seem to care. He may also have been desperate to find *any*one for the part.

Robowar shot for six weeks. Early each morning a small bus would collect the cast from their hotel and drive for an hour to the filming location at Mt. Makiling, a dormant volcano covered in extensive, sweltering rainforest. Fortunately, the shoot itself was relatively straightforward: "The crew was well oiled," Dulaney recalls, and "Bruno was such an even tempered director. Never raised his voice, always in command in a smooth and cool manner." However, a minor misfortune put Mattei very briefly out of action, requiring someone else to fill in. So Claudio Fragasso, filming *Oltre la morte* (*After Death*, 1989) nearby for the same company, was drafted to direct a sequence at the film's climax—without, he claimed, being told what had come before.

His scene couldn't have been too much of a mystery, however, as the film was effectively a carbon copy of *Predator* (1987) that he had helped to write. Drudi's script and Mattei's direction replicated even the minutiae, from the dead soldiers who appear to have been firing at nothing ("They shoot in all directions," intones the tracker); to the discovery of an old comrade's dog tags; to the raid on the enemy camp, during which the major pins a baddie to the wall of a hut with a knife and a quip.

Only the iconic mandibled alien was altered, replaced by a RoboCop-style

The Omega One suit attempted to blend elements of Predator and RoboCop, but for a fraction of the price.

cyborg with terrestrial origins (Mattei had been keen on incorporating elements from *RoboCop* as well). Mascher reveals in the final act that inside Omega One are the reanimated remains of Major Black's former compatriot, a casualty of a Viet Cong landmine. Behind the scenes, however, the suit was inhabited by several different actors including Romano Puppo, who pulled double duty as Omega One and one of the commandos. The economical robo-outfit consisted merely of a black suit with plastic armor and a modified motorcycle helmet. "I heard it was done by two Italian guys in their garage," recalls Dulaney, referring to Francesco and Gaetano Paolocci, who built creatures for several of Mattei and Fragasso's films. No one was particularly happy with the final design.

After *Robowar*, which saw a limited home video release in Asia and Europe, Mattei stayed on in the Philippines to finish his slate of movies for Flora Film, including Lucio Fulci's uncompleted *Zombi 3* (1988). In the 2000s Mattei would return once again to the islands where, along with actress Yvette Yzon, he would make nine more genre films—erotic, women-in-prison, and horror—before his death in 2007.

Shocking Dark

INSPIRED BY: *Aliens* (1986), *The Terminator* (1984)
COUNTRY: Italy
YEAR: 1989
PRODUCTION: Flora Film
DIRECTOR: Vincent Dawn (Bruno Mattei)
WRITER: Clyde Anderson (Rossella Drudi, Claudio Fragasso)
STARS: Haven Tyler, Christopher Ahrens, Dominica Coulson

Venice, "tomorrow." A toxic cloud has rendered the city uninhabitable. The Tubular Corporation, charged with the years-long decontamination effort, has built

198   5. Androids, Aliens, and the Apocalypse

a sprawling underground complex connecting Venice to the safe zone. But after losing contact with the facility's research team, the authorities send in an elite squad of marines known as Megaforce to investigate. Accompanying them are scientist Dr. Sara Drumbull (Haven Tyler) and the taciturn, suspicious Tubular representative, Samuel Fuller (Christopher Ahrens).

The group ventures into the sealed tunnels, but they're immediately waylaid by a madman who abducts one of the soldiers. They soon find their comrade alongside the corpses of the research team—all plastered to the wall in cocoons. Barely alive, he begs for death just before a monstrous claw bursts from his chest—while elsewhere a humanoid, fishlike creature attacks two more of their number. Pushing further into the facility, the marines pick up life signs that turn out to be those of a young girl, Samantha (Dominica Coulson), who's been hiding from the monsters for some time. Sara takes the orphan under her wing.

Their route leads them to the facility's genetics lab where they discover that the creatures are the result of a synthetic parasite that "reprograms" its host's DNA. Under protest from Fuller, they make for the compound's control center for more answers. However, according to their sensors, more of the beasts are rapidly approaching. The team retreats into a shelter, but the creatures still close in—so near that they should be visible, yet the room remains empty. Suddenly they burst into the chamber from below, forcing the marines to flee under cover fire.

Gaining enough distance, they stop to rest. Sara and Samantha take a side room, but they're locked in and attacked by a monster. As they gesture frantically for help at a security camera, Fuller quietly turns off the monitor. Fortunately, pulling a fire alarm brings their colleagues to the rescue and the team continues onward. Arriving in the control center, Sara and Megaforce learn the truth: The Tubular Corporation

(From left to right) Geretta Geretta, Mark Steinborn, Haven Tyler, Christopher Ahrens, Cortland Reilly, and Fausto Lombardi prepare to enter the polluted ghost city of Venice.

was responsible for the poisoning of Venice—one of the company's many ventures into biological weapons. Moreover, Samantha realizes that another of its weapons is Fuller himself—an android. Thus outed, Fuller kills the remaining marines and activates the facility's self-destruct mechanism—an action which will contaminate the entire planet. Sara and Samantha flee for their lives, pursued by Fuller, but creatures seize the girl. And even if Sara can rescue her in time, their only hope to escape the end of the world is a mysterious prototype transport pod built by Tubular....

∽∽∽

In Hollywood, movies are often pitched to less-than-imaginative investors using glib comparisons like "*Tomb Raider* meets *Transformers*" or "*Spider-Man* meets *Pulp Fiction*," providing an easy-to-digest but often inaccurate picture of the final film. But when Franco Gaudenzi, the Italian producer of *Predator* (1987) clone *Robowar* (1988) and Rambo knock-off *Double Target* (1987), asked for a script that was *Aliens* (1986) meets *The Terminator* (1984), that was precisely what he wanted. The overseas market was lucrative and locally-made copycat films were doing well. Ridley Scott's original *Alien* (1979) had already spawned *Alien 2: Sulla Terra* (*Alien 2: On Earth*, 1980) and *Contamination* (1980), and *The Terminator* had inspired the variation-on-a-theme *Vendetta dal futuro* (*Hands of Steel*, 1986). So why not the best of both worlds?

Gaudenzi commissioned his mash-up screenplay from husband-and-wife team Claudio Fragasso and Rossella Drudi. He specifically demanded numerous elements be lifted wholesale from *The Terminator*, including character names, which resulted in a protagonist called Sara. Drudi chafed at the micromanagement, refusing such requests where she could, and ultimately worked out a story built heavily upon James Cameron's *Aliens* (1986). Her original concept featured an extraterrestrial ship crashing into the Venetian Lagoon and wreaking new havoc on an already pollution-ravaged Earth.

Although very little of this concept survived, the pollution subplot remained. In fact, a 1990 MIFED film market brochure would describe *Shocking Dark* as simply "an ecological thriller set in Venice"—a breathtaking example of missing the forest for the trees. Nevertheless, Drudi's novel contribution to an otherwise by-the-numbers *Aliens* copy reflected Italy's contemporary environmental concerns. In the mid–1980s, the country could only process around 20 percent of the toxic waste it produced each year. This led to an international scandal when it was discovered that companies were offloading thousands of drums of toxic waste to developing nations like Nigeria—and that many of those containers were leaking. Separately, after the 1986 Chernobyl disaster, fear of a similar incident prompted the decommissioning of the country's nuclear power plants. Italy was greening, and ecological messages were already permeating its films, including the earlier *Terminator*-inspired *Vendetta dal futuro*.

With a screenplay in place, director Bruno Mattei, in an effort to make *Shocking Dark* look like an American production, cast several Americans living in Italy. He found his lead in Haven Tyler, a model from Connecticut who was studying abroad in Florence. Going in for her audition, Tyler was informed that the project was a horror film, but "I could quickly understand that it was an *Aliens* rip-off from the way they were describing it," she recalls. "I went in, and they just asked me to scream. That was it. That was the whole audition." She credits her casting to the fact that "I had red hair and freckles, and I kinda looked a little bit like Sigourney Weaver." However, committing to the film meant temporarily abandoning her studies—and breaking the news to her father, a conservative lawyer: "I had to call him and say, 'Yeah, I'm going to be dropping out of school second semester senior year in college to do this film in Italy.' And I remember there was a long pause. And he said, 'Are there monsters?' I said yes. He said, 'Do you get to kill them?' and I said yes. And he was like, 'Fantastic!' So once I had his approval I was good to go."

From there, Tyler and the rest of the cast and crew embarked on six weeks of shooting in various locations throughout Italy. Much of the underground complex was filmed at the decommissioned Latina Nuclear Power Plant near the west coast, where Rossella Drudi had a connection. The underground tunnels at Roma Termini railway station in Rome served as other parts of the facility. And the finale was shot on location in Venice. The only set built for the film was the transport pod.

Throughout production Mattei recreated *Aliens* in often shot-perfect detail, including the pursuit and introduction of Samantha (Newt in *Aliens*); the discovery of the cocooned corpses—with one victim still alive and begging for death before a chestburster finishes the job; Sara giving Samantha a good luck charm and promising not to leave her ("I cross my heart" and "And hope to die?"); the attack on Sara and Samantha which Fuller (Burke in *Aliens*) tries to hide by turning off the security monitor; the advance of an apparently invisible horde ("The reading is correct, look!" and "You can't be reading that right!"); the desperate flight from the facility's imminent destruction; and Samantha's capture by creatures at the eleventh hour.

Only at the film's climax does it really begin to emulate *The Terminator*, with

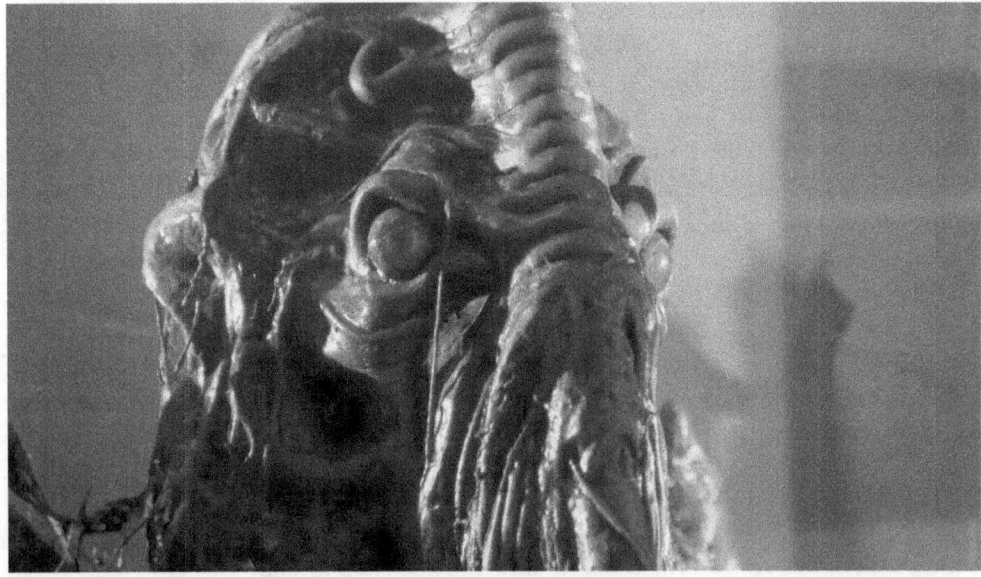

One of two styles of monster suits created for the film by the Paolocci brothers, the same duo who built the Omega One for *Robowar* (1988).

Fuller revealed as an unstoppable, murderous robot that pursues Sara and Samantha through the complex just as the T-800 chased Sarah Connor and Kyle Reese through the Cyberdyne factory. (Coincidentally, the revelation of a character as a deadly android with loyalties to a scheming corporation is also an element of 1979's original *Alien*.) And once the heroes reach the Tubular transport pod—a time machine that sends them back to the pollution-free present day—the film plants itself firmly in *Terminator* territory. In fact, Gaudenzi even managed to release the movie in some territories as *Terminator 2*, beating the official sequel to the punch.

After *Shocking Dark*, Mattei was done with killer robots, but he'd revisit *Aliens* in 2007 for his final film, *Zombi: La creazione* (*Zombies: The Beginning*), the sequel to *L'isola dei morti viventi* (*Island of the Living Dead*, 2007). Following Cameron's movie beat for beat, only swapping Xenomorphs for zombies, the film follows the sole survivor of an undead-infested isle as she's rescued from the ocean, discredited by the insurance company that underwrote the ship she was forced to destroy (on account of zombies), and sent back with a squad of soldiers after they lose contact with a medical team on the island. The film comes complete with a Burke surrogate, zombie chestbursters, flamethrowers, and even a Zombie Queen that births baby zombies.

Starcrash

INSPIRED BY: *Star Wars* (1977)
COUNTRY: Italy
YEAR: 1978
PRODUCTION: Film Enterprises Productions
DIRECTOR: Luigi Cozzi
WRITERS: Luigi Cozzi, Nat Wachsberger
STARS: Marjoe Gortner, Caroline Munro, Christopher Plummer, David Hasselhoff, Robert Tessier, Joe Spinell, Judd Hamilton

Daredevil galactic smuggler Stella Star (Caroline Munro) and her mystical companion Akton (Marjoe Gortner) find themselves in a strange situation. Caught and imprisoned by Imperial police, they're granted a miraculous reprieve when the Emperor of the Universe (Christopher Plummer) singles them out for a mission of cosmic importance.

It appears the evil Count Zarth Arn (Joe Spinell) has built a secret weapon so large that it would require an entire planet to conceal it. One of the Emperor's spaceships was close to discovering its location when it came under attack and disappeared. The Emperor entreats Stella and Akton to find and destroy the Count's secret planet and, if possible, locate the ship and its commander—the Emperor's only son. Accompanying them on their mission are the scowling, green-skinned Chief Thor (Robert Tessier), and Elle (Judd Hamilton), an affable robot with a Darth Vader chassis and a Texas drawl.

The team narrows its focus to three planets in the heart of the Haunted Stars. They strike out on the first, discovering only a race of hostile Amazons and a sword-wielding robotic colossus. They fare poorer still on the second planet, a frozen wasteland and the last resting place of the Emperor's ship. As Stella and Elle search vainly for survivors among the wreckage, Thor reveals himself as a traitor, dealing

Akton a deadly blow and leaving the others to freeze to death outside. Fortunately, Akton is no ordinary mortal and survives. He kills Thor and rescues the castaways in the nick of time.

Arriving on the third planet, Stella and Elle are promptly set upon by a tribe of cavemen who capture the heroine and destroy the robot. But before Stella can be killed, she's rescued by a mysterious figure who turns out to be the Emperor's son, Simon (David Hasselhoff). Joined by Akton, they discover that this planet is the very one they've been searching for: the location of the Count's weapon. Unfortunately, the revelation is dampened by the appearance of the Count himself. Flanked by two skeletal robot golems, the despot reveals that he has lured the Emperor to the planet and set it to explode upon his arrival. With only minutes remaining, Stella and her companions must destroy the golems and prevent the assassination of the Emperor so that together they might stop the Count from conquering the universe.

～～～

By the mid–1970s, Italian writer/director Luigi Cozzi was dying to make a science fiction movie. He had been an avid fan of the genre ever since he was a child. Yet although he had established an excellent reputation for himself as a filmmaker, he just couldn't get a sci-fi movie off the ground. Outer space stuff was box office poison, said Italian producers; nobody wanted to make it.

Then *Star Wars* arrived in 1977 and everything changed.

When producer Nat Wachsberger telephoned Cozzi in the summer of '77 and asked him if he could make a space opera just like *Star Wars*, how could he refuse? Wachsberger said, "Be ready [with a story] in 10 days from now when I come to meet

A big Ray Harryhausen fan, Luigi Cozzi based the robot golems on the "children of the Hydra's teeth" skeletons from *Jason and the Argonauts* (1963). The creatures themselves were built and animated by Armando Valcauda.

you in Rome." Cozzi readily agreed, but there was just one problem he failed to mention. He had never seen *Star Wars*.

That's hardly surprising; *Star Wars* wouldn't be released in Italy for another six months. But as luck would have it, Cozzi just happened to own the novelization of the film which had been published the previous year. That became his key to experiencing the story of *Star Wars*, and from there he began work on his own version: *Empire of the Stars*—a title later changed at Wachsberger's insistence to the more dynamic *Starcrash*.

True to his word, Cozzi's story had all the requisite *Star Wars* hallmarks, from massive ships traveling through hyperspace, to laser battles and lightsabers, to robot sidekicks and mysterious spiritual superpowers. It even had, in a sense, *two* Death Stars. One is Count Zarth Arn's planet-sized ultimate weapon, and the other is his flagship-cum-space-station, an immense metal claw where the final battle takes place—a sequence that echoes the iconic trench-run from the climax of *A New Hope*.

However, *Starcrash* is no mere clone. Despite his orders for a knock-off, Cozzi wasn't really interested in copying *Star Wars*. He was a huge fan of all things science fiction and fantasy, and he chose instead to make his film a love letter to the entire genre. The first spaceship we see, for example, is named after sci-fi author Murray Leinster—and the movie is littered with references to Robert Heinlein, Leigh Brackett, Roberta Rambelli, Edmond Hamilton, and other literary visionaries. The film borrows freely from *Flash Gordon*, *Barbarella* (1968), and *Forbidden Planet* (1956). Because Cozzi was particularly enamored with the filmography of Ray Harryhausen, Stella's battle with the Amazons' robot guardian is a near-duplicate of the Talos sequence from *Jason and the Argonauts* (1963), while the coastline used for the spaceship wreckage on the Amazons' planet is a location straight out of 1973's *The Golden Voyage of*

U.S. one-sheet for *Starcrash* (1978). The robot Elle may look like an evil Sith lord, but he's really just a friendly, folksy lawman. Also, because the spaceship *Murray Leinster* was accidentally printed upside down on some of the promotional photos, it was mistakenly drawn the same way on the poster.

Sinbad (in which Caroline Munro also starred). In fact, Cozzi describes his original concept as "Sinbad on Mars," a moniker that suits the film perfectly.

The producers also had some peculiar non–*Star Wars* suggestions. One of the film's backers was American International Pictures, which had just had a big hit with *The Land that Time Forgot* (1974). AIP apparently felt that the movie's success was due primarily to its inclusion of dinosaurs and cavemen, and therefore they demanded that *Starcrash* have them as well. Thus, our heroes do face a horde of troglodytes on Zarth Arn's weapon planet, but although a dinosaur sequence was filmed for Stella's escape from prison, it was not included in the final cut.

Overzealous studio executives were the least of Cozzi's problems. The entire production of *Starcrash* was a study in adversity. The cast and crew wrestled with extreme temperatures, union strikes, and constant money troubles. During the most difficult days, wages and per diems might be paid out of the producers' own pockets, from shady suitcases full of cash, or occasionally not at all.

The film's financial difficulties were a particular burden on special effects director Armando Valcauda, who had merely been shown a bootleg videotape of *Star Wars* and instructed to make spaceships that looked like that. Yet the entire budget for *Starcrash* was a mere $4 million (compared to *Star Wars*'s $11 million), and less than $30,000 of that was allotted for special effects. Valcauda was being asked to do the impossible.

His splashy outer space vistas were created using little more than black construction paper and colored lights. The spaceships, carefully built and textured, were a harrowing exercise in "kitbashing"—creating original models out of pieces from existing model kits. To save money Valcauda even made use of the molding sprue framework that held the model pieces together in the box! Moreover, all of the film's visual effects, from the outer space dogfights to the swordplay with the robot golems, were achieved using classic in-camera techniques like rear-projection, stop-motion, and double exposure, rather than optical printing which would have been far too expensive.

Cozzi and his team continuously fought hardship with perseverance, and in the end they were rewarded. *Starcrash* sold over one million tickets in Italy, and when the film was exported to the United States it was released to the tune of $16 million in box office revenue. Wachsberger got his Italian *Star Wars*, and Cozzi finally got his vibrant science fiction epic. "And for a little time, at least," says the Emperor at the end of the film, no doubt echoing Cozzi's sentiments, "we can rest."

Time of the Apes

INSPIRED BY: *Planet of the Apes* (1968)
COUNTRY: Japan
YEAR: 1987
PRODUCTION: Tsuburaya Productions
DIRECTORS: Fukazawa Kiyosumi, Okunaka Atsuo
WRITER: Abe Keiichi
STARS: Tokunaga Reiko, Saitō Hiroko, Kaji Masaaki, Ushio Tetsuya, Hatakeyama Baku, Takita Kazue, Ōmae Wataru

Time of the Apes

Schoolchildren Jirō (Kaji Masaaki) and Yurika (Saitō Hiroko) are touring a cryogenics lab when a massive earthquake suddenly strikes. Lab assistant Kazuko (Tokunaga Reiko) bundles herself and the children into shielded cryo pods to protect them from falling debris, but the chambers are accidentally activated, putting the trio into cold sleep. When they awake in an unfamiliar hospital, they discover that they've been frozen for centuries and the Earth is now ruled by intelligent apes!

The three are seized by a chimpanzee army and placed before a firing squad, but they make a desperate break for it. Reaching a nearby village, they sneak into a house and meet a friendly ape child named Pepe (Takita Kazue). Before they can be formally introduced, the humans are chased off and flee to a forbidden area in Green Mountain. There they discover a lone human, Gōdo (Ushio Tetsuya), who has lived there as a hermit his entire life.

Led by the unrelenting Police Chief Gebā (Hatakeyama Baku), the ape army closes in on its prey and smokes them out. Pepe attempts to warn them of the danger, but she's too late and the humans are captured. Gōdo is very nearly executed, but Cabinet Minister Bippu (Ōmae Wataru), a gorilla with human sympathies, arrives and forces Gebā's army to stand down. The humans are taken into custody and civilly detained.

The last remaining humans on Earth find themselves in the clutches of their ape masters. From left to right: Gebā (Hatakeyama Baku), Jirō (Kaji Masaaki), Yurika (Saitō Hiroko), Kazuko (Tokunaga Reiko), Secretary Goby (Yanami Jōji), Sabo (Watabe Takeshi), Gōdo (Ushio Tetsuya).

Pepe sneaks into the jail and succeeds in breaking out Jirō and Gōdo. The three escape into the country, intending to return for Yurika and Kazuko once the heat is off. They notice, however, that their progress is being monitored by a mysterious flying saucer. Eventually the fugitives reach a military outpost where Yurika and Kazuko have been transferred. They stage a jailbreak. Gebā and his soldiers very nearly recapture the prisoners, but the UFO appears and disables their weapons, allowing the heroes to flee in a jeep. Gōdo and Kazuko deduce that the flying saucer is controlled by a shadowy organization called UECCOM. Believing it to be on their side, the humans decide to seek it out and ask for protection.

Unfortunately, their path to UECCOM is blocked by Gebā. The ape has abandoned his post to demand a one-on-one showdown with Gōdo, who he believes is responsible for the death of his wife and son years ago. However, the flying saucer returns and reveals the truth: Gōdo was actually trying to rescue the ape's family, not kill them, and that child's death was caused by Gebā himself. Horrified, Gebā breaks down, and Gōdo and the humans drive away to discover the sinister secret of UECCOM.

~~~

Viewers will notice right away that *Time of the Apes* moves at a breakneck, almost dizzying pace. There's a very good reason for this: it isn't really a film at all, but rather a movie-length abridgment of a 26-episode TV series!

Its story begins with 20th Century–Fox's *Planet of the Apes* (1968), based on Pierre Boulle's novel of the same name. The movie was a sensation in Japan, doing big business at the box office and spawning two separate manga adaptations. Its four sequels were also hits across the Pacific, and an extended cut of *Conquest of the Planet of the Apes* (1972) was even produced exclusively for the Japanese market.

Eager to cash in on the *Apes* craze, local studios got in on the action. Fuji TV debuted kids' adventure series *Uchū Enjin Gori* ("Space Apeman Gori," later *Spectreman*) in 1971, and Toho dropped a race of simian invaders into its 1974 theatrical offering *Gojira Tai Mekagojira* (*Godzilla vs. Mechagodzilla*). However, both of these productions made the frugal choice to bring just a handful of apes down to the planet of the humans, rather than the other way around. But when TBS aired the Japanese network premiere of *Planet of the Apes* in 1974 to enormous ratings, it was emboldened to go a step further and commission a full-on *Apes*-style show of its very own. Consequently, TBS joined forces with Tsuburaya Productions, the company behind the wildly successful series *Urutoraman* (*Ultraman*, 1966) and founded by the late special effects wizard Tsuburaya Eiji.

However, TBS and Tsuburaya were aware that any such series would inevitably invite comparisons with *Planet of the Apes* and possibly even legal action from 20th Century–Fox. It was vital that, beyond its ape-world premise, the show be otherwise original. To that end, the production team approached prominent sci-fi author Komatsu Sakyō, whose recent novel *Nihon Chinbotsu* (*Japan Sinks*) had just been adapted into a major motion picture. Komatsu, together with collaborators Tanaka Kōji and Toyota Aritsune, developed the unique storyline for their new show, *Saru no Gundan* ("Army of the Apes," 1974).

Following a catastrophic earthquake that recalls Komatsu's recent disaster tale, *Saru no Gundan*'s stranded humans are led on a journey through an abandoned human outpost tenanted by a boxy caretaker robot, into the clutches of an ape spy masquerading as a surviving human, to a rural village whose religious ceremonies feature clever inversions of Japanese mythology, and into a deadly forest where the heroes are ambushed by ape ninjas—yes, *ninjas*—who leap from the trees wielding automatic weapons.

Meanwhile, in spite of the show's more outlandish aspects, Komatsu and company worked to incorporate into their universe various elements of zoological realism that *Planet of the Apes* had overlooked or misrepresented. Therefore, *Saru no Gundan*'s apes display such stereotypical behavior as chest-beating, social grooming, and fear of snakes. (Unlike ordinary apes, however, they have machine guns and the snakes do not.) The show also authentically portrays its gorillas as a gentler species and the chimpanzees as aggressive—traits which *Planet of the Apes* had flipped. In fact, a major series plotline involves a violent chimpanzee military coup staged against the gorillas.

In crafting its own story separate from *Planet of the Apes*, Komatsu's team was, quite possibly by accident, more faithful to Boulle's original novel than the official adaptation in one important respect. Here, as in the book, the apes have a modern civilization with electricity, automobiles, airplanes, and other contemporary technology. This stands in marked contrast to the 20th Century–Fox films in which the apes

Gōdo (Ushio Tetsuya) is surrounded by the Army of the Apes. ***Saru no Gundan*** **(1974) would premiere less than a month after the debut of the official *Planet of the Apes* (1974) live action TV series.**

live in primitive architecture (inspired by the work of Antoni Gaudí) and make use of even more primitive technology. It wasn't until a year after the premiere of *Saru no Gundan* that the official animated series *Return to the Planet of the Apes* (1975) would finally bring Dr. Zaius, Zira, and the other canonical simians up to date.

Saru no Gundan aired on TBS Sunday nights between October 1974 and March 1975. Then, some thirteen years after its original broadcast, the series was picked up for American distribution by producer Sandy Frank. Frank had been distributing Japanese entertainment in the U.S. since 1977, when he bought and recut the superhero anime *Kagaku Ninja Tai Gatchaman* ("Science Ninja Team Gatchaman," 1972) into a *Star Wars* cash-in called *Battle of the Planets*, rewriting the story and adding new scenes. By the mid–1980s Frank had moved on to selling bundles of dubbed Japanese sci-fi films, like the *Gamera* franchise, to television for syndication. Realizing perhaps that *Saru no Gundan* could tap into *Apes* fandom in the States just as it once had in Japan, Frank licensed the show from Tsuburaya Productions. But rather than release it as a series, he chopped it down to movie length to match his other offerings, titling his new version *Time of the Apes*.

Of course, condensing 650 minutes into 97 is bound to cause some narrative incoherence. Focusing its edit job primarily on the main arc of the series, numerous plot elements—including major revelations—were marginalized or expunged, with swaths of episodes vanishing in a single splice. Thus, American viewers missed out on the chimpanzee coup, the ape ninjas, a wicked mandrill witch doctor, and a guitar-strumming ape troubadour—none of which directly served the stripped-down narrative.

It only remains for some even wilier editor to re-edit that discarded footage into *Time of the Apes 2*.

Turist Ömer Uzay Yolunda ("Ömer the Tourist in Star Trek")

INSPIRED BY: *Star Trek* (1966)
COUNTRY: Turkey
YEAR: 1973
PRODUCTION: Saner Film
DIRECTOR: Hulki Saner
WRITER: Ferdi Merter
STARS: Sadri Alışık, Cemil Şahbaz, Erol Amaç, Ferdi Merter, Kayhan Yıldızoğlu, Şule Tınaz

Stardate 2520.1. The Federation starship *Enterprise* is dispatched to the barren planet Orin 7 for a routine medical check-up of archaeologist Professor Crater (Kayhan Yıldızoğlu) and his wife Nancy (Şule Tınaz). When ship's doctor McCoy (Ferdi Merter) teleports to the surface with First Officer Spock (Erol Amaç) and two crewmen, Crater receives them testily. He insists the pair are perfectly healthy and require no supplies beyond some salt. Suddenly a scream draws them outside where Nancy stands horrified over the body of a dead crewman. According to Nancy, he died from eating a native toxic plant, but Crater knows better. And in a preemptive move to protect his wife, he prepares to offer a scapegoat.

Meanwhile in Turkey on present-day Earth, a loud-mouthed rural vagrant named Ömer the Tourist (Sadri Alışık) is being railroaded into a literal shotgun wedding. But just before he's made to say "I do" he suddenly disappears, rematerializing on Orin 7. Dr. Crater presents the confused man to the *Enterprise* crew as the murderer. Brought to the ship for examination, the irreverent oaf gets up to all manner of mischief, from fiddling with buttons on the bridge to mercilessly razzing the alien Mr. Spock about his pointed ears and cold logic. However, the fellow is found to pose no real threat and is therefore given freedom to roam the ship.

Back on the planet, Nancy has murdered another crewman. She is, in reality, a shapeshifting creature that leaches salt from living organisms. In search of more prey, she mimics her latest victim and beams aboard the *Enterprise*. Soon more crew turn up dead, and Spock and Captain Kirk (Cemil Şahbaz) beam down with Ömer and McCoy to confront the professor. Crater eludes them, leading Kirk into the grasp of a fire-breathing monster. Spock rescues the captain just in time, and together they discover the body of the man Nancy impersonated.

Unfortunately, the salt monster is among them in the guise of McCoy. But seizing an opportunity, it takes the form of Spock's dead lover T'Pau and coaxes him into battling Kirk. Suspicious, Ömer approaches T'Pau, who ducks behind a rock and again impersonates the doctor, breaking the creature's hold over Spock. However, Crater promptly unleashes a horde of fighting androids from his hideout, and their superior numbers spell doom for the *Enterprise* crew and its bumbling guest.

~~~

Captain Kirk, Turist Ömer, and Mr. Spock are surrounded by a swarm of fighting-mad androids. Turkish lobby card.

Although experimented with more than a decade earlier, television wouldn't be introduced to Turkey in earnest until 1968. At a time when hardly anyone in the country could afford a TV set—they had to be imported from Germany—the state-run Turkish Radio and Television Corporation (TRT) launched a single station in Ankara. TRT broadcast its black-and-white signal just three evenings a week, eventually expanding to four in 1970. The duration increased over the course of the decade as TV sets slowly became more common, but with limited production facilities TRT turned to foreign programs to fill its lineup. Before long, foreign series and movies made up two thirds of TRT's programming. These imports were dubbed into Turkish by local stage actors, often classically trained, resulting in a level of quality that Turks still remember fondly. Through TRT, the nation was introduced to Golden Age Hollywood stars like Clark Gable, Katharine Hepburn, and Burt Lancaster, while shows like *The Fugitive* (1963), *Mission: Impossible* (1966), *Little House on the Prairie* (1974), and *Rich Man, Poor Man* (1976) became part of daily life. Tough guys were called "Falconetti," kids would emulate the Six Million Dollar Man by walking to school in slow motion, and passengers would spur on cab drivers by demanding "Işınla beni Skati!"—"Beam me there, Scotty!"

Star Trek first reached Turkish TV screens in 1972, six years after its initial airing in the States—a time when TRT's viewership was about half of Turkey's population. It was a sensation. Captain Kirk's swaggering heroism made him an instant role model for kids, and Mr. Spock was a proper phenomenon. "Spockmania" wasn't unique to Turkey, but part of what made the character resonate with Turks was his particular brand of wisdom and stoicism. Film and TV historian Ali Murat Güven compares the half–Vulcan to a quintessential Sufi wise man—thoughtful, methodical, and in strict control of his hands, tongue, and loins. Yet as popular as the characters were individually, it was their friendship, solidarity, and teamwork as a unit that made them beloved. That warmth and camaraderie gave *Star Trek* an edge over its British competition like *UFO* (1970) and *Space: 1999* (1975), whose heroes struck many Turkish viewers as cold and impersonal.

Recognizing enormous potential for the show beyond the small screen, filmmaker Hulki Saner approached actor Ferdi Merter, the Turkish voice of *Star Trek*'s Dr. McCoy, about the possibility of adapting it into a domestic theatrical feature. At first Merter was dubious. They couldn't simply imitate it, he argued. He was concerned that without visual effects on par with the series, audiences wouldn't take the film seriously. But if, on the other hand, it were intentionally played for laughs, it might work. However, it would need something unique; a fresh perspective. It needed Ömer the Tourist.

Ömer was a popular character from a series of Turkish comedies produced and directed by Saner and based on his uncle, a friendly, eccentric traveler. A lower-class fish-out-of-water and vagabond, Ömer had traveled to Germany, Spain, Arabia, and the jungles of Africa, offering humorous observations about the people and customs he encountered. Merter suggested that through Ömer, their *Star Trek* could be transformed from a lackluster imitation into a playful commentary on the material. Saner agreed.

Tasked with writing the screenplay, Merter pored through episodes of the TV series. For the majority of his script he borrowed the plot of "The Man Trap"—the first episode to air on NBC in 1966. But to fill out a feature run time, he also lifted elements from other *Star Trek* stories, including androids from "What Are Little Girls Made Of" and "I, Mudd," the Gorn from "Arena," and the fight between Kirk and Spock from "Amok Time." Yet all the while Merter consciously kept the focus on Ömer.

Going into production, Saner made the savvy decision to cast the show's Turkish voice actors as their onscreen counterparts. Unfortunately, Oytun Şanal was unavailable to reprise his role as Kirk, so another actor, Cemil Şahbaz, played him on screen and Şanal still provided the dubbing. Ferdi Merter also did much of the production design, and through his efforts the *Enterprise* interior, the uniforms, and the salt monster were all slavishly duplicated. And although Spock uncharacteristically wears yellow instead of blue and Scotty sports green instead of red, local fans were unlikely to have noticed; color TV wouldn't be introduced to Turkey until 1981.

In spite of Merter's fears, Saner's production values hewed fairly closely to those of *Star Trek*, as American television shows and Turkish features were similarly forced to shoot quickly and cheaply. They merely had different strengths. To save time and manpower, series like *Star Trek* were filmed exclusively on sound stages, giving the crew greater control over the environment, lighting, and final image, but resulting in small and noticeably artificial sets. However, in Turkey, where there were no major studio facilities, the best way to contain costs was to shoot on location. Therefore, much of *Turist Ömer Uzay Yolunda* was shot among the sprawling ruins of Ephesus, site of the Temple of Artemis, one of the Seven Wonders of the Ancient World. This spectacular tourist attraction gave the film a much grander scope than an American TV budget would have allowed, even though its technical resources may have been restricted.

Speaking to website *Sabah*'s Olkan Özyurt in

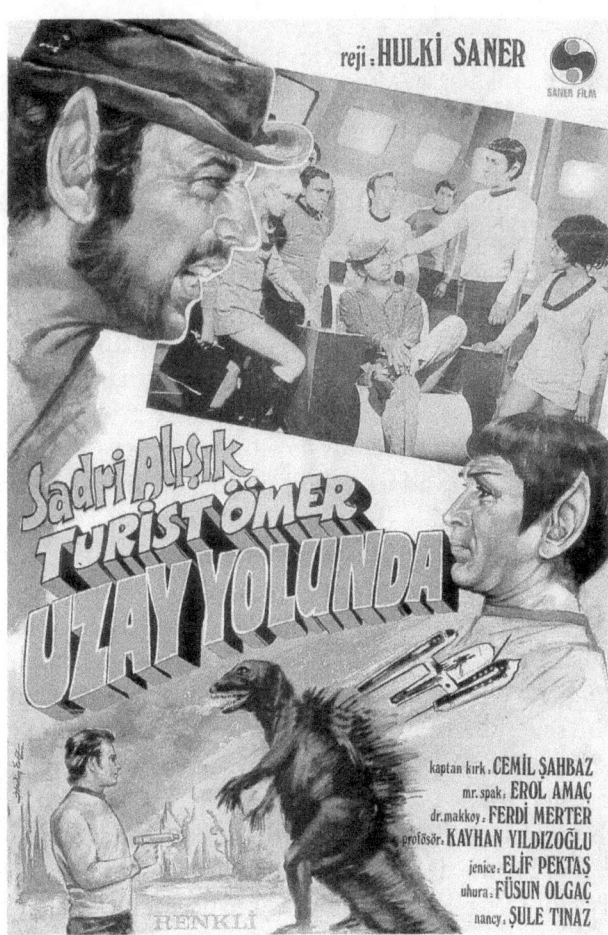

The first *Star Trek* movie, predating *Star Trek: The Motion Picture* (1979) by six years. Turkish one-sheet.

2009, Merter recalled that, just as Saner anticipated, audiences loved the movie: "[N]o one could believe it. We were constantly giving interviews and attending events." The film has remained fairly popular, regularly airing on television and receiving a high-definition restoration in 2016. Reportedly it was also the inspiration for comedian Cem Yılmaz's record-breaking sci-fi parody *G.O.R.A.* (2004), which tells the story of another uncouth local abducted by spacemen. Featuring numerous references to the scrappy films of Yeşilçam in addition to the Hollywood movies it spoofs, *G.O.R.A.* spawned two sequels of its own, firmly establishing Yılmaz as one of the Turkish *Star Trek*'s next generation.

Uchū kara no Messēji (*Message from Space*)

INSPIRED BY: *Star Wars* (1977)
COUNTRY: Japan
YEAR: 1978
PRODUCTION: Tōei Company, Ltd
DIRECTOR: Fukasaku Kinji
WRITER: Matsuda Hirō
STARS: Vic Morrow, Chiba Shin'ichi, Philip Casnoff, Peggy Lee Brennan, Shihomi Etsuko, Narita Mikio, Sanada Hiroyuki, Okabe Masazumi

The once-beautiful planet Jillucia has been ravaged, converted into a giant fortress by the conquering Gavanas and their leader, Emperor Rockseia XXII (Narita Mikio). In a last-ditch attempt to save his people, the Jillucians' elderly ruler casts eight magical Liabe seeds into space in search of eight saviors. Two of these land in the possession of space hotrodders Shiro (Sanada Hiroyuki) and Aaron (Philip Casnoff). Another appears in the drink of the disenchanted General Garuda (Vic Morrow). A fourth falls into the hands of cowardly hustler Jack (Okabe Masazumi).

None know what to make of the seeds until Jack, the pilots, and their rich-kid friend Meia (Peggy Lee Brennan) spy a wrecked Jillucian ship in the middle of an asteroid belt. On board they discover an unconscious royal, Emeralida (Shihomi Etsuko), and pull her out just as a Gavana ship attacks. They escape to Shiro and Aaron's home, where Garuda has been sleeping off his liquor. When Emeralida recovers, she sees their Liabe seeds and tries in vain to enlist them to her cause.

Jack does worse than refuse. With the complicity of Shiro and Aaron, he betrays Emeralida, selling her into slavery and delivering her into the Gavanas' hands. When Meia discovers what they've done, she's horrified and abandons them. Nightmares about the fate of the Jillucians trigger a change of heart in her friends, however, and when Meia discovers a fifth Liabe seed, she returns. They join forces to save Emeralida, and along the way they pick up the recipient of the sixth seed: the benevolent Prince Han (Chiba Shin'ichi), true heir to the Gavana throne.

Meanwhile, Rockseia travels to Earth in his warship with the entire planet of Jillucia in tow. He makes short work of Earth's defenses and gives humanity three days to surrender. General Garuda is sent to stall for time but is unsuccessful. Remembering the Liabe seed, he decides instead to join the Jillucians' cause and rendezvous with the other chosen ones.

The heroes learn that the only way to defeat the Gavanas is to pilot a small fighter

Uchū kara no Messēji (Message from Space)

The heroes cram into the cockpit of the *Liabe Special*, more than a little reminiscent of the *Millennium Falcon*'s interior. Top row, from left to right: Satō Makoto, Sanada Hiroyuki, and Philip Casnoff. Bottom row, from left to right: Chiba Shin'ichi, Peggy Lee Brennan.

ship into the planet and blow up the reactor that powers their fortress. It will require expert flying down a narrow tunnel and even more expert shooting. Unfortunately, they learn too late that they have a traitor in their midst, and the Gavanas' army has them surrounded....

~~~

Jaws from space. That was more or less how *Uchū kara no Messēji* began. The folks at Tōei Company had just abandoned a British co-production called *Kongorilla*, and following the staggering success of Steven Spielberg's *Jaws* (1975) they decided to switch gears, emulating the killer shark film but on a cosmic scale. *Debirumanta* ("Devil Manta") would detail the arrival of a giant manta ray from space that wreaks havoc on Earth. (It's hard to close the beaches when the beaches are the entire planet!) But before the project could get past the development phase, *Star Wars* (1977) arrived. Giant fish paled in comparison to galactic dogfights and laser sword battles, so word came down from Tōei's top brass to start over. Good-bye space monster, hello space opera.

Star Wars wouldn't actually reach Japan until the middle of 1978, but awareness of the film was like the Force: it was everywhere. Several Japanese studios were eager to cash in on audience anticipation and rushed their own space adventures into production. Toho cranked out *Wakusei Daisensō* (*The War in Space*, 1977) in just a few months, cobbling it together with elements from several of the studio's earlier sci-fi offerings. Looking to the small screen, Tsuburaya Productions bought the rights to American novelist Edmond Hamilton's *Starwolf* trilogy from the '60s, retrofitted it with *Star Wars* style ships and lightsabers, and broadcast it as *Sutā Urufu* (*Star Wolf*, 1978). And Tōei had already reaped the benefits of *Star Wars* mania once, albeit inadvertently, when its 1977 *Uchū Senkan Yamato: Gekijōban* (*Space Battleship Yamato:*

The Movie), edited down from Matsumoto Leiji's sci-fi anime TV series, hit theaters at just the right time.

Tōei boss Okada Shigeru had a penchant for chasing Hollywood film trends. Following the popularity of '70s American disaster movies like *Airport* (1970) and *The Towering Inferno* (1974), he produced the runaway-train thriller *Shinkansen Daibakuha* (*The Bullet Train*, 1975). Later, his horror film *Jigoku* (*The Inferno*, 1979) would piggyback on *The Exorcist* (1973) and *The Omen* (1976), and *Kyōryū Kaichō no Densetsu* (*Legend of Dinosaurs and Monster Birds*, 1977) would finally give him the *Jaws*-esque killer animal movie he had been looking for. *Uchū kara no Messēji* was a similar endeavor, and in preparation Okada sent a team consisting of his son Okada Yūsuke, screenwriter Matsuda Hirō, and special effects artist Yajima Nobuo to Hawaii to watch *Star Wars* and see how it could be adapted for Japan.

On his return, Matsuda worked with manga artist Ishinomori Shōtarō and author Noda Masahiro to develop the story in detail. Searching for inspiration, Matsuda looked to Takizawa Bakin's 19th-century epic *Nansō Satomi Hakkenden* ("Satomi and the Eight Dog Warriors"). The 106-volume saga tells of a princess of the Satomi clan who, upon her death, casts eight magical rosary beads to the wind. The beads fall into the hands of eight unrelated youngsters who grow up to become samurai. Over time the warriors discover each other, eventually banding together to help the Satomi family battle its enemies in the shogunate. Matsuda and his team would change the Satomi clan to a conquered planet, the beads to seeds, the samurai to a ragtag bunch of misfits, and the shogunate to a warlike race of invaders.

To direct the film, Okada tapped Fukasaku Kinji, best known for his violent yakuza films like the seminal *Jingi Naki Tatakai* (*Battles Without Honor or Humanity*, 1973). His career was a varied one, however, and had already included science fiction. His *Ganmā Daisan Gō: Uchū Daisakusen* (*The Green Slime*, 1968) was a loose sequel to Antonio Margheriti's Gamma One quadrilogy about the adventures of a space station crew. For this new sci-fi project, Fukasaku cast several of his yakuza regulars, including Chiba Shin'ichi—better known in the West as Sonny Chiba—and Narita Mikio. He and Okada also brought in American actors to give the film more international appeal. Vic Morrow was well known in Japan thanks to airings of the ABC television series *Combat!* (1962), while Philip Casnoff and Peggy Lee Brennan were stage actors selected from New York auditions.

The budget for *Uchū kara no Messēji*, between $5–6 million, was massive for a Japanese production, but still only half that of *Star Wars*. Fukasaku and company made the most of it, however, incorporating multiple state of the art technologies to achieve the film's visual effects. These included the Snorkel Camera System, a remote-controlled periscope camera for photographing miniatures, and the Totsu ECG System, a video-to-film process that allowed for instant compositing and on-set review. These techniques complemented the massive sets built for the film, including a full-size recreation of the Jillucian ship *Prayer Star*—a space-faring galleon complete with sails.

Even though the film was by no means a carbon copy of *Star Wars*, the production design still owes a great deal to Lucas's film. Blasters and electric swords abound, General Garuda gets a pint-sized robot companion in the vein of R2D2 and C3PO,

Uchū kara no Messēji (Message from Space)

General Garuda (Vic Morrow) and his stubby robot pal Beba-2 enter the Gavanas' fortress. Mini lobby card.

Meia's ship bears a notable resemblance to the Millennium Falcon down to its turret gun wells, and of course the Gavanas' planet fortress is the film's own Death Star complete with the power to destroy worlds—and concealing a fatal, hard to reach weakness. The music, too, echoes *Star Wars*, emulating the Gustav Holst stylings of composer John Williams. On the other hand, one might consider all of these similarities a case of turnabout as fair play, since *Star Wars* was itself heavily influenced by Japanese samurai films like Kurosawa Akira's *Kakushi toride no san akunin* (*The Hidden Fortress*, 1958).

Ultimately, *Uchū kara no Messēji* found only mediocre success at the box office. However, Tōei promptly continued the story for television with the 27-episode spin-off *Uchū kara no Messēji: Ginga Taisen* (*Message from Space: Galactic Wars*, 1978). A blend of space opera and Super Sentai–style action, the series included even more *Star Wars* elements, such as a Chewbacca-like ape-man called Baru. The show found its way to the U.S. in the early '80s when 3B Productions licensed it and tasked Michael Part, who had worked on the Americanization of *Supekutoruman* (*Spectreman*, 1971), to edit it down to a feature-length film. By that time, *Raiders of the Lost Ark* (1981) was the hot new property, so Part enterprisingly titled his film *Swords of the Space Ark*. With that decision, he fittingly ended the *Uchū kara no Messēji* story where it started: with a cash-in on a Steven Spielberg movie.

Warrior of the Lost World

INSPIRED BY: *Mad Max 2: The Road Warrior* (1981)
COUNTRY: Italy
YEAR: 1983
PRODUCTION: Royal Film
DIRECTOR: David Worth
WRITER: David Worth
STARS: Robert Ginty, Persis Khambatta, Donald Pleasence, Fred Williamson, Harrison Muller

The radiation wars have ended and the world's nations have collapsed. Upon their remains, a despot named Prossor (Donald Pleasence) has established a new martial regime called the Omega, maintaining law and order through drugs and mind control. Outside the Omega's domain are a wasteland populated by tribal gangs and mountains home to a cabal of rebels and mystics. Through these speeds the Rider (Robert Ginty), a scruffy loner on a high-tech talking motorcycle.

Pursued by Omega soldiers in deadly souped-up junk cars, the Rider is forced into a head-on collision with the side of a cliff. When he wakes, he finds himself in the rebels' camp, his injuries healed by mystics. The rebels, under the temporary command of an unnamed officer (Fred Williamson), require the Rider's help to rescue their leader, Professor McWayne (Harrison Muller), from the Omega's clutches. The Rider prefers not to get involved, but McWayne's daughter Nastassia (Persis Khambatta) forcefully changes his mind.

Disguised as municipal workers, the Rider and Nastassia travel on foot through underground caverns, avoiding hostile mutants, and finally arrive inside the city. They're not a moment too soon, either, as McWayne's execution is imminent. They stage a daring rescue and steal a helicopter, but Nastassia is hit by a bullet as the vehicle lifts off, leaving her stranded behind.

McWayne, now free and in need of larger forces, uses the Rider to enlist the support of the Wasteland gangs for a final assault on Omega HQ. As some of them infiltrate the HQ covertly, McWayne, the Rider, and the rest march on the city, gathering a convoy of vehicles from the Omega soldiers they kill along the way. All goes well until their path is blocked by Megaweapon, a massive armored truck carrying intense firepower. Its only weakness is a computer terminal on its underside, so the Rider launches himself beneath the chassis, sacrificing his bike. His gambit proves successful, and he fatally disables the supertruck.

The heroes arrive in the city, now under complete revolution, and the Rider and McWayne storm Prossor's headquarters. But the tyrant is far from beaten. He reveals a brainwashed Nastassia and orders her to kill her father and the Rider.

~~~

Strictly speaking, the original *Mad Max* movies aren't Hollywood films, hailing instead from half a world away in the Land Down Under. However, their cultural impact in the States was so substantial, incidentally launching the career of soon-to-be Hollywood star Mel Gibson, that Warner Bros. was eventually moved to co-produce an official entry in the series. So I'm going to stretch a point for the sake of a good story.

Warrior of the Lost World

After the modest success of *Mad Max 2: The Road Warrior* (1981) in the States, America produced a smattering of its own low budget junk-cars-in-the-desert flicks, including *Metalstorm: The Destruction of Jared-Syn* (1983) and *Wheels of Fire* (1985). But in Italy, where it was released as *Interceptor: Il guerriero della strada*, it generated an entire *filone*—or "thread"—of similar films. More than a dozen, in fact, including *I nuovi barbari* (*The New Barbarians*, 1983), *Il giustiziere della strada* (*Exterminators of the Year 3000*, 1983), and *Rage—Fuoco incrociato* (*A Man Called Rage*, 1984). Producer Eduard Sarlui had one too. He had already sold it internationally based on a poster of a masked biker in a post-apocalyptic futurescape. The only problem was, it didn't exist. He had pre-sold the movie based on the artwork and intended to use the profits to finance the film. But Sarlui didn't even have a script.

Enter David Worth, American cinematographer. Worth was the DP on two Clint Eastwood movies, and he had imagined those gigs would springboard him to other high-profile work. When the phone didn't ring, he eventually took matters into his own hands, calling around Hollywood with a movie treatment of his own. He pitched it as "*High Plains Drifter* on a motorcycle," about "a guy [who] rides out of the heat waves on a high-speed motorcycle, comes into town, kills all the bad guys, kisses the girl ... [and] disappears again into the heat waves on the highway." After striking out a few times, he finally caught a break with indie producer Sandy Howard, who pointed Worth to an Italian colleague named Eduard Sarlui.

It was a Wednesday when Worth telephoned Sarlui and gave him the pitch. The producer's response was brief: "Put it in the future." "Fine," replied Worth nonchalantly, "it's in the future." Sarlui asked, "How would you like to go to Rome and direct that movie?" The next day Worth was in Sarlui's Los Angeles office signing a contract, and on Friday he

German A1 poster for *Warrior of the Lost World* (1983). This final poster was based on director David Worth's own sketch which adorned the cover of his storyboards.

was on a plane to Rome. Stunned by the speed and his good fortune, he didn't realize at the time that he had just saved Sarlui's bacon by providing his missing futuristic biker film.

Now in Rome, Worth's first task was scouting locations. These included specimens of fascist architecture which would serve as Prossor's citadel and an automobile graveyard that could suggest the remains of the Golden State Freeway. Then over the next two weeks he wrote a comprehensive 40- to 60-page treatment based around those locations. When Sarlui returned to Rome, Worth showed up in his office, treatment in hand. The producer leaned back and closed his eyes. "Read it to me," he said. Worth did as he was told. "Okay," said Sarlui, "make the movie." Surprised, Worth asked, "Don't you want me to turn this into a script?" "No," Sarlui replied, "It's all there."

As an American making an Italian genre film, Worth was in an unusual situation. Faced with the prospect of working with a crew unlikely to speak much English, he decided to hire a translator. He found an American student, Susan Adler, who was studying Italian in Rome. Adler, who had never worked on a film, translated Worth's instructions to the local crew during pre-production. Worth's next order of business was communicating the story visually to the crew over the course of filming. To that end he drew 200 pages of storyboards, illustrating virtually every shot in the film. These became the "bible" for the shoot.

Casting for the lead roles was done remotely in Los Angeles with options sent to Worth for review. The director was impressed with Robert Ginty's vengeful performance in *The Exterminator* (1980) and selected him as the Rider. A long-time James Bond fan, he was thrilled to get Donald Pleasence, even styling Prossor's uniform after Blofeld's in *You Only Live Twice* (1967). Fred Williamson was a different story. He was already in Rome, having just made several films there including *I nuovi barbari*. He was just about to return to the States when he approached Worth at a party and asked the filmmaker to write him a part in *Warrior of the Lost World* so that he could extend his stay. Worth was happy to oblige, and Sarlui, also at the party, was delighted to have another bankable actor.

Worth never heard Sarlui mention *The Road Warrior* by name, but it was clear enough the kind of film

A leather-jacketed Robert Ginty does his best Mad Max impression while mounted on his supersonic speed cycle, Einstein.

the producer had in mind. Thus, he delivered the broad strokes of a *Mad Max* flick: a dystopian future, a jaded drifter, a vast wasteland, wildly costumed gangs of marauders, cars customized with mismatched hardware and assorted junk, a convoy of vehicles for the final battle with the bad guys, plenty of action, and minimal dialogue.

Mad Max wasn't Worth's only influence. In crafting the story, he structured the film like the classic adventure serials he enjoyed as a kid, with every couple pages of dialogue setting up the next five to ten minutes of action. The Rider's sassy talking motorcycle, Einstein, who speaks in short bursts of jive and surfer slang, borrowed elements of KITT from TV's *Knight Rider* (1982) and the droids from *Star Wars* (1977), all filtered through Worth's self-described "demented sense of humor." And of course, true to Worth's original treatment, the Rider enters and leaves the story through the heat waves on the highway, à la *High Plains Drifter*.

The film was released first in Italy as *Il giustiziere della terra perduta*, though *Warrior of the Lost World* was Worth's original title and appeared on the American home video release. It would eventually see replay on Italian television as *I predatori dell'anno omega*, and it gained most of its fame in the U.S. from its appearance on *Mystery Science Theater 3000* (1989). A sequel was planned, but it failed to materialize due to a falling-out between Worth and Sarlui over an aborted film in Argentina.

6

Outlaws, Outsiders, and Oscar Winners

12

INSPIRED BY: *12 Angry Men* (1957)
COUNTRY: Russia
YEAR: 2007
PRODUCTION: Three T Productions
DIRECTOR: Nikita Mikhalkov
WRITERS: Nikita Mikhalkov, Aleksandr Novototskiy-Vlasov, Vladimir Moiseenko
STARS: Sergey Makovetskiy, Nikita Mikhalkov, Sergey Garmash, Valentin Gaft

Twelve mismatched jurors are charged with deciding the fate of a Chechen teenager accused of killing and robbing his adoptive father, a former officer in the Russian army. The courthouse is being renovated, however, so the men are forced to deliberate in a repurposed middle school gymnasium.

The evidence of the boy's guilt appears overwhelming, so eleven jurors are horrified when Juror 1 (Sergey Makovetskiy) votes not guilty. The outlier believes the boy's life is not worth throwing away without discussion. However, after much protest from his peers he begins to buckle. He proposes a second vote—a secret ballot. If the others vote guilty, he'll go along; if not, they'll keep talking. Juror 4 (Valentin Gaft), an old Jewish man, comes to his rescue. He's had his own doubts, recalling the defense attorney's indifferent performance.

These arguments raise the ire of Juror 3 (Sergey Garmash), who lashes out with racist attacks against the old man. He believes the foreigners to be nothing more than capitalist savages who commit murder and buy up all of Moscow's businesses from honest Russian citizens. His faith in the boy's guilt is unshakable.

Juror 1 brings up the crux of the prosecution's case: the murder weapon, a knife which the boy once owned but claims he sold. It's a rare special forces combat knife, brought from Chechnya, and supposedly unobtainable in Moscow. The juror dramatically produces an identical knife, which he purchased easily, and suggests that the prosecution did not present their facts in good faith.

Others begin to agree with him. They reconstruct the floor plan of an elderly witness and determine it unlikely that he could have seen or heard what he claimed. Juror 3 rages and fearmongers, but another juror makes a convincing case for a frame-up, and yet another calls the once-solid testimony of an eyewitness across the street into question.

Juror 5 (Aleksey Petrenko, right) tells a story about his uncle's redemption in order to advocate for kindness.

Yet once the evidence unravels, they learn that whatever verdict they agree on, delivering it will only be the beginning of the story.

~~~

In 1991, following the collapse of the Soviet Union, Chechnya declared independence from Russia. What followed were two distinct, briefly separated wars in which Chechens attempted to permanently secure that independence. They met instead with hardship and loss. Russia prevailed, leaving an estimated 100,000 Chechen civilians dead and thousands more displaced. Meanwhile, any sympathy the average Russian may have had toward the oft-persecuted Chechen populace evaporated after the war's incursion into Moscow and the relentlessly negative coverage of the separatists in the state-owned media. Xenophobia seized hold. In 2007, ex-KGB Russian president Vladimir Putin, whose rise to power owed much to the second Chechen war, installed ally Ramzan Kadyrov as president of the Russian satellite state and began the process of authoritarian peace building.

Renowned filmmaker Nikita Mikhalkov, Oscar winner and president of the Russian Filmmakers' Union, was a longtime Putin supporter. He had directed a campaign ad for the president and famously co-authored an open letter urging him to take an unconstitutional third term of office. The same year as *12* he would produce *55*, a television special celebrating Putin on his 55th birthday. Mikhalkov's affinity for the leader and his autocratic policies had begun to show more strongly in his work, and it would transparently influence his approach to bringing *12 Angry Men* to Russian screens.

Reginald Rose originally wrote *12 Angry Men* as a 1954 episode of the anthology TV series *Studio One in Hollywood* (1948), later adapting it into a stage play that became the basis for Sidney Lumet's famous film. Powerful and inexpensive to shoot, it was an attractive subject for remakes all over the world—in Germany (*Die zwölf Geschworenen*, 1963), Norway (*Tolv edsvorne menn*, 1982), India (*Ek Ruka Hua Faisla*, 1986), France (*Douze hommes en colère*, 2010), and Hong Kong (*Shi'er gongmin*, 2014). *12* would not even be the first time that Mikhalkov had staged *12 Angry Men*; he had produced the play in 1966 while attending the Boris Shchukin Theatre Institute.

In adapting the story for a 2007 audience, Mikhalkov seized on the aftermath of the still-raw Chechen conflict to provide its backdrop. He transformed the young Puerto Rican defendant of *12 Angry Men* into the Chechen son of parents murdered by separatists (not, it should be noted, by Russian soldiers). Mikhalkov then populated his jury with a haphazard cross-section of Russian society: a racist cabbie, a Caucasian surgeon, an irreverent actor, an American-educated TV producer, a liberal democrat, and more. "The basis," Mikhalkov told *Reuters* at the Venice International Film Festival, "was the wish to see 12 people who are a reflection of our society, bound together because they have to solve the problem of a life that is unknown to all of them." Each gets their say, bringing their experiences, perspectives, prejudices, insecurities, and humanity to bear on the case. However, Mikhalkov left the last word for himself.

The mysterious foreman, played by director Nikita Mikhalkov. This photo was also used as the primary image for the film's Russian poster.

In *12*'s surprising finale, the aloof foreman, played by Mikhalkov, admits that he's always known the Chechen to be innocent. He believes, however, that the boy will be safer in jail than on the streets, where the real murderers will undoubtedly find and kill him. The foreman also hints at his own past as a GRU officer, not quite finishing the phrase, "Once an officer, always an officer." The line echoes Putin's oft-repeated "There is no such thing as a former *chekist*," using a term for someone in Russian intelligence. He proposes a solution he deems better than what the law can offer. Since the Russian population cares little about the boy, he suggests that the jurors take responsibility for him. When they demur, the foreman takes the teen under his own wing and promises to help him punish the murderers of his stepfather. Mikhalkov's role mirrors strongman Putin, and his authoritarian gesture of swooping in to take charge of the foreign boy depicts, as the director explained to the *Los Angeles Times*, "what I wish was true."

Mikhalkov also applied some dramatic license in his portrayal of Russia's judicial system. Just as in the American version, the film's judge obligates the jury to reach a unanimous verdict. This is of course the driving force of the story; until all the jurors are convinced one way or the other, they cannot leave the gym. In reality, however, Russian juries are only required to deliver a unanimous decision if deliberations last fewer than three hours. After that, if no consensus is reached, a majority vote is sufficient to convict, with a tie resulting in acquittal.

Trial by jury had only been reintroduced to the country in 1993 with the establishment of the Russian Federation, and it's not the default mode of criminal trial. In fact, jury trials compose only about 0.06 percent of all trials each year. Moreover, their history in Russia is rife with stories of corruption, with state security officials attempting to cajole or threaten jurors on the verge of acquittal into withdrawing, and verdicts of not guilty being conspicuously overturned. Mikhalkov paints a much rosier picture.

It's worth recalling, however, that Lumet's *12 Angry Men* is no bastion of realism either. With jurors instructed to examine only the facts presented in the case, Henry Fonda's solo investigation and purchase of an identical knife is blatant juror misconduct. Furthermore, throughout the film various jurors make speculative guesses or give their own "expert testimony" on elements of the case that would not be considered appropriate behavior for a real jury. The story has never been a documentary.

It's likely that Mikhalkov believed that, given the relative rarity of Russian juries, combined with viewers' greater familiarity with the American jury system through movies, he could get away with some legal legerdemain. Nevertheless, when *12* won the 2007 Themis Award in Law and Art, members of the Russian legal community were understandably uncomfortable. Lawyer and professor Ekaterina Mishina recalled,

> Their confusion had nothing to do with the artistic merits of the film: if my colleagues and I were not lawyers, if we didn't live in Russia and had never heard anything about the Chechen war, we would have absolutely loved this movie. Our problem was that the movie had nothing to do with the reality of Russian jury trials.

In any event, Mishina was certainly correct about the opinions of non–Russians. The film received a Golden Lion at the Venice International Film Festival and was nominated for an Academy Award in America. Back in Russia, Putin himself screened the film with Chechnya's Ramzan Kadyrov, declaring afterward, per news outlet *Prague Watchdog*, that the film "brought a tear to the eye." For Mikhalkov, there could almost certainly be no more favorable verdict.

Akounak Tedalat Taha Tazoughai ("Rain the Color of Blue with a Little Red in It")

INSPIRED BY: *Purple Rain* (1984)
COUNTRY: Niger
YEAR: 2015
PRODUCTION: Sahel Sounds
DIRECTOR: Christopher Kirkley
WRITERS: Mdou Moctar, Christopher Kirkley, Jérôme Fino
STARS: Mdou Moctar, Ahmoudou Madassane, Rhaicha Ibrahim, Kader Tanoutanoute

Agadez, Niger. The young, purple-clad electric guitarist Mahamadou "Mdou" Moctar, whose songs are widely shared via Saharan cell phones, has just moved to town. Astride his equally purple motorcycle, he rides to a wedding reception where he impresses the crowd with his skill. He also catches the ear of another musician, Ahmoudou (Ahmoudou Madassane), who's quick to befriend the newcomer. Afterward, Mdou returns home to practice in secret, as his religious father disapproves of his musical ambitions in the strongest possible terms.

The next day, Mdou explores the town and visits a shop where he inquires about a guitar for sale. At the same time, neighborhood girl Rhaicha (Rhaicha Ibrahim) has noticed Mdou. She follows him into the shop on the pretext of asking about a necklace, then contrives to get him to take her home. Smitten, he makes her a gift of the jewelry.

Mdou then visits Ahmoudou. He and his bandmate have been struggling in Agadez, where competition between artists for low-paying gigs is fierce. They convince Mdou to lend his talent to their group. There's an upcoming battle of the bands at the Alliance Française club, and Mdou signs them up. Hot shot Kader (Kader Tanoutanoute) is expected to win, but he's shaken when he hears of Mdou's arrival. He tries to recruit Mdou for his own band, but when he's rebuffed, Kader resorts to sabotage.

Mdou is working on a new song for the competition, and Kader pays a child to secretly record the rehearsal on his phone. Kader then invites Mdou and Rhaicha to a group picnic where he debuts Mdou's song as his own. Angry, Mdou storms off, stranding a disgruntled Rhaicha. Ahmoudou suggests one of his own compositions as a replacement contest entry, but Mdou refuses to play anyone else's music.

Things only get worse when Mdou's father finds his guitar and burns it. Mdou soon understands why: he discovers a book of poetry in his father's belongings, and his mother reveals that her husband used to write song lyrics. However, eventually his musician friends turned to drink and drugs, souring him on the profession forever.

Now, with hardly any time until the competition, Mdou will have to find an

Akounak Tedalat Taha Tazoughai ("Rain the Color of Blue...")

Rhaicha Ibrahim rides with Mdou Moctar, clad in a purple jacket on his purple motorcycle.

instrument, a song, and possibly some humility in order to defeat Kader, recover Rhaicha's affection, and regain Ahmoudou's respect.

～～～

Christopher Kirkley, a self-described "guerrilla ethnomusicologist" from Oregon, discovered Sub-Saharan Africa's unique music network as he traveled the Sahel in the late 2000s. Inspired by scholars like Alan Lomax, he had set out across West Africa with a guitar and a sound recorder with the goal of capturing something significant. He visited several young musicians, but when he'd ask to hear some of their regional music, he didn't get the live folk performances he expected. Instead, they'd take out their phones and play mp3s from tinny speakers—modern tracks with electronic instruments and even autotuning. At first Kirkley was put off, but after having the same experience over and over, he became fascinated. He realized he was witnessing a modern tradition: with internet access scarce or non-existent, popular local music was still going viral, traveling hundreds of miles one phone at a time via Bluetooth and memory cards. By the time Kirkley heard the songs, they were often stripped of any identifying information. But with effort he tracked down several of the artists, negotiated rights to their recordings, and in 2011 released an album called *Music from Saharan Cellphones* via his blog-turned-label Sahel Sounds.

Many of the tracks he collected were Tuareg guitar music. Traditionally a nomadic people, the Tuareg inhabit a vast swath of the Sahara and Sahel. Without a nation of their own, their tumultuous history has seen them battling the French, Malian, and Nigérien governments for independence. By the '90s the fighting—and severe droughts—had forced many Tuareg into exile in Libya and Algeria. There many musicians learned to play the electric guitar and began fusing its modern sound with traditional melodies. Bands like Tinariwen and Group Bombino sprang up playing songs about rebellion and democracy. Eventually, as Tuareg rock expanded both in geography and subject matter, it incorporated new elements like drum machines, synthesizers, and Auto-Tune. "Desert blues" were quickly embraced by Sahelian youth as part of the pop music scene. One of its hubs was Agadez, the fifth largest city in Niger.

Agadez would eventually become the home of Mahamadou Souleymane, a.k.a. Mdou Moctar. Moctar found his calling at age 12 when he witnessed a performance by Tuareg rock pioneer Abdallah Ag Oumbadougou. Unable to buy a proper guitar, Moctar cobbled one together out of old wood and bicycle cables. Then he hung out around older musicians to learn how they played. Years later, when his older brother acquired a real guitar, Moctar promptly commandeered it. Despite objections from his strict Muslim parents, he played with friends and composed his own songs. Eventually, however, responsibility reared its ugly head and he was compelled to move to Libya to find work. After a two-year stint digging wells, he returned to his family and his music. He played local gigs and soon began to acquire a following. In 2008 he traveled to Nigeria where he recorded his first album, *Anar*, influenced by Hausa music and its use of Auto-Tuned vocals. It never received a traditional release, but its songs circulated widely via the vast network of Saharan cellphones.

Thus, Moctar's music kept popping up throughout Kirkley's travels, and the Portlander was dying to know more about this "Hendrix of the Sahara." With the help of Tuareg rock fans on Facebook, he located Moctar, struck up a friendship over the phone, and visited him in Niger in 2012. Together they recorded Moctar's second album, *Afelan*, which Kirkley released on his Sahel Sounds label.

Before long, Kirkley had a crazy idea. He had often joked about remaking Hollywood movies for the Sahara, and now he had noted real parallels between Moctar's life story and *Purple Rain* (1984), Prince's loosely autobiographical film about struggling to make it in the Minneapolis music biz. Taking a page from filmmaker Jean Rouch's "ethnofictions," which presented fictional stories in authentic cultural settings, he proposed remaking *Purple Rain* with Moctar as its star—trading Prince's rococo outfits for a purple robe and tagelmust—and set against the backdrop of Agadez's flourishing music scene. He imagined a film shot entirely in Tamasheq, the Tuareg language, and made for a Tuareg audience. With luck it could also be used to promote desert blues to an international community in a way that documentaries never could. Moctar was amenable to the idea, though he had never heard of Prince. Kirkley gladly filled in the cultural gap with a DVD.

Since there's no word in Tamasheq for "purple," they did the best they could for the title, settling on "Rain the Color of Blue with a Little Red in It." In 2013 they shot a trailer, using that as the basis for a Kickstarter fundraising campaign. Their goal was to raise $12,000, and by the end they had topped that by nearly 50 percent. They were in business.

Kirkley and Moctar teamed up with French video artist Jérôme Fino, and together they worked out the story. Much of the structure was taken from *Purple Rain*, but a great deal had to be removed to accommodate a conservative Muslim audience. No nudity. No sex. No kissing. Not even hugging. The domestic violence angle disappeared as well, but the filmmakers incorporated real elements of Moctar's

Mdou Moctar, in his purple robe and tagelmust, performs at the battle of the bands.

relationship with his parents. What wasn't taken from the original or Moctar's own life came from the experiences of other Agadez musicians, including one whose devout mother really did burn his guitar. Cellphones naturally played a vital part in the story as well, spreading Moctar's music and allowing his Morris Day-esque rival to steal his composition.

For the ten-day shoot, Kirkley and Moctar recruited friends to form their Nigérien crew. No fiction films had ever been made in Agadez, so finding actors proved a challenge, especially with many locals concerned that the rock-oriented movie might be something sacrilegious. Fortunately, fellow musicians, family, and neighbors came to their aid to fill out the cast. Dialogue was entirely improvised based on the needs of each scene, and the story was often rewritten on the fly to accommodate production obstacles or moral objections. Together, the team weathered dust storms, blackouts, and vehicle breakdowns to get the movie in the can.

When the finished film finally premiered in Agadez, the crowd was ecstatic. Since then, *Akounak* has traveled to film festivals around the world, garnering considerable praise from the press. As for Moctar himself, his star has risen substantially. He has continued to release albums of increasing complexity and now alternates between touring the world and playing extravagant weddings in Agadez.

Cemo ile Cemile ("Cemo and Cemile")

INSPIRED BY: *Bonnie and Clyde* (1967)
COUNTRY: Turkey
YEAR: 1971
PRODUCTION: Erman Film
DIRECTOR: Çetin İnanç
WRITER: Çetin İnanç
STARS: Yılmaz Köksal, Ülkü Özen, Turgut Boralı, Kudret Karadağ

After a three-year sentence, Cemo (Yılmaz Köksal) is released from prison and met by his fiancée Cemile (Ülkü Özen). They return to their village in Anatolia where they're met with a grisly scene. A gang of bandits known as the Seven Mehmets has pillaged, raped, and slaughtered. Not a soul is left alive. Over the body of his sister, Cemo vows to hunt the men responsible and destroy them. Cemile, with no ties remaining, joins him.

The Mehmets have divided their plunder and split up, but Cemo tracks two of them to a blacksmith's shop and metes out deadly vengeance. He guns down three more Mehmets in another village and rescues a young woman from their clutches. The couple finds and kills the sixth Mehmet on the coast and the seventh in another village. Just as their mission is complete, however, the couple is ambushed by the authorities. Cemile takes a bullet, but the two shoot their way out and make a bold escape across a river. They stagger back to the village of the woman they saved, where they're taken in and cared for.

Once they've recovered, Cemo and Cemile leave on a bus, but when they spy a police roadblock ahead, they get out early and circumvent it on foot. Making their way into a city, they jump a train to the outskirts of another town, then steal a convertible at a gas station. Cemo, who learned to drive in the military, chauffeurs them to Istanbul where they plan to lose themselves in the metropolis.

Cemil (Yılmaz Köksal) gets his vengeance against one of the Seven Mehmets (Yavuz Selekman).

They quickly realize that their rural garb makes this plan untenable, so they rob a boutique for some fancier city clothes. Dressed for success, they check out the nightlife and steal a swankier car. Aware that they won't be able to get by for long without money, Cemo breaks the windows of a jewelry store and steals everything in the display. Unfortunately, he's spotted by the police. The lovers make a getaway, but now they're being hunted by both city and rural authorities.

With Istanbul too dangerous, they decide to spend much of their newfound wealth on fake passports. The police, anticipating their flight, try a ruse. They make it known that the duo is believed to have already escaped to the east, suggesting that the coast is now clear. In reality, however, a deadly trap awaits them.

～～～

For years, actor and filmmaker Yılmaz Güney, whose gruff, atypical leading-man looks earned him the nickname "the Ugly King," was the face of low-budget Anatolian Westerns. In the 1960s he was frequently seen slinging guns and riding horseback. However, following the success of his award-winning social drama *Umut* (*Hope*, 1970), he began focusing on political films and became harder to obtain for genre quickies. İzzettin Yılmaz of Erman Film, which produced some of Güney's early work, may have seen the writing on the wall. In 1970 he asked director Çetin İnanç, a frequent collaborator, to make an inexpensive Western starring the second tier but charismatic Yılmaz Köksal. With his Anatolian features and ever-present moustache, Köksal looked remarkably similar to Güney, and İzzettin may have intended to reintroduce him as a sort of Maurizio Merli to Güney's Franco Nero. The film was *Çeko* (1970) and it was a hit, particularly in Anatolia. Its success ensured stardom for Köksal and a free hand for İnanç on his next project, so long as it could be done on the cheap.

İnanç was an inveterate collector of ideas. Another movie, a newspaper item, a casual remark from a friend or relative—any of these might contain the germ of an idea for a film. He'd jot them all down on pocketed scraps of paper. When he saw Arthur Penn's *Bonnie and Clyde* in 1971 at Istanbul's Atlas Cinema, he recognized plenty of material he could use. "It was a good movie," he wrote in his memoir, *Jet Rejisör*, and "it had a theme that could be adapted for us. Imagine, a man and a woman who love each other come from the village to the big city because of a vendetta, experience a number of events, and then they become gangsters and rob a bank."

İnanç reteamed with Köksal, casting him in the Clyde role and ingénue Ülkü Özen as his partner. He named their characters—and the film—after songwriter Cemil Cankat's 1930s folk standard "Ay Cemo, Ay Cemile." This may have been a calculated move on his part, capitalizing on the song's popularity in southern Turkey and hoping that name recognition would sell tickets. He also got pop singer Berkant to record a cover of it, which would be featured in the film and released as a tie-in 45 by record label Televizyon Plâk.

It would be easy to forgive the viewer for not at first recognizing the film as a remake of *Bonnie and Clyde*. The first half bears very little resemblance to it. Perhaps capitalizing on Köksal's new cowboy screen persona, İnanç instead began the story like an Anatolian Western straight out of the Yılmaz Güney playbook: all horses and rifles and bandits and revenge. It's not until the latter half that İnanç begins to hew closer to his source material. Once in Istanbul, Cemo and Cemile acquire the Barrow Gang's penchant for fancy clothes, including Bonnie's iconic beret. As they leave a nightclub, they trade up their stolen car for a nicer one, just like Bonnie and Clyde outside the diner ("But we came in this one!" and "Don't mean we have to go home in it"). And of course, like their American counterparts, they rob banks—but more on that later.

One scene from *Bonnie and Clyde* that İnanç was particularly keen to recreate was Penn's gruesome, stylized ending. Penn filmed the American outlaws' demise using a mixture of full speed and slow motion, then intercut them for maximum effect. İnanç intended to do the same, but he had one major obstacle: Yeşilçam's typical 35mm cameras lacked the ability to shoot slow motion. He tried manually wiring in a second battery to give the mechanism enough juice to overcrank, but no dice. Then he had a brainstorm: what if he used a 16mm camera, which *did* have a slow-motion function, and blew up the footage to 35mm? İnanç had spent enough years in film labs to know it should be feasible. His colleagues, on the other hand, were skeptical. "They said, 'No, it'll be grainy,' and so on," wrote the director. "At the time, there was İlhan Arakon, Erman Films' chief cameraman. We consulted him, and even he said, 'it won't be any good.'" However, İnanç wouldn't hear it. He went ahead anyway.

With the film completed, İnanç then had to get it past the censors. That didn't go well. "They rejected the film," explained the director in Cem Kaya's documentary *Remake Remix Rip-Off*, "saying that there had never been a bank robbery in Turkey. They called me a traitor to the nation." Their justification may have been absurd, but it was certainly not unusual. Turkish censors were notorious for arbitrary rulings,

Cemil (Yılmaz Köksal) and Cemile (Ülkü Özen) rob a bank in a scene that, due to censorship, was cut from the final film.

and they were quick to challenge any element that might possibly portray the country in a poor light, however imaginary. Begrudgingly, İnanç chopped out the bank robbery and replaced it with a new scene of Cemo looting a jewelry store display. Over fifteen days, *Cemo ile Cemile* would go back and forth with the censors seven times due to additional charges of excessive violence. "I cut out so many scenes," İnanç complained, "the film became a plucked chicken."

It's not surprising that the final product didn't perform well. In addition to the many edits, the film was seen as something of a misfire. Shot in black-and-white when color was becoming the standard even in Turkey, it was relegated primarily to the cheaper venues in the provinces. But to rural audiences it was puzzling. It wasn't quite a Western, but it also didn't have the glitz that they expected from a movie set in the big city. Moreover, the finale was problematic. The idea of the Turkish National Police massacring a young couple in a hail of bullets, even if they were criminals, was appalling and difficult for viewers to accept.

After *Cemo ile Cemile*'s box office failure, Çetin İnanç and Erman Film parted ways. Erman opted to invest in more established directors, and İnanç continued to make low budget films through his own company, Osmanlı Film, which he founded the same year. One bit of good news, though: his pioneering use of slo-mo didn't go unnoticed. "[A] thousand people came and asked how I did it," he wrote. "I even heard that it was mentioned in *Cinematheque*."

Fight Club: Members Only

INSPIRED BY: *Fight Club* (1999)
COUNTRY: India
YEAR: 2006
PRODUCTION: Sohail Khan Productions
DIRECTOR: Vikram Chopra
WRITERS: Sohail Khan, Vikram Chopra
STARS: Suniel Shetty, Sohail Khan, Zayed Khan, Dino Morea, Riteish Deshmukh, Aashish Chaudhary, Yash Tonk

Mumbai is the home of four best friends: personal trainer Karan (Dino Morea), straightlaced Somil (Riteish Deshmukh), clownish boozehound Diku (Aashish Chaudhary), and their de facto leader, the fun-loving Vicky (Zayed Khan). During a night of partying, Vicky notices pockets of antagonism throughout the club—macho duos with a beef, itching for a one-on-one fight. He begins to notice this kind of conflict everywhere, and he's struck with an idea. He convinces his friends to start a new venture: a space where adversaries can pay to sort out their grievances once and for all, fist-to-fist. The name? Fight Club, of course.

It's a success. Inevitably, however, one fight goes too far. A hot-headed young gangster, Mohit (Yash Tonk), beats his opponent nearly to death. Forcibly removed by the friends, he vows revenge. His protests also draw the police, scuttling the night's event. The next Fight Club brings a more personal challenge when a victim of Vicky's high school bullying calls out his former abuser. Once an overweight kid, now a buff bouncer, challenger Sameer (Sohail Khan) displays impressive fighting skills—until the police burst in and send everyone scattering.

Meanwhile, Somil's uncle is in trouble. He owns a club in Delhi called Crossroads, and a crime syndicate wants it. It's close to the border, making it an ideal front for smuggling. When the uncle won't sell, he turns up dead. Somil and his friends travel to Delhi where they decide to take over the club and renovate it with a vaguely American Western theme. However, some of the patrons, possibly agents of the syndicate, are too rowdy and destructive for them to handle. The friends realize they need a talented head bouncer, so Vicky hires his old frenemy Sameer.

The friends repel the syndicate's escalating attacks until a devious new opportunity presents itself to the crooks. One of the gang's junior members has a history with the old Fight Club crew: Mohit, who's also the kid brother of the syndicate's fearsome former boss, Anna (Suniel Shetty). Exploiting Anna's love for his brother, the gang murders Mohit and frames the Crossroads owners, drawing Anna back into the fold and out for blood.

~~~

The year of 1999 saw the release of *Fight Club*, David Fincher's violent meditation on nihilism and masculinity based on the 1996 novel by Chuck Palahniuk. Unfortunately, a misguided marketing campaign and scathing reviews from mainstream critics nearly consigned the darkly comic film to obscurity. Once it hit home video, however, it began to find its audience, speedily accumulating a cult following and becoming one of Fox's best-selling DVDs. A sleeper sensation around the world, *Fight Club* and its success was, therefore, unlikely to escape the notice of Indian actor-filmmaker Sohail Khan.

The younger brother of major star Salman Khan, Sohail got his showbiz start behind the camera. His debut, however, was an inauspicious one: *Auzaar* ("Weapon," 1997), an actioner written and directed by Khan, flopped at the box office. Though he'd soon add acting and producing to his repertoire, founding Sohail Khan Productions in 2004, he would continue to struggle with action-focused films. He produced the disastrous self-starring *I Proud to Be an Indian* in 2004 and appeared in the similarly ill-fated *Lakeer: Forbidden Lines* (2004) for another producer. His only hits, meanwhile, were romantic comedies headlined by his more famous brother. Worse, his own acting rarely received much critical praise. So for his next attempt at an action-oriented *masala*, he may have felt he needed every advantage at his disposal—and a recognizable title wouldn't hurt.

However, *Fight Club*'s graphic violence, sex, and anarchism, which very nearly shelved the film in the States thanks to gun-shy executives, would have utterly buried a Hindi film in censorship-conscious Bollywood. Fortunately, Khan had a new, less controversial story in mind. "Whenever I saw two guys get into a fight," he explained in the film's making-of featurette, "they always made a statement, you know, 'Tu akele mein mil … yahaan bahut log hain isiliye main kuch kar nahin paya'"—"Meet me alone … there are too many people around, so I can't do anything here." He imagined an underground arena where those kinds of one-on-one altercations could happen without drawing the attention of authorities.

To help develop the screenplay and direct the film, Khan turned to his longtime friend—and first-time director—Vikram Chopra. Nephew of established filmmaker

Vidhu Vinod Chopra, Vikram had been keen to direct for some time, observing his uncle and taking small roles in various films to gain an actor's perspective on the process. This was his chance to prove himself. "Sohail and I have been buddies for more than 15 years," Chopra related to website Glamsham.com, "so when he asked me whether I would direct this project for his banner, I jumped at the idea." Intrigued by the title, he saw it as exploiting the story's action scenes, not copying a Hollywood film.

He wasn't really wrong; the screenplay Khan and Chopra developed had little to do with Fincher's *Fight Club*. The exception, of course, is the club itself. Though their *raisons d'être* are different, both films' clubs are underground affairs that begin with their founders laying down some familiar ground rules. First and foremost in India's version is "there is no Fight Club," an obvious play on "you do not talk about Fight Club." Others include "if one of the fighters raises his left hand [read: taps out], the fight is over" and "two guys to a fight."

Yet although Khan and Chopra borrowed little from their film's namesake, they did lift liberally from another Hollywood film. A roadside bar, under threat from a criminal organization, plagued by unruly patrons and in need of a proficient bouncer to clean the place up, perfectly describes Rowdy Herrington's 1989 *Road House*. The Patrick Swayze film provided the template for much of the Delhi section of the story, so it should come as little surprise that bouncer Sameer (the Swayze role) falls for the doctor who treats his fighting injuries, or that gangsters damage a truck delivery and start a major brawl that nearly overwhelms him.

With *Road House* as a model, the film was distanced even further from the countless objectionable elements in Fincher's *Fight Club*. Chopra even toned down *Road House*'s R-rated violence in an effort to make the film family-friendly, opening it to the widest possible audience for its best chance at box office success. "Going by the popularity of ... action cartoon series," Chopra explained to *The Hindu*, "it is a fact that kids love violence.

VCD box art for *Fight Club: Members Only* (2006). "Fight Club" baseball bats like the one Sohail Khan is holding were sent out as invitations to the film's premiere.

But we have taken care that there is not too much of blood and fights should not look filthy."

For the film's musical duties, Khan hired Pritam Chakraborty, who had recently made a name for himself with the soundtracks to hits like *Mere Yaar Ki Shaadi Hai* ("My Friend's Wedding," 2002) and *Dhoom* ("Boom," 2004). Some of *Fight Club*'s musical numbers would have already been familiar to certain audiences, however. Pritam's "Chhore Ki Baatein" reworked Pakistani artist Ali Zafar's "Channo," while the title-dropping "Joshile Java Ho" (with the lyrics "go go Fight Club!") borrowed heavily from uncredited Egyptian singer Ehap Tawfik's "Allah Aleik Ya Sidi" as well Pritam's own track "Mummy Ko Nahi Hai Pata" from *Chocolate: Deep Dark Secrets* (2005). Pritam's career has been fraught with well-founded accusations of plagiarism, with the composer reworking songs from America, Pakistan, Egypt, Turkey, Indonesia, and elsewhere. He doesn't dispute the charges; interviewed by *Rolling Stone*, he admitted, "Everyone, including my lawyer back then told me that I should deny, [but I couldn't].... It was only in 2009 that I sat back and realized that something had really gone wrong."

Production on *Fight Club* began in December 2004 and wrapped in October 2005. By the time the film was released the subsequent February it had picked up the *Members Only* subtitle. Key art mimicked the layout of the 1999 *Fight Club* poster and logo, and the movie's grungy opening credits sequence mirrored the aesthetic of Fincher's film. Ultimately, however, *Members Only* flopped, barely making back its costs. Subsequently, Chopra's directing career foundered. An action-oriented hit would continue to elude Khan until *Jai Ho* ("Let There Be Victory") in 2014—which, perhaps not coincidentally, starred his brother Salman.

Kara Şimşek ("Black Lightning")

INSPIRED BY: *Rocky* (1976)
COUNTRY: Turkey
YEAR: 1985
PRODUCTION: Anıt Ticaret
DIRECTOR: Çetin İnanç
WRITER: Çetin İnanç
STARS: Serdar Kebapçılar, Serhan Kebapçılar, Hüseyin Peyda, Sümer Tilmaç, Maurizio Martina, Fuat Okan, Ece Berkant

Young Turkish boxer Serhan (Serhan Kebapçılar) has just won the European Championship belt from the German incumbent. Thanks to his successful career, Serhan and his avaricious father/manager Osman (Sümer Tilmaç) have been living the good life in Germany. But for fifteen years they've also been away from Serhan's mother and two brothers in Turkey. Serhan suggests they send more money home, but Osman tells him not to worry about it. Osman, a former migrant worker, has a bone to pick with Germany; he believes it has treated him and his fellow Turks inhumanly, turning them into wage slaves with menial jobs. Now he's finally getting what he deserves.

But his family in Turkey lives in a ghetto. Serhan's elder brother Serdar (Serdar Kebapçılar) works an oppressive job at a scrapyard where he suffers abuse from the cruel foreman. However, when a heavy tank nearly falls on his co-workers, Serdar comes to the rescue without a thought for his own safety. In appreciation, his boss Necati (Fuat Okan) takes Serdar home to his large estate and offers to help Serdar financially, but the young man's pride won't allow him to accept charity.

Meanwhile, hotheaded Italian boxer Maurizio Martina crashes Serhan's celebration and challenges him to a fight. The match is arranged to be held in Turkey with a large cash prize, finally bringing Osman and Serhan home. But Osman is embarrassed by his poor, backward family, and wants little to do with them, focusing instead on Serhan and the fight. Unfortunately, the bout is fixed by the mafia. Its goons drug Serhan's water bottle, causing his death in the ring.

At the scrapyard, the foreman picks a fight with a disconsolate Serdar who, having finally had enough, beats the tar out of him. However, the scene is witnessed by Necati and Serhan's former trainer Hulusi (Hüseyin Peyda). Realizing that Serdar has the makings of a fighter, they offer him an opportunity for vengeance with Necati's sponsorship and Hulusi's training. The preparation is intense, involving not just speed bags and pushups, but also climbing crane ropes, punching rocks, and jogging wrapped in plastic bags. As Serdar rises through the ranks, his father spurns him, gambling away his fortune. But this perfectly suits the mafia, which offers Osman some desperately-needed money to force Serdar to forfeit his final match against Martina.

~~~

Serdar Kebapçılar takes on Germany's fighter. Turkish lobby card.

After World War II, a shattered Germany took radical steps to recover its economy, halting inflation, removing price controls, and slashing taxes. Its effect was immediate and profound, resulting in the nation's celebrated "economic miracle." By the 1960s West Germany had created more jobs than it could fill, and it looked to migrant workers from countries like Turkey to cover its unskilled labor shortage. Although these "guest workers" were originally contracted for just two years, that limit was soon extended indefinitely in order to avoid the hassle and expense of continually training replacements. Unfortunately, in spite of their contributions to society and long-term residence, these migrants faced discrimination, enduring segregation, anti–Turkish marches, and vandalism. And while they navigated intolerance, inadequate housing, and backbreaking work, in their free time they unknowingly sowed seeds that would dramatically alter the landscape of cinema back home.

In the 1980s, videocassette companies like Kalkavan Video sprang up throughout Germany to market Turkish films to homesick guest workers. Comparatively flush with cash, the displaced Turks gladly bought pricey VCRs in order to enjoy a slice of home. They even purchased additional machines to bring back to their families on their return visits to Turkey. These imported cassette players became immensely popular, and before long Turkish cinemas were fighting a losing battle with home video.

Among the many filmmakers who felt the squeeze was the wildly prolific Çetin İnanç. Turkey's answer to Roger Corman, İnanç directed nearly 200 theatrical films between 1967 and 1987. But when the video boom hit, İnanç and his business partner Mehmet Karahafız saw the writing on the wall and branched out, opening a video rental shop in İzmir called Osmanlı Video.

One of Osmanlı's regular customers was champion bodybuilder Serdar Kebapçılar, who owned the gym next door. İnanç was impressed with Kebapçılar's physique, and with Rambo and Rocky currently box office heavyweights, İnanç immediately saw the potential: he had found Turkey's Sylvester Stallone. He concocted a scenario for a Turkish version of *Rocky* (1976), casting Serdar as its hero and his real-life brother Serhan as his doomed onscreen sibling. Despite his stars' lack of experience, İnanç preferred working with unknown actors over highly paid marquee names. "If they make more money than me," he'd explain, "I can't ask them to do what I want them to do."

Other new faces included Italian karateka Maurizio Martina and his girlfriend Angela Howell. But while Serdar was easy to work with, İnanç's son Murat recalls that Martina and Howell quickly proved to be a problem, often showing up to set hours late. ("In Turkey, we respect the job," explains Murat.) This frequent absenteeism finally prompted the mercurial director to threaten Martina with a camera tripod. (Martina would eventually get himself in trouble with officials for taking unauthorized photos of a navy base, forcing a frustrated İnanç to replace him with a body double in their second and last film together, *Ölüm Vuruşu* ["Death Shot," 1986].)

Although the film was intended as a variation on *Rocky*, İnanç's scenario was written to speak more specifically to the Turkish experience. *Kara Şimşek* explores the subject of guest workers in Germany through the character of Serdar's father. When Osman vents about his subhuman treatment and slavery to the Deutsche Mark, his

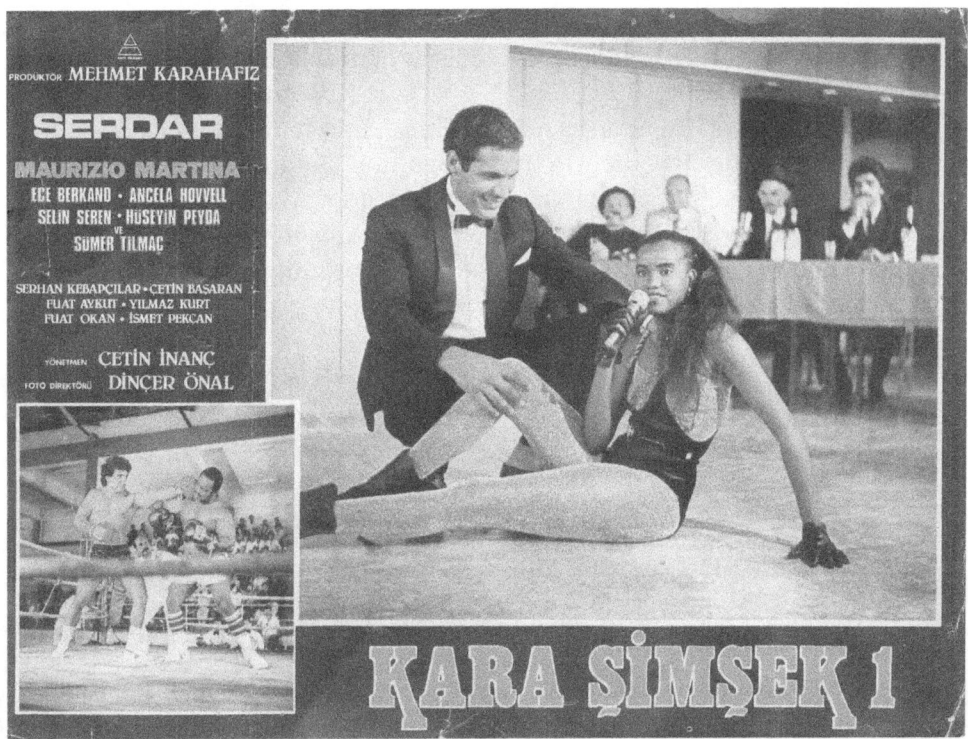

Maurizio Martina admires Angela Howell's stage number in *Kara Şimşek* (1985). Turkish lobby card.

frustration would have been relatable to countless migrant workers and their families (who would have been able to rent the film on VHS and Betamax thanks to Kalkavan Video). And Serhan's success in boxing and victory over the German champion—perhaps inspired by *Rocky III* (1982) in which Rocky also KO's the German champ—are a symbolic victory for Turkey over Germany itself.

The boxing milieu also gave İnanç a novel way to dress up the classic Turkish melodrama, which frequently explored the conflict between rich, Westernized characters and lower class, traditionally Eastern ones. This clash afforded storytellers a bottomless well of dramatic material ever since the Republic of Turkey was founded in 1923, when massive reforms impelled the country to modernize and move away from its Ottoman roots. Here both sides are represented within the same family; the father has become accustomed to Western luxury and its excesses—gambling, drinking, and infidelity—while his wife and two other sons live in the slums of Turkey, maintaining a poor but honest life. Meanwhile, a subplot involving Serdar and his wealthy boss's daughter provides a classic rich-girl-poor-boy love story that was also much repeated among Turkish melodramas.

But *Kara Şimşek* still has plenty of familiar material for *Rocky* fans. Osman convincingly fills in for Paulie as the drunken lout; Serdar's fatherly trainer Hulusi employs Mickey's brand of tough love; the obligatory training montage is in place with Serdar donning Rocky's signature sweat suit; and while Serdar practices, his opponent lives the easy life, making a movie about himself in sequences that bring to mind Rocky's grandstanding in the first act of *Rocky III*. The music, too, is very familiar, as much of the score is made up of needle drops from the *Rocky III* soundtrack.

Kebapçılar recalls that upon its release, *Kara Şimşek* topped the box office. Some of that success may be due purely to title recognition. But if the name "Black Lightning" is puzzling, that's because it has nothing to do with the film, or even *Rocky*. *Kara Şimşek* was the Turkish title of the TV series *Knight Rider* (1982), which was extremely popular in Turkey. Çetin İnanç saw an opportunity to cash in on the familiarity of the name, so he took it KITT and caboodle.

Kartal Yuvası ("Eagle's Nest")

INSPIRED BY: *Straw Dogs* (1971)
COUNTRY: Turkey
YEAR: 1975
PRODUCTION: Çağdaş Film
DIRECTOR: Natuk Baytan
WRITER: Tarık Dursun Kakınç
STARS: Yıldız Kenter, Ceyda Karahan, Cemil Şahbaz, Yılmaz Gruda, Oktar Durukan, Ülkü Akbaba, Güner Sümer

Young Turkish doctor Murat (Cemil Şahbaz) and his English fiancée Mary (Ceyda Karahan) have relocated to Murat's hometown in Cyprus to live with his mother, Makbule (Yıldız Kenter). Unfortunately, the political climate there has become hostile. The Christian Greeks have chased nearly all of the Muslim Turks from the village except for Makbule and two brothers—one of whom, Musa (Oktar Durukan), is mentally handicapped. Arriving in town, Murat and Mary receive a cold reception at a local pub, where the natives eye Mary meaningfully. And before the couple can even settle into their deceptively peaceful rural life, a band of Turkish guerrilla fighters urgently request Murat's help to tend to their wounded comrades far away. Murat leaves with them, not knowing when he might return.

Meanwhile, for her forthcoming marriage Mary has agreed to convert to Islam, infuriating the local Greeks. They begin a campaign of harassment and terror against her: firing rifles outside the house, attempting to run Mary down with a tractor, and murdering her pet cat (*warning: this film features sequences of unsimulated animal cruelty*).

Presently Makbule, a midwife, is called away to assist with a birth, leaving Mary home alone. Seizing the opportunity, two of the local Greek gang break into the house. And while elsewhere Makbule is delivering a baby, the two fiends beat and rape Mary. But when her future mother-in-law returns, Mary tells her nothing, except that she has decided to leave on the next ship in two days.

That night, a local girl, Eleni (Ülkü Akbaba), seduces Musa. But she's discovered by one of the gang, who attempts to rape her. She fights him off but he kills her and frames Musa for the crime. Enraged, the girl's father hunts down the hapless scapegoat with a rifle and shoots him. Fleeing, the wounded Musa is discovered by his brother and Makbule, who take him to Makbule's house. The brother goes to fetch a doctor but the gang murders him, then continues to the house to demand the injured

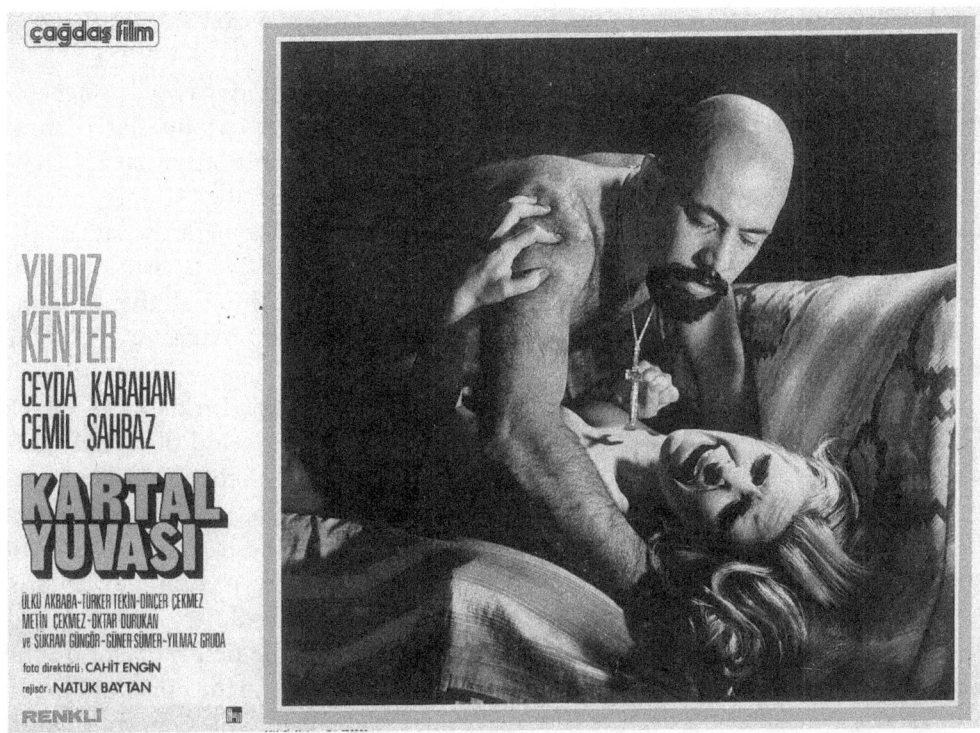

Dimitri (Dinçer Çekmez) rapes Mary (Ceyda Karahan). The scene incorporates an unsettling POV shot of his swinging cross. Turkish lobby card.

man. When Makbule refuses to give him up, the mob lays siege to her home. Makbule and Mary fight back with every weapon available to them, but with no one to come to their aid, it appears that their only hope might be nothing short of a full-scale invasion of Cyprus....

∽∼∽

Acclaimed nationalist director Natuk Baytan nearly had a very different career. Enrolling at Istanbul University, he graduated with a degree in archaeology. But after taking unrelated jobs as a city clerk and a photographer, he was cast in some small movie roles that introduced him to the local film industry. Discovering a passion for the art, he established Doğan Film in 1960 to direct his own movies, becoming one of the few right-wing filmmakers in the business. Drawing on his passion for history, he specialized in swashbuckling historical adventure movies, often reworking classic stories like *Michael Strogoff* and *The Count of Monte Cristo* for their plots—a far cry from violent thrillers like *Straw Dogs* (1971).

Loosely based on Gordon Williams's novel *The Siege of Trencher's Farm*, *Straw Dogs* was Sam Peckinpah's cynical response to American violence in the midst of Vietnam and the wake of the Kennedy and King assassinations. Released stateside in 1971, it hit Turkey two years later, and its story about a couple trapped in a village of hostiles suggested to Baytan a unique framework for tackling not textbook history, but history in the making. Teaming up with film critic, novelist, and screenwriter

Tarık Dursun Kakınç, he reworked the story as a commentary on a crisis that was currently unfolding on the island of Cyprus.

Located just south of Turkey, Cyprus has long been a nation of two distinct cultures. Settled by Mycenaean Greeks during the Bronze Age, it was the island's three hundred years of Ottoman rule some two and a half millennia later that led to its dual—and dueling—ethnic heritage. Cyprus became an independent country in 1960 but it remained ideologically divided, with the Greek Cypriot majority campaigning for unification with Greece, and the Turkish Cypriots favoring a partition of the island. A neutral or impartial government was unlikely from the start, thanks to the election of the Greek Cypriots' communal leader, Archbishop Makarios III, as the Republic's first president.

On December 21, 1963, violence broke out between the Turkish and Greek Cypriot communities, marking the beginning of a brutal period of island-wide carnage that would become known as "Bloody Christmas." Nikos Sampson, a former Greek Cypriot hit man and member of the EOKA ("National Organization of Cypriot Struggle") guerrilla movement, was responsible for some of its most infamous bloodshed. (In the 1950s, when Cyprus was a Crown colony of Britain, Sampson had made a name for himself by murdering British soldiers and their collaborators in the guise of a photojournalist—and then, as the first reporter on the scene, reporting their assassinations.) On December 23, 1973, in the midst of Bloody Christmas, Sampson led a team of Greek Cypriot irregulars into the Omorphita suburb of Nicosia and massacred the Turkish Cypriot population, women and children included.

Sampson's raids and others like it resulted in Turkish Cypriots being forced from their homes in villages and rural areas and into enclaves. But some, like *Kartal Yuvası*'s fictional Makbule, held out. The Greek government exerted considerable pressure on the island, but when Makarios attempted to shake off its militant influence, Athens staged a coup. On July 15, 1973, Greek forces stormed the presidential palace intending to kill the archbishop, but Makarios managed to escape to London with the help of the British government. The Greek junta nevertheless installed a new president: Nikos Sampson. Infuriated, Turkey invaded Cyprus five days later, forcing the Greek Cypriots out of the northern portion of the island. And after a mere eight-day presidency, Sampson was deposed.

Brought together by their mutual anger at the oppression of the Turkish Cypriots, both left- and right-wing citizens on the Turkish mainland had clamored for their relief, urging the government to take action under its rights as a guarantor power. Meanwhile, Turkish filmmakers did their part, turning out politically-charged melodramas depicting the harsh lives of their Cypriot kinsmen that galvanized public opinion. These nationalist, propagandistic films often featured noble Turks doing battle against barbarous, fanatical Greeks.

Natuk Baytan added his voice to the chorus with *Kartal Yuvası*, beginning its story just prior to the coup against Makarios and ending it during the Turkish invasion of Cyprus, which was still recent news when the film went into production. The movie's gang of Greek Cypriots is explicitly shown to be in league with Sampson and is given orders by one of his agents. Finally, the climactic siege on Makbule's home is

Makbule (Yıldız Kenter) tries to beat it into Mary (Ceyda Karahan) that if she leaves the house, she'll be killed. Turkish lobby card.

intercut with Turkish forces heroically storming Pentemilli beachhead—as depicted by repurposed documentary footage.

Baytan also altered *Straw Dogs*' main character to suit both the new ripped-from-the-headlines backdrop and his audience's expectations. Dustin Hoffman's conceited and cowardly David Sumner would have made an unlikely hero for Yeşilçam, which traditionally favored strong, macho male protagonists. (In fact, Peckinpah saw David as the villain, inciting the violence against him.) But as the story's structure required an apparent weakling to be pushed to the edge, that role became Murat's elderly mother. Baytan cast Makbule in the mold of Cyprus's many female Turkish freedom fighters, some of whom fought side by side with their husbands to protect their villages from EOKA guerrillas. At the film's finale, as she fends off the invaders, she proudly wears the Turkish flag and plays a record of Turkish Army Band music in an act of defiance against the Greek gang.

The record-playing scene directly mirrors a sequence in *Straw Dogs*, albeit with an added nationalistic overtone. In fact, in spite of the various cultural tweaks, Baytan follows the 1971 film nearly beat for beat, even including some of the stylistic touches like Peckinpah's violent bursts of slow motion—with slo-mo shots lifted directly from *Straw Dogs* itself.

Kartal Yuvası wasn't the last international movie to repurpose *Straw Dogs* as a tale of ethnic displacement and oppression. Jacques Audiard's 2015 semi-remake *Dheepan*, a French film that explores the plight of Tamil refugees from Sri Lanka, even won the Palme d'Or at Cannes. Both *Kartal Yuvası* and *Dheepan* reimagined the David Sumner character as a hero defending a peaceful life for their family in their arguably rightful home, however distant it may be from their ancestral one. Interestingly, Rod Lurie's Hollywood *Straw Dogs* remake from 2011, which effectively transformed the story into an Americentric home invasion film, specifically avoided politics. "I just said I couldn't do another political project," Lurie elaborated to *Film School Rejects*, "and then *Straw Dogs* came along. I thought I could do a thriller and an audience film, for sure." His movie was a critical and financial failure, suggesting that, whether its protagonist is a hero or a villain, *Straw Dogs* is a story that lives or dies by its ideology.

Kılıç Bey ("Mr. Kılıç")

INSPIRED BY: *The Godfather* (1972)
COUNTRY: Turkey
YEAR: 1978
PRODUCTION: Sezer Film
DIRECTOR: Natuk Baytan
WRITER: Safa Önal
STARS: Cüneyt Arkın, Perihan Savaş, Bilal İnci, Nejat Özbek, Batı Aldemir, Turgut Özatay

Ruthless businessmen are fixing prices, abusing their workers, and swindling the poor. Innocent men are dragged in front of the court on trumped-up charges. The only hope of the desperate men and women of Istanbul is Kılıç Bey (Cüneyt Arkın), a wealthy industrialist who's always willing to bend or break the law in defense of the common man. Possessed of enormous influence and sturdy fists, he strongarms crooked business owners into repenting for their sins, usually by making them give back to the underprivileged.

However, these shady tycoons don't appreciate getting their comeuppance, so they hire gangster Cemal (Bilal İnci) to take care of Kılıç for good. Cemal attempts to intimidate Kılıç by roughing up his men, but the plan backfires when Kılıç tracks down Cemal, smacks him around, and advises him to stick to his own territory.

Meanwhile, Kılıç receives word that Mr. Oflaz (Turgut Özatay), an old family friend from his rural hometown, is on his deathbed. Kılıç travels to be by his side, and with his dying words Oflaz entrusts Kılıç with the safety of his daughter Cennet (Perihan Savaş). Kılıç takes her to live with his mother, and as the old woman urges Kılıç to move back the country, Cennet begins to fall in love with her new protector. But all too soon he must return to the city.

Back in Istanbul, Cemal invites Kılıç in on a share of the drug trade. Kılıç refuses, but his brother-in-law Serhat (Nejat Özbek), seized by greed, urges him in front of Cemal to accept. Serhat realizes he has overstepped his bounds, but Cemal recognizes that if he can kill Kılıç, he'll have an ally in Serhat. Cemal gives orders to execute Kılıç, and his men gun down the philanthropist in broad daylight. Wounded but not dead, Kılıç is taken to the hospital. When Cemal learns he's still alive, he brings a squad to finish the job. Fortunately, Kılıç, now conscious, anticipates Cemal's move and convinces his nurse to transfer him quickly to another room, thereby saving his life.

Kılıç returns to the country and his mother to recuperate. There Cennet tries to minister to his needs, but Kılıç rebuffs her and returns to Istanbul, where Cemal has convinced the scheming Ahmet (Batı Aldemir) to lure Kılıç into a trap. Ahmet comes home drunk and beats his wife, causing her to telephone Kılıç for help. Enraged, Kılıç rushes to her aid and right into an ambush....

~~~

The 1970s were a turbulent time in Turkey's history. Sandwiched between the 1971 and 1980 military coups, it was a politically violent decade, with the nation bearing witness to an average of ten assassinations every day. At the same time the country was in the midst of an economic and industrial crisis. The 1973 OPEC oil embargo had a devastating effect on Turkey, which was entirely dependent on foreign oil. As petroleum prices skyrocketed, so too did inflation and the national debt. Transportation was crippled and daily power cuts became commonplace. Meanwhile, the government's policy of import substitution—banning foreign goods when the often-inferior domestic versions were deemed adequate—led to rampant smuggling across borders. And the local industries had their own problems, as many factory bosses learned they could get away with swindling their workers without fear of consequences. Such practices led to labor unrest and violence in the streets, infamously erupting in 1977 during Labor Day demonstrations in Taksim Square with a massacre that robbed dozens of their lives.

Keying in on the desperation and anxiety of Turkish citizens, Yeşilçam responded to the crisis in its own way, with a new genre: the "men's film." Not merely action flicks, men's films specifically featured strong male characters, often father figures, who used their fists and their guns to single-handedly resolve this new epidemic of social and moral decay. These were men with no faith in the law and who acted alone as judge, jury, and executioner—with no one immune from their violent brand of justice. It was this formula for populist, macho wish-fulfillment that would provide the foundation for director Natuk Baytan's Turkish take on *The Godfather* (1972).

Francis Ford Coppola's iconic mob film wasn't quite the same pop phenomenon in Turkey as it was in the States, but it still had impact. Nino Rota's memorable musical score, for one thing, was lifted for use in dozens of Yeşilçam movies—everything from crime thrillers to comedies. And it was because of *The Godfather* that Turkish journalists and politicians began to adopt the terms "mafia" and *baba* ("father," the film's Turkish title) when referring to large criminal enterprises and their ringleaders.

Yet although it was topical, a compassionate story about the head of a mafia family would have been incompatible with the men's film format, since criminals like the Corleones were precisely the sort of baddies that the genre's heroes normally fought against. Moreover, the nation's conservative censors took issue with films that glorified criminals, and those that made it through tended to end the same way, with the evildoers all apprehended or killed by the valiant and dogged police force. But Natuk Baytan and writer Safa Önal had a different tactic—one already suggested in the original film. In the opening scene of *The Godfather*, Don Vito exercises his influence to punish a rapist whom the law refuses to touch. If the hero of the Turkish version was more like that—more vigilante than thug, righting society's wrongs—he'd be a perfect fit.

244   6. Outlaws, Outsiders, and Oscar Winners

To embody that hero, Baytan cast actor Cüneyt Arkın. The ideal choice, Arkın was the man's man—Turkey's number one action superstar. He learned stunt riding from a Tatar circus, trained in acrobatics, and attained a black belt in karate. These skills, combined with good looks, natural charisma, and powerful screen presence, earned him a career that has spanned five decades and hundreds of films. In the '70s he too jumped on the men's film bandwagon. His 1975 *Cemil* and its sequel *Cemil Dönüyor* ("Cemil Returns"), about an idealist cop rebelling against corrupt politicians and corporations, were exemplars of the genre. He also starred in several others featuring "Baba" in the title, capitalizing on the *Godfather* name. And like Marlon Brando with his portrayal of Don Vito Corleone, Arkın's talent and larger-than-life persona made him a perfect choice for the role of Mr. Kılıç.

With a star onboard, Baytan and his team reworked *The Godfather* to reflect the domestic problems of the day, trading organized crime for corporate crime. In several vignettes throughout the film, Kılıç takes on such villains as a produce wholesaler who has dumped eight tons of perfectly good spinach into the sea to keep prices high, a manufacturer who's smuggled in foreign machinery while paying his workers one fifth of a fair wage, and a foundry owner who staged a bogus strike as part of a ploy to fire his workforce and move his business to a more lucrative location.

But in spite of these modifications, a great deal of *The Godfather*'s framework still remained intact. Baytan and Önal retained the central family, the crime ring that invites the don into a new drug venture (which he refuses on moral grounds), the attempted assassination, the hospital room deception, and the wife-beating brother-in-law who tries to scheme his way into the family business. And in other areas they simply condensed or streamlined material to fit a standard 75-minute runtime. They merged the Don Vito and Michael roles, giving Kılıç the wisdom of one

Cüneyt Arkın is both the world-weary don and the gun-toting enforcer on the Turkish one-sheet for *Kılıç Bey* (1978).

and energy of the other, and folded *The Godfather*'s Sollozzo and the rival crime families into Cemal, giving Kılıç a primary focal point for his war on injustice.

Surprisingly, Baytan also reinstated a "lost" sequence from *The Godfather*. The scene in which Oflaz entrusts his daughter to Kılıç is visually identical to a scene originally cut from Coppola's film in which Don Vito visits the deathbed of his old consigliere Genco. (The sequence was restored in 1977 when the first two *Godfather* movies were extended and re-edited as a television miniseries.)

Although *Kılıç Bey*'s title character and his fellow men's film heroes did a great deal to help a legion of oppressed people, that aid didn't extend beyond the movie screen. In real life it would take more than a tough but benevolent Godfather to solve society's ills. On September 12, 1980, the Turkish military seized control of the government, restoring order to an unstable nation on the brink of economic collapse, but exacting a terrible toll in lives and freedoms. In the wake of the coup, Yeşilçam charted a new course that, for the most part, would steer well clear of politics. Filmmakers like Natuk Baytan decided it would be wiser to turn their attention to safer genres—arabesque musicals, melodramas, and comedies.

Lim jing dai yat gik (*First Shot*)

INSPIRED BY: *The Untouchables* (1987)
COUNTRY: Hong Kong
YEAR: 1993
DIRECTOR: David Lam Tak-luk
PRODUCTION: David Lam Films
WRITERS: Samuel So Man-sing, Chan Kiu-ying
STARS: Ti Lung, Waise Lee Chi-hung, Maggie Cheung Man-yuk, Simon Yam Tat-wah, Andy Hui Chi-on, Canti Lau Sek-ming, Chow Hong-chiu

It's the early 1970s and corruption has consumed the Hong Kong civil service. Crime boss Lui Tai-chiu (Waise Lee Chi-hung) has virtually the entire city in his pocket—especially the police. So when honest cop Wong Yat-chung (Ti Lung) refuses to accept a payoff during a drug bust, his crooked subordinate Sam Mok (Simon Yam Tat-wah) shoots him in the back.

Incoming governor Sir Murray MacLehose is determined to curb this rampant corruption, appointing Sir William Alexander "Alastair" Blair-Kerr to head an investigation. But when, after giving testimony, a witness and his young son are murdered, Blair-Kerr decides on a new approach. He sends his aide Annie Ma (Maggie Cheung Man-yuk) to see Wong.

Wong has recovered only to find himself discharged from the force. Ma offers him a new job: gathering evidence of police corruption. Skeptical, Wong refuses, but Ma guarantees direct reporting to the governor and a firm intention of taking the dirty cops down. Wong finally accedes, but he'll need some good eggs to help. In order to avoid anyone already on Lui's payroll, Wong recruits two top students from the police academy: hot shot marksman Lo Kam-shui (Andy Hui Chi-on) and Bruce Lee fan Yip Chun-wan (Canti Lau Sek-ming). The team is given a secret headquarters in a laundry and a cover as agents of the Inland Revenue Department.

Seeking Lui's financial records, Wong interrogates a remorseful Sam Mok who reveals their location. The team's official inquiry yields only legitimate documents, but a nighttime break-in turns up a secret, coded ledger in a safe.

With the ledger in the hands of the authorities, Lui orders the death of his accountant, Mak Kay (Chow Hong-chiu), the only man who can decipher it. Wong's squad arrives in time to scare off the hitman, but the police arrive and arrest everyone. The cops plot to murder the anti-corruption squad and Mak Kay together, staging it as a breakout, but Annie Ma arrives in the nick of time.

Mak Kay agrees to testify against Lui, but Lui's hitman murders both the accountant and Lo Kam-shui in the courthouse before the beans can be spilled. Incensed, Wong confronts Lui, who retaliates by bombing the laundry and incinerating all of Wong's evidence.

Wong refuses to give up, however, and meets with the governor to propose a new, independent anti-corruption force. With his support, the Independent Commission Against Corruption is formed—Hong Kong's last hope to end Lui's reign.

~~~

Brian De Palma's *The Untouchables* (1987), only nominally inspired by the 1959 TV series, was a fictionalized account of the U.S. Treasury department's pursuit of prohibition-era gangster Al Capone. In the late 1920s and early '30s, the infamous Chicago crime boss operated illegal breweries, smuggled alcohol across the Canadian border, and ran gambling, protection, and prostitution rackets. He maintained power thanks to a wicked combination of violence and graft. He had the mayor on his payroll. He bribed cops. It took Eliot Ness's incorruptible team of agents, independent from the tainted police, to finally take the gangster down.

Across the Pacific, Hong Kong had its own movie-worthy stories of corruption. In the late 1960s, thanks to a dramatic increase in industrialization, the British colony enjoyed a thriving economy. The government, however, was struggling to meet the needs of a population that had surged eight-fold since World War II. It offered only minimal salaries for civil servants. Government employees fought to make ends meet, and backdoor opportunities to supplement their incomes became increasingly tempting. Fire fighters began demanding money to put out blazes. Hospital workers charged patients for basic amenities. Police shook down business owners for "tea money" and took large bribes to look the other way as Triads trafficked in drugs and prostitution. The police department's Anti-Corruption Branch was of little help since, as part of the force, it was just as bribable as the rest. Eventually, like tips for sub-minimum-wage waitstaff, graft became a fundamental part of civil service income. For some, it would even be their ticket to riches. Many accepted this arrangement as an unfortunate part of life, but by the early '70s the public was losing its patience.

In 1973, Chief Superintendent Peter Fitzroy Godber provided the match in the powder barrel. Upon his retirement, the government discovered that the 20-year veteran of the Hong Kong Police had squirreled away HK$4.4 million—nearly six times as much as he made on the force—in bank accounts all over the world. For years Godber had been selling "franchises," offering subordinates plum assignments where they could profit most from the pyramid scheme of bribery. When called to account for his extra income, Godber fled to the UK. An outraged public demanded justice. Some legal wrangling later, Godber was extradited back to Hong Kong and finally tried, convicted, fined, and sentenced to four years in prison.

In the midst of the Godber affair, Hong Kong governor Sir Murray MacLehose, with the recommendation of Sir Alastair Blair-Kerr and under pressure from a furious populace, established the Independent Commission Against Corruption (ICAC) in 1974. A completely separate entity from the police force, the ICAC proved startlingly effective at ferreting out corruption. Within three years it had arrested hundreds of officers and uncovered nearly 20 police-run syndicates.

One of ICAC's employees was director David Lam Tak-luk, who worked for the organization's community relations office. ICAC's mission went beyond investigation and enforcement; part of its charter involved educating the public about the dangers of corruption. To that end it produced commercials and documentaries as well as movies and TV series that dramatized real cases and showed ICAC agents in action. Lam, already a director of television dramas, joined ICAC in 1980, where he lensed series like *Lian zheng xian feng* ("Integrity Pioneer," 1981). His dream, however, was to make feature films, and he finally left to pursue it in 1986.

Lam's experiences at ICAC stuck with him. He was contractually prohibited from making films about the ICAC for a set number of years after his employment with the agency, but in 1992 he dipped his toe in the water with *Si da tan zhang* (*Powerful Four*). The film follows a quartet of Chinese officers in Godber's police force who rise to the rank of sergeant major—the highest position open to local Chinese at the time—and profit from its corruption.

By 1993 Lam's ICAC embargo had fully expired and the filmmaker went all in with *Lim jing dai yat gik*. He used *The Untouchables* as a framework to tell a highly fictionalized account of the founding of the ICAC, much as De Palma had taken liberties with the real events of the 1930s. Lam cast Maggie Cheung Man-yuk as a

Hong Kong DVD cover for *Lim jing dai yat gik* (1993). Evoking the *Untouchables* movie and series, the silhouetted lineup of heroes was featured in much of the film's advertising.

backstage "Eliot Ness" and Ti Lung as the equivalent of Sean Connery's Jim Malone, now elevated to the lead role. Rather than setting his heroes against, for example, Peter Godber, Lam and screenwriters Samuel So Man-sing and Chan Kiu-ying invented a grandiose Capone-like puppet master who keeps officials loyal by offering them as much cash as they can carry. Though Lam's characters were mostly invented for the film, he did include such real-life figures as Governor MacLehose, his predecessor David Trench, Sir Alastair Blair-Kerr, and vocal anti-corruption activist Elsie Elliott.

Lam also replicated many specific sequences from *The Untouchables* in detail. A witness and his young son are murdered by a bomb, just like the shop owner and little girl at the beginning of De Palma's film. A tailor makes a near-fatal mistake when he accidentally pricks Lui with a pin, just as the barber risks Capone's deadly ire when he nicks the gangster with a razor. Lui mutilates a subordinate at a dinner party, echoing the baseball bat murder during Capone's banquet. Wong offers his new employers a variation of Malone's "He pulls a knife, you pull a gun" speech. And when Mak Kay refuses to decipher Lui's ledger, Wong takes another page from Malone, staging a phony scene of excessive police brutality that cows the accountant.

Bringing in just HK$5.5 million, *Lim jing dai yat gik* wasn't an especially big hit. Lam would still go on to make more films in the '90s, mostly romance and dramas, but the 1997 Asian financial crisis and widespread movie piracy forced him out of the business at the end of the decade. Lam made a comeback in 2014, returning to his roots with the ICAC thriller *"Z" fung bou* (*Z Storm*) about the investigation of a massive charity fraud. The year of 2016 saw a sequel, *S Storm*, which was a hit in mainland China and launched an alphabet soup of ICAC follow-ups that included *L Storm* (2018), *P Storm* (2019), and *G Storm* (2021).

Masoyiyata / *Titanic* ("My Beloved / Titanic")

INSPIRED BY: *Titanic* (1997)
COUNTRY: Nigeria
YEAR: 2003
PRODUCTION: Ashu Film
DIRECTOR: Farouk Ashu-Brown
WRITER: Farouk Ashu-Brown
STARS: Sadiya Abdu Rano, Ahmad S. Nuhu, Farouk Ashu-Brown

The remains of the sunken ship *Titanic* have been discovered, and divers have recovered relics from the wreckage. Among them is a portrait which an elderly woman, watching the news at home, recognizes as a drawing of herself. Phoning the television station, she offers to tell her story.

Decades previous, the *Titanic* embarks on its maiden voyage from Nigeria to America. The woman, Binta (Sadiya Abdu Rano), then a young lady from an upper-class family, is making the journey to be married against her will to Zayyad (Farouk Ashu-Brown), the abusive son of the richest man in Nigeria. Attempting one night to throw herself overboard to escape her fate, she is rescued by a penniless artist, Abdul (Ahmad S. Nuhu), who has become smitten with her. The two strike up a surreptitious romance while Zayyad vainly attempts to buy Binta's love with a priceless necklace.

Unfortunately, Binta's parents find her out and forbid her from seeing Abdul again. However, she defies them, returning to Abdul and asking him to draw her portrait. Meanwhile Zayyad discovers her infidelity and, enraged, sends his entourage to hunt the lovers down. The men chase Abdul and Binta through the ship, but the pair hide out in the ship's kitchen just before the liner strikes an unseen iceberg. Unbeknownst to the passengers, the ship begins to fill with water.

Zayyad's men finally catch up to Abdul and Binta, seizing them. One of the thugs slips the precious necklace into Abdul's pocket, allowing Zayyad to frame him for theft. As punishment, Abdul is locked in a cabin and cuffed to a post. Zayyad then turns his attention to Binta when a steward informs them that the ship is sinking. Frantic, Binta breaks free from her fiancé and rushes to her lover, cutting him free with a meat cleaver.

As the *Titanic* goes down, passengers plunge into the icy water and become a meal for a swarm of hungry sharks. In a last-ditch attempt at survival, Abdul leads Binta on deck to the stern of the ship where they cling for dear life as the liner finally submerges. A small piece of driftwood provides a platform for Binta to keep above the water and Abdul, still immersed, clings to it. But time is nearly out for any hope of rescue.

~~~

Because of the expense of shooting on celluloid, the developing nation of Nigeria has never been able to support a traditional film industry. That's not to say that no films were made there, but they were not plentiful, and many were simply filmed performances of traveling Yoruba theater troupes. However, in the early 1990s, in predominantly Christian southern Nigeria, an alternative technology would empower the country to become the second largest producer of movies in the world.

Thanks to an economic spike caused by the oil boom, many middle-class Nigerian households owned videocassette players. What they lacked, however, was content. Demand breeds opportunity, and soon black marketeers were importing foreign films on VHS, dubbing them onto blank tapes ordered in bulk from China, and distributing them to an eager public.

However, VHS wasn't just a distribution medium, and Okechukwu Ogunjiofor reckoned he could shoot an entire movie on the format. He had developed a paranormal thriller about a man ensnared in a money cult, and he calculated that he'd only need about $12,000 to shoot it on videotape. After failing to raise the money on his own, he approached Lagos businessman Kenneth Nnebue, a movie pirate with some videography experience. Nnebue provided the resources, including a video camera purchased from Japan and plenty of tapes for distribution, and he hired television director Chris Obi Rapu to make the movie. The result, *Living in Bondage* (1992), wasn't the first Nigerian film shot on video, but thanks to a flashy Hollywood-style cover it was the first one that hit big, selling a staggering 200,000 copies.

Nollywood was born. Soon scores of would-be filmmakers were producing their own shot-on-video opuses. Many of these self-starters had no formal training, but not all of them were totally green. In 1990, under Ibrahim Babangida's administration, the state-run Nigerian Television Authority (NTA) began to commercialize, letting go of much of its in-house talent. Suddenly there was a pool of writers, directors, producers, and actors in need of jobs, and a burgeoning video industry that needed them. It wasn't easy work; they were making movies under miserable conditions—meager budgets, urban crime, and daily power blackouts that necessitated gas-powered generators on set. Their production values were extremely low, but for audiences hungry for stories reflecting local issues, culture, morality, and religion, it didn't matter. Before long Nollywood was turning out 1,500 movies per year, distributing them first on VHS and later, as the technology became more available, VCD and DVD.

The home video bug quickly spread to the Muslim north, where the state of Kano became the center of Hausa-language moviemaking. Focusing on melodramas and romances, "Kannywood" was modeled not on Hollywood, but rather on India's Bollywood. Indian films were enormously popular in Hausa culture thanks to greater similarities of morality, family values, and gender relations. Not only were Kannywood films thematically akin to Bollywood, but many were outright remakes of Indian films—and nearly all came complete with the obligatory musical numbers.

So with Bollywood as the standard template for Hausa language films, it's strange that in 2003 newcomer Farouk Ashu-Brown would opt to remake James Cameron's $200 million *Titanic* (1997), the quintessential Hollywood blockbuster. However, its central conflict between an arranged and a love-based marriage, only plausible to Western audiences in a period piece, was still a reality in modern Nigeria, giving the film unique relevance. It's perhaps for this reason, in addition to the more pressing necessity of thrift, that Ashu-Brown ignored time period entirely, dressing his cast in modern clothes and setting his film in the present day.

To place his characters aboard the largest passenger steamship in the world, Ashu-Brown lifted footage from Cameron's *Titanic*, using exteriors of the ship and shots in which the original actors' faces are obscured. He intercut these with his own material shot in ordinary urban buildings and a local pool, or chroma-keyed them behind his actors. As a final touch, he crudely superimposed the word "Nigeria" onto the ship's sinking stern, just below "Titanic," to cement the liner's connection to its new homeland. (Ashu-Brown's borrowing wasn't restricted to *Titanic*, either; as the ship sinks, the passengers are confronted not only with freezing ocean water, but also vicious sharks—courtesy of footage cribbed from Renny Harlin's 1999 *Deep Blue Sea*.)

Although the plot mostly follows the 1997 film, with Abdul and Binta's romance mirroring that of Jack and Rose, certain changes were absolutely essential. In June 2000 Kano implemented Sharia Law, and the movie industry was only allowed to continue under the strict oversight of an Islamic censorship board. This meant, for example, that Abdul could not win his passage on the *Titanic* in a hand of poker like Jack—gambling is considered a sin—but instead wins it in a national lottery, suggestive of the American Diversity Visa Lottery. Nudity, too, was taboo, so Abdul could only draw Binta fully clothed. And it was strictly forbidden for men and women to touch on screen, let alone make love, so a musical number between the two leads takes the place of Jack and Rose's sex scene.

There are in fact three song-and-dance sequences in *Masoyiyata/Titanic*. Two of these, love songs between Abdul and Binta, feature the actors lip synching to Hindi music tracks. The third, a Hausa language version of Céline Dion's "My Heart Will Go On" with lyrics altered to fit the plot of the movie, is staged like a music video. Superimposed over various backgrounds (clouds, fireworks, the ocean), Binta sings to the camera in a variety of costumes, including a traditional Indian sari.

Speaking in *Masoyiyata/Titanic*'s making-of documentary, Ashu-Brown declared, "We're making a statement with this movie." It's unclear, however, precisely what that statement is, although he did dedicate the film to "all the Africans who died when the real *Titanic* sank in 1929"—a message that appears in a text box near the beginning of the video. Yet while the sentiment is noble, it's not particularly well-researched, as only one African actually perished aboard the real *Titanic*—Joseph Philippe Lemercier Laroche, a Haitian engineer—and the *Titanic* sank in 1912.

Whatever the message Ashu-Brown had in mind, it was apparently lost on the public, which was not particularly enamored with the movie. *Masoyiyata/Titanic* was a flop, with the director denounced by his peers for the use of pirated footage—ironically sinking Ashu-Brown's filmmaking career on its maiden voyage.

Pi li da niu (Girl with a Gun)

INSPIRED BY: *Ms .45* (1981)
COUNTRY: Taiwan
YEAR: 1982
PRODUCTION: Yung Sheng Film Company
DIRECTOR: Richard Chen Yao-chi
WRITER: Lu Chia (Richard Chen Yao-chi)
STARS: Ying Hsia, Alan Tam Wing-lun, Chan Chi-jan

Liang Pi-ho (Ying Hsia), a shy, mute dressmaker living in Hong Kong, is the tragic victim of a brutal double rape. She suffers her first attack while walking home from work, dragged into an alley by a man in a mask. When she finally arrives at her apartment, she interrupts an armed burglar who also violates her. This time, however, she kills the rapist in self-defense. Faced with a dead body in her apartment and no apparent way to dispose of it, she dismembers the corpse with a hacksaw. She then stores the pieces in her freezer and slowly discards them one by one throughout the city. But on one of these occasions a laborer, believing she's left her grisly parcel behind by accident, chases her down to return it. Frightened, Pi-ho shoots him dead with the burglar's gun and flees.

Later, after a luncheon with her co-workers, Pi-ho is hit on by a persistent and sleazy photographer. She willingly accompanies him to his studio, but the moment they step inside, Pi-ho shoots him. Shattered by her experiences and believing herself surrounded by a sea of scummy and brutal men, she has decided to take action. Forging herself into a vigilante, she dresses the part of a femme fatale and stalks the streets at night, gunning down any man who approaches her with evil intentions. In a series of vignettes, she murders a violent pimp, a subway gang, and a lecherous middle-aged businessman in a limousine. Soon her targeted hate becomes unconditional misandry.

Pi-ho's killing spree does not escape the notice of the police, however. And on the night of a party for the dressmakers to celebrate a big contract, the cops stake out a nearby park. An officer witnesses a man mug Pi-ho on her way to the party and arrests him, but Pi-ho slips away in the confusion. Meanwhile, Pi-ho's nosy landlady (Chan Chi-jan), suspicious of her tenant's recent strange behavior, enters her apartment and discovers the remaining body parts in the freezer. Terrified, she calls the police.

Pi-ho arrives at the party, and presently one of her boss's friends takes her upstairs. He drunkenly paws at her, unaware that he's the catalyst for one final, vengeful massacre.

~~~

As awareness of rape culture in America increased in the 1970s, a controversial new kind of movie emerged: the rape-revenge film. A varying mixture of sexual violence, gender politics, and exploitation, films like *Rape Squad* (1974), *Lipstick* (1976), and *I Spit on Your Grave* (1978) generated an abundance of critical attention and notoriety. Abel Ferrara's *Ms .45* (1981) epitomized the genre, telling the story of a mute dressmaker who, after being raped twice in one day, remakes herself as a deadly vigilante.

Ferrara's film was released just as a similar cinematic trend was gaining traction overseas: Taiwan's euphemistically-named "social realism." Tsai Yang-ming's 1979 true crime thriller *Cuo wu de di yi bu* (*Never Too Late to Repent*), starring real-life criminal Ma Sha in his own sensational life story, set off a wave of copycats featuring lurid tales ripped from the headlines. In the beginning, many of these films included political themes and anti–Communist messages. But producers quickly noticed that audiences were responding more favorably to occasional glimpses of women's bare flesh than to serious social or political content, so they adjusted accordingly. Soon social realism became synonymous with outlandish female avenger movies showcasing tough, sexy women enacting savage justice against the sleazy men who violated them.

Ms .45, then, was a kindred spirit, even if it wasn't an international blockbuster. Realizing its potential, Taiwanese production company Yuen Sheng Films assigned contract director Richard Chen Yao-chi to remake *Ms .45* for domestic audiences— on short notice and without a script. And as producers would regularly bank on a film's success based solely on its stars, its lead actors were hired simultaneously. Well-known folk singer Ying Hsia was cast in the title role, and pop idol and recent award-winner Alan Tam Wing-lun was signed on for an extended cameo as Pi-ho's boss. From there Chen and his team had just six weeks to write and produce a film. Fortunately, they already had a blueprint.

Indeed, with *Pi li da niu*, Chen painstakingly recreates *Ms .45*, often shot-for-shot. There are, for instance, the symbolic rows of packaged meat at the supermarket, Pi-ho huddled in a corner of the frame after her attack in the alley, and her reflection in a vanity mirror as she kisses the bullet that will begin her final murder spree. But even if Chen had wanted to simply Xerox the film with local actors, it wouldn't have been so easy. He was to a certain extent hamstrung by Taiwan's rigorous and often arbitrary censorship standards, particularly with regard to gore and sex. So he knew he'd have to make some changes.

First and foremost, Chen had to deal with the gory scenes. Often when censors flagged material as objectionable, Taiwanese filmmakers were forced to crudely chop out the offending frames from an otherwise-completed movie. These sometimes occurred in the middle of a shot and would result in jarring jump-cuts. However, from the outset Chen foresaw that, given the nature of his film, he was bound to run into trouble. So even before production began, he devised a novel solution that would help him avoid having to mangle his film. He shot the necessary sequences of blood, dismemberment, and severed body parts without restraint, but he presented them in the finished film as negative images. By altering and obscuring the more graphic imagery in this way, he was able to avoid the ire of the censors.

An assailant (uncredited) rapes Pi-ho (Ying Hsia) in an alley. In *Ms .45* (1981), the attacker was played by the film's director, Abel Ferrara.

In a further effort to pass scrutiny, Chen collaborated with a team of educational psychologists to develop new bookends that, at least superficially, presented the film as a cautionary tale rather than purely exploitation. Beginning with television broadcasts and newspaper headlines declaring the rise in mental illness cases in Hong Kong, the film then transitions to a mental hospital where, following her killing spree, Pi-ho has been committed. There Pi-ho's doctor discusses her case with a reporter in terms of social injustice. Later, at the end of the film, the hospital is revisited and the psychologist reassures the reporter that Pi-ho's condition has improved with treatment.

Other new scenes follow the CID's attempts to solve Pi-ho's murders. These do little to advance the story but were included to reinforce, if only for the sake of the censors, the presence and efficacy of the police force—and to add a few kung fu fights. Furthermore, they feature a novel use of *Ms .45*'s iconic nun costume when a policewoman dons a habit for her stakeout in the park.

Even the movie's overseas locale was tied into making *Pi li da niu* more acceptable. Setting films in Hong Kong permitted Taiwanese filmmakers to show prohibitive levels of crime and violence by justifying that, although such events might not occur in Taiwan, anything could happen "over there." And as an added bonus, shifting the action to a cosmopolitan stage made these films more attractive to foreign markets.

Chen's efforts paid off; the film passed censorship intact. And although not a box office smash in Taiwan, *Pi li da niu* was ultimately purchased and distributed internationally by IFD Films and Arts in Hong Kong. IFD also produced a *second* version that, unbeknownst to Chen, spliced in newly-shot scenes starring local Caucasian actors and a subplot involving a satanic cult that has allegedly mesmerized Pi-ho. This Frankensteined film was sold to the West under the unlikely title *American Commando 5: Fury in Red* (1988).

Pyaar Tune Kya Kiya... ("Love... What Have You Done")

INSPIRED BY: *Fatal Attraction* (1987)
COUNTRY: India
YEAR: 2001
PRODUCTION: Varma Corporation
DIRECTOR: Rajat Mukherjee
WRITER: Rajat Mukherjee
STARS: Fardeen Khan, Urmila Matondkar, Sonali Kulkarni, Ravi Baswani

Flirtatious photographer Jai (Fardeen Khan) is on assignment in Goa when he spies a beautiful woman practicing yoga on a cliff. He surreptitiously snaps some shots of her, but when he belatedly approaches to ask permission she fiercely rebuffs him.

Forgoing permission, he gives the photos to his editor, Wispy (Ravi Baswani), for the cover of his new fashion magazine. Wispy invites the local bigwigs to a launch party, and who should arrive but the woman herself! Her name is Ria (Urmila Matondkar), and it turns out she's the daughter of a wealthy industrialist. When she discovers that she's the new cover girl for the magazine, she's livid.

Wispy is eager to continue to feature Ria, so Jai charms her and convinces her to give modeling a shot. Before long, she begins to fall for him. However, slowly her infatuation begins to look a bit like obsession. She's soon determined to marry Jai, and she visits his house to propose only to discover....

He's already happily married.

Ria breaks down, accusing Jai of hiding his marriage. She asks if he ever loved her, and Jai, attempting to placate her, suggests that he might have if he wasn't already married. The situation escalates that night when she calls Jai and threatens to commit suicide. He goes to her and succeeds in talking her down. His wife Geeta (Sonali Kulkarni), believing Ria is mad, insists on informing the police, but Jai wants to save Ria from scandal.

Ria calls the next day to apologize and ask if they can remain friends. However, she continues to call incessantly, driving Geeta to distraction. Jai and Geeta see her again at a party, where Ria attempts to make Geeta jealous by implying a secret romance. It starts to work. Back at home the couple argues and Geeta storms out, leaving the door open for Ria to sneak in and stage a compromising scene for Geeta's benefit. Another argument follows and Geeta stumbles, crashing through a glass table and cutting herself badly. Jai rushes her to the hospital.

Jai decides the only option is for him and Geeta to move away. Discovering his plan, Ria asks to meet him one last time at the studio. Jai agrees, but instead he goes to her house with the intention of explaining everything to her father. However, Ria has also lied. She drives to Jai's house with a kitchen knife....

A steamy publicity photo of Urmila Matondkar and Fardeen Khan, suggesting an affair that doesn't actually occur in the film.

Remaking *Fatal Attraction* was supposed to be impossible. In 1996, scholar Tejaswini Ganti sat with an unnamed filmmaking team—a director, a screenwriter, actors, and technicians—as they watched a laserdisc of the '87 Adrian Lyne thriller. They were attempting to determine whether the film, about a man who commits casual adultery with a woman who becomes obsessed with him, was worth adapting for a Hindi audience. What they discovered were a number of obstacles. The writer found it too boring, the actress who'd be playing the Glenn Close role felt that mentally unstable characters were passé, the director realized he'd have to handle the sex scenes gingerly to get them past the censors, and all were concerned about making sure the "other woman" wasn't seen as just another Bollywood "vamp." For this last point they debated making her unaware that the man was married, but that only underscored the story's biggest problem: the protagonist was kind of a jerk. The director believed that, at the end of the day, Indian audiences simply wouldn't accept a hero who cheated on his wife for no compelling reason. "We can't make this film," he finally declared, and the project was scrapped.

What he and his team may not have realized was that *Fatal Attraction* had already been remade in India. I.V. Sasi's *Aksharathettu* (1989), shot in the Malayalam language, followed the original much more closely than one might have expected given the Hindi filmmakers' reservations. Sasi, however, made sure that the affair could safely be blamed on the other woman, who this time drugs the protagonist in order to sleep with him. (Also, be warned: whereas *Fatal Attraction* features a dead rabbit, *Aksharathettu* ups the ante—and discomfort factor—by showing many additional animal corpses, all apparently genuine.) Even the Hindi language industry had previously attempted a remake to an extent. Avtar Bhogal's *Haar Jeet* (1990) blended *Fatal Attraction* with Ridley Scott's *Someone to Watch Over Me* (1987), about a married cop who has an affair with a witness.

Since 1990, other Hindi directors like Sanjay Gupta and Arbaaz Khan have attempted to mount adaptations of Lyne's film, but it would take a first-timer to finally pull it off. Rajat Mukherjee was a former ad man from Rajasthan who moved to Mumbai to become a filmmaker. He sought out well-known producer-director Ram Gopal Varma, who permitted the hopeful to assist on his films in an unofficial capacity. Toward the end of production on Varma's *Mast* ("Easy Going," 1999), the director asked Mukherjee what he'd really like to do. The newbie replied that he'd like to direct a film and pitched the story for *Pyaar Tune Kya Kiya...* Varma, a fan of thrillers, was tempted to helm it himself, but he finally consented to produce the film with Mukherjee in the director's seat.

Mukherjee has gone on record stating that his film is not a remake of *Fatal Attraction*, but in Bollywood, where a large percentage of films are remakes (one source put it at 46 percent in 2008), "not a remake" is an old and dubious refrain. Some filmmakers say it to avoid legal trouble when the remake is unauthorized. Others may simply use a more narrow definition of "remake"; for them, only a movie that duplicates every scene may qualify. However, Mukherjee's denials didn't stop the press from almost exclusively referring to his film as a version of *Fatal Attraction*, or the studio from using the phrase "fatal attraction" in its marketing.

A disconsolate Ria (Urmila Matondkar) can't bring herself to tell her father (Suresh Oberoi) the truth about her obsession with a married man.

And there's another reason, discussed later, that casts further doubt on the sincerity of his claim.

Certainly the similarities between the two films are primarily in the broad strokes: the unhinged obsessive woman, the "if I wasn't with somebody else" concession, the suicide attempt, the phone calls, the attempted murder of the wife with a butcher knife, etc. At the same time, however, some of the differences appear to be designed to solve exactly the kinds of story problems that Ganti's filmmakers encountered in '96. Mukherjee avoided making Ria a vamp by creating a scenario in which Ria is unaware of Jai's marriage. But he also took it a step further by removing the affair altogether, sidestepping both the unsympathetic hero who cheats on his wife and any sex scenes that would have to pass censorship. As for whether it would be boring, that would be up to audiences to decide, but there were always the obligatory songs to liven things up.

Mukherjee placed composer Sandeep Chowta, a Ram Gopal Varma regular, in charge of both the songs and the score. Crediting him as a composer was a bit of a stretch, however, as the film is a master class in musical plagiarism. The title song "Pyaar Tune Kya Kiya" was based on Ennio Morricone's "Regan's Theme" from *Exorcist II: The Heretic* (1977); "Kambakth Ishq" lifted Afro Celt Sound System's "Éireann" with visuals copied from Madonna's music video for "Human Nature"; "Raundhe Hain" reworked Wojciech Kilar's "Vampire Hunters" from *Bram Stoker's Dracula* (1992); and "Jaana" was a rehash of Chowta's own "Devudu Karunisthadani" from *Prema Katha* ("Love Story," 1999). For the rest of the score, Chowta put together a smorgasbord of stolen cues from *Close Encounters of the Third Kind* (1977), *The Lost World: Jurassic Park* (1997), *Onegin* (1999), *Sleepy Hollow* (1999), *The Thomas Crown Affair* (1999) and Chowta's *Satya* (1998). Bizarrely, while promoting the film, Mukherjee would claim that Chowta's music was all totally original. It's possible he made the statement in good faith, but it unfortunately also calls into question his denial of the film's connection to *Fatal Attraction*.

Pyaar's below average box office performance—it still brought in double its budget—might appear to reinforce the idea that *Fatal Attraction* simply isn't a story that appeals to Indian audiences. However, it's important to understand that filmmakers' generalizations of what Indian viewers will or will not accept are not based on substantial market research, but rather, as Ganti explains, "a mix of intuition, observation of box-office successes and failures, and first-hand viewing of films in theaters with audiences." All it takes is a surprise hit for the preferences of 1.4 billion people to, in the eyes of producers, miraculously transform.

Sangharsh ("Conflict")

INSPIRED BY: *Silence of the Lambs* (1991)
COUNTRY: India
YEAR: 1999
PRODUCTION: Vishesh Films
DIRECTOR: Tanuja Chandra
WRITER: Mahesh Bhatt
STARS: Preity Zinta, Akshay Kumar, Ashutosh Rana

Rookie CBI officer Reet Oberoi (Preity Zinta) is assigned to locate escaped convict Lajja Shankar Pandey (Ashutosh Rana), a religious fanatic who sacrifices children to attain immortality. To start, she's asked to interview the man who originally helped put Pandey behind bars: criminal genius "Professor" Aman Varma (Akshay Kumar).

Varma, locked away in a prison cellar, is handsome, probing, and disturbingly insightful. He initially refuses to help, but he's impressed with Oberoi's spirit and intelligence and finally relents, putting her in touch with an associate. From him Oberoi learns that Pandey has offered to buy a child from a ringleader of street urchins. Using this knowledge, Oberoi sets up a sting operation to catch Pandey. Unfortunately, Pandey, who arrives in disguise as a woman, spots Oberoi and the sting quickly goes south. Pandey escapes.

Oberoi returns to Varma who withholds further assistance, instead pressing her for personal details. In spite of themselves, the two begin to develop an attraction.

Having failed to buy a victim, Pandey abducts the son of a government minister. Now desperate for Varma's aid, Oberoi offers him better accommodations. Unfortunately, Oberoi's superiors condemn the bargain and pull her off the case. Instead they spirit Varma away to a secret location for interrogation. The Professor refuses to speak to anyone but Oberoi, so the officers torture him. Oberoi, tenacious, bluffs her way into Varma's new jail, where the bruised Professor suggests that Pandey is awaiting the appearance of "stars in the daytime" to kill the child.

That night, Varma lock-picks his handcuffs and assaults the guards. The police arrive to discover one man dead, the other barely alive, and Varma gone. They send the wounded guard off in an ambulance and discover what appears to be Varma's dead body atop the elevator. But the corpse isn't him; Varma has disguised himself as the injured guard to make his escape.

Meanwhile, Oberoi consults an astronomer and realizes that Pandey's zero-hour is an upcoming solar eclipse. But before she can act on the information, she's forced to evade the police who believe that she aided Varma's escape. Fortunately, the Professor comes to her rescue; he has a lead and wants to help before surrendering himself. Dodging the cops, they duck into a costume ball

It's Preity Zinta and Akshay Kumar against the world in *Sangharsh* (1999).

where Varma dons a series of disguises (including a Zorro getup!) to avoid detection before finally taking a bullet from the police. Now wounded and on the run, they're racing time to stop Pandey and save the child.

~~~

Sangharsh was the brainchild of renowned producer Mahesh Bhatt. Previously a director, Bhatt helmed a number of Bollywood remakes including *Kabzaa* ("The Capture," 1988), inspired by *On the Waterfront* (1954); *Junoon* ("Obsession," 1992), based on *An American Werewolf in London* (1981) and parts of *Cat People* (1942); and a remake of *The Fugitive* (1993) called *Criminal* (1995). In the late '90s, however, he refocused his cinematic energies on writing in addition to producing alongside his brother Mukesh. At the same time, he also began working in television, where he discovered an up-and-coming young director who he took on as a protégé: Tanuja Chandra.

Despite contributing to the industry since 1926, female directors in Bollywood have always been scarce. Those who succeeded in joining its boys' club tended to confine their talents to social dramas. However, Chandra, who went to film school in the U.S., had a yen to make raw, intense, violent films in the vein of Francis Ford Coppola. This would have her treading even more heavily on the toes of her male colleagues, who felt such films were their exclusive domain.

Most heretically of all, she wanted her heroes to be women. "Telling female stories has been my abiding passion right from the start of my career," she explains. Tackling sexism both in the industry and the world at large, she acknowledges that "it's a struggle and an uphill journey. However, we must be committed to bringing about equality, and my endeavour of telling female stories is to move toward that goal."

Even with the support of her mentor, Chandra struggled to be taken seriously in Bollywood's male-dominated world. She found herself meeting with stars and distributors who would speak only to the men in the room, ignoring her completely. Once she was even evicted from her own set by an overzealous crewmember who assumed she was a trespassing fan.

Fortunately, Bhatt offered Chandra a debut project that was virtually tailor-made for her: *Dushman* ("Enemy," 1998), a remake of John Schlesinger's *Eye for an Eye* (1996), about a woman who avenges the brutal rape and murder of her sister. Unfortunately, Chandra quickly discovered that a female-centric action-thriller was too much for Bollywood gatekeepers to swallow: even with a marquee actress in the lead, money men invariably wanted to know who her male co-star would be. A masculine hero was non-negotiable. So was a love story. Bowing to pressure, Chandra added both. And while *Dushman* garnered critical acclaim, it was a box office flop. In an interview with Nandita Dutta for her book *F-Rated: Being a Woman Filmmaker in India*, Chandra lamented over the love story, "The thing that is supposed to assure you footfalls is the very thing that drives them away and possibly compromises the film."

But Chandra had shown her chops, and Bhatt was happy to assign her next to an Indianization of *The Silence of the Lambs*. It was another ideal project—a dark thriller with a driven heroine at its forefront. Bhatt, credited with the screenplay, had also reworked the story with a new baddie ripped straight from the headlines. "There was a story in the newspaper," explains Chandra, "about a man who had murdered people because he believed that these 'human sacrifices' would enable him to live a very long life.... The Ashutosh Rana character was inspired by this story. We wanted to denounce the completely ridiculous belief that killing a child will add those years onto the life of a person, allowing them to live forever." So out went Buffalo Bill, woman-skinner—and in came Lajja Shankar Pandey, child-murderer.

Unfortunately, as with *Dushman*, Chandra and Bhatt still needed a male star to sell the film to distributors. That meant they had to craft a substantial role—a romantic one, naturally—to attract a suitably prominent actor. The clear choice was to rewrite the Hannibal Lecter character as Oberoi's star-crossed lover. Chandra's attitude toward this striking change was pragmatic: "The film could've been made without that angle ... however the addition of romantic love does complicate matters. And hurdles and conflicts are what propel a story forward." It did mean, however, that Varma certainly couldn't be a cannibal: "Come on, be more realistic," Chandra entreated in an interview for Sify.com, "you can't have a hero with a past of eating human beings suddenly fall in love with the heroine."

Fundamental changes notwithstanding, Chandra's six-month shoot included a number of sequences carefully replicated from *Silence of the Lambs*. Like Clarice Starling, Reet Oberoi is introduced under the opening credits on her early-morning run. She visits Varma in a familiar cell (albeit fronted with bars instead of plexiglass), and after she's assaulted by another prisoner, Varma metes out a grisly punishment for the rudeness. Varma's jailbreak, too, is a note-perfect recreation of its *Silence* counterpart. Other examples abound.

Sangharsh premiered on September 3, 1999. Just a few days later, however, Chandra was horrified to discover her film already

Poster for *Sangharsh* (1999) featuring Akshay Kumar, Preity Zinta, and Ashutosh Rana in his female disguise.

playing on television! Piracy has plagued India's film industries for decades, evolving far beyond bootleg DVDs and VCDs. In this instance, cable channels in the Mumbai suburbs had acquired a print of the film from an international distributor and had been broadcasting it illegally, damaging the movie's box office during its crucial opening week. Through a friend, Chandra reached out to the "boss" of those cable channels who agreed, as a personal favor—and for a consideration of 50,000 rupees (roughly $1,100 in 1999)—to hold off on airing the movie for a month.

Sangharsh still underperformed financially, but it was a critical success, earning Ashutosh Rana two awards for his chilling performance as Pandey. The film continues to resonate two decades later: on September 3, 2018, Preity Zinta tweeted, along with a video clip of the movie, "After all these years this film remains closest to my heart. If I was not an actor I would probably be #ReetOberoi from #Sangharsh." As for Chandra, her passion for women-oriented films continues unabated, and it remains a battle. "The budgets are of course lower in female driven films," she points out, and "there may not be much interest from producers, but it's better now than it was when I made *Sangharsh*. It's not a trend yet though, far from it. I hope it does become a trend someday soon."

Sarkar ("Overlord")

INSPIRED BY: *The Godfather* (1972)
COUNTRY: India
YEAR: 2005
PRODUCTION: RGV Film Company
DIRECTOR: Ram Gopal Varma
WRITER: Manish Gupta
STARS: Amitabh Bachchan, Abhishek Bachchan, Kay Kay Menon, Zakir Hussain, Raju Mavani, Priyanka Kothari

When common folk are unable to obtain justice from the law, they come to Subhash Nagre (Amitabh Bachchan), better known to the oppressed as "Sarkar." The honorific means, roughly, "overlord." He holds no official political position, but he is nevertheless one of India's most powerful men. He uses that power for the benefit of the people, sometimes operating outside the law. Subhash has two sons: Shankar (Abhishek Bachchan), just arrived from America with a new sweetheart, and Vishnu (Kay Kay Menon), a sleazy Bollywood producer who's attempting to woo his latest starlet, Sapna (Priyanka Kothari).

Trouble begins when Dubai-based criminal Rasheed (Zakir Hussain) requests an audience with Subhash. Rasheed has consignments of drugs arriving by ship, but he requires the elder Nagre's blessing before they can dock. He offers Subhash a cut of the profits, but Sarkar does not deal in drugs. He's committed to using his influence only for good, and he promises to stop Rasheed altogether.

In revenge, Rasheed conspires with Subhash's former associate Vishram (Raju Mavani), a crooked member of the State Legislative Assembly. Together they consult a devious swami who proposes that they disgrace Sarkar before eliminating him. To that end they frame Subhash for the assassination of a vocal but peaceful political opponent. Riots break out.

An awkward family dinner as Sarkar admonishes Vishnu for using foul language in front of his own child. Standing, from left to right: Rukhsaar Rehman and Supriya Pathak. Sitting, from left to right: Kay Kay Menon, Amitabh Bachchan, Chintan Atul Shah, and Abhishek Bachchan.

As a follow-up, Vishram uses evidence of Sapna's secret relationship with her co-star to manipulate Vishnu into publicly murdering the actor in cold blood. Disgusted, Subhash banishes his son. However, Vishram shelters the fugitive young Nagre and promises to take care of everything.

Meanwhile, the assassin has been arrested and testifies, per the plan, that he was hired by Subhash. Left with no choice, Sarkar surrenders himself to the police. Shankar takes over the family business and presently learns that Rasheed is arranging to have Subhash killed in prison. When the commissioner will do nothing, Shankar appeals to one of his father's associates for help, but he finds himself in a trap orchestrated by Rasheed. As Shankar is about to be murdered, his aide sacrifices himself instead. Shankar rushes to the jail and saves his father's life, but Sarkar is gravely wounded and rushed to the hospital.

With Rasheed and his network now exposed to the Nagre family, and public support for Sarkar returning, the villains play their last remaining card. They convince Vishnu to murder his father.

~~~

Ram Gopal Varma was first introduced to *The Godfather* in his school days. A friend, handing him Mario Puzo's novel, urged him to read the steamy sex scene between mafia heir Sonny Corleone and his girlfriend. He had plenty of free time, so Varma read not only the naughty bits, but the entire book cover to cover—several times. The word "mafia" meant nothing to him then, but he was fascinated by the characters and the drama. The book, as well as Francis Ford Coppola's film adaptation, would continue to stick with him through an aborted career as a civil engineer and the owner of a Hyderabad video store.

By the time he broke into Bollywood and was considering adapting the mafia epic for an Indian audience, *The Godfather* (1972) had already become a touchstone for a host of local crime films. Perhaps the most famous, and certainly the first, was Feroz Khan's *Dharmatma* ("Saint," 1975). Following the basic outline of Coppola's film, *Dharmatma* featured more romance and several musical numbers, both of which are typical elements of Bollywood *masala* films. In reimagining the story, Khan had also sought out a more Indian brand of "godfather," modeling his version of Don Vito on Ratan Khatri, king of India's largest betting racket.

Varma, too, was in search of a real-life Indian mafia don. He found him in the person of Balasaheb Thackeray, the head of Shiv Sena ("Shiva's Army"), a nationalist political party in the state of Maharashtra. Styling itself as a social service organization, Shiv Sena fought for jobs for local Hindus and maintained vital public works for the poor and underprivileged. Though he never sought political office, Thackeray had devoted followers from all walks of life—including police and politicians—who granted him, as he once claimed, "remote control" of the Maharashtra government. It was no idle boast, and even foreigners recognized his clout. Negotiating a deal for a Maharashtra power plant in 1995, for example, Enron officials prioritized a meeting with Thackeray over one with the Chief Minister.

A man with that kind of power, effectively the head of a parallel government, was the perfect template for Varma's Sarkar. Well, except for Thackeray's fierce anti-immigrant and anti–Muslim politics. Thackeray was linked with, among other things, violent Islamophobic riots in Mumbai in the 1980s and '90s. *Sarkar*'s Godfather would be more benevolent.

Varma began work on his Bollywood *Godfather* in 1993. At the time it was titled *Nayak* ("Hero") and starred Sanjay Dutt. However, Varma was 20 days into production when Dutt was arrested for conspiracy in the 1993 Mumbai bombings that killed 257 people. Suddenly without a star, the director had no choice but to shelve the film indefinitely. Nevertheless, the idea stuck with him, and in subsequent years he would incorporate elements from *The Godfather* into several of his films. *Satya* ("Truth," 1998), for instance, includes narration lifted directly from Puzo's prose.

In 2002, Varma resurrected *Nayak*, retitled *Sarkar*, and took the project to superstar Amitabh Bachchan. The actor had rocketed to fame in the '70s starring in anti-establishment "angry young man" films, and by the 2000s he had aged into playing the patriarch. His son Abhishek had also become a famous actor, and Varma's timing put him in the unique position to cast the two together for the first time, something that their schedules had never previously allowed.

Varma made no secret of his film's connection to *The Godfather*. *Sarkar* begins with the personal statement, "Like countless directors all over the World, I have been deeply influenced by 'THE GODFATHER.' 'SARKAR' is my tribute to it." The dedication is followed by an introductory scene straight out of Coppola's film (it comes later in the novel), in which an anguished man begs Sarkar for justice following the rape of his daughter. However, although Varma recreated several additional moments from his inspiration—including Sarkar's refusal to get involved with drug trafficking, the attempt on his life, and Shankar's coordinated hit on his father's betrayers—the similarities remain primarily in the broad strokes.

Unlike *Dharmatma*, Varma boldly chose to forego Bollywood's ever-present musical numbers. The director has been a vocal critic of the preponderance of songs in Indian movies. In an interview with *Filmfare* he condemned them as "principally responsible for 70 per cent of the bad films we make today,"

Holding a string of prayer beads, Sarkar (Amitabh Bachchan) prepares to hear Rasheed's request to allow a shipment of drugs to dock.

emphasizing that they only work "when they are integral to a film." Songless Bollywood movies had certainly existed for decades, but they were generally viewed as less commercial "art films." However, Varma's popular 2003 horror flick *Bhoot* ("Ghost") proved a notable exception to the rule. Soon other filmmakers were following suit, producing commercially successful pictures without musical numbers like *Black* (2005), *Iqbal* (2005), *Chak De India* (2007), and *A Wednesday!* (2008). Varma limited *Sarkar*'s musical voice to an orchestral score by frequent collaborator Amar Mohile—with an occasional sample from the *Rambo: First Blood Part II* (1985) soundtrack.

Before *Sarkar*'s release, Varma arranged a special screening for Balasaheb Thackeray and his family. (Thackeray had, in a *Godfather*-esque move, recently handed the reins of Shiv Sena to his son Uddhav.) After the film, according to *The Telegraph*, Thackeray embraced the director, exclaiming, "You've captured my life so perfectly I can't believe this isn't my story! Every incident you've shown has happened at one time or the other in my life." He would go on to comment in interviews that even Amitabh Bachchan's mannerisms echoed his own.

Sarkar was a box office success, and Varma would follow it with two sequels, *Sarkar Raj* (2008) and *Sarkar 3* (2017). Neither was based on Coppola's *Godfather* sequels. He also revisited *Sarkar* via a Telugu-language remake, *Rowdy* (2014), starring another popular father-son combo, Mohan Babu and Vishnu Manchu.

Varma never did get to recreate that love scene from the book, though.

Yurusarezaru mono (*Unforgiven*)

INSPIRED BY: *Unforgiven* (1992)
COUNTRY: Japan
YEAR: 2013
PRODUCTION: Warner Bros. Pictures
DIRECTOR: Lee Sang-il
WRITER: Lee Sang-il
STARS: Watanabe Ken, Satō Kōichi, Emoto Akira, Yagira Yūya, Kutsuna Shiori

Yurusarezaru mono (Unforgiven)

At a brothel in Washiro, Hokkaido, two settlers disfigure an innocent prostitute named Natsume (Kutsuna Shiori). When the chief lawman, Oishi Ichizo (Satō Kōichi), merely fines the brothers for their crime, the other prostitutes pool their money and put a price on the men's heads.

Kamata Jubei (Watanabe Ken), once a merciless samurai for the shogunate, is now a widower eking out a pitiful living for himself and his two young children on a barren Hokkaido farm. He receives a visit from his old war buddy, Baba Kingo (Emoto Akira), who's on his way to Washiro to collect the bounty. Kingo asks Jubei to be his partner, but the ex-samurai declines; he promised his wife he'd give that life up. However, when Jubei discovers that his measly crops are inedible, he reconsiders. He takes up his grungy old sword and meets up with Kingo.

The two assassins are soon joined by a boastful young half–Ainu named Sawada Goro (Yagira Yūya) who offers to show them a faster route to the city in exchange for a shot at the action and a third share of the bounty. Traveling through a storm, the three eventually reach the Washiro establishment, but Jubei catches a fever. Goro and Kingo meet with their clients upstairs, but down in the bar Oishi enters and confronts Jubei. Recognizing "Jubei the Killer," Oishi beats him to a pulp, slices his face, and makes him crawl out of town. At a shack at the outskirts, Kingo stitches up his friend and Natsume watches over him while he heals.

Once Jubei is fit to move, the trio sets out to kill the brothers. Kingo incapacitates one with his rifle but can't bring himself to deliver the final shot, forcing Jubei to do the job with his sword. Realizing that he no longer has the stomach for murder, Kingo gives his rifle to Jubei and leaves. Jubei and Goro stake out the second brother's home, and Goro ambushes the target when he uses the outhouse.

Oishi Ichizo (Satō Kōichi) provokes a feverish Kamata Jubei (Watanabe Ken).

The experience traumatizes Goro, causing him to break down and swear off killing. Things get worse when Natsume delivers their money—and some news. Kingo was caught on the road. Oishi tortured him for information about Jubei and the Ainu, then killed him. Realizing what he has to do, Jubei sends Goro and Natsume to his home with the reward money. Then he picks up Kingo's rifle and goes back to town for bloody revenge.

~~~

In 1992, after more than 30 years of being associated with the Western film, Clint Eastwood had come a long way from his "white hats vs. black hats" adventures on TV's *Rawhide* (1959). He had made his name portraying anti-heroes and morally questionable gunfighters in revisionist Westerns like *Per un pugno di dollari* (*A Fistful of Dollars*, 1964), *Hang 'Em High* (1968), and *The Outlaw Josey Wales* (1976). He had evolved from a television actor to a movie star and auteur. But now he was finally ready to hang up his Stetson. *Unforgiven* (1992), his final entry in the genre and perhaps the ultimate revisionist Western, was a film with no good guys or bad guys. It featured dubious gunslingers and civilians alike, an unglamorous depiction of killing, and a cynical look at the frontier dream. It was a Wild West swan song that won him major critical acclaim and four Oscars.

Korean-Japanese director Lee Sang-il first saw *Unforgiven* at age 19. He didn't fully appreciate the film at the time, but it struck a melancholy chord that resonated with him. Rewatching it years later, he was moved by its tragic chain of violence and was fascinated by Eastwood's break with traditional Western movie stereotypes. Lee would go on to incorporate similar themes of moral ambiguity in his own films, notably his critically acclaimed *Akunin* (*Villain*, 2010). He wanted to continue to explore those ideas in a *jidaigeki*, or period drama, since he felt that the genre—especially its samurai films—frequently fell into the same good guys vs. bad guys tropes that colored typical American Westerns. So what better way to shake up the conventions, he reasoned, than with a remake of *Unforgiven*?

Clint Eastwood's films have always been popular in Japan, so taking on one of his most respected movies was no small thing. First, though, Lee needed permission. He was working with Warner Bros.' Japanese branch, and through the studio he submitted his request to Eastwood's production company. He received a pithy response from the American filmmaker's producer: "Boss says ok!" It probably didn't hurt that Eastwood was himself interested in Japanese history; only a few years earlier he directed *Letters from Iwo Jima* (2006), a compassionate portrayal of the Japanese Imperial Army during the famous World War II battle.

Lee set his adaptation of *Unforgiven* in the same year as Eastwood's film, 1880—shortly after the dawn of the Meiji Era. Japan's previous government, the Tokugawa shogunate, had ruled since the 17th century. Japan technically had an emperor, but the position was effectively symbolic; the shogunate was a feudal military dictatorship with little need for a monarch. However, after the shōgun gave in to a series of unfavorable trade agreements in the late 1850s, opposition to his governance grew. The powerful rival domains of Satsuma and Chōshū conspired with others to reconsolidate political power under young Emperor Meiji. Shōgun Tokugawa Yoshinobu, realizing his position was untenable, abdicated in the vain hope of retaining some political standing in the new government. Instead, an official decree stripped him of his lands and titles, leading to a civil war in which the ex-shōgun's samurai fought against the supporters of the emperor. Meiji's forces, armed with superior Western firepower and organization, eventually won out over the comparatively outmoded Tokugawa allies. The abolition of the samurai class soon followed.

This was the tumultuous environment into which Lee transferred *Unforgiven*'s story, rewriting its protagonist, now Kamata Jubei, as one of the former shōgun's elite samurai. In a prologue set after Tokugawa's defeat in 1869, Kamata is hunted by the agents of the new government in an effort to wipe out all remnants of the old regime. He brutally murders his pursuers and flees into the frontierland of Hokkaido, Japan's northern island.

Thanks to a program of modernization, Hokkaido was Meiji Era Japan's answer to the Wild West. The government realized that, given the superior might of foreign powers, building Japan up as a technologically progressive nation was the best way to avoid colonization. Its mantra was "fukoku kyōhei"—"enrich the country, strengthen the military." As part of the former, it looked to scientific agriculture. In particular, it set its sights on Hokkaido which had been mostly undeveloped. Many of the island's settlers would be former samurai recruited both to farm the land and protect it against invasion from foreign powers. Not only did the Hokkaido settlements have much in common with the American West, but experts were even brought in from America to share knowledge of modern agriculture and ranching.

There was one problem, though. Hokkaido was already inhabited. The indigenous Ainu, a separate ethnic group of hunter-gatherers, had been living there for centuries. As the Japanese government encroached on Ainu land, it implemented a series of reforms to forcibly assimilate and subdue the native population. The authorities forbade their language and traditional ceremonies, prohibited fishing and hunting, regulated their appearance by banning tattooing and facial hair, encouraged alcoholism, and drove many from their homes. These measures took their psychological toll. Missionary John Batchelor, who moved to Hokkaido in the late 1870s, wrote that the Ainu's exposure to the Japanese had left them "one and all imbued with the inferiority complex."

In adapting *Unforgiven*, Lee was keen to give the Ainu and their plight a substantial presence in the story. Crafting his version of the original film's hot-headed young gun, he wrote Sawada Goro as a half–Ainu struggling with self-hatred and his dual identity. Lee conceived Kamata as the widower of an Ainu woman who taught him a more peaceful life than the one he left behind. (Her *shitoki*, a traditional beaded necklace, becomes a recurring symbol of his oath of nonviolence.) And in one scene original to the Japanese film, the assassins pass an Ainu village where the militia is punishing and humiliating its inhabitants for the performance of funeral rites.

In general, Lee's film translated the pieces of Eastwood's movie comfortably into the Meiji Era. Like *Unforgiven*'s Big Whiskey, the town of Washiro forbids weapons of any kind—a stinging reminder to Kamata since Imperial edict already banned the wearing of swords in its effort to dissolve the samurai class. Richard Harris's "English Bob" gets an analogue in the form of a pompous Chōshū samurai who, traveling with his biographer, picks a fight with a Satsuma samurai before getting beaten, humiliated, and ousted by the Washiro sheriff. And most of all, killing is portrayed as, if anything, an even grimmer business than in the original, as both assassinations are painfully drawn-out affairs ultimately concluded with messy sword and knife stabs.

Though *Yurusarezaru mono* was something of a creative risk for Lee Sang-il, his revisionist *jidaigeki* won not only the approval of critics, but five Japan Academy Prizes, the domestic equivalent of the Oscars. It also earned a commendation from Clint Eastwood himself, who wrote a letter to the crew expressing his enjoyment of the movie and appreciation of its historical and cultural spirit.

It's worth pointing out that Eastwood's breakthrough Western, *Per un pugno di dollari*, was in fact an adaptation of a Japanese film, Kurosawa Akira's samurai classic *Yojimbo* (1961). So perhaps it's only appropriate that his final entry in the genre should be reborn as a samurai tale.

Japanese poster for *Yurusarezaru mono* (2013). Alternate art featured a recreation of the *Unforgiven* (1992) theatrical poster, with Watanabe Ken's back to the camera and his head angled down.

Bibliography and Filmography

"Aabra Ka Daabra—India's First 3-D Plus Film." *3D Review*, Aug. 2004, www.rollanet.org/~vbeydler/van/3dreview/3dr0408.htm.
Adarsh, Taran. "Venus & Tips Fight It Out." *IndiaFM*, 24 May 2003, www.indiafm.com/scoop/03/may/2405venus/index.shtml. *Internet Archive*. web.archive.org/web/20030805144715/www.indiafm.com/scoop/03/may/2405venus/index.shtml.
Akçay, Zeynep Gültekin. "Pamuk Prenses ve Yedi Cüceler Masalının Üç Hali: Grimm Kardeşler, Walt Disney Ve Ertem Göreç [Three Versions of the Snow White and the Seven Dwarfs Tale: Brothers Grimm, Walt Disney and Ertem Göreç]." *Erciyes İletişim Dergisi 7 [Erciyes Communication Magazine 7]* (2020): pp. 965–988.
"Akounak: The Feature Film of a Tuareg Guitarist in Agadez." *Kickstarter*, www.kickstarter.com/projects/454629120/akounak-the-feature-film-of-a-tuareg-guitarist-in.
Alaniz, José. *Komiks: Comic Art in Russia*. University of Mississippi, 2010.
Alper, Max. "The Best Guitar Music in the World Is Coming from Agadez." *Soundfly*, 29 Oct. 2017, flypaper. soundfly.com/play/best-guitar-music-world-coming-agadez/.
al-Saadi, Yazan. "No Zombies in Gaza: Horror in Arabic Cinema." *Al Akhbar English*, 31 Oct. 2012, english.al-akhbar.com/node/13233. *Internet Archive*. web.archive.org/web/20161222083646/https://english.al-akhbar.com/node/13233.
Altıner, Birsen. *Metin Erksan Sineması [Metin Erksan Cinema]*. Pan Yayıncılık, 2005.
Amita. "Nafisa Ali's Love Story." *Film World*, August 1980, pp. 28–32.
Arınç, Cihat. "Postcolonial Ghosts in New Turkish Cinema: A Deconstructive Politics of Memory in Dervis Zaim's 'The Cyprus Trilogy.'" Goldsmiths, University of London, 2015.
Arslan, Savaş. *Cinema in Turkey: A New Critical History*. Oxford University Press, 2011.
Ashraf, Syed Firdaus. "'People Will Love Dhoom!'" *Rediff.com*, 26 Aug. 2004, www.rediff.com/movies/2004/aug/26gadhvi.htm.
Bahree, Megha. "Thackeray Controlled Mumbai for Four Decades." *Wall Street Journal (Online)*, Nov 17, 2012. ProQuest, https://search.proquest.com/docview/1157732368?accountid=14553.
Bailey, Keith. "FVI: What You Didn't Know." *The Unknown Movies*, www.the-unknown-movies.com/unknownmovies/reviews/fvi.html.
"Balasaheb's Real-Life Roars Inspired Reel Drama." *The Times of India*, 18 Nov. 2012, timesofindia.indiatimes.com/city/mumbai/Balasahebs-real-life-roars-inspired-reel-drama/articleshow/17262487.cms.
Balina, Marina, and Birgit Beumers. "'To Catch Up and Overtake Disney?' Soviet and Post-Soviet Fairy-Tale Films." *Fairy-Tale Films Beyond Disney: International Perspectives*, edited by Jack David Zipes et al., Routledge Taylor & Francis Group, 2016, pp. 124–138.
Banerjee, Arpan. "Political Censorship and Indian Cinematographic Laws: A Functionalist Liberal Analysis." *Drexel Law Review*, Vol. 2, p. 557, 2010.
Banerjie, Adite. "Pages from a Storyboard." *The Life and Art of Desh Mukerji*, 7 Apr. 2014, deshmukerji.wordpress.com/2014/04/07/pages-from-a-storyboard/.
Barber, Tony. "But Movies Undermine Kremlin Control: Illicit Videos Entertain Moscow Masses." *Los Angeles Times*, 19 Jan. 1986, p. 5.
Barrot, Pierre, editor. *Nollywood: The Video Phenomenon in Nigeria*. James Currey, 2008.
Barry, Ellen. "In Russia, Jury Is Something to Work Around." *The New York Times*, The New York Times, 16 Nov. 2010, p. A1.
Batchelor, John. "Steps by the Way." *Early European Writings on Ainu Culture: Travelogues and Descriptions*, edited by Kirsten Refsing, vol. 5.
Baum, L. Frank. *The Wonderful Wizard of Oz*. Hill, 1900.
Baumgärtel, Tilman. "Imitation, Indigenization, Assimilation? No, Globalization! The Cinema of Bobby Suarez." Asia Culture Forum, 2006.

Beasley, W.G. *The Modern History of Japan*. Praeger Publishers, 1974.
Behrend, Heike. "The Titanic in Kano." *Gender and Islam in Africa: Rights, Sexuality, and Law*, edited by Margot Badran, Stanford University Press, 2011.
Ben-Yehuda, Ayala. "'High School Musical' Retunes to Suit Latin America." *Reuters*, 11 July 2008, www.reuters.com/article/us-highschool/high-school-musical-retunes-to-suit-latin-america-idUSN1126047920080712.
Berenguer, Andre. "The Adventure of Photographing Jules Verne's 'Fabulous Journey to the Center of the Earth.'" *American Cinematographer*, Dec. 1977, pp. 1294–1309.
Besas, Peter. "Spain's Film Biz a Question." *Variety*, 31 Jan. 1973, pp. 31–32.
Bhowmik, Someswar. "From Coercion to Power Relations: Film Censorship in Post-Colonial India." *Economic and Political Weekly*, vol. 38, no. 30, 2003, pp. 3148–3152.
"'Bionic Boy' Hopefuls Turn up for Film Interviews." *The Straits Times*, 16 October 1977, p. 9.
Blake, Matt, and David Deal. *The Eurospy Guide*. Luminary Press, 2004.
Blaxploitalian: 100 Years of Blackness in Italian Cinema. Dir. Fred Kuwornu. Blue Rose Films, 2016. Film.
Blood, Guts, and Bad Acting: Inside the Indonesian B Movies of the 1980s. Prod. Jonathan Vit. Vice, 2017. Film.
Boivin, Jennifer. "Animation and the National Ethos: The American Dream, Socialist Realism, and Russian Émigrés in France." *University of Alberta*, 2017.
Borowiec, Andrew. *Cyprus: A Troubled Island*. Praeger, 2000.
Bose, Sumantra. *Secular States, Religious Politics: India, Turkey, and the Future of Secularism*. Cambridge University Press, 2018.
"Breaking the Ice: South Korea Lifts Ban on Japanese Culture." *Trends in Japan*, Japan Echo Inc., 7 Dec. 1998, web-japan.org/trends98/honbun/ntj981207.html.
"Bridey Murphy? Southland Hypnotist Has Hundreds of Them!" *Independent Press-Telegram*, 5 Feb. 1956, pp. A1–A3.
Broughton, Lee. "*Captain Swing the Fearless*: A Turkish Film Adaptation of an Italian Western Comic Strip." *Impure Cinema: Intermedial and Intercultural Approaches to Film*, edited by Lúcia Nagib and Anne Jerslev. I.B. Tauris, 2014. 102–18.
Bryanski, Gleb. "Putin: On the Pulse or Out of Touch with Russia?" *Reuters*, 15 Dec. 2011, www.reuters.com/article/us-russia-putin-showman/putin-on-the-pulse-or-out-of-touch-with-russia-idUSTRE7BE1PG20111215.
Castellari, Enzo G., et al. Audio commentary. *1990: The Bronx Warriors*. Dir. Enzo G. Castellari. Blue Underground, 2018. Blu-ray.
Cerone, Daniel. "The New TV Season : Lassie Comes Home—Again." *Los Angeles Times*, 7 Sept. 1989, pp. VI:1–VI:4.
Chan, Kenneth. "The Shaw-Tarantino Connection: Rolling Thunder Pictures and the Exploitation Aesthetics of Cool." *Mediascape*, Fall 2009, http://digscholarship.unco.edu/engfacpub/1.
Chandrahas, K., and K. Lakshminarayana. *NTR, a Biography*. CLS Publishers, 2019.
Chatterji, Shoma A. "Desh Mukherjee." *Upperstall.com*, 11 Mar. 2016, upperstall.com/profile/desh-mukherjee/.
Chiang, Sing-chen Lydia. *Collecting the Self: Body and Identity in Strange Tale Collections of Late Imperial China*. Brill, 2005.
Chukhno, Irina. "Отряд Советских Супергероев. Интервью с Режиссёром Фильма «Защитники» [Otryad Sovetskikh Supergeroyev. Interv'yu s Rezhissorom Fil'ma «Zashchitniki»; Detachment of Soviet Superheroes. Interview with the Director of the Film 'Guardians']." *Aif.ru*, 23 Feb. 2017, www.aif.ru/culture/person/otryad_sovetskikh_supergeroev_intervyu_s_rezhissyorom_filma_zashchitniki.
Chung, Stephanie Po-Yin. "Moguls of the Chinese Cinema: The Story of the Shaw Brothers in Shanghai, Hong Kong and Singapore, 1924–2002." *Modern Asian Studies*, vol. 41, no. 4, 2007, pp. 665–682.
"The Cinematographer Behind the Glossy 'Bike' Film." *Hindu, The* (Madras, India), 30 Aug. 2004. *NewsBank: Access World News*, infoweb.newsbank.com/apps/news/document-view?p=AWNB&docref=news/104CC76C925FE1BF.
Clements, Jonathan, and Motoko Tamamuro. "Army of the Apes." *The Dorama Encyclopedia: A Guide to Japanese TV Drama since 1953*, Stone Bridge, 2004, p. 12.
Clover, Carol J. *Men, Women, and Chain Saws: Gender in the Modern Horror Film*. Princeton University Press, 2015.
Coll, Steve. "The Stand-Off." *The New Yorker*, 13 Feb. 2006, pp. 126–139.
Collett-White, Mike. "'12 Angry Men' Gets Russian Remake." *Reuters*, Thomson Reuters, 7 Sept. 2007, www.reuters.com/article/us-venice-russia/12-angry-men-gets-russian-remake-idUSPAR75794020070907.
Collier, Kevin Scott. *Fyodor Khitruk's Vinni-Pukh: Russia's Animated Winnie-the-Pooh*. Cartoon Research, 2018.
Collins, Ace. *Lassie: A Dog's Life, The First Fifty Years*. Penguin Books, 1993.
Conrad, Andreas. "Der Erste Deutsche Lassie—Film Feiert Premiere [The First German Lassie Film Celebrates Its Premiere]." *Der Tagesspiegel [The Daily Mirror]*, 16 Feb. 2020, www.tagesspiegel.de/berlin/familienkino-mit-hund-der-erste-deutsche-lassie-film-feiert-premiere/25550188.html.
Coonan, Clifford. "'HSM' to Sing for Disney in China." *Daily Variety Gotham*, 23 Nov. 2009, pp. 8, 30.
Corporatisation of Indian Film Industry. India Brand Equity Foundation, 2013.

Cosmatos, George P. Audio commentary. *Rambo: First Blood Part II*. Dir. George P. Cosmatos. Lionsgate, 2008. Blu-ray.
Cothern, Keegan J. "Training for Empire and Modernity: Japan's Development of Hokkaido from the 1870s-90s." *Boise State University*, 2012.
Cotter, Robert. *The Mexican Masked Wrestler and Monster Filmography*. McFarland, 2005.
"Critic Calls Film a Peasant's View of 'Jaws.'" *The Age*, 3 Aug. 1982, p. 19.
Cuevas, Antonio. "100 Pix Per Year: Who Wants Them?" *Variety*, 11 Sept. 1974, pp. 27–44.
Dadyburjor, Farhad J. "All Actresses Need to Treat Women-Oriented Roles as an Agenda, Says Tanuja Chandra." *Hindustan Times*, 27 May 2017, www.hindustantimes.com/brunch/all-actresses-need-to-treat-women-oriented-roles-as-an-agenda-says-tanuja-chandra/story-3tsMJgsXa5ggIsMctn9eeL.html.
Dutta, Nandita. *F-Rated: Being a Woman Filmmaker in India*. HarperCollins India, 2019.
Danna, Corey. "Fred Williamson Interview." *The Action Elite*, 25 Jan. 2016, theactionelite.com/fred-williamson-interview/.
Das, Ronjita. "'Urmila Was the First Person I Thought of.'" *Rediff.com*, 22 Mar. 2001, www.rediff.com/entertai/2001/mar/22rajat.htm.
Dasgupta, Shamya. *Don't Disturb the Dead: The Story of the Ramsay Brothers*. HarperCollins Publishers India, 2017.
Daugherty, Julia. "'Bridey Murphy' Theory Getting Linkletter Test." *The Indianapolis Star*, 15 Feb. 1956, p. 15.
Demick, Barbara. "South Korea Makes Way for Anime." *Los Angeles Times*, 28 Dec. 2003, p. 29.
Denison, Rayna. "American Superheroes in Japanese Hands: Superhero Genre Hybridity as Superhero Systems Collide in Supaidāman." *Superheroes on World Screens*, edited by Rayna Denison and Rachel Mizsei-Ward, University Press of Mississippi, 2015, pp. 53–72.
Dennison, Stephanie, and Lisa Shaw. *Popular Cinema in Brazil, 1930–2001*. Manchester University Press, 2004.
Derendorf, Kevin. "Japlanet of the Apes." *Maser Patrol*, 11 July 2017, maserpatrol.wordpress.com/2017/07/11/japlanet-of-the-apes/.
Deshpande, Manisha. "Vikram Chopra to Begin Shooting of 'Fight Club' in December." *Glamsham.com*, 19 Oct. 2004, www.glamsham.com/movies/scoops/04/oct/19bshah.asp. *Internet Archive*. web.archive.org/web/20070217001013/www.glamsham.com/movies/scoops/04/oct/19bshah.asp.
Desser, David. "Remaking *Seven Samurai* in World Cinema." *East Asian Cinemas: Exploring Transnational Connections on Film*, edited by Leon Hunt and Wing-Fai Leung. I.B. Tauris, 2008. 17–40.
Dhananjayan, G. *Pride of Tamil Cinema 1931–2013: Tamil Films That Have Earned National and International Recognition*. Blue Ocean Publishers, 2014.
"Dhoom: The Making." *Dhoom*, directed by Sanjay Gadhvi. Yash Raj Films, 2004. Blu-ray.
"Dhoom 2 Is like Amar Akbar Anthony." *Rediff.com*, 22 Nov. 2006, www.rediff.com/movies/2006/nov/22sanjay.htm.
"Director H. Tjut Djalil: Mystic from Bali." *Dangerous Seductress*, directed by H. Tjut Djalil. Mondo Macabro, 2004. DVD.
Dugger, Celia W. "Gunmen Kill 30, Including 10 Children, in Kashmir." *The New York Times*, 15 May 2002, p. A3.
Dugger, Celia W. "India Raises the Pitch in Criticism of Pakistan." *The New York Times*, 19 Dec. 2001, p. A18.
Dwyer, Rachel. *Filming the Gods: Religion and Indian Cinema*. Routledge, 2006.
Eig, Jonathan. *Get Capone: The Secret Plot That Captured America's Most Wanted Gangster*. Simon & Schuster, 2011.
Elley, Derek. "Disney High School Musical China." *Film Business Asia*, 29 Dec. 2010, www.filmbiz.asia/reviews/disney-high-school-musical-china. *Internet Archive*. web.archive.org/web/20141213084329/http://www.filmbiz.asia/reviews/disney-high-school-musical-china.
"Enzo G. Castellari & Fabrizio De Angelis in Conversation. Part 1." *1990: The Bronx Warriors*, directed by Enzo G. Castellari. Blue Underground, 2018. Blu-ray.
"Enzo G. Castellari & Fabrizio De Angelis in Conversation. Part 2." *The New Barbarians*, directed by Enzo G. Castellari. Blue Underground, 2018. Blu-ray.
"Enzo G. Castellari & Fabrizio De Angelis in Conversation. Part 3." *Escape from the Bronx*, directed by Enzo G. Castellari. Blue Underground, 2018. Blu-ray.
Essoe, Gabe. *Tarzan of the Movies: A Pictorial History of More than Fifty Years of Edgar Rice Burroughs' Legendary Hero*. Citadel Press, 1979.
Exley, Charles. "No Land's Man: On Remaking the Last Western in Japan and the Politics of Revision." *Journal of Japanese and Korean Cinema*, vol. 10, no. 2, 2018, pp. 147–162.
Exploitation Aesthetics of Cool." *Mediascape*, Fall 2009, digscholarship.unco.edu/cgi/viewcontent.cgi?article=1001&context=engfacpub
"Fantasy Films from Indonesia." *Mondo Macabro*, written by Andrew Starke and Pete Tombs, season 1, episode 5, Channel 4, 2002.
Fedina, Anna. "Актер и Режиссер Михаил Пореченков: 'Я Меньше Шварценеггера, Но Актерских Данных у Меня Больше' [Akter i Rezhisser Mikhail Porechenkov: 'YA Men'she Shvartseneggera, No Akterskikh Dannykh u Menya Bol'she'; Actor and Director Mikhail Porechenkov: 'I Am Smaller than

Schwarzenegger, but I Have Better Acting Skills']." Известия *[Izvestiya; The News]*, 5 Sept. 2007, iz.ru/news/328387.
"Fight Club Members Only—The Making of the Film." *Fight Club: Members Only*, directed by Vikram Chopra. Shemaroo, 2006. DVD.
Fischer, Dennis. "Luigi Cozzi." *Science Fiction Film Directors, 1895–1998*, by Dennis Fischer, McFarland, 2011, pp. 139–143.
Flores, Emil M. "The Concept of the Superhero in Filipino Films." *Plaridel*, vol. 2, no. 2, Aug. 2005, pp. 23–38.
Frater, Patrick. "IM Global Sells 'Paranormal Activity.'" *Variety*, 13 Nov. 2008, variety.com/2008/film/markets-festivals/im-global-sells-paranormal-activity-1117995812/.
Fukasaku, Kinji, and Sadao Yamane. 映画監督深作欣二 *[Eiga kantoku Fukasaku Kinji; Kinji Fukasaku, Film Director]*. Waizu Shuppan, 2003.
Galbraith, Stuart. *Monsters Are Attacking Tokyo! The Incredible World of Japanese Fantasy Films*. Feral House, 1998.
Ganti, Tejaswini. "And Yet My Heart Is Still Indian: The Bombay Film Industry and the (H)Indianization of Hollywood." *Media Worlds: Anthropology on New Terrain*, edited by Faye D. Ginsburg et al., University of California Press, 2002, pp. 281–300.
Gelgeç, Gökay. "Yeşilçam'in Remake'leri: Cemo ile Cemile—Turkish Bonnie and Clyde (1971) [Remakes of Yeşilçam: Cemo ile Cemile—Turkish Bonnie and Clyde (1971)]." *Sinematik Yeşilçam [Cinematic Yeşilçam]*, 22 Apr. 2013, sinematikyesilcam.com/2013/04/cemo-ile-cemile-turkish-bonnie-and-clyde/.
Giordano, Michele. *Giganti Buoni: Da Ercole a Piedone (e Oltre) Il Mito Dell'uomo Forte Nel Cinema Italiano [Good Giants: From Hercules to Piedone (and Beyond) The Myth of the Strong Man in Italian Cinema]*. Gremese Editore, 1998.
Giovacchini, Saverio. "John Kitzmiller, Euro-American Difference, and the Cinema of the West." *Black Camera*, vol. 6, no. 2, Apr. 2015, pp. 17–41.
Giroux, Jack. "Interview: Rod Lurie's 'Straw Dogs' Loves Women and Searches for the Inner Man." *Film School Rejects*, 17 Sept. 2011, filmschoolrejects.com/interview-rod-luries-straw-dogs-loves-women-and-searches-for-the-inner-man-bc9afcf60e17/.
Giusti, Marco. *Dizionario Dei Film Italiani Stracult [Stracult Italian Film Dictionary]*. Sperling & Kupfer, 1999.
Gomarasca, Manlio, and Davide Pulici, editors. "Intervista a Bruno Mattei [Interview with Bruno Mattei]." *Nocturno Dossier*, Apr. 2006, pp. 6–28.
Greene, Doyle. *Mexploitation Cinema: A Critical History of Mexican Vampire, Wrestler, Ape-man, and Similar Films, 1957–1977*. McFarland, 2005.
Grobler, Craig. "I Talk Remaking Unforgiven Yurusarezaru mono with Director Sang-Il Lee, His Influences, What Clint Eastwood Said about the Remake, Why It Is the Right Time for His Film & the Possibility of a Sequel." *The Establishing Shot*, 28 Feb. 2014, www.theestablishingshot.com/2014/02/i-talk-remaking-unforgiven-yurusarezaru.html.
Gullo, Christopher. *The Films of Donald Pleasence*. BookBaby, 2012.
Gunter, M.M. "Transnational Sources of Support for the Kurdish Insurgency in Turkey." *Journal of Conflict Studies*, vol. 11, no. 2, Mar. 1991, pp. 7–29.
Gupte, Pranay. "Germany's Guest Workers." *The New York Times*, 19 Aug. 1984, pp. 88–101.
Güven, Ali Murat. Interview with Metin Erksan (unpublished). July 2004.
Guy, Randor. "Kuzhandaiyum Deivamum 1965." *The Hindu*, 30 July 2011, www.thehindu.com/features/cinema/kuzhandaiyum-deivamum-1965/article2308458.ece.
Hall, William. "Big Brother Is Watching Him." *Photoplay*, June 1967, pp. 46–52.
Hampton, Mark. "British Legal Culture and Colonial Governance: The Attack on Corruption in Hong Kong, 1968–1974." *Britain and the World*, vol. 5, no. 2, 2012, pp. 223–239.
Haynes, Jonathan. *Nollywood: The Creation of Nigerian Film Genres*. The University of Chicago Press, 2016.
Hendrix, Grady. "Kaiju Shakedown: The Ramsays of Bollywood." *Film Comment*, 13 July 2015, www.filmcomment.com/blog/kaiju-shakedown-the-ramsays-of-bollywood/.
Hofius, Jason, and George Khoury. *Age of TV Heroes*. TwoMorrows, 2010.
Homenick, Brett. "The Brains Behind Brain 17! Michael Part on Americanizing a Japanese Cult Classic!" *Vantage Point Interviews*, 16 Sept. 2018, vantagepointinterviews.com/2018/09/16/the-brains-behind-brain-17-michael-part-on-americanizing-a-japanese-cult-classic/.
Horn, John. "The Film That Jolted Spielberg into 'Yes.'" *Los Angeles Times*, 20 Sept. 2009, pp. D1–D8.
Hughes, Howard. *Cinema Italiano: The Complete Guide from Classics to Cult*. I.B. Tauris, 2011.
"Interview with Aytekin Akkaya." *3 Dev Adam*. directed by Tevfik Fikret Uçak. Onar Films, 2006. DVD.
"Interview with Doğan Tamer." *3 Dev Adam*, directed by Tevfik Fikret Uçak. Onar Films, 2006. DVD.
"Interview with Kunt Tulgar." *Tarzan İstanbul'da*, directed by Orhan Atadeniz. Onar Films, 2007. DVD.
"Interview with Luigi Cozzi." *Starcrash*, directed by Luigi Cozzi. Shout! Factory, 2010. DVD.
"Interview with Tevfik Fikret Uçak." *3 Dev Adam*, directed by Tevfik Fikret Uçak. Onar Films, 2006. DVD.
"Introduction by August Ragone." *Mystery Science Theater 3000: Volume XXII*. Shout! Factory, 2011. DVD.
Irina, Isaeva. "'Мы с Тобой Одной Крови, Ты и я' ['My s Toboy Odnoy Krovi, Ty i ya'; 'We Are of

the Same Blood, You and I']." *Собеседник [Sobesednik; Interlocutor]*, 20 May 2019, sobesednik. ru/kultura-i-tv/20190514-maugli-my-s-toboj-odnoj-krovi-ty-i-ya.
Isayev, Ruslan. " Mikhalkov's Film '12' Screened in Moscow and Chechnya." *Prague Watchdog*, 6 Nov. 2007, www.watchdog.cz/?show=000000-000015-000006-000023&lang=1.
"Italy's Movie Boom for Negro Actors." *Jet*, 13 May 1954, pp. 60–62.
Izharuddin, Alicia. *Gender and Islam in Indonesian Cinema*. Palgrave Macmillan,2017.
Jaundrill, D. Colin. *Samurai to Soldier: Remaking Military Service in Nineteenth-Century Japan*. Cornell University Press, 2016.
Jha, Subhash K. "'I Want to Bring Sex out of the Closet.'" *Rediff.com*, 25 Apr. 2003, www.rediff.com/movies/2003/apr/25sanjay.htm.
Jha, Subhash K. "Here Comes the Real Agent Vinod." *The Times of India*, 26 Mar. 2012, timesofindia.indiatimes.com/entertainment/hindi/bollywood/news/Here-comes-the-real-Agent-Vinod/articleshow/12412673.cms.
Kazmi, Fareeduddin. "How Angry Is the Angry Young Man? 'Rebellion' in Conventional Hindi Films." *The Secret Politics of Our Desires: Nation, Culture, and Gender in Indian Popular Cinema*, edited by Ashis Nandy, Zed Books, 1998, pp. 135–155.
McGilligan, Patrick. *Clint: The Life and Legend*. St. Martin's Press, 2002.
Jimenez-Varea, Jesus, and Miguel Ángel Pérez-Gómez. "Marvel and Toei." *Marvel Comics into Film: Essays on Adaptations since the 1940s*, edited by Matthew J. McEniry et al., McFarland, 2016, pp. 84–93.
Johnson, Randal. "Popular Cinema in Brazil." *Studies in Latin American Popular Culture*, vol. 3, no. 1, 1984, pp. 86–96.
"Juan Piquer Sets an Example, So, Why No More Like Him?" *Variety*, 30 Sept. 1981, p. 47.
K, Sangeetha Devi. "Devgan guns for action with Qayamat." *Times of India, The (Mumbai, India)*, sec. Hyderabad Times, 12 June 2003. *NewsBank: Access World News*, infoweb.newsbank.com/apps/news/document-view?p=AWNB&docref=news/15680599610BDAA8.
Kalat, David. *A Critical History and Filmography of Toho's Godzilla Series*. 2nd ed., McFarland, 2017.
Kalat, David. *J-Horror: The Definitive Guide to The Ring, The Grudge and Beyond*. Vertical, 2007.
Kamovnikova, Natalia. "'Once, Twice and Again!' Kipling's Works in the Russian Twentieth Century Retranslations." *TranscUlturAl: A Journal of Translation and Cultural Studies*, vol. 20, no. 1, 6 Aug. 2020, pp. 140–156.
Kansteiner, Wulf. "Nazis, Viewers and Statistics: Television History, Television Audience Research and Collective Memory in West Germany." *Journal of Contemporary History*, vol. 39, no. 4, 2004, pp. 575–598.
Kelts, Roland. *Japanamerica: How Japanese Pop Culture Has Invaded the U.S.* Palgrave Macmillan, 2008.
Kennel, Glenn. *Color and Mastering for Digital Cinema*. Focal Press, Taylor & Francis Group, 2013.
Kim, Hyuk. 나는 장난감에 탐닉한다 *[Naneun jangnangam-e tamnighanda; I Indulge in Toys]*. 갤리온 [Gaellion; Galleon], 2014.
Kim, Yungduk. "Review of South Korea's Acceptance of Japanese Animation." *Japan Spotlight*, 2009, pp. 44–45.
Kinnard, Roy, and Tony Crnkovich. *Italian Sword and Sandal Films, 1908–1990*. McFarland, 2017.
Kirkley, Christopher. "All Gold Everything—Akounak Film Shoot Recap." *Sahel Sounds*, 18 Mar. 2014, sahelsounds.com/2014/03/allgoldeverything/.
Kirkley, Christopher. "Rain the Color of Blue with a Little Red in It." *Sahel Sounds*, 17 Jan. 2014, sahelsounds.com/2014/01/rain-the-color-of-blue-with-a-little-red-in-it/.
Kleiman, Dena. "Now 60, Milne's 'Pooh' Is Big in Soviet Union." *The New York Times*, 27 Dec. 1986, p. 15.
Kohli, Suresh. "Dharmatma (1975)." *The Hindu*, 13 June 2016, www.thehindu.com/features/cinema/dharmatma-1975/article4316386.ece.
Kokas, Aynne. *Hollywood Made in China*. University of California Press, 2017.
Krings, Matthias. "Black Titanic: Pirating the White Star Liner." *African Appropriations: Cultural Difference, Mimesis, and Media*, Indiana University Press, 2015, pp. 84–119.
Krivoruchko, Anna. "Who Has a Right to Speak? The Word and Silence in Nikita Mikhalkov's Twelve (2007)." *Studies in Russian and Soviet Cinema*, vol. 9, no. 3, Feb. 2015, pp. 184–199.
Krueger, Anne O. "Partial Adjustment and Growth in the 1980s in Turkey." *Reform, Recovery, and Growth: Latin America and the Middle East*, edited by Rudiger Dornbusch and Sebastian Edwards, University of Chicago Press, 1995, pp. 343–368.
Kulkarni, Damini. "They Suffer in Life and Become Powerful after Death: Meet Cinema's Female Ghosts." *Scroll.in*, 15 Mar. 2017, scroll.in/reel/830851/they-suffer-in-life-and-become-powerful-after-death-meet-cinemas-female-ghosts.
Kumar, Anuj. "Time to Swing into Action." *The Hindu*, 19 Jan. 2006, www.thehindu.com/todays-paper/tp-features/tp-metroplus/time-to-swing-into-action/article3185905.ece.
"Kurd Rebels Kill 9 Turks." *Los Angeles Times*, 27 Oct. 1985, p. I:8.
Kushner, David. "The Hendrix of the Sahara." *Esquire*, Winter 2020, pp. 86–117.
Kutty, N.G. "Bionic Boy Johnson Signed on for Part II" *The Straits Times*, 27 November 1977, p. 11.
Kuznetsov, Sergey. "Уйти Из Джунглей [Uyti Iz Dzhungley; Get Out of the Jungle]." *Искусство Кино [Iskusstvo Kino; Film Art]*, Mar. 2004, old.kinoart.ru/archive/2004/03/n3-article15.
Kwok, Ching-ling, and Ng Grace, editors. *Director Chor Yuen*. Hong Kong Film Archive, 2006.

Lacaba, Jose F. *The Films of ASEAN*. ASEAN Committee on Culture and Information, 2000.
Lam, Stephanie. "Hop on Pop." *Cineaction*, no. 78, Dec. 2009, pp. 46–51.
Landreth, Jonathan. "'HSM' China Shooting in Shanghai." *The Hollywood Reporter*, 22 Nov. 2009, www.hollywoodreporter.com/news/hsm-china-shooting-shanghai-91630.
Laughlin, Will. "Child's Play in India: Four Adaptations." *Braineater.com*, braineater.com/bolly_tolly_dolly.html.
Lawagan, Ernesto. "The Lost Works of Mars Ravelo." *Ernee's Corner*, 23 Feb. 2012, erneelawagan.blogspot.com/2012/02/lost-works-of-mars-ravelo.html.
Lawagan, Ernesto. "The Untold True Beginning of Darna." *Ernee's Corner*, 12 May 2017, erneelawagan.blogspot.com/2017/05/the-untold-true-beginning-of-darna.html.
Lăzărescu, Emanuel. "Lassie Come Home—Interview with Director Hanno Olderdissen: 'The Audience Can Look Forward to a Modern Film with a Nostalgic Feel and Lots of Fun.'" *Prorom*, 8 Sept. 2020, www.prorom.com/en/news/lassie-come-home---interview-with-director-hanno-olderdissen-the-audience-can-look-forward-to-a-modern-film-with-a-nostalgic-feel-and-lots-of-fun.
Leavold, Andrew. "Bionic Guts and Exploding Huts! The Filipino Pulp Factory of Bobby A. Suarez, Part Two." *Weng's Chop*, Aug. 2016, pp. 84–103.
Leavold, Andrew. "On Lady Terminator: Interview with Barbara Anne Constable." *Plaridel*, vol. 11, no. 2, Aug. 2014, pp. 189–207.
Leeder, Mike. "Hong Kong's Roger Corman, Joseph Lai." *Impact*, Oct. 2000, pp. 50–53.
Levy, Frederic Albert. "Contamination." *Cinefantastique*, Sept. 1981, p. 8.
Lewis, Meredith. *Ask for the Moon: Innovation at Shaw Brothers Studios*. Meredith Lewis, 2018.
Lewis, Paul. "Nikos Sampson, 66, Cyprus President After Coup, Dies." *The New York Times*, 11 May 2001, p. C13.
Linson, Art. *What Just Happened? Bitter Hollywood Tales from the Front Line*. Grove Press, 2008.
Logan, Bey. Audio commentary. *The Mighty Peking Man*. Dir. Ho Meng-hua. 88 Films, 2017. Blu-ray.
Luo, Yadong, et al. "Emerging Economy Copycats: Capability, Environment, and Strategy." *Academy of Management Perspectives*, vol. 25, no. 2, 2011, pp. 37–56.
Lupi, Gordiano, and Ivo Gazzarrini. *Bruno Mattei: L'ultimo Artigiano [Bruno Mattei: The Last Craftsman]*. Il Foglio, 2013.
Lupi, Gordiano. *Written and Directed by Lewis Coates*. Profondo Rosso, 2011.
Machete Maidens Unleashed! Dir. Mark Hartley. Dark Sky Films, 2011. Film.
Macias, Patrick, and August Ragone. "Message from Space: There Are More Beautiful Dreams in Space." *Message from Space*, directed by Kinji Fukasaku. Shout! Factory, 2013. Blu-ray.
Magalhães, Antônio Rocha. "Life and Drought in Brazil." *Drought in Brazil: Proactive Management and Policy*, edited by Nathan Engle et al., Taylor & Francis, 2017, pp. 1–18.
Majumder, Rishi. "Ramsay International." *Motherland Magazine*, May 2012, pp. 52–61.
Manley, Lance. "Interview with Director Enzo G. Castellari." *Bronx Warriors—The Website*, 28 Oct. 2003, www.bronxwarriors.co.uk/enzoint.htm.
Manley, Lance. "Interview with Enzo Castellari in Rome, 2004." *Bronx Warriors—The Website*, www.bronxwarriors.co.uk/enzoint2.htm.
Marak, Katarzyna. *Japanese and American Horror: A Comparative Study of Film, Fiction, Graphic Novels and Video Games*. McFarland, 2015.
Marengo, J.A., Torres, R.R. & Alves, L.M. "Drought in Northeast Brazil—past, present, and future." *Theoretical and Applied Climatology*, vol. 129, 2017, 1189–1200.
Margheriti, Edoardo. "Biography." *The Official Website of Antonio Margheriti*, www.antoniomargheriti.com/English_Version/biography/Page3.htm. *Internet Archive*. web.archive.org/web/20110311022834/http://www.antoniomargheriti.com/English_Version/biography/Page3.htm.
"Market Guide: For Sale in Milan." *Variety*, 19 Oct. 1992, pp. 142–144.
Martina, Maurizio. "Biography—Maurizio Martina." *Prof Antonio Maurizio Martina*, 16 May 2013, antoniomauriziomartina.blogspot.com/2013/05/biography-maurizio-martina.html.
McCormick, Moira. "Monarch Enters Sell-Thru with 'Mowgli.'" *Billboard*, vol. 110, no. 18, May 1998, p. 72.
Mehta, Suketu. *Maximum City: Bombay Lost and Found*. Alfred A. Knopf, 2005.
Merelo, Alfonso. "Juan Piquer Simón, Director Del Fantástico Español [Juan Piquer Simón, Spanish Director of the Fantastic]." *Sitio De Ciencia-Ficción [Science-Fiction Site]*, 17 Apr. 2006, www.ciencia-ficcion.com/opinion/op01030.htm.
"Mermaid Hooker." *Film World*, May 1980, p. 23.
Mibu, Tomohiro. "『ハリー・ポッター』最終章がぶっちぎり！3D化断念の影響もはねのけ首位発進！『パラノーマル』日本版続編も初登場!! ['Harī pottā' sai shūshō ga butchigiri! 3 D-ka dan'nen no eikyō mo hanenoke shui hasshin! 'Paranōmaru' Nihon-ban zokuhen mo hatsu tōjō!!; The Final Chapter of 'Harry Potter' Is Just Right! The Influence of the 3D Abandoned Is Also the First Start! The Japanese Version of 'Paranormal' Is Also Available for the First Time!!]." シネマトゥデイ *[Shinematoudei; Cinema Today]*, 24 Nov. 2010, www.cinematoday.jp/news/N0028579.
"Михаил Пореченков и Братья Пресняковы Представили Ремейк 'Командо' [Mikhail Porechenkov i Brat'ya Presnyakovy Predstavili Remeyk 'Komando'; Mikhail Porechenkov and the Presnyakov

Brothers Presented a Remake of 'Commando']." *РИА Новости [RIA Novosti; RIA News]*, 9 July 2007, ria.ru/20070709/68621745.html.

Mikhailin, Yuri. "О Зарождении Идеи Фильма [O Zarozhdenii Idei Fil'ma; On the Origin of the Idea of the Film]." *Киноведческие Записки [Kinovedcheskiye Zapiski; Film Studies Notes]*, no. 73, 2005, pp. 55–65.

Mishina, Ekaterina. "Trial by Jury in Russia: Revival and Survival." *Institute of Modern Russia*, 26 Jan. 2012, imrussia.org/en/rule-of-law/186-trial-by-jury-in-russia-revival-and-survival.

Modlin, E Nelson. "A Big-Budget Blitz to Beat the Crisis." *Screen International*, 3 Mar. 1979, p. 9.

Mohan, Devendra. "The New Experience." *Business Insider*, 24 Nov. 2003, p. 153.

Mora, Carl J. *Mexican Cinema: Reflections of a Society, 1896–2004*. McFarland, 2012.

Morton, Ray. *King Kong: The History of a Movie Icon from Fay Wray to Peter Jackson*. Applause Theatre & Cinema Books, 2005.

Muir, John Kenneth. *The Encyclopedia of Superheroes on Film and Television*. McFarland, 2004.

Murray, Jeremy A., and Kathleen M. Nadeau, editors. *Pop Culture in Asia and Oceania*. ABC-CLIO, 2016.

Murray, Nick. "'Purple Rain' Falls on the Sahara in African Adaptation." *Rolling Stone*, 8 May 2015, www.rollingstone.com/music/music-news/purple-rain-falls-on-the-sahara-in-brilliant-african-adaptation-173222/.

Nadeau, Josh. "Eastern Partners: the Russian-Chinese Film Collaborations Trying to Hit the Big Time." *The Calvert Journal*, 11 July 2018, www.calvertjournal.com/articles/show/10463/eastern-partners-will-joint-russian-chinese-films-hit-the-big-time.

Narayanan, Nirmal. "Inspired by Dhoom? Bikers rob 25 kg of gold worth Rs 6 crore in Kochi." *International Business Times: Indian Edition (India)*, sec. News, 10 May 2019. *NewsBank: Access World News*, infoweb.newsbank.com/apps/news/document-view?p=AWNB&docref=news/173F9112E8E77750.

Nelson, Michelle R., and Sameer Deshpande. "The Prevalence of and Consumer Response to Foreign and Domestic Brand Placement in Bollywood Movies." *Journal of Advertising*, vol. 42, no. 1, 2013, pp. 1–15.

"'Нет, я Не Ален Делон' ['Net, ya Ne Alen Delon'; 'No, I'm Not Alain Delon']." *Золотое Кольцо [Zolotoye Kol'tso; Gold Ring]*, 20 July 2007, goldring.ru/news/show/86516.

"New Interviews with Cast and Crew." *Guardians*, directed by Sarik Andreasyan, Shout! Factory, 2017. Blu-ray.

Nikita. "Interview De Alberto De Martino." *Nanarland*, www.nanarland.com/interview/interview-albertodemartino-page-1.html.

Öğünç, Pınar. *Jet Rejisör Çetin İnanç*. Roll, 2006.

Olsen, Mark. "12 Angry … Russian Men?" *Los Angeles Times*, 8 Mar. 2009, p. D6.

Oltmanns, Torsten. "Das Öffentlich-Rechtliche TV-Angebot 1952 Bis 1991 Und Seine Nutzung [The Public Television Service 1952 to 1991 and Its Use]." Universität zu Köln, Instituts Für Rundfunkökonomie [University of Cologne, Institute for Broadcasting Economics], 1993, www.rundfunkoek.uni-koeln.de/sites/rundfunk/Arbeitspapiere/006_93.pdf.

Operation: RAMBU!. Dir. Steve Austin. SPV Films, 2019. Film.

Osava, Mario. "No More Mass Deaths from Drought in Northeast Brazil." *Inter Press Service*, 30 Dec. 2016, www.ipsnews.net/2016/12/no-more-mass-deaths-from-drought-in-northeast-brazil/.

Osman, Tarek. *Egypt on the Brink: From Nasser to the Muslim Brotherhood*. Yale University Press, 2013.

Ou, Mirian, and Alessandro Constantino Gamo. "Brazilian Children's Cinema in the 1990s: Tensions Between the National-Popular and the International-Popular." *Family Films in Global Cinema: The World Beyond Disney*, edited by Noel Brown and Bruce Babington, I.B. Tauris, 2015, pp. 207–222.

Özçınar, Meral. "A Cornerstone of Turkish Fantastic Films: From Flash Gordon to Baytekin." *Comics as a Nexus of Cultures: Essays on the Interplay of Media, Disciplines and International Perspectives*, edited by Mark Berninger et al., McFarland & Co., 2010, pp. 164–174.

Özkaracalar, Kaya, and David White. "Yilmaz Atadeniz: Superman of Turkish Cinema." *Video Watchdog*, Feb. 2002, pp. 26–41.

Özkaracalar, Kaya. "Between Appropriation and Innovation: Turkish Horror Cinema." *Fear Without Frontiers: Horror Cinema Across the Globe*, edited by Steven Jay Schneider, FAB Press, 2003, pp. 205–217.

Özkaracalar, Kaya. "Debut of Flash Gordon in Turkey." *The Mysterious Flame of Queen Loana*, 25 Oct. 2009, kayaozkaracalar.blogspot.com/2009/10/debut-of-flash-gordon-in-turkey.html.

Özkaracalar, Kaya. "Horror Films in Turkish Cinema." *European Nightmares: Horror Cinema in Europe since 1945*, edited by Patricia Allmer et al., Wallflower Press, 2012, pp. 249–260.

Özkaracalar, Kaya. "Phantom Comics in Turkey." 22 Aug. 2005, 3 July 2016, http://www.geocities.ws/rick40s2002/turk_phantom.html.

Pais, Arthur. "4 'Ghosts' Meet 3 'Pretty Women' in India's Ripoffs." *Variety*, 12 Nov. 1990, pp. 1–85.

Paksoy, H.B. *The Bald Boy and the Most Beautiful Girl in the World*. ATON, 2003.

Palmer, Stephen. "'People Around Me Often Say I Should Start Doing More Cheerful Movies'—In Conversation with Lee Sang-Il." *EasternKicks*, 27 Feb. 2014, www.easternkicks.com/features/people-around-me-often-say-i-should-start-doing-more-cheerful-movies-in-conversation-with-lee-sang-il.

Palmerini, Luca M., and Gaetano Mistretta. *Spaghetti Nightmares: Italian Fantasy-Horrors as Seen through the Eyes of Their Protagonists*. Fantasma, 1996.

Pandya, Sonal. "Seeing Double: Twins and Hindi Cinema." *Cinestaan*, 1 Dec. 2015, www.cinestaan.com/articles/2015/dec/1/220.
"『パラノーマル・アクティビティ第2章 / TOKYO NIGHT』メイキング ['Paranōmaru akutibiti dai 2-shō: tōkyō naito' meikingu; The Making of 'Paranormal Activity 2: Tokyo Night']." *Paranormal Activity 2: Tokyo Night*, directed by Nagae Toshikazu. Presidio Corporation, 2010. DVD.
"「パラノーマル・アクティビティ第2章」の結末は女子高生100人が決める!? ['Paranōmaru akutibiti dai 2-shō' no ketsumatsu wa mesukōsei 100-ri ga kimeru!?; 100 High School Girls Decide the Ending of 'Paranormal Activity Chapter 2'!?]." 映画.com *[Eiga.com]*, 21 Oct. 2010, eiga.com/news/20101021/20/.
Patil, Vimla. "Making Miracles on the Silver Screen!" *The Tribune*, The Tribune Trust, 11 May 2003, www.tribuneindia.com/2003/20030511/spectrum/main7.htm.
Paul, Louis. *Italian Horror Film Directors*. McFarland, 2011.
Pendakur, Manjunath. "New Cultural Technologies and the Fading Glitter of Indian Cinema." *Quarterly Review of Film and Video*, vol. 11, no. 3, 1989, pp. 69–78.
Pérez Molina, Jesús Manuel. *Golden Ninja Operation: Los Secretos De Las IFD y La Filmark*. Applehead Team Creaciones, 2015.
Phipps, Keith. "The Great Lost Jaws Rip-Off." *The Dissolve*, 10 July 2014, thedissolve.com/features/movie-of-the-week/654-the-great-lost-jaws-rip-off/.
Pikkov, Ülo. "On the Topics and Style of Soviet Animated Films." *Baltic Screen Media Review*, vol. 4, no. 1, 2016, pp. 16–37.
Player, Mark. "Intergalactic Tokusatsu: Charting the Japanese Space Opera, Part 2." *Midnight Eye*, 7 July 2014, www.midnighteye.com/features/intergalactic-tokusatsu-charting-the-japanese-space-opera-part-2/.
Pontieri, Laura. *Soviet Animation and the Thaw of the 1960s: Not Only for Children*. John Libbey, 2012.
Pope, Nicole, and Hugh Pope. *Turkey Unveiled: A History of Modern Turkey*. Overlook Duckworth, 2011.
Porteous, Phelan. "Our Friend Power 5 (TMNT) - Phelous." *YouTube*, 16 Mar. 2018, www.youtube.com/watch?v=iRuNZqqVmbE.
Prynn, Jonathan. "Firm Ordered to Destroy 'Mockbusters' of Disney's Top Movies." *Evening Standard*, 26 Nov. 2012, www.standard.co.uk/news/uk/firm-ordered-to-destroy-mockbusters-of-disneys-top-movies-8352016.html.
Ragone, August. *Eiji Tsuburaya: Master of Monsters*. Chronicle Books, 2007.
Rainville, Keith J. *Zombi Mexicano*. From Parts Unknown Publ., 2012.
Ram Gopal Varma, "Interview," *Filmfare*, March 2003, 64–65.
Ramachandran, T.M. "Another Box-Office from A.V.M." *Sport & Pastime*, 18 Dec. 1965, p. 51.
Raphael, Raphael. "Planet Kong: Transnational Flows of King Kong (1933) in Japan and East Asia." *Transnational Horror Cinema*, edited by Sophia Siddique and Raphael Raphael, Palgrave Macmillan, 2016, pp. 205–220.
Ravi, P.R. "I Want to Tell My Story from the Woman's Point of View." *The Tribune India*, 26 Sept. 1999, www.tribuneindia.com/1999/99sep26/sunday/view.htm.
@realpreityzinta. "After all these years this film remains closest to my heart. If I was not an actor I would probably be #ReetOberoi from #Sangharsh. Thank you to the #Bhatts & #Tanuja for this opportunity. Thank you @akshaykumar & #AshutoshRana for making it so special! ⭐ #19YearsOfSangharsh." *Twitter*, 3 Sep. 2019, 1:06 a.m., twitter.com/realpreityzinta/status/1036495622453514240.
Reinhart, Mark S. *The Batman Filmography: Live-Action Features, 1943–1997*. McFarland, 2005.
Remake Remix Rip-Off. Dir. Cem Kaya. Drop-Out Cinema, 2014. Film.
"Режиссер 'Защитников': Мы Не Пытаемся Бросить Вызов Голливуду [Rezhisser 'Zashchitnikov': My Ne Pytayemsya Brosit' Vyzov Gollivudu; 'Guardians' Director: We're Not Trying to Challenge Hollywood]." *Sputnik*, 17 Feb. 2017, sputnik.by/culture/20170217/1027500952/rezhisser-zashchitnikov-my-ne-pytaemsya-brosit-vyzov-gollivudu.html.
Riera, Emilio García. *Historia Documental Del Cine Mexicano*. Vol. 6, Era, 1974.
Rodrigues, Christina. "Search on for Bionic Boy No. 2." *The Straits Times*, 14 October 1977, p. 14.
Romano, Stephen. "Compromising Hyperspace: The Making of Starcrash." *Stephen Romano Express*, www.stephenromanoshockfestival.com/compromising-hyperspace-the-making-of-starcrash/.
Romano, Stephen. Audio commentary. *Starcrash*, directed by Luigi Cozzi. Shout! Factory, 2010. DVD.
Rossi, Jones. "Estúdio Brasileiro Faz Sucesso 'Clonando' a Disney [Brazilian Studio Is Successful at 'Cloning' Disney.]." *Globo.com*, 7 Aug. 2007, g1.globo.com/Noticias/Cinema/0,,MUL83997-7086-244,00.html.
Said, Salim, and John H. McGlynn. *Cinema of Indonesia*. Festival of Indonesia Foundation, 1991.
Sampath, Janani. "Remakes Are Never Passé in Tamil." *The New Indian Express*, 10 June 2013, www.newindianexpress.com/entertainment/tamil/2013/jun/10/Remakes-are-never-passé-in-Tamil-485453.html.
Savlov, Marc. "Way, Way Outer Space." *The Austin Chronicle*, 10 Sept. 2010, www.austinchronicle.com/screens/2010-09-10/1080026/.
Schild, Susana. "Renato Aragão Quer Também o Mercado Externo." *Jornal do Brasil*, 29 June 1980, p. B9.
Schmidt, Eric J. "Akounak Tedalat Taha Tazoughai (Rain the Color of Blue with a Little Red in It)." *Ethnomusicology*, vol. 63, no. 1, 2019, pp. 156–158.
Schmidt, Eric J. "Interview: Christopher Kirkley, Sahel Sounds, and Guerrilla Ethnomusicology." *Ethnomu-

sicology Review, UCLA, 26 Jan. 2014, ethnomusicologyreview.ucla.edu/content/interview-christopher-kirkley-sahel-sounds-and-guerilla-ethnomusicology.
Schwartz, Todd David. "RoboCopies … or RoboCoincidences?" *Los Angeles Times*, 13 Mar. 1988, p. 29.
Scognamillo, Giovanni, and Metin Demirhan. *Fantastik Türk Sineması [Turkish Fantastic Cinema]*. Kabalcı Yayınevi, 1999.
Sengul, Ali F. "On the Spatial Ideology of Turkish Cinema (The West as 'Outside'): Reading *Seyyit Han* as Western." *International Westerns: Re-locating the Frontier*, edited by Cynthia J. Miller and A. Bowdoin Van Riper. Scarecrow, 2014. 37–62.
Seta, Keyur. "15 Years of Dhoom: Aditya Chopra Took a Brave, Unconventional Step, Recalls Vijay Krishna Acharya." *Cinestaan*, 27 Aug. 2019, www.cinestaan.com/articles/2019/aug/27/22234.
Seyfioğlu, Ali Rıza, and Bram Stoker. *Dracula in Istanbul: The Unauthorized Version of the Gothic Classic*. Translated by Necip Ateş, Neon Harbor Entertainment, 2017.
Shaan, Asim. "Sex, Violence and Cheap Thrills: The Making of a C-Grade Hindi Film." *Youth Ki Awaaz*, 29 Nov. 2016, www.youthkiawaaz.com/2016/06/c-grade-bollywood-films/.
Shafik, Viola. "Egypt: A Cinema Without Horror?" *Horror International*, edited by Steven Jay Schneider and Tony Williams, Wayne State University Press, 2005, pp. 273–289.
Shah, Arjun. "Is Bollywood Unlawfully Copying Hollywood? Why? What Has Been Done About It? And How Can It Be Stopped?" *Emory International Law Review*, vol. 26, no. 1, 2012, pp. 449–487.
Sharma, Srijan. "Operation Parakram—When India and Pakistan Were on the Verge of War after Parliament Attacks." *Woodward Journal*, 20 Aug. 2020, www.woodwardjournal.com/analysis/operation-parakram-when-india-and-pakistan-were-on-the-verge-of-war-after-parliament-attacks.
Sharma, Unnati. "Laxmikant Berde, Marathi Superstar Who Was Much Beyond the Characters He's Remembered For." *ThePrint*, 16 Dec. 2019, theprint.in/theprint-profile/laxmikant-berde-marathi-superstar-who-was-much-beyond-the-characters-hes-remembered-for/334347/.
Shattuc, Jane. *Television, Tabloids, and Tears: Fassbinder and Popular Culture*. University of Minnesota Press, 1995.
Simons, Marlise. "Relief Stalled as Drought Ravages Northeast Brazil." *The New York Times*, 25 Mar. 1984, p. 13.
Singer, Matthew. "Africa High-Tech." *Willamette Week*, 23 Oct. 2012, www.wweek.com/portland/article-19788-africa-high-tech.html.
Singh, Mauli. "The Really Dirty Picture." *Mid-Day*, 26 Jan. 2012, mid-day.com/articles/the-really-dirty-picture/152041.
Singh, Nirmika. "Pritam and the Politics of Bollywood Music." *Rolling Stone India*, 23 Mar. 2017, rollingstoneindia.com/pritam-and-the-politics-of-bollywood-music/.
Skal, David J. *Hollywood Gothic: The Tangled Web of Dracula from Novel to Stage to Screen*. Deutsch, 1992.
Skidmore, Max J. "Promise and Peril in Combating Corruption: Hong Kong's ICAC." *The Annals of the American Academy of Political and Social Science*, vol. 547, 1996, pp. 118–130.
Sloan, Will. "'A Black Clint Eastwood with Martial Arts': An Interview with Fred 'The Hammer' Williamson." *Torontoist*, 12 Feb. 2015, torontoist.com/2015/02/a-black-clint-eastwood-with-martial-arts-an-interview-with-fred-the-hammer-williamson/.
Smith, Brian. "Bond of Brothers." *Cinema Retro*, Sept. 2008, pp. 12–19.
Smith, Iain Robert. "'Tu Mera Superman': Globalization, Cultural Exchange, and the Indian Superhero." *Superheroes On World Screens*. University Press of Mississippi, 2016.
Smith, Iain Robert. *The Hollywood Meme*. Edinburgh University Press, 2017.
Smith, Patrick. "We don't wanna be like you: how Soviet Russia made its own, darker Jungle Book—Don't expect singing bears and swing-dancing apes—the Adventures of Mowgli is a very different beast." *Daily Telegraph, The/The Sunday Telegraph: Web Edition Articles (London, England)*, 15 Apr. 2016. *NewsBank: Access World News*, infoweb.newsbank.com/apps/news/document-view?p=AWNB&docref=news/15C488281AB8BE78.
Smithers, Rebecca. "Disney Challenges UK Film Company Over 'Misleading' DVDs." *The Guardian*, Guardian News and Media, 6 Sept. 2012, www.theguardian.com/money/2012/sep/06/disney-challenges-uk-film-company-misleading-releases.
Smorodinska, Tatiana. "Rule of Law vs. 'Russian Justice': Nikita Mikhalkov's 12." *Studies in Russian and Soviet Cinema*, vol. 4, no. 2, 2010, pp. 161–170.
Spotnitz, Frank. "Study in Contrast: 'Rambo' And His Creator." *Chicago Tribune*, 28 June 1985, p. 7K.
"Spurting Blood 'Definitely' Sets Violent Climate." *The Pocono Record*, 29 June 1972, p. 23.
Stadtman, Todd. *Funky Bollywood: The Wild World of 1970s Indian Action Cinema*. FAB Press, 2015.
Stallone, Sylvester. Audio commentary. *First Blood*. Dir. Ted Kotcheff. Lionsgate, 2007. Blu-ray.
Standish, Dominic. "Nuclear Power and Environmentalism in Italy." *Energy & Environment*, 1 Oct. 2009, pp. 949–960.
Stein, Daniel. "Of Transcreations and Transpacific Adaptations: Investigating Manga Versions of Spider-Man." *Transnational Perspectives on Graphic Narratives: Comics at the Crossroads*, edited by Shane Denson et al., Bloomsbury, 2014, pp. 145–161.

Strassoldo, Raimondo. "The Greening of the Booth: Environmental Awareness, Movements and Policies in Italy." *Innovation: The European Journal of Social Science Research*, vol. 6, no. 4, 1993, pp. 457–471.
Subba, Vibhushan. "The Bad-Shahs of Small Budget: The Small-Budget Hindi Film of the B Circuit." *BioScope: South Asian Screen Studies*, vol. 7, no. 2, 2016, pp. 215–233.
Sulim, Alexandra. "Сарик Андреасян Про «Защитников»: «Мы Создаём Киновселенную» [Sarik Andreasyan Pro «Zashchitnikov»: «My Sozdayom Kinovselennuyu»; Sarik Andreasyan On 'Guardians': 'We Create the Cinematic Universe']." *ФильмПРО [Fil'mPRO; FilmPRO]*, 25 May 2016, www.filmpro.ru/materials/48031.
Süzgün, İlhan. "Natuk Baytan." *TSA Türk Sineması Araştırmaları [TSA Turkish Cinema Studies]*, www.tsa.org.tr/en/kisi/kisigoster/1493/natuk-baytan.
Taiwan Black Movies. Dir. Hou Chi-jan. Shih Kuang Creative, 2005. Film.
Talbot, Paul. *Bronson's Loose! The Making of the Death Wish Movies*. iUniverse, Inc., 2006.
Tangari, Joe. "Rebel Blues in the Sahara: A Desert Guitar Primer." *Pitchfork*, 25 Mar. 2008, pitchfork.com/features/article/6814-rebel-blues-in-the-sahara-a-desert-guitar-primer/.
Tanmayi, Bhawana. "Letha Manasulu Was Released in 1966 and Was One of the Big Hits of the Year." *Telangana Today*, 10 Sept. 2017, telanganatoday.com/letha-manasulu-released-1966-and-was-one-big-hits-year.
"Tanuja Chandra." *Sify.com*, 1999, www.sify.com/movies/bollywood/interview.php?id=6006581&cid=2398.
Temmy Plays! Comment on "Our Friend Power 5 (TMNT) - Phelous." *YouTube*, 16 Mar. 2018, 4:58 p.m., https://www.youtube.com/watch?v=iRuNZqqVmbE&lc=UgyUfnUb9SSzmGZyBMF4AaABAg.
Teo, Edmund. "'Dynamite' Johnson to Star as Bionic Boy." *The Straits Times*, 13 June 1976, p. 7.
Teo, Edmund. "Black Belt Johnson Yap, 10, to Star in HK Film." *The Straits Times*, 16 May 1976, p. 1.
Tereschenko, Maria. "Russian Animation in Search of a Hero." *Russia Beyond*, 17 Dec. 2009, www.rbth.com/articles/2009/12/17/171209_animation.html.
"Terminator in Venice." *Shocking Dark*, directed by Bruno Mattei. Severin, 2018. Blu-ray.
Thakkar, Ashish J. *The Lion Awakes: Adventures in Africa's Economic Miracle*. St. Martin's Press, 2015.
Thomas, Bob. "Schwarzenegger Bares Most in Near-Nude Fight Scene." *Los Angeles Times*, 14 July 1988, p. VI:3.
Tombs, Pete. *Mondo Macabro: Weird & Wonderful Cinema around the World*. St. Martin's Griffin, 1998.
"TV-Films: 'Lassie' in Yugoslavia." *Variety*, vol. 217, no. 4, Dec 23, 1959, pp. 26.
"TV-Films: Reiner Sees Foreign Market in '57 Hitting 30% of TPA's Total Gross." *Variety*, vol. 207, no. 2, Jun 12, 1957, pp. 32–32, 58.
Uluer, Utku. "Yeşilçam Arkeolojisi: İsveçli Cecilia'nın Altın Çocuk Filmini Kendisine Nasıl Ulaştırdık? [Yeşilçam Archeology: How Did We Deliver Swedish Cecilia's Golden Boy Film?]" *Sinematik Yeşilçam [Cinematic Yeşilçam]*, 15 June 2014, http://sinematikyesilcam.com/2014/06/isvecli-cecilianin-altin-cocuk-filmi/.
"Urban Legends." *Hindustan Times* (New Delhi, India), 4 Dec. 2004. *NewsBank: Access World News*, infoweb.newsbank.com/apps/news/document-view?p=AWNB&docref=news/106D61E10D3F6CA7.
"'Urmila Is Just Wonderful in My Film.'" *Rediff.com*, 12 Apr. 2001, www.rediff.com/chat/trans/0412rajt.htm. Internet Archive. web.archive.org/web/20190408140328/www.rediff.com/chat/trans/0412rajt.htm.
"Uzay'daki Sahte Gordon! [Fake Gordon in Space]" *Müsekkin [Sedative]*, 18 Sept. 2012, teskin.blogspot.com/2012/09/uzaydaki-sahte-gordon.html.
Varma, Ram Gopal. *Guns & Thighs: The Story of My Life*. Rupa, 2016.
Vātave Bāpu. *Dadasaheb Phalke, the Father of Indian Cinema*. National Book Trust, 2004.
Vierra, Sarah Thomsen. *Turkish Germans in the Federal Republic of Germany: Immigration, Space, and Belonging, 1961–1990*. Cambridge University Press, 2018.
Vishnu, J.T. "ISI Supervised Parliament Attack." *The Tribune*, 16 Dec. 2001, www.tribuneindia.com/2001/20011217/main1.htm.
von der Leyen, Katharina. "Immer Wieder Lassie [Again and again Lassie]." *Lumpi4.de: Hundemagazin [Lumpi4.de: Dog Magazine]*, 1 Mar. 2020, www.lumpi4.de/immer-wieder-lassie/.
Wagner, Alex. "Pakistan Tests Three Nuclear-Capable Ballistic Missiles." *Arms Control Today*, vol. 32, no.2, June 2002, p. 28.
"Walk the Talk with Bal Thackeray." *Walk the Talk*, hosted by Shekhar Gupta, NDTV 24x7, January 2007.
"The Warlord and the Spook—Russia and Chechnya; Russia and Chechnya." *The Economist*, vol. 383, no. 8531, Jun 02, 2007, pp. 47.
Wei, Liu. "Disney Taps Sophomores for High School Musical." *China Daily*, 24 Nov. 2009, www.chinadaily.com.cn/showbiz/2009-11/24/content_9031276.htm.
Weinbaum, Marvin G. "Egypt's 'Infitah' and the Politics of US Economic Assistance." *Middle Eastern Studies*, vol. 21, no. 2, 1985, pp. 206–222.
Weisselberg, Charles D. "Good Film, Bad Jury." *Chicago-Kent Law Review*, vol. 82, no. 2, Apr. 2007, pp. 717–731.
Wells, Robert G. "I, P-T Staff Man Helps Expose Diploma Mill." *Independent Press-Telegram*, 31 Mar. 1957, pp. A1–A4.
Welsh, Frank. *A History of Hong Kong*. HarperCollins Publishers, 1997.
"Winnie the Pooh Is 90 Today, But the Soviet Cartoon Remains Timeless." *The Moscow Times*, 14 Dec. 2016, www.themoscowtimes.com/2016/10/14/winnie-the-pooh-is-90-today-but-the-soviet-cartoon-remains-timeless-a55761.

Witt, Emily. *Nollywood: The Making of a Film Empire*. Columbia Global Reports, 2017.
Yajima, Nobuo. "撮影報告『宇宙からのメッセージ』[Satsuei hōkoku 'Uchū kara no messēji'; Shooting Report: 'Message from Space']." 日本映画撮影監督協会 *[Nihon eiga satsuei kantoku kyōkai; Japanese Society of Cinematographers]*, no. 65, 20 July 1978, pp. 16–18.
Yalçınkaya, Can. "Homoti: The Turkish Gay E.T. Remake." *Sequentials*, vol. 1, no. 2, 2018.
Yeo, Joseph. "'Bionic Boy' Star Gets Second Lead Role Offer." *The Straits Times*, 21 August 1977, p. 9.
Yiwu, Liao. *The Corpse Walker*. Anchor, 2009.
"You've Captured My Life So Perfectly I Can't Believe This Isn't My Story—Bal Thackeray." *Telegraph India*, 1 July 2005, www.telegraphindia.com/india/you-ve-captured-my-life-so-perfectly-i-can-t-believe-this-isn-t-my-story-bal-thackeray/cid/969271.
"全米大ヒット作の続編が日本で製作されたのはなぜ？ プロデューサーが語る [Zenbei dai hitto-saku no zokuhen ga Nihon de seisaku sa reta no wa naze? Purodeyūsā ga kataru; Why Was the Sequel to the Nationwide Blockbuster Made in Japan? The Producer Speaks]." チケットぴあ *[Chikettopia; Ticket Pia]*, 19 Oct. 2010, ticket-news.pia.jp/pia/news.do?newsCd=201010190005.
Zhang, Mingmeng. "当年情：听导演林德禄说港片往事 [Dāngnián qíng: Tīng dǎoyǎn líndélù shuō gǎng piàn wǎngshì; At That Time: Listen to Director Lin Deluo Telling the Past of Hong Kong Films]." 南方人物周刊 *[Nánfāng rénwù zhōukān; Southern People Weekly]*, 18 Nov. 2018, www.nfpeople.com/article/8712.
Zhu, Weijing. "The Real Walking Dead." *The World of Chinese*, no. 2, 2014, pp. 24–25.
"专访陈士争：《歌舞青春》讲述梦开始的地方 [Zhuānfǎng chén shì zhēng: 'Gēwǔ qīngchūn' jiǎngshù mèng kāishǐ dì dìfāng; Interview with Chen Shizheng: 'High School Musical' Tells Where Dreams Begin]." *Mtime*, 4 Aug. 2010, news.mtime.com/2010/08/03/1437849.html.

Index

Aabra Ka Daabra: The School of Magic (2004) 5, 96–99
Aadamkhor Hasina (2002) 136
Aatank (1996) 130–133
Aathma Bandhana (1992) 171
Aaya Toofan (1964) 84
Abelhinhas (2009) 104
The Abyss (1989) 40
Adiós Amigo (1975) 68
Adventure of Haunted House (2012) 138
Adventures of Captain Marvel (1941) 37, 40, 44
The Adventures of Mowgli (1973) see Maugli (1973)
After Death (1989) see Oltre La Morte (1989)
Agadez, Niger 226–227
Agent Vinod (1977) 85
Agente 077 Dall'oriente Con Furore (1965) 64
Ainscough, Jane 111, 113–114
Ainu 265, 267
Airport (1970) 214
Airport (series) 168
Akounak Tedalat Taha Tazoughai (2015) 224–227
Aksharathettu (1989) 255
Alemdar, Mehmet 142–144
Alien (1979) 40, 199, 201
Alien 2: On Earth (1980) see Alien 2: Sulla Terra (1980)
Alien 2: Sulla Terra (1980) 199
Aliens (1986) 197, 199–201
Altın Çocuk (1966) 62–66
Altın Çocuk Beyrut'ta (1967) 66
American Commando 5: Fury in Red (1988) 254
American International Pictures 68, 204
An American Werewolf in London (1981) 2, 259
Ammo Bomma (2001) 172–173
The Amos 'n' Andy Show (1951) 67
Anasının Gözü (1974) 71
Anatolian Western 57, 229–231
Andreasyan, Gevond 53–55

Andreasyan, Sarik 52–55
animation 46–47, 103–105, 116–118, 127–129, 181–183
Anyab (1981) 5, 133–135
Apocalypse Now (1979) 195–196
arabesk 143
Aragão, Renato 122–125
Argentina 39, 106, 219
Arkın, Cüneyt 73, 86, 183–185, 187, 242, 244
Arsoy, Göksel 63–66
Ashu-Brown, Farouk 248, 250–251
Asi Kabadayı (1986) 86
Atadeniz, Orhan 41, 43–44
Atadeniz, Yılmaz 23, 41, 57, 71
Atasoy, İrfan 56, 58–59, 71
Atatürk, Mustafa Kemal 87
Ator L'invincibile (1982) 13–16
Ator Il Guerriero Di Ferro (1987) 16
Ator the Fighting Eagle (1982) see Ator L'invincibile (1982)
Ator 2: L'invincibile Orion (1982) 16
Attack of the Mayan Mummy (1963) 158
Automan (1983) 181
The Avengers 53–54
The Avengers (2012) 6, 52
Avengers: Age of Ultron (2015) 54
Ayşecik (1960) 120
Ayşecik Fakir Prenses (1963) 120
Ayşecik Ve Sihirli Cüceler Rüyalar Ülkesinde (1971) 122
The Aztec Mummy (1957) see La Momia Azteca (1957)

Bacalhau (1975) 131
Bach Ke Zara (2008) 135–138
Badi (1984) 99–102
Bağdat Hırsızı (1968) 120
Balıkçı Güzeli: Bin İkinci Gece (1953) 119
The Bamboo House of Dolls (1973) see Nu Ji Zhong Ying (1973)

Banda Yeh Bindaas Hai 6
Banditi a Milano (1968) 71
Bang Bang! (2014) 6
Bao Hu Lu De Mi Mi (2007) 106
Bat Woman (1968) see La Mujer Murciélago (1968)
Batas Impian Ranjang Setan (1986) 189
Batman 3, 10, 24–26, 48–51
Batman (1966) 24–26, 48–49, 135
Batman Fights Dracula (1967) 178
Batman: The Movie (1966) 23–24, 49
Batoru Fībā Jei (1979) 29
Batoru Rowaiaru (2000) 4
Battle Beyond the Stars (1980) 57
Battle Fever J (1979) see Batoru Fībā Jei (1979)
Battle of the Planets (1978) see Kagaku Ninja Tai Gatchaman (1972)
Battle Royale (2000) see Batoru Rowaiaru (2000)
Battles Without Honor or Humanity (1973) see Jingi Naki Tatakai (1973)
Battlestar Galactica (1978) 40, 185
Baweja, Harry 92, 94–95
Baytan, Natuk 238–245
Bayteкin Fezada Çarpışanlar (1967) 174–176
Bee Movie (2009) 104
Beverly Hills Cop (1984) 69
Beyond the Door (1974) see Chi Sei? (1974)
Bhatt, Mahesh 2, 257, 259–260
Bhayam (2007) 136–137
Bie Ai Mosheng Ren (1982) 192
The Big Bird Cage (1972) 167
The Big Doll House (1971) 167
The Bionic Boy (1977) 176–179
The Bionic Woman (1976) 178
Black Caesar (1973) 68
Black Cobra (1987) 66–69

The Black Cobra 2 (1989) 69
Black Cobra 3: The Manila Connection (1990) 69
Black Star and the Golden Bat (1979) see *Geomeunbyeolgwa Hwanggeumbakjwi* (1979)
The Blade Master (1982) see *Ator 2: L'invincibile Orion* (1982)
Blair-Kerr, Sir William Alexander 245, 247–248
Blaxploitation 68, 178
The Blue Lagoon (1980) 80
Bollywood 1–2, 6, 32, 83–85, 93, 98, 131–33, 137–38, 153, 232, 250, 255–256, 259, 261–264
Bond, James 12, 51, 53, 64–66, 75, 84–85, 90–92, 111, 146–147, 178, 218
Bonnie and Clyde (1967) 227, 229–230
Das Boot (1981) 40
Born in China (2016) 108
Brave (2012) 104
Britannica's Tales Around the World (1991) 104
Bronze Soldier of Tallinn 75
A Bug's Life (1998) 57
The Bullet Train (1975) see *Shinkansen Daibakuha* (1975)
Bul-sa-jo Roboteu Pinikseu-King (1984) 181

Cabiria (1914) 14
Çakır, Levent 48–51
Caligula (1979) 15
Captain America 1, 9–12, 53
Captain America (1944) 3, 9, 11
Captain America: Civil War (2016) 11, 53
Captain Barbell (1986) 19
Captain Marvel 18, 23, 37
Cardona, René 24–26
Cars (2006) 102–104
Casino Royale (1967) 92
Casper the Friendly Ghost 98
Castellari, Enzo G. 59–62, 148–151
Casus Kıran (1968) 22
Cat People (1942) 259
Çeko (1970) 229
Cellat (1975) 69–73
Cemil (1975) 244
Cemil Dönüyor (1975) 244
Cemo Ile Cemile (1971) 227–231
censorship 2, 22, 38, 50–51, 72, 75, 83, 85, 87, 93, 117, 134–135, 163, 177, 180–181, 184, 189–190, 226, 230–231, 232, 243, 250, 252–253, 255, 257
Chakraborty, Pritam 234
Chandra, Tanuja 2, 257, 259–261

Charlie and the Chocolate Factory 98
Chechnya 220–224
Chen, Richard Yao-chi 251–254
Chen, Shi-zheng 105–106
Chi Sei? (1974) 166
Child's Play (1988) 169–171
China Town (1962) 110
Chocolate: Deep Dark Secrets (2005) 234
Chōjikū Yōsai Makurosu (1982) 47, 181
Chopra, Aditya 77
Chopra, Vikram 231–234
Chowta, Sandeep 257
The Church (1989) 153
C.I.D. 909 (1967) 84
Çığlık (1949) 140
Cilalı İbo Ve Kırk Haramiler (1964) 119–120
Çılgın Kız Ve Üç Süper Adam (1973) 51
Cinderella (1950) 122
Cleopatra Jones (1973) 178
Cobra (1986) 66, 69
Çöl (1983) 131
Columbia 48, 50
Commando (1985) 73–75
Computer Haekjeonham Pokpa Daejakjeon (1983) 180–183
Conan the Barbarian (1982) 13–16, 75
Connery, Neil 89–92
Conquest of the Planet of the Apes (1972) 206
Contamination (1980) 199
Corman, Roger 167, 195, 236
Cosa Nostra Asia (1974) 192
Cozzi, Luigi 149, 201–204
Crazy Joe (1974) 68
The Creature from the Black Lagoon (1954) 26
Criminal (1995) 259
Cruel Jaws (1995) 151
Cuo Wu De Di Yi Bu (1979) 252
Cure (1997) 160
The Curse (2005) see *Noroi* (2005)
The Curse of the Aztec Mummy (1957) see *La Maldición De La Momia Azteca* (1957)
Cyprus 238–241

D-Day (2008) see *Den'D* (2008)
Daikaijū Baran (1958) 145
Dariya Dil (1988) 31
Darna 16–20
Darna (1951) 18–19
Darna (1991) 16–20
Darna at Ding (1980) 19
Davydov, Roman 115, 117–118

Dawn of the Dead (1978) 60, 149, 196
Day of the Dead (1985) 154
Day of the Owl (1968) see *Il Giorno Della Civetta* (1968)
The Dead Poets Society (1989) 77
De Angelis, Fabrizio 60–62, 150
Death Wish (1974) 69, 71–73
Death Wish (2018) 72
Death Wish 2 (1982) 72
Deep Blood (1990) see *Sangue Negli Abissi* (1990)
Deep Blue Sea (1999) 250
The Deer Hunter (1978) 195
Defenders of Space (1984) see *Bul-sa-jo Roboteu Pinikseu-King* (1984)
Değirmencioğlu, Hamdi 119–122
Değirmencioğlu, Zeynep 119–122
Deja View 2
De Martino, Alberto 89, 91
Demir Pençe: Korsan Adam (1969) 22–23
Demirağ, Turgut 138, 140
Demircioğlu, Haşim 34, 36–37
Den'D (2008) 73–73
Derman (1983) 100, 102
Detective Malone: The Black Cobra 4 (1991) 69
Devgn, Ajay 92–93, 95
Devil Dynamite (1987) 194
Devil Fish (1984) see *Shark: Rosso Nell'oceano*
devotional 32–33
Dharmatma (1975) 262–263
Dheepan (2015) 241–242
Dhoom (2004) 76–79, 234
Dhoom 2 (2006) 78
Dhoom 3 (2013) 78–79
Diamonds Are Forever (1971) 12
Dikiy Vostok (1993) 57
Dirty Harry (1971) 69, 71, 82–85
Disney 3, 6, 103–109, 116–118, 120–122, 127, 129, 181
Disney High School Musical: China (2010) see *Ge Wu Qing Chun* (2010)
Djalil, H. Tjut 187–190
Do Gaz Zameen Ke Neeche (1972) 153
Do Kaliyaan (1968) 111
Dr. Cyclops (1940) 84
Donner, Richard 16, 32, 34–35, 37, 39–40
Don't Look Up (1996) see *Joyū-rei* (1996)
Don't Trust a Stranger (1982) see *Bie Ai Mosheng Ren* (1982)
Dört Hergele (1974) 71
Double Target (1987) 81, 199

Douze Hommes En Colère (2010) 222
Dracula 44, 80, 133–135, 138–141, 167
Dracula (1931) 3, 138–140, 156
Dracula (1958) 135
Drakula İstanbul'da (1953) 3, 44, 138–142
The Dreaming Man (2017) *see Jia Ru Wang Zi Shui Zhao Le* (2017)
Drudi, Rossella 194, 196–197, 199–200
Dry Summer (1963) *see Susuz Yaz* (1963)
Duel (1971) 77
Dulaney, John P. 194, 196–197
Dünyayı Kurtaran Adam (1982) 5, 183–187
Dünyayı Kurtaran Adam'ın Oğlu (2006) 187
Dynamite Johnson (1979) 179

Earthquake (1974) 168
Eastwood, Clint 69, 83–85, 217, 266–268
Ek Nanhi Munni Ladki Thi (1970) 153
Ek Ruka Hua Faisla (1986) 222
El Santo 9–11, 25, 157
Emanuelle Nera (1975) 15
Emmanuelle (1974) 15
The Empire Strikes Back (1980) 184–185
Enter the Dragon (1973) 179
Enter the Ninja (1981) 192
Ercole Al Centro Della Terra (1961) 15
Erksan, Metin 162–166
Escape from New York (1981) 62
Escape from the Bronx (1983) *see Fuga Dal Bronx* (1983)
Eşici, Savaş 49–50
Estambul 65 (1965) 64
Estonia 75
E.T.: The Extra Terrestrial (1982) 40, 99–102, 181
Eurospy 51, 64, 90–91
An Evening in Paris (1967) 98
The Evil Dead (1981) 3, 135–138, 154, 160
Evil Dead: The Musical 138
Evil Dead 2 (1987) 160
The Exorcist (1973) 1, 80, 161, 163–166, 214
The Exterminator (1980) 218
Exterminators of the Year 3000 (1983) *see Il Giustiziere Della Strada* (1983)
Extra Terrestrial Visitors (1983) *see Los Nuevos Extraterrestres* (1983)
Eye for an Eye (1996) 259

Fair Game 69
A Fairy Tale Christmas (2005) 104
Fantoma İstanbul'da Buluşalım (1967) 49
The Fast and the Furious (2001) 76–78
Fatal Attraction (1987) 254–257
Le Fatiche Di Ercole (1958) 14
Ferber, Henning 113–115
Fight Club (1999) 231–234
Fight Club: Members Only (2006) 231–234
Finding Nemo (2003) 103
First Blood (1982) 86, 89
First Shot (1993) *see Lim Jing Dai Yat Gik* (1993)
A Fistful of Dollars (1964) *see Per Un Pugno Di Dollari* (1964)
Flash Gordon 39, 174–176, 203
Flash Gordon (1936) 174
Flash Gordon Conquers the Universe (1940) 176
Flashdance (1983) 15
Forbidden Planet (1956) 135, 185, 203
Four for All (1974) *see Dört Hergele* (1974)
Fragasso, Claudio 196–197, 199
Frank, Sandy 208
Frankenstein (1931) 26
The Frog Prince (2009) *see a Princesa E O Sapo* (2009)
From Istanbul, Orders to Kill (1965) *see Da Istanbul Ordine Di Uccidere* (1965)
From Russia with Love (1963) 37, 64–65, 91–92
From the Orient with Fury (1965) *see Agente 077 Dall'oriente Con Furore* (1965)
Fuga Dal Bronx (1983) 62
The Fugitive (1993) 259
Fukasaku, Kinji 4, 212, 214

Gadhvi, Sanjay 76–78
Ganmā Daisan Gō: Uchū Daisakusen (1968) 214
Gaudenzi, Franco 199, 201
Ge Wu Qing Chun (2010) 6, 105–108
Geomeunbyeolgwa Hwanggeumbakjwi (1979) 181
Geung Si Sin Sang (1985) 193
Ghidrah, the Three-Headed Monster (1964) *see Sandai Kaijū: Chikyū Saidai No Kessen* (1964)
Il Giorno Della Civetta (1968) 71
Girl with a Gun (1982) *see Pi Li Da Niu* (1982)

Il Giustiziere Della Strada (1983) 217
Godber, Peter Fitzroy 246–248
The Godfather (1972) 3, 71, 242–245, 261–264
Godzilla (1954) *see Gojira* (1954)
Godzilla Raids Again (1955) *see Gojira No Gyakushū* (1955)
Godzilla Vs. Mechagodzilla (1974) *see Gojira Tai Mekagojira* (1974)
Godzilla Vs. the Sea Monster (1966) *see Gojira, Ebira, Mosura Nankai No Daikettō* (1966)
Gojira (1954) 145
Gojira, Ebira, Mosura Nankai No Daikettō (1966) 146
Gojira No Gyakushū (1955) 145
Gojira Tai Mekagojira (1974) 206
The Golden Voyage of Sinbad (1973) 203–204
Goldfinger (1964) 37, 92
Goldwing (1978) *see Hwang Geumnalgae 1.2.3.* (1978)
G.O.R.A. (2004) 187, 212
Göreç, Ertem 119–120, 122
Gören, Şerif 100–102
Görünmeyen Adam İstanbul'da (1955) 44
The Green Slime (1968) *see Ganmā Daisan Gō: Uchū Daisakusen* (1968)
Guardians (2017) *see Zashchitniki* (2017)
guest workers 236–237
Güney, Yılmaz 3–4, 56, 58–59, 73, 100, 229–230

Haar Jeet (1990) 256
Hamburger Hill (1987) 195
Hanada, Yasutaka 159–160
Hands of Steel (1986) *see Vendetta Dal Future* (1986)
Harry Potter (series) 97–99
Harry Potter and the Sorcerer's Stone (2001) 5, 96
Hell Up in Harlem (1973) 68
The Hidden Fortress (1958) *see Kakushi Toride No San Akunin* (1958)
High Plains Drifter (1973) 217, 219
High School Musical (2006) 105–107
High School Musical: El Desafío (2008) 106
High School Musical: O Desafio (2010) 106
Hills of Home (1948) 114
Himitsu Sentai Gorenjā (1975) 28, 29

Index

Hitchcock, Alfred 142–144
Ho, Godfrey Chi-keung 192
Hokkaido, Japan 265, 267
Honto Ni Atta Kowai Hanashi (1991) 160
Hope (1970) *see Umut* (1970)
Hum Dono (1961) 110
Hussain, Mohammed 82, 84–85
Hwang Geumnalgae 1.2.3. (1978) 46

I Nuovi Barbari (1983) 150, 217–218
I Proud to Be an Indian (2004) 232
I Sette Magnifici Gladiatori (1983) 57
IFD Films and Arts 192, 254
İnanç, Çetin 20, 22–23, 85–89, 143, 183–187, 227, 229–231, 234, 236–238
The Incredible Hulk 27, 28, 53–54
Independent Commission Against Corruption (ICAC) 246–248
The Inferno (1979) *see Jigoku* (1979)
Infra-Man (1975) *see Zhong Guo Chao Ren* (1975)
İntikam Hırsı (1963) 57
İntikamcı (1986) 86, 88
The Intruder (1986) 79–82
Invasion USA (1985) 71
The Invisible Man (1933) 158
Irma La Douce (1963) 85
Iron Man 2 (2010) 54
Iron Warrior (1987) *see Ator Il Guerriero Di Ferro* (1987)
Ishinomori, Shōtarō 28, 214
Island of the Living Dead (2007) *see L'isola Dei Morti Viventi* (2007)
Da Istanbul Ordine Di Uccidere (1965) 64

J-horror 160
Jack the Giant Killer (1962) 84
Jai Ho (2014) 234
Jaka Sembung (1981) 189
Jaka Sembung & Bergola Ijo (1985) 189
Japanese occupation of Korea 180–181
Jason and the Argonauts (1963) 202–203
Jaws (1975) 6, 130–131, 133, 135, 149–151, 213–214
Jaws 2 (1978) 150
Jeong, Su-yong 180–181
Jia Ru Wang Zi Shui Zhao Le (2017) 108
jiangshi 193–194

Jigoku (1979) 214
Jingi Naki Tatakai (1973) 214
Joyū-rei (1996) 160
The Jungle Book (1976) 115–117
Junoon (1992) 259
Ju-on (2002) 160

Kaakum Karangal (1965) 110
Kabzaa (1988) 259
Kader Diyelim (1995) 142–144
Kadyrov, Ramzan 221, 224
Kagaku Ninja Tai Gatchaman (1972) 208
Kakushi Toride No San Akunin (1958) 215
Kamen Raidā (1971) 28, 167
Kamen Rider (1971) *see Kamen Raidā* (1971)
Kandhei Akhire Luha (1997) 171
Kannywood 250
Kara Şimşek (1985) 234–238
Kartal Yuvası (1975) 238–242
Kashmir 92, 94–95
Kazıklı Voyvoda 140–141
Kebapçılar, Serdar 85–86, 88–89, 234, 236–238
Keloğlan (1965) 120
Khan, Sohail 231–234
Khitruk, Fyodor 125, 127–129
Khoon Khoon (1973) 82–85
Khooni Murdaa (1989) 154
Kidō Senshi Gandamu (1979) 181
Kılıç Bey (1978) 242–245
Kilink İstanbul'da (1967) 23
Kilink: Soy Ve Öldür (1967) 23
Killing (character) 10, 23
King Kong 145–147
King Kong (1933) 3, 84, 135, 144, 147
King Kong (1976) 147, 166, 168–169
King Kong Escapes (1967) *see Kingu Kongu No Gyakushū* (1967)
The King Kong Show (1966) 146
King Kong Vs. Godzilla (1962) *see Kingu Kongu Tai Gojira* (1962)
Kingdom Under the Sea (2001) 103
Kingu Kongu No Gyakushū (1967) 144–147
Kingu Kongu Tai Gojira (1962) 145
Kirkley, Christopher 224–227
Kitzmiller, John 68
Kızıl Maske (1968, dir. Çetin İnanç) 20–23
Knight and Day (2010) 6
Knight Rider (1982) 219, 238
Köksal, Yılmaz 227–230
Kollywood 109–110
Komatsu, Sakyō 206–207

Korkusuz (1986) 81, 85–89
Kothare, Mahesh 169, 171
Kumar, Dheeraj 96–99
Kung Fu Panda (2008) 104
Kurds 87–89
Kuril Islands 75
Kurtlar Vadisi (2003) 66
Kuwornu, Fred Kudjo 68
Kuzhandaiyum Deivamum (1965) 108–111
Kyōryū Kaichō No Densetsu (1977) 214
Kyōryū Sentai Zyuranger (1992) 29–30

Lady Terminator (1988) *see Pembalasan Ratu Pantai Selatan* (1988)
Lai, Joseph San-lun 182–183, 192
Lai, Terry Siu-ping 191–192
Lakeer: Forbidden Lines (2004) 232
Lam, David Tak-luk 245, 247–248
The Land That Time Forgot (1974) 204
Lanka Dahan (1917) 32
Lassie (1954) 113
Lassie (2014) 113
Lassie Come Home (1943) 111–112, 115
Lassie Come Home (2020) *see Lassie—Eine Abenteuerliche Reise* (2020)
Lassie—Eine Abenteuerliche Reise (2020) 111–115
The Last Hunter (1980) *see L'ultimo Cacciatore* (1980)
The Last Shark (1981) *see L'ultimo Squalo* (1981)
The Last Starfighter (1984) 181
Leák (1981) 189
Lee, Sang-il 264, 266–268
Legend of Dinosaurs and Monster Birds (1977) *see Kyōryū Kaichō No Densetsu* (1977)
The Legend of the 7 Golden Vampires (1974) 167
Letha Manasulu (1966) 111
Lim Jing Dai Yat Gik (1993) 245–248
L'isola Dei Morti Viventi (2007) 201
Little Bee (2009) *see Abelhinhas* (2009)
The Little Cars in the Great Race (2006) *see Os Carrinhos Em: A Grande Corrida* (2006)
Little Panda Fighter (2008) *see Ursinho Da Pesada* (2008)
Living in Bondage (1992) 249
The Lord of Akili (1990) 16

Index

lucha libre 24–25, 84
Las Luchadoras Contra El Médico Asesino (1962) 25
Las Luchadoras Contra El Robot Asesino (1969) 25

MacLehose, Sir Murray 245, 247–248
Mad Max (1979) 15, 69, 149
Mad Max (series) 216, 219
Mad Max 2: The Road Warrior (1981) 89, 216–218
Magdalena, Possessed by the Devil (1974) *see Magdalena, Vom Teufel Besessen* (1974)
Magdalena, Vom Teufel Besessen (1974) 166
The Magic Sword (1962) 185
The Magnificent Seven (1960) 3–4, 56–59
Mahaan (1983) 171
Mahakaal (1993) 5, 151–155
Maikeuro Teukgongdae Daiya Teuron 5 (1985) 181
Makkala Bhagya (1967) 111
La Maldición De La Momia Azteca (1957) 157
Malegaon Ka Superman (2009) 34
A Man Called Rage (1984) *see Rage—Fuoco Incrociato* (1984)
The Man Who Saves the World (1982) *see Dünyayı Kurtaran Adam* (1982)
Marcos, Ferdinand 177, 195
Margheriti, Antonio 195–196
martial law 87, 177, 184
Marvel 6, 13, 27–30, 52–54
MASH (1970) 68
Masoyiyata / Titanic (2003) 248–251
Massaccesi, Aristide 13, 15–16, 151
Massi, Danilo 66, 69
Massi, Stelvio 66, 69
Master Samurai (1974) 192
The Matrix (1999) 3
The Matrix Reloaded (2003) 78
Matsuda, Hirō 212, 214
Mattei, Bruno 151, 194, 196–197, 199, 201
Maugli (1973) 115–119
Mazinger Z 28, 46, 181
Meiji Restoration 266–267
Meiyappan, A.V. 110–111
men's film 243–245
Mere Yaar Ki Shaadi (2002) 77, 234
Merter, Ferdi 208, 210–212
Message from Space (1978) *see Uchū Kara No Messēji* (1978)
Message from Space: Galactic Wars (1978) *see Uchū Kara*

No Messēji: Ginga Taisen (1978)
Metalstorm: The Destruction of Jared-Syn (1983) 217
MGM 42–43, 92, 112–113, 120
Micro-Commando Diatron-5 (1985) *see Maikeuro Teukgongdae Daiya Teuron 5* (1985)
Mighty Morphin' Power Rangers (1993) 30
The Mighty Peking Man (1977) *see Xingxing Wang* (1977)
Mikhalkov, Nikita 220–224
Minority Report (2002) 99
Missing in Action (1984) 71, 195
Mission: Impossible (1966) 51, 210
Mission Thunderbolt (1983) 192
Missione Speciale Lady Chaplin (1966) 91
Mr. Deeds Goes to Town (1936) 110
Mr. Vampire (1985) *see Geung Si Sin Sang* (1985)
Mister X (1967) 23
Mobile Suit Gundam (1979) *see Kidō Senshi Gandamu* (1979)
Moctar, Mdou 224–227
La Momia Azteca (1957) 155–158
La Momia Azteca Contra El Robot Humano (1958) 157
Las Momias De Guanajuato (1972) 157
Mosura (1961) 145
Mothra (1961) *see Mosura* (1961)
movie piracy 5, 75, 143, 186, 204, 248, 261
Ms .45 (1981) 251–253
La Mujer Murciélago (1968) 23–26
Las Mujeres Panteras (1967) 25
Mukherjee, Desh 131–133
Mukherjee, Rajat 254, 256–257
The Mummy (1932) 26, 155–156
The Mummy's Hand (1940) 156
Murphy, Bridey 156–157
Music from Saharan Cellphones 225
My Best Friend's Wedding (1997) 77
My Cousin Vinny (1992) 6
My Dear Kuttichathan (1984) 98
The Mysterious Doctor Satan (1940) 40
Mystery Science Theater 3000 (1989) 92, 219
Mystics in Bali (1981) *see Leák* (1981)
mythological 32–33

Nagae, Toshikazu 158, 160–161
Nallathambi (1949) 110

Nazarov, Eduard 128–129
Nero, Franco 71, 229
Never Too Late to Repent (1979) *see Cuo Wu De Di Yi Bu* (1979)
The New Barbarians (1983) *see I Nuovi Barbari* (1983)
The New Original Wonder Woman (1975) 16, 19
Ni, Kuang 166, 168
A Nightmare on Elm Street (1984) 3, 5, 151, 153–155
A Nightmare on Elm Street 2: Freddy's Revenge (1985) 154, 194
A Nightmare on Elm Street 4: The Dream Master (1988) 154
1990: I Guerrieri Del Bronx (1982) 59–62
1990: The Bronx Warriors (1992) *see 1990: I Guerrieri Del Bronx* (1982)
Ninja, Phantom Heros U.S.A. (1987) 192
Nollywood 249–250
Noroi (2005) 160
Nosferatu (1922) 141
Nosferatu the Vampyre (1979) 135
Nu Ji Zhong Ying (1973) 167
Los Nuevos Extraterrestres (1983) 40

O'Brian, Peter 79–80, 82
Ocean's Eleven (2001) 78
OK Connery (1967) 89–92
Okada, Shigeru 214
O'Keeffe, Miles 13, 16
Olderdissen, Hanno 111, 113
Oltre La Morte (1989) 196
The Omen (1976) 214
On the Waterfront (1954) 2, 259
Önal, Safa 71, 242–244
One Million B.C. (1940) 44
OPEC oil embargo 243
Operation Kid Brother (1967) *see OK Connery* (1967)
Operation Thunderbolt (1977) 192
Oran, Bülent 69, 71–72
Ortaşark Yanıyor (1967) 66
Os Carrinhos em: A Grande Corrida (2006) 102–105
Os Trapalhões 5, 122–125
Os Trapalhões E O Mágico De Oróz (1984) 122–125
Os Trapalhões Na Serra Pelada (1982) 124
Os Vagabundos Trapalhões (1982) 124
OSS 117 Se Déchaîne (1963) 66
Özonuk, Şinasi 174, 176

Index

Padhye, Ramdas 171–173
Pakistan 92, 94–95, 234
Pamuk Prenses Ve 7 Cüceler (1970) 119–122
Par, Zafer 99–101
Paranōmaru Akutibiti Dai 2 Shō: Tōkyō Naito (2010) 158–161
Paranormal Activity (2007) 158–161
Paranormal Activity 2 (2010) 161
Paranormal Activity 2: Tokyo Night (2010) see *Paranōmaru Akutibiti Dai 2 Shō: Tōkyō Naito* (2010)
Paranormal Effect (2010) 159
Paranormal Entity (2009) 159
The Parent Trap (1961) 108
Pelc, Gene 27–8, 30
Pembalasan Rambu (1982) 82
Pembalasan Ratu Pantai Selatan (1988) 187–190
peplum 14–15, 149
Per Un Pugno Di Dollari (1964) 3, 266, 268
Perestroika 54
Pha Loka Nt (1984) 194
Phalke, Dhundiraj Govind 32
The Phantom 10, 20–23, 31, 49, 51
The Phantom (1943) 20
Pi Li Da Niu (1982) 251–254
Pirhasan, Barış 99–101
Pixar 103–104
Planet of the Apes (1968) 5, 185–186, 204, 206–208
Platoon (1986) 195
poliziottesco 69, 71
Porechenkov, Mikhail 73–76
Powerful Four (1992) see *Si Da Tan Zhang* (1992)
Predator (1987) 194, 196, 199
The Prestige (2006) 79
A Princesa E O Sapo (2009) 104
The Princess and the Frog (2009) 104
product placement 98, 101
Psycho (1960) 142–144
The Pumaman (1980) see *L'uomo Puma* (1980)
Punjabi, Raam 80
Purana Mandir (1984) 154
Purple Rain (1984) 224, 226
Putin, Vladimir 118–119, 221, 223–224
Putuler Protisodh (1998) 171
Pyaar Tune Kya Kiya… (2001) 254–257
Pyasa Shaitan (1984) 136

Qayamat: City Under Threat (2003) 92–95
The Quest for Fire (1981) 16
Quest for the Mighty Sword (1990) see *the Lord of Akili* (1990)

racism 67–68
Rage—Fuoco Incrociato (1984) 217
Raiders of the Lost Ark (1981) 69, 185, 215
Raja Harishchandra (1913) 32
Rama Rao, Nandamuri Taraka 30, 32–33
Rambo, John 3, 6, 80–82, 86–89, 195–196, 199, 236
Rambo: First Blood Part II (1985) 74–75, 79–80, 85–89, 192, 196, 264
Rambo: The Force of Freedom (1986) 81
Rampage (1986) see *Korkusuz* (1986)
Ramsay Brothers 151–154
Ramudu Bheemudu (1964) 110
Rankin/Bass 146–147
rape-revenge film 252
Ratatoing (2007) 104
Ratatouille (2007) 104
Ratu Buaya Putih (1988) 189
Ravelo, Mars 18–19
Raza, Salim 135, 137–138
Red Heat (1988) 75
Republic 11, 40
The Return of Mr. Superman (1960) 31–32
Return to the Planet of the Apes (1975) 208
Revenge of the Ninja (1983) 192
The Rift (1990) 40
Ring (1998) 160
Road House (1989) 233
Robo Vampire (1988) 190–194
RoboCop (1987) 190, 192, 196–197
Robot Taekwon V 46–47, 181
The Robot Vs. the Aztec Mummy (1958) see *La Momia Azteca Contra El Robot Humano* (1958)
Robowar (1988) 194–197, 199
The Rock 92–95
Rocky (1976) 234, 236–238
The Rocky Horror Picture Show (1975) 5, 133–135
Rocky III (1982) 237–238
Rodan (1956) see *Sora No Daikaijū Radon* (1956)
Rowdy (2014) 264

Sabatello, Dario 90–92
Salazar, Abel 155–156
Salazar, Alfredo 24–26, 155–158
Sampson, Nikos 240
Sandai Kaijū: Chikyū Saidai No Kessen (1964) 146

Sandhu, Mahendra 82, 84–85
Saner, Hulki 163–166, 208, 210–212
Sangharsh (1999) 1, 257–261
Sangue Negli Abissi (1990) 151
Sarkar (2005) 261–264
Sarkar Raj (2008) 264
Sarkar 3 (2017) 264
Şarlo İstanbul'da (1954) 44
Sarlui, Eduard 217–219
Saru No Gundan (1974) 206–208
Satan's Bed (1986) see *Batas Impian Ranjang Setan* (1986)
Satya (1998) 263
Savior of the Earth (1983) see *Computer Haekjeonham Pokpa Daejakjeon* (1983)
Scary True Stories (1991) see *Honto Ni Atta Kowai Hanashi* (1991)
Schwarzenegger, Arnold 74–75, 196
The Secret of the Magic Gourd (2007) see *Bao Hu Lu De Mi Mi* (2007)
serial 11, 21, 23–25, 37, 40, 48, 50, 176, 219
Serpico (1973) 71
Sert, Ahmet 50, 57
Sethubandhanam (1974) 111
7 Belalılar (1970) see *Yedi Belalılar* (1970)
Seven Magnificent Gladiators (1983) see *I Sette Magnifici Gladiatori* (1983)
Seven Samurai (1954) see *Shichinin No Samurai* (1954)
Şeytan (1974) 161–166
The Shakiest Gun in the West (1968) 147
Shark: Rosso Nell'oceano (1984) 131
Shaw Brothers 166–169
The She-Creature (1956) 157
Shebl, Mohamed 5, 133–135
Shichinin No Samurai (1954) 57
Shi'er Gongmin (2014) 222
Shikari (1963) 84
Shin, Hyun-hwan 46–47
Shinkansen Daibakuha (1975) 214
Shocking Dark (1989) 197–201
Si Da Tan Zhang (1992) 247
Silaha Yeminliydim (1987) 81
The Silence of the Lambs (1991) 1, 257, 259–260
Simón, Juan Piquer 38–40
The Six Million Dollar Man (1973) 176, 178–179
Snow White and the Seven Dwarfs (1937) 119–120, 122
social realism 252

Sodom and Gomorrah (1962) 185
Solaris (1972) 75
Someone to Watch Over Me (1987) 256
Sora No Daikaijū Radon (1956) 145
Soyuzmultfilm 115, 117–118, 125, 127, 129
Space Adventure Cobra (1982) see *Supēsu Adobenchā Kobura* (1982)
Space Battleship Yamato: The Movie (1977) see *Uchū Senkan Yamato: Gekijōban* (1977)
Space Gundam V (1983) 47
Space Thunder Kids (1991) 183
Spaghetti Western 3, 57, 149
Special Mission Lady Chaplin (1966) see *Missione Speciale Lady Chaplin* (1966)
Spectreman (1971) see *Uchū Enjin Gori* (1971)
Speed (1994) 110
Spider-Man 1, 9–11, 26–30, 31, 53
Spider-Man (1977) 26, 28
Spider-Man (1978) see *Supaidāman* (1978)
Spielberg, Steven 40, 77, 100–101, 131, 159, 213, 215
Spy Kids 3-D (2003) 97
Spy Smasher 10
The Spy with Ten Faces (1966) see *Upperseven, L'uomo Da Uccidere* (1966)
Stallone, Sylvester 69, 80, 236
Star Trek (1966) 208–212
Star Wars (1977) 4, 5–6, 40, 123, 183–187, 201–204, 212–214, 219
Star Wolf (1978) see *Sutā Urufu* (1978)
Starcrash (1978) 6, 201–204
Straw Dogs (1971) 238–239, 241–242
Straw Dogs (2011) 242
Strike Commando (1987) 81
Studio One in Hollywood (1948) 222
Suarez, Bobby A. 177–179, 191
Summertime Killer (1972) see *Un Verano Para Matar* (1972)
Supaidāman (1978) 26–30
Super Dimension Fortress Macross (1982) see *Chōjikū Yōsai Makurosu* (1982)
Super Taekwon V (1982) see *Syupeo Taegwon V* (1982)
Superman 18, 20, 30–37, 39–40, 49, 51, 53
Superman (1960) 31–32
Superman (1978) 16, 30, 32–35, 37–39

Superman (1980) 30–34
Superman (1987) 34
Süpermen Dönüyor (1979) 32, 34–37, 186–187
Supermen of Malegaon (2012) 34
Supersonic Man (1979) 32, 38–40
Supēsu Adobenchā Kobura (1982) 182
Susuz Yaz (1963) 163
Sutā Urufu (1978) 213
Syupeo Taegwon V (1982) 46–47

Tahkhana (1986) 153
Taksim Square massacre 243
Tamer, Doğan 9, 11–12
Tang, Tomas Kaak-yan 192–194
Tangled! (2010) 104
Tarkan: Camoka'ya Karşı (1969) 10
Tarzan 40, 41–44, 80, 168
Tarzan İstanbul'da (1952) 41–44
Tarzan Korkusuz Adam (1974) 44
Tarzan the Ape Man (1932) 41–43
Tarzan, the Ape Man (1981) 16
Tarzan's New York Adventure (1942) 42
Tarzan's Revenge (1938) 44
Taxi (1998) 78
Teenage Mutant Ninja Turtles 45–47
Teenage Mutant Ninja Turtles: The Epic Begins (1988) 44–45
Tentacles (1977) see *Tentacoli* (1977)
Tentacoli (1977) 131
Țepeș, Vlad 140
The Terminator (1984) 1, 80, 187–190, 197, 199–201
Thackeray, Balasaheb 263–264
That Man in Istanbul (1965) see *Estambul 65* (1965)
They Call Her Cleopatra Wong (1978) 179
3D (stereoscope) 5, 97–99, 173
3D Saamri (1985) 98
3 Dev Adam (1973) see *Üç Dev Adam* (1973)
Three Giant Men (1973) see *Üç Dev Adam* (1973)
3 Süpermen Olimpiyatlarda (1984) see *Üç Süpermen Olimpiyatlarda* (1984)
Three Tough Guys (1974) 68
Thunderball (1965) 3, 51, 62, 64–66, 91
Time of the Apes (1987) 204–208
Tintorera (1977) 131
Titanic (1997) 248, 250–251
To Live in Peace (1947) see *Vivere in Pace* (1947)

Tōei 26, 28–29, 46, 212–215
Toho 131, 144–146, 206, 213
tokusatsu 28–30, 167
Tollywood 32
Tolv Edsvorne Men (1982) 222
Top Gun (1986) 69
The Towering Inferno (1974) 168, 214
Trader Horn (1931) 43
Trail of the Panda (2009) see *Xiong Mao Hui Jia Lu* (2009)
The Transformers (1984) 181
Troll 2 (1990) 16
Tron (1982) 1, 180–182
The Truth About Cats & Dogs (1996) 77
Tsuburaya, Eiji 147, 169, 206
Tuareg people 222–226
Tucci, Ugo 149–150
Tulgar, Kunt 34–37, 43–44, 184–187
Tulgar, Sabahattin 35, 42–44
Turist Ömer Uzay Yolunda (1973) 208–212
Türkiye (1973) 36
12 (2007) 220–224
12 Angry Men (1957) 3, 220–223
12 Citizens (2014) see *Shi'er Gongmin* (2014)
20th Century-Fox 5–6, 52, 68, 206–207, 232
2 Fast 2 Furious (2003) 78
Tyler, Haven 197, 199–200

Üç Dev Adam (1973) 9–13
Üç Süpermen Olimpiyatlarda (1984) 51
Uçak, Tevfik Fikret 9–12, 143
Uçan Daireler İstanbul'da (1955) 44
Uchū Enjin Gori (1971) 206, 215
Uchū Kara No Messēji (1978) 212–215
Uchū Kara No Messēji: Ginga Taisen (1978) 29, 215
Uchū Senkan Yamato: Gekijōban (1977) 213–214
UFOReul Tagoon Oegyein Wangja (1983) 181
L'ultimo Cacciatore (1980) 195–196
L'ultimo Squalo (1981) 6–7, 131, 148–151
Ultraman (1966) see *Urutoraman* (1966)
Umut (1970) 229
Ün, Memduh 69, 71, 73
The Undead (1957) 157
Unforgiven (1992) 264, 266–267
Unforgiven (2013) see *Yurusarezaru Mono* (2013)
Universal 3, 6, 13, 26, 85, 131,

139–140, 147, 150–151, 155–156, 158, 176
The Untouchables (1987) 245–148
L'uomo Puma (1980) 32
Upperseven, L'uomo Da Uccidere (1966) 91
Ursinho Da Pesada (2008) 104
Urutoraman (1966) 28, 167, 206

Vaa Arugil Vaa (1991) 171
Vahşi Kan (1983) 81, 86
Valcauda, Armando 202, 204
The Vampire Is Alive (1987) 194
El Vampiro (1957) 156, 158
Varan the Unbelievable (1958) see *Daikaijū Baran* (1958)
Varma, Ram Gopal 256–257, 261–264
Veendum Lisa (1987) 136
Vendetta Dal Future (1986) 199
Un Verano Para Matar (1972) 192
Verma, Suparn 92, 94
Viaje Al Centro De La Tierra (1977) 39
Vídeo Brinquedo 102–105
video clubs 75
Vietnam War 71, 80–81, 87, 195–196, 239
Vinni-Pukh (1969) 3, 125–129
Vinni-Pukh I Den Zabot (1972) 126–127, 129
Vinni-Pukh Idyot V Gosti (1971) 126, 129
The Violent Four (1968) see *Banditi a Milano* (1968)
Vivere in Pace (1947) 68
Vural, Vahdet 143

Wakusei Daisensō (1977) 213
The War in Space (1977) see *Wakusei Daisensō* (1977)
Warner Bros. 85, 97, 216, 264, 266
The Warrior (1981) see *Jaka Sembung* (1981)
The Warrior and the Ninja (1985) see *Jaka Sembung & Bergola Ijo* (1985)
Warrior of the Lost World (1983) 216–219
The Warriors (1979) 59–60, 62
Wheels of Fire (1985) 217
When Harry Met Sally... (1989) 77
When Worlds Collide (1951) 185
Where Time Began (1977) see *Viaje Al Centro De La Tierra* (1977)
While You Were Sleeping (1995) 108
Wild East (1993) see *Dikiy Vostok* (1993)
The Wild World of Batwoman (1966) 26
Williamson, Fred 59, 61–62, 66, 68–69, 218
Winner, Michael 71–72
Winnie the Pooh and the Honey Tree (1966) 3, 5, 125, 127, 129
The Wizard of Oz (1939) 3, 5, 122, 125
Wonder Woman 18–20
World War II 11, 18, 32, 54, 68, 180, 236, 246, 266
Worth, David 216–219
Wurideul-Ui Chingu Pawo 5 (1989) 44–47

X-Men (2000) 52
Xingxing Wang (1976) 166–169
Xiong Mao Hui Jia Lu (2009) 106

Yaandein (2001) 98
Yap, Johnson 177–179
Yarasa Adam: Bedmen (1973) 48–51
Yedi Belalılar (1970) 56–59
Yeşilçam 10, 12, 71, 86, 120, 143–144, 163–164, 212, 230, 241, 243, 245
Yojimbo (1961) 3, 268
Yol (1982) 4, 100
You Only Live Twice (1967) 65, 92, 218
Yurusarezaru Mono (2013) 264–268

"Z" Fung Bou (2014) 248
Z Storm (2014) see *"Z" Fung Bou* (2014)
Zakhoder, Boris 125, 127–129
Zanjeer (1673) 85
Zapatlela (1993) 169–173
Zapatlela 2 (2013) 173
Zashchitniki (2017) 6, 52–55
Zhong Guo Chao Ren (1975) 167
Zombi: La Creazione (2007) 201
Zombi 2 (1979) 149
Zombi 3 (1988) 197
Zombies: The Beginning (2007) see *Zombi: La Creazione* (2007)
Zorro 1, 22–23, 57, 80, 259
Die Zwölf Geschworenen (1963 222

www.ingramcontent.com/pod-product-compliance
Lightning Source LLC
Chambersburg PA
CBHW060336010526
44117CB00017B/2855